Intel's SL Architecture

Designing Portable Applications

Desmond Yuen

McGraw-Hill, Inc.

New York San Francisco Washington, D.C. Auckland Bogotá
Caracas Lisbon London Madrid Mexico City Milan
Montreal New Delhi San Juan Singapore
Sydney Tokyo Toronto

Library of Congress Cataloging-in-Publication Data

Yuen, Desmond.
Intel's SL architecture : designing portable applications /
Desmond Yuen.
p. cm.—(Intel/McGraw Hill series)
Includes bibliographical references and index.
ISBN 0-07-911336-2
1. Intel i386SL (Microprocessor) 2. Portable computers—Design and construction. I. Title. II. Series.
QA76.8.I266Y84 1993
004.165—dc20 92-43722
CIP

1 2 3 4 5 6 7 8 9 0 DOH/DOH 9 8 7 6 5 4 3

ISBN 0-07-072693-0

The sponsoring editor for this book was Neil Levine, and the production supervisor was Pamela A. Pelton. This book was set in Century Schoolbook by North Market Street Graphics.

Printed and bound by R. R. Donnelley & Sons Company.

Intel Literature may be obtained from: Intel Corporation, Literature Sales, P.O. Box 7641, Mt. Prospect, IL 60056-7641 (1-800-548-4725)

Intel's SL Architecture

Other Books in the Intel/McGraw-Hill Series

BUNZEL AND MORRIS • *Multimedia Applications Development: Using DVI® Technology*

EDELHART • *Intel's Official Guide to 386™ Computing*

GUREWICH • *Communication Systems: Practical Hardware and Firmware Implementation of LANs*

INTEL • *i486 Microprocessor Programming Reference Manual*

INTEL • *Intel386™ Family Binary Compatibility Specification 2*

LUTHER • *Digital Video in the PC Environment, 2nd edition*

MARGULIS • *i860 Microprocessor Architecture*

RAGSDALE • *Parallel Programming*

To Angelina, Annie, Jimmy, Lisa, and Patricia

Contents

Foreword

This book contains a wealth of technical information about how to design an Intel486™ SL CPU and Intel386™ SL CPU-based portable computer. It is designed to help you better exploit the pioneering SL architecture. It provides concise overviews of the various features of the SL CPU, and the 82360SL peripheral controller. It also gives a great many examples of how these features can be used in your designs, with emphasis on System Management Mode (SMM), power management, and memory subsystem design. Finally, it provides many software and hardware design tips to help you avoid some of the common pitfalls inherent in portable computer design. Before you begin your portable computer design journey, I would like to give you some insight into the birth and development of the SL architecture.

The SL architecture was conceived as a product that would help spur the growth of the portable computer market. When Intel began the SL project, portables were quite heavy (ranging from 12 to 20 lbs) and had battery lives of 30 minutes to just over 2 hours. Many were also limited in the kind and amount of software that the users could run. Although the market for portable computers was growing rapidly, users were clamoring for lighter-weight, longer-battery-life machines.

Let me offer a personal anecdote that I hope will help you better understand the demands of the portable computer user. Several years ago, my job required me to work in two different states with a lot of airplane travel in between. In an attempt to simplify my life, I decided to get a portable computer so that I could carry my office with me in electronic format. The idea seemed simple enough, but in practice it turned into a new kind of nightmare! The weight of the portable machine I chose gave me a constantly bruised shoulder, and it was so big that it took up most of my leg room on the plane. Its limited battery life caused me to constantly seek wall outlets. I also found it cumbersome to open up the computer, boot the system, and load my application, especially during short waits in airports. As a result of my experiment with the electronic office, I was actually getting less work done using this wonderful "productivity enhancer" than when I was using paper!

Initially, I didn't think that a silicon company like Intel could really impact any of these problems. But as I started piecing together technical and marketing information, I realized that electronics could play a key role in solving all of my problems. Hardware support for power management could extend battery life. Greater component integration could make machines smaller and lighter. And performance could be improved by using an Intel386 CPU in place of the 80286 technology.

As I visited our customers and discussed the problems of portable computer design, I quickly realized that everyone was trying to solve the same problems and that Intel could offer viable solutions.

Many people were involved in nurturing the concepts that became the SL architecture. The team included people from both inside and outside of Intel. Most of the team was composed of silicon and system engineers; however, it also included people from marketing, fabrication, applications, software development, and product validation.

The resulting SL architecture introduced many advances to microprocessor architectures, including on-chip power management facilities, suspend/resume capability, high integration, a high-speed Peripheral Interface bus (PI bus), a faster parallel port, and support for emerging technologies like Flash Memory. It also brought 32-bit computing to the portable computer arena, giving PCs the processing power to run any software package at the required level of performance.

Perhaps the greatest achievement of the SL architecture was the introduction of System Management Mode. SMM is an environment which provides system designers—Intel's customers—with the ability to take control of the system regardless of the software being run. Not only does SMM provide a simple and robust mechanism for implementing power management facilities in a portable computer, but it also enables system designers to add other product-specific features to their machines without having to worry about compatibility with the operating system and application programs. Portable computer designers can thus easily "differentiate" their machines by adding features that offer unique benefits to their users. Our customers continue to find innovative ways of using the SMM "tool box."

I would like to give credit to everyone involved with making the SL architecture a reality. This includes well over a hundred Intel employees, as well as many of our customers and design partners. Without them our better mouse trap would simply be collecting dust in a corner of a dark shelf. Worse, I'd still be looking for a way to protect my bruised shoulder.

DAVE VANNIER
Chief Architect of the SL Architecture and
Co-Architect of the Intel386 Architecture

Preface

Since the introduction of the Intel386 SL Microprocessor Superset, many exciting things have happened in the laptop world. The introduction of the Intel386 SL microprocessor has certainly changed the way people think about laptop computers.

While working at Intel as an applications engineer, I accumulated a wealth of knowledge about how to design SL architecture-based products through working with PC manufacturers and the BIOS vendors. Instead of letting this information get lost, I decided to write this book to share the experience and knowledge I have gained over the years. Hopefully, the information contained in this book will spur further growth in the PC industry.

This book has been written primarily for system designers and programmers who are developing products based on the Intel486 SL microprocessor and the Intel386 SL microprocessor. This book is for anyone who wants to understand the SL architecture to improve their hardware, BIOS, and support software designs. The main goal of this book is to show readers how to design innovative products using the SL architecture.

This book should be of particular interest to readers wishing to use the system management mode of the SL processor for better power management. Even though the concept of power management has been around for a long time (probably since the day the battery was invented), power management on PCs is still a myth to many people. One of the goals of this book is to demystify power management.

I believe that the best way to learn about the SL architecture is to experiment with it. Many examples are given throughout the book to assist readers in experimenting with the Intel486 SL microprocessor and the Intel386 SL microprocessor. To make it easier to use this book, the software (including program listings) and examples are included on a disk.

It is difficult to master a subject that is continuously evolving. You have to constantly adapt to changes and take advantage of the new technology. Instead of trying to catch up with the technology, my advice is to be innovative and stay ahead of the technology. I hope this book will help many of you to achieve that goal.

DESMOND YUEN

Acknowledgments

There are many people at Intel who provided tremendous support on this project. Dave Ryan sponsored my book and his confidence in me helped me to take the initiative to write it. Without Dave's support, this book would not exist. Dave Vannier, co-architect for the Intel386 microprocessor and grandfather of the SL architecture, wrote an excellent foreword. Tom Rossi, my boss and my coach, provided continuous support and encouragement.

Pauline Albert, Janet Brownstone, and Barbara Holtz provided continuous encouragement to keep me going. Janet, my coordinator for the book, has been very protective and supportive. She took care of a lot of details for me so that I could concentrate on writing.

Gregg Wyant deserves special thanks for spending a lot of time (including weekends) working with me on the organization and technical contents of the book. Bob Albers did a thorough critique of the first draft of the manuscript and made many valuable suggestions. Simon Ellis, one of the key architects for the Intel386 SL microprocessor, wrote an excellent chapter on the history of the SL architecture.

Betsy Jones provided very useful input and suggestions throughout this project. Darci Worth has done a lot of work with power consumption measurements and some of the information used in the book is based on her work. Patrick Murray and Phil Cloud were very helpful in checking the accuracy of the technical contents of the book. Jessie Garcia built the flash disk card for the PI bus. My thanks to Suresh Marisetty for writing the appendix on hardware emulation using SMI. K. J. Jun reviewed the page proofs for technical accuracy.

It is extremely hard to find qualified reviewers who can spend time to evaluate a book of this magnitude. I am fortunate enough to have many good technical reviewers who sacrificed their spare time to review my book. I would like to thank the following people for providing suggestions on the manuscript. Bill Rallis of SystemSoft Inc. and Dennis Chang of Award Software Inc. reviewed the source listing and the chapters related to programming. Scott Schaefer of Micron Technology checked materials related to DRAM, SRAM, and cache RAM and also put forth extra effort to review in detail the other chapters as well. Jim Williams of Linear Technology evaluated the power supply material. Paul Cahill of Gates Energy Products checked battery information. Mark Singer and Ed Garcia of Cirrus Logic Inc. checked chapters on PI bus and graphics-related chapters. Frank Barry of IBM reviewed the overall organization of the book. David Schwabe did an excellent job on the copyediting. Special thanks to my acquisition editor Neil Levine and his production staff at McGraw-Hill for their excellent support.

Chapter

1

Introduction

From the day the personal computer (PC) was invented, people have anxiously awaited the PC on a chip. Intel took a big step toward this goal with the introduction in 1990 of the SL architecture. This architecture offers two important features that foster the development of small, lightweight PCs. First, the SL architecture embraces almost all of the CPU, memory management, system control, and peripheral control functions required to make a PC. When implemented in silicon using very large scale integration (VLSI) circuitry, the SL architecture allows a PC to be designed with only a handful of components.

Second, the SL architecture offers several power management features that allow the design of PCs that can run for many hours on a single battery. The most important of these features is the system management mode (SMM), a unique operating mode that allows the CPU to execute system management software transparently from the operating system and application programs. In the first implementation of the SL architecture, Intel engineers were able to pack all the SL circuitry into two components: the Intel386 SL CPU and the 82360SL peripheral controller. (See Figs. 1.1 and 1.2.)

Using Intel's CMOS IV chip technology, these components provide Intel386 CPU-class computational power, plus all the memory management, system management, bus control, and peripheral control hardware required to build a PC. In fact, Intel386 SL CPU-based notebook PCs that use only ten components (not counting the memory devices) are already on the market. These chips also provide a wide range of power management features that have allowed designers to extend the operating time of battery-powered notebooks to eight hours or more. (See Fig. 1.3.) In the spring of 1992, Intel introduced a 3.3-volt version of the Intel386 SL CPU, and in the fall of 1992, they introduced the Intel486 SL CPU.

This book describes the SL architecture and its implementation in the Intel486 SL CPU, Intel386 SL CPU, and 82360SL peripheral controller components. It also discusses a broad selection of system design considerations, divided into various topic areas. The design tips given in each topic area include sample circuits and assembly-language routines.

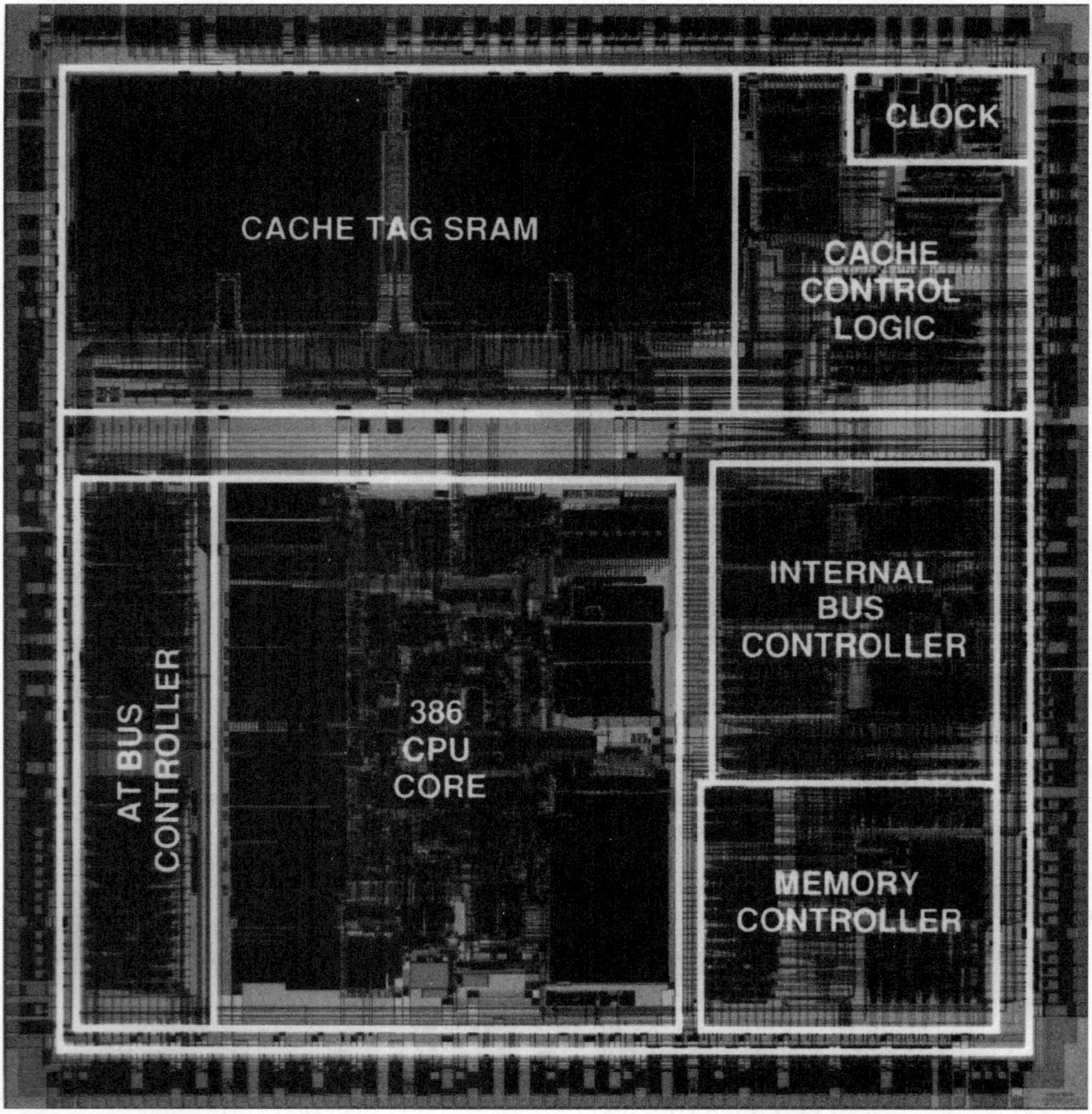

Figure 1.1 Die photograph of the Intel386 SL microprocessor.

The intention of this book is to help you understand the operation of the SL CPU and 82360SL components and learn how to exploit various features of these components to develop profitable and innovative portable PCs, pen-based systems, and Personal Application Devices (PADs).

Organization of the Book

Your introduction to the SL architecture begins in Chap. 2 with an insightful look at the history of the architecture written by Simon Ellis, one of the archi-

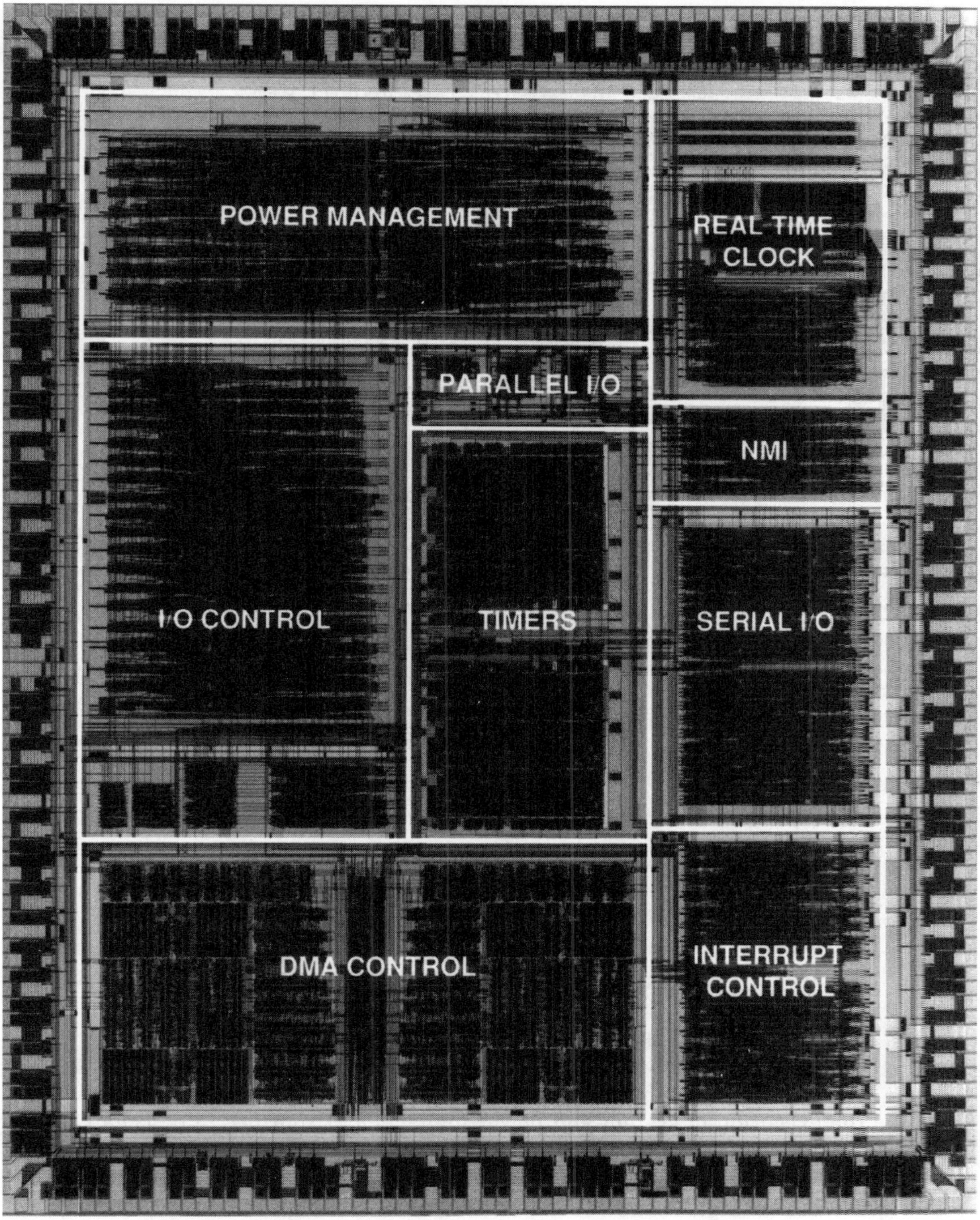

Figure 1.2 Die photograph of the 82360SL peripheral controller.

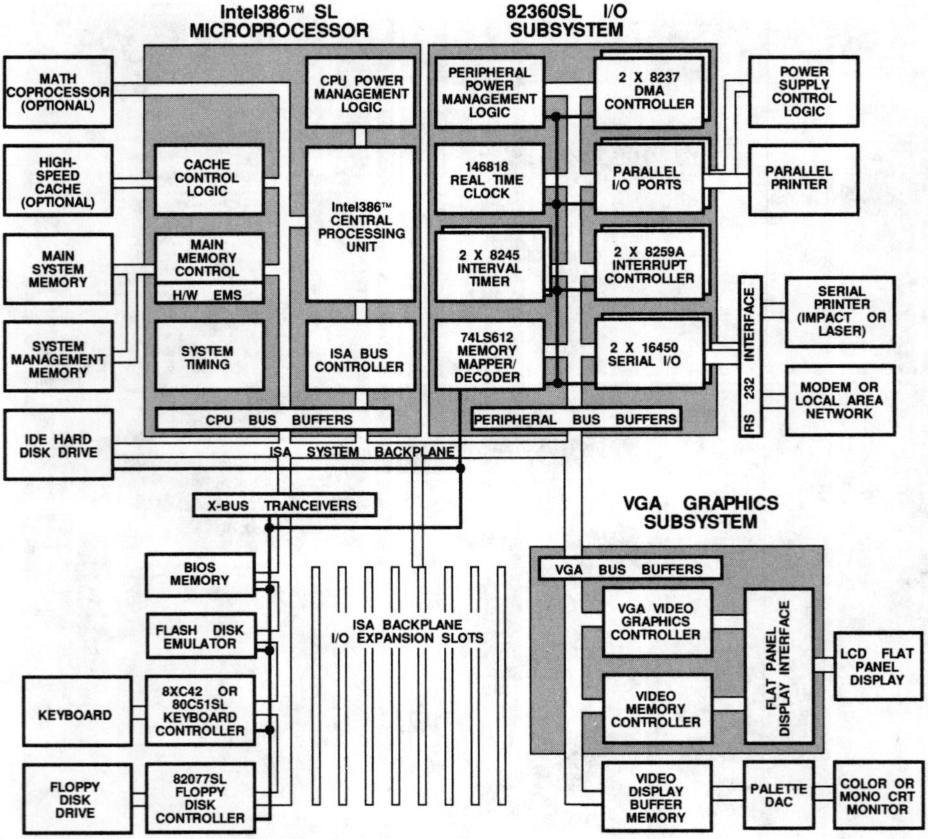

Figure 1.3 Block diagram of PC system based on the Intel386 SL microprocessor and 82360SL.

tects of the SL architecture. This chapter explains the motivation behind the "Genesis Project," the Intel code name for the SL development project, and the reasons for many of the features in the architecture.

Chapter 3 provides a brief overview of the SL architecture. It describes the underlying design of the architecture and introduces you to the basic components of a PC system. The remaining chapters of this book cover system design considerations and give valuable hardware and software design tips.

Chapter 4 describes the most innovative feature of the SL architecture: the System Management Mode. The SMM is a special operating mode that allows the execution of system and power management routines to be isolated from the operating system and application program to prevent incompatibility with BIOS routines. This chapter describes the architecture of the SMM and gives several examples of how it can be used in a PC design.

Chapters 5, 6, and 7 describe the power management features provided in the SL architecture to reduce power consumption in a battery-operated portable computer. These features include using the SMM to execute power management routines; a mechanism for powering down idle peripheral devices; the ability to stop the clock to the CPU and other system components; and the suspend/resume mechanism that enables a system to be powered down, then powered up again without losing the state of the machine.

Chapter 8 discusses several issues that must be considered in portable computer designs and how the SL architecture addresses these issues.

Chapter 9 describes the clock control facilities and the mechanisms available to slow or stop various system clocks to reduce power consumption in system components.

Chapters 10 and 11 describe the memory management facilities of the Intel486 SL CPU and Intel386 SL CPU. The emphasis in these chapters is on the facilities provided to reduce the power consumption of memory components during normal operation and in a number of power-down modes.

Chapter 12 describes a special enhanced version of the ISA bus, called the *peripheral interface bus* (PI bus), which the SL CPUs support. This chapter also shows how this bus can be used as an interface to a flash disk and a VGA graphics frame memory.

Chapter 13 describes the ISA-bus interface and ISA peripheral controllers provided in the 82360SL. It also gives guidelines for interfacing other peripheral controllers such as a keyboard controller, floppy-drive controller, and IDE hard disk controller to the 82360SL.

Chapter 14 describes the 82360SL's enhanced parallel port, a simpler and faster parallel port interface that shares the same signal lines as the ISA parallel port.

Chapter 15 gives guidelines for writing BIOS routines to control various aspects of system operation in SL CPU-based products of an operating system.

Chapter 16 gives some guidelines for debugging SL architecture-based products. It also shows how to build some of your own debugging tools using the SMM mode to execute debugging routines.

Chapter 17 describes several mechanisms and issues that affect the performance of the SL CPU-based products.

Chapter 18 offers some insights into the future of the SL architecture.

Basic Concepts

Before we start looking at the SL architecture in great detail, it is important to review some of the fundamental concepts we will be using throughout this book.

System management

System management mode is a special execution mode of the Intel486 SL CPU and Intel386 SL CPU used to support applications such as power management software and to ensure compatibility with existing operating systems and applications software.

Power management

Power management is a mechanism of controlling the power consumption of a system to extend battery life.

Battery management

Battery management involves performing functions like monitoring the battery temperature and voltage, recharging the battery, and detecting battery-low condition. Do not get battery management confused with power management—they are not the same.

Power mode

Power mode is a representation of the power consumption level of a device or system. An SL CPU-based system can be programmed for local standby, global standby, or suspend mode to conserve power. (See Table 1.1.)

Hardware Platform

Most of the examples and programs in this book were designed to run on the SL microprocessor evaluation board. This board was chosen because the configuration jumpers, test points, connectors, ISA-bus expansion slots, and the breadboarding area on the evaluation board make experimentation easy. The schematics for the evaluation board are available from your local Intel sales office.

Notation

The following notation and conventions are used throughout this book.

Signal descriptions. # denotes active low signal.

Bit notation. Bits field within a byte or word are shown as a range of decimal numbers separated by a dash, such as y-x. (*Example:* Bits [2-0].)

Hexadecimal numbers. Hexadecimal numbers are represented by a string of hexadecimal digits followed by the character H. A leading zero is added if the number would otherwise begin with one of the digits A–F. (*Example:* 38H, 0FFH.)

TABLE 1.1 Summary of Power Modes in a Typical Intel386 SL CPU-based System

Mode	Relative power	Typical power	User overhead	Main advantage
Full on	Full	8410 mW @ 20 MHz	None	Full speed operation
Local standby	Low	4410 mW @ 20 MHz	Low	Peripherals disabled
Global standby	Medium low	2455 mW @ 20 MHz	Moderate to high	Code execution stopped
Suspend	Lowest	53 mW @ 20 MHz	High	Long battery life

Bytes, words, double words. A byte is 8 bits. A word is 16 bits. A double word (dword) is 32 bits.

Configuration spaces. The following abbreviations are used to represent the five hidden configuration spaces in the SL architecture:

IBU	Internal Bus Unit configuration space
OMCU	On-board Memory Controller configuration space
CU	Cache controller Unit configuration space
EBU	External Bus Unit configuration space
INDEX	82360SL configuration space

Configuration space addresses. The following format is used to show the configuration space address for registers inside the SL architecture configuration spaces:

mnemonic (configuration space address, configuration space)

For example:

MCMODE (300H, OMCU)

In this example, MCMODE is the mnemonic for the Memory Controller Mode Register, 300H is the configuration space address, and OMCU is the configuration space where MCMODE register resides.

Normal I/O space addresses. The following format is used to show the address for registers inside the normal I/O address space:

mnemonic (address)

For example:

CPUPWRMODE (22H)

In this example, CPUPWRMODE is the mnemonic for the CPU Power Mode register and 22H is the I/O address.

Units of measure. The following units of measure are used throughout the book.

Symbol	Unit
A	ampere
Kbyte	kilobyte
Mbyte	megabyte
MHz	megahertz
mA	milliamp
ms	millisecond

Symbol	Unit
mW	milliwatt
ns	nanosecond
s	second
W	watt
μs	microsecond
V	volt

Useful References

You will find the following books, papers, and data sheets useful when designing an SL CPU-based product. All of these publications are available from Intel.

The Intel486 SL Microprocessor SuperSet Programmer's Reference Manual, Order Number 241327-001

The Intel486 SL Microprocessor SuperSet System Design Guide, Order Number 241326-001

The Intel486 SL Microprocessor SuperSet Data Sheet, Order Number 241325-001

"The Intel486 SL Microprocessor SuperSet Family Product Brief"

"The Intel486 SL Microprocessor Family Overview"

The Intel386 SL Microprocessor SuperSet Programmer's Reference Manual, Order Number 240815-004

The Intel386 SL Microprocessor SuperSet System Design Guide, Order Number 240816-002

The Intel386 SL Microprocessor SuperSet Data Sheet, Order Number 240814-005

"The Intel386 SL Microprocessor Family Overview," Order Number 240865-001

"The Intel386 SL Microprocessor SuperSet Family Product Brief," Order Number 240851-001

"Notebook Market Overview—The New Computers," Order Number 240864-001

Summary

The most interesting thing about the Intel386 SL PCU project is how the architecture evolved along the course of development. The changes are largely due to changes in the market and feedback from customers. We worked with the customers to find out what they really needed. The process involved talking with the notebook computer manufacturers and software vendors. Input from the alpha and beta sites was key in defining the SL architecture. The end result is a highly flexible architecture. Direct input from customers also influenced the design specification process. The most significant thing we have heard from customers is that they want a better mechanism to handle power management. In response, the system management mode was implemented. Not only does system management mode make power management much more efficient and reliable, it also opens up a world of opportunity for new applications.

Chapter

2

The History and Future of the Intel SL Architecture*

The Intel SL research and development program started in the middle of 1988, at which time Intel established a task force to evaluate the PC marketplace and determine where we could add value. At the time, the industry was based on the 80286 CPU with the Intel386 architecture about to overtake it. The portable PC market was taking off and was proclaimed by industry observers to be the fastest growing market segment. Because of this predicted growth potential, we decided to focus on battery-operated portable computers.

The SL Challenge

Having evolved from desktop designs, the first portable computers contended with power management and form factor as their chief design challenges. Intel's development team was driven by three motivating challenges: to make significant progress toward the "PC on a chip"; to provide on-board power management facilities; and to provide a transparent "suspend/resume" capability from any Intel386 CPU operating mode. (*Suspend/resume* is the ability to suspend operation while the computer is powered off, then to resume the exact state from which the machine was suspended when the computer is powered up again.)

The original PC was made from 180 components, which were reduced to about 30 by 1988. Intel decided on a target of ten or fewer components.

Our power management research centered around finding ways to add new power saving functions to an architecture that was originally designed for the desktop. We believed that the most convenient way to preserve battery life is to control the power going to the PC subsystem and to provide power only when necessary. However, this particular power management technique does not

* The author wishes to gratefully acknowledge that this chapter has been contributed by Simon Ellis.

always maintain strict PC compatibility. The compatibility problem became even more severe in systems that used the Intel386 CPU architecture. The Intel386 CPU architecture extended the capabilities of the PC platform by adding more sophisticated operating modes, such as extended memory management and paging. As the PC operating system software was developed to utilize these capabilities, the problem of managing power transparently suddenly became more difficult by an order of magnitude.

After deciding which market to address and diagnosing the major problems in that segment, we began to engage our customer base. Fortunately, most portable computer manufacturers were already Intel customers and were willing to listen to our proposal. Moreover, most of them were already trying to solve these very same portable PC design problems in their own ways.

For Intel to provide the solutions, we knew we would have to take a full-system approach. The problem of PC compatibility was equal to that of the power management, however, and Intel did not have a proven track record in the compatibility arena. We understood that we would have to learn more and to prove that our power management strategy would yield PC-compatible computers before our customers would take us seriously. Intel of course had some major competencies to offer in other areas. We understood X86 compatibility and PC performance, and we were able to manufacture high-transistor-count devices at high volume. In the end, we partnered with one major customer and began designing the detailed architecture.

The Solution

When we began our design phase, high-volume Intel silicon processes were capable of integrating one million transistors, and our packaging was in the 196 lead range. The Intel386 CPU core has about 275,000 transistors, giving us room for some significant integration. We established a two-chip solution that consisted of the Intel386 SL CPU, containing the CPU and high-performance devices, and the 82360SL peripheral unit, containing the PC peripherals and the bulk of the power management logic.

System Partitioning

The Intel386 SL CPU contains about 880,000 transistors. It has a modified Intel386 CPU core, memory controller, EMS 4.0 mapper, ISA-bus controller, cache controller, and PC address mapper. Intel's ability to integrate these devices on a single piece of silicon offers many design benefits. For example, interfacing between the modules is done in the metal layers on the die. The signals are not limited in number and do not have to be buffered to drive pins and high loads. The addresses coming out of the CPU core are available two clocks earlier than the equivalent stand-alone CPU. These benefits were utilized to increase performance and reduce the number of cycles. The full cache lookup is done internally before the cycle and only goes to the memory controller if the cycle is a cache miss or write.

The 82360SL is a complete IBM PC-AT-compatible peripheral subsystem chip that contains: Programmable Interval Timer (PIT), Programmable Interrupt Controller (PIC), DMA (plus, mapper), dual serial ports, enhanced (fast) parallel port, Real Time Clock plus CMOS (RTC), and the system monitoring functions for power management.

Power Management

Transparent power management presented a different problem. Chip vendors offered many partial solutions, including: static CPUs, power management controllers with system event timers and monitors, sleep modes, low-power devices, and software drivers. None of these solutions addressed the fundamental problem of how to maintain PC compatibility while power managing the computer. Existing notebook computers used standard PC resources, such as Nonmaskable Interrupt (NMI) handlers or TSRs, as interfaces between the power management software and hardware and the rest of the system. These notebooks achieved a level of "compatibility by testing." Once systems had been designed, they had to be extensively tested with many applications to ensure that applications would not clash with power management code. These systems were then prey to any changes or new releases of software. The Intel386 CPU architecture is established as the basis for today's operating systems and applications. The protected mode programs such as Windows 3.0, UNIX and the various DOS extenders make the traditional power management approaches even more difficult to implement.

When Intel started assessing portable computing requirements, it soon became apparent that the Intel386 CPU architecture itself had to be extended with a system management mode (SMM). Only with SMM can a system achieve "compatibility by design" for all operating systems and applications, including those that use the Intel386 protected modes.

The SL architecture's SMM enables the CPU and peripheral controller to combine the power management elements, such as static CPU and system event timers, in a complete solution. Vendors can fine-tune power management for their boxes. The whole system tradeoff between performance, latency, weight, and battery life can be also be improved. Once implemented in the BIOS, the system performance is enhanced and unaffected by operating systems, applications, and the way the user has set up his or her machine. The thousands of PC compatibility features have been resolved with the transparent power management functions such as suspend/resume and are offered as a foundation whereby PC vendors add to their own special differentiation for a new class of notebook computers.

Notebook Computer Functions

The next generation of notebook PCs must support power management functions and special utilities for on-the-road operation. They must be simple to operate, automatic if possible, and foolproof if they are to change the behavior of the computer user. To maintain strict PC compatibility and utilize the huge base of existing PC software, these operations must run independently from an application or operating system. The SMM architecture is ideally suited to these tasks. It allows these functions to be implemented in such a way that they are robust, yet transparent to the user.

Suspend/Resume

After we had settled on our SMM design, the implementation of suspend/resume became much easier. To understand the power of suspend/resume, imagine a notebook computer user in an airport, working on his or her expense or trip report and account database while waiting for a plane. The multitasking Intel386 operating system is finely tuned, and provides the necessary functions to perform these multiple tasks. When the flight is called, the user closes the lid of his or her notebook, without saving the work or exiting the applications. A suspend request is immediately initiated, causing a graceful shutdown of the machine that leaves it in a low power state which could last 30 days or more. After dinner on the plane, the user opens the notebook lid, and the machine instantly resumes its state prior to the initiation of the suspend (perhaps with the cursor blinking in the "$" column of the expense report spreadsheet).

The scenario just discussed presents the SL architecture's suspend/resume functionality in a nutshell. We designed this function to be very simple to initiate, highly reliable, and very fast. We knew that if there were a 10-second delay for the suspend to take effect, the function would seldom be used.

Global Standby

Another important feature of the SL power management architecture is global standby. In global standby mode, a machine that is left idle for a programmable period of time will shut down to a lower-powered state. The idle state is detected when the global standby timer count expires. This counter is reset by system events. When the time-out occurs, a system management interrupt (SMI) is generated and the CPU is placed in SMM. Power management routines running in SMM then turn off the display, power down the disk drives, and stop the CPU clock. Code execution also stops in the middle of the power management routine. The system is restarted by a STOP_BREAK event (similar to system events). The CPU clock is then restarted and power management code continues to execute, restoring power to the screen and disk drives and executing the RSM instruction to exit SMM. We estimated that this mode would save up to 60 percent of the total system power.

While the system is in global standby, the Auto Power off timer can optionally be used to put the machine into the lower-power suspend state. When this timer expires during a standby, the CPU clock is restored and an SMI is generated to initiate the suspend sequence.

Detailed Design

After defining the high-level architecture, our engineering team then had to engage in the internal design. We had to learn all about the PC platform—compatibility, function, performance, and how different companies had extended the architecture over the past 10 years.

We approached compatibility from two different directions: ISA-bus compatibility for the more than 1000 plug-in adapters, and software compatibility for the more than 25,000 available software packages. We knew a lot about the original IBM AT-339 design; most of the components were designed by Intel, and we had accurate schematic and BIOS information. The biggest challenges facing us included third-party vendors' usage of the PC and how they had extended the platform. To aid us in our ISA-bus design, we decided to create a "compatibility bible." Six specs had been given to us by various customers, and we also had the IEEE-996 document. The "bible" was created by performing extensive experiments on ISA hardware and comparing them to the specifications and our detailed knowledge of the inner working of the devices. The programming model was developed in a similar way. Our X86 knowledge gave us most of the information required. This, along with customer input and many experiments with applications, enabled us to create the specifications for our part.

After defining the Intel386 SL architecture, we started to evaluate the BIOS. To separate the initial powering up of hardware from new software, we made the chips power up in a default state so that a regular AT BIOS would boot and work. After that, the configuration and power management software could be brought up. We worked closely with our partner, a major BIOS vendor, and with internal programming teams to validate our defined programming model.

The silicon development teams were also very active. One of these teams, in charge of "full-chip" simulation, was developing the capability to simulate the entire PC platform on our models. The team had to generate models of all the PC peripherals and system behavior. Their efforts enabled us to boot DOS on the silicon model. This involved executing the system configuration, POST tests, system initialization, and BIOS calls. All of this ran on the low-level transistor model of our product—a task which took our largest mainframe approximately two weeks to execute.

First Silicon and Debug

After 18 months of definition and development, we finally produced the first silicon. This was a very exciting time—would our baby work? It took us six days to get to the point of booting DOS. The part was functional! We were able to get our test board to work with the first silicon—a miracle! Working on one platform with some applications is one thing, but getting to a full "worst-case" design and PC compatibility is another. At the Intel386 SL Microprocessor introduction in October 1990, we were able to demonstrate a fully transparent suspend/resume sequence while the board, with less than 10 components, was running in enhanced 386 mode. We had met our challenge.

First Customer Shipment

Before our first partner could announce and ship product, we had to prove that the Intel386 SL CPU was compatible, competitive, and functional, and had met the performance and power expectations in a mass-produced notebook product. We also had to prove that it could run any of the 25,000 PC applications in any combination at any time of day. This took some time. For all of the engineers, this was an important time, and we gained significant PC experience.

General Marketing of the Product

After the introduction of our first partner's notebook PC, we started to engage with more customers. The Intel386 SL CPU worked, and we had proved that we could resolve some of the system and compatibility issues. The power management architecture was a success. We made some changes to the parts to support the needs of the rest of the PC industry: increasing the operating frequency to 25 MHz and adding more flexible configurations so that the whole customer base could implement their own specific features.

The Success of the SMM Architecture

The power management architecture was working, but we needed to separate power management from the system management mode (SMM). (Power management is just one of the applications for SMM.) Customers were beginning to use SMM for some other applications. A longer-term strategy and road map for SMM was thus required.

To distinguish SMM from power management facilities in the Intel386 SL processor, we decided to make it the sixth operating mode of the extended Intel386 architecture. This mode will be implemented in all future X86-compatible CPUs produced at Intel.

Support for Product-Specific Functions

A common request from our customers is to give them the ability to differentiate their boxes. The Intel SL architecture provides this support with more than 120 configuration registers and the flexibility of SMM. There are many, very different, Intel386 SL CPU-based systems in the market today. The features and functions of the SL architecture that will be used in a product are up to the system designer. He or she has to consider several tradeoffs: performance, system weight, battery life, features, and peripherals. What the SL architecture offers to all of these designers is the base of a compatible PC with many extensions and hooks. Product design teams can spend their resources on these new differentiating features and can rely on the Intel386 SL CPU to provide the base-compatible platform for all of the available PC applications.

Future SL Generations

After completing the first generation of SL products, we started to plan for future products. We believe that the SL SMM and power management architecture and system partitioning will be good for the next three or four generations of products.

Performance and battery life are two major areas identified for new development. Intel had solutions to both the problems in the next X86 core, as well as the ability to reduce the core voltage to 3.3 volts. With these two mechanisms alone, we estimated that we could easily double the system performance and halve the power consumption. The next X86 core is easily implemented and keeps the programming interface the same. This keeps binary compatibility with SL BIOS and power management software. The only changes required are in the system configuration and setup.

Reducing the supply voltage in CMOS technology has a square proportionality to power. Going from 5 volts to 3.3 volts results in a 60 percent power saving. The speed of the silicon switching is proportional to the supply voltage. Both of these facts provided Intel with challenges, including performance to be reclaimed, reliability issues, and reduced system noise margins. All of this requires us to tune the silicon process.

In the spring of 1992, Intel announced the low-voltage Intel386 SL CPU which uses a hybrid voltage design in which any circuit that operates above 8 MHz runs at 3.3 volts, and the rest of the circuitry runs at 5 volts. In the fall of 1992, Intel announced the Intel486 SL CPU that combines an Intel486 SX core with 3.3-volt operation.

Conclusion

Working on the design and development of the SL architecture was gratifying for many reasons. The most gratifying feeling for us derives from witnessing the success of Intel386 SL-based products and the great strides that have been taken toward making portable computers more useful, more convenient, and more reliable.

Chapter

3

SL Architecture Overview

The Intel SL architecture is the first microprocessor architecture to be designed specifically for notebook computer and hand-held computer applications. It was designed with two goals in mind:

- To capture as many of the components required to make an ISA-compatible PC as possible on a few VLSI chips
- To provide power management tools that work transparently to the operating system and applications programs and that give designers complete control over power usage by system components

Figure 3.1 shows a block diagram of an ISA-compatible PC, implemented with the SL architecture. As this diagram illustrates, all you need to build a complete PC in addition to the SL CPU and 82360SL I/O are memory chips, a VGA controller, a floppy disk controller, a keyboard controller, an optional math coprocessor (MCP), and buffers for optional I/O peripherals, such as a flash disk.

The following sections describe the internal design of the Intel486 SL CPU, Intel386 SL CPU and the 82360SL peripheral controller. It also describes the various buses in the system.

Intel386 SL CPU and Intel486 SL CPU

Intel386 SL microprocessor

The Intel386 SL microprocessor is the first processor for portable computers. The memory controller inside the Intel386 SL CPU contains all the control and interface logic to drive a 20-Mbyte DRAM memory system or a 32-Mbyte SRAM memory system and a cache controller to maximize performance. The memory controller supports common memory options such as shadowing and memory roll-over. Also, the on-chip hardware implements LIM 4.0-compatible expanded memory system (EMS). (See Fig. 3.2.)

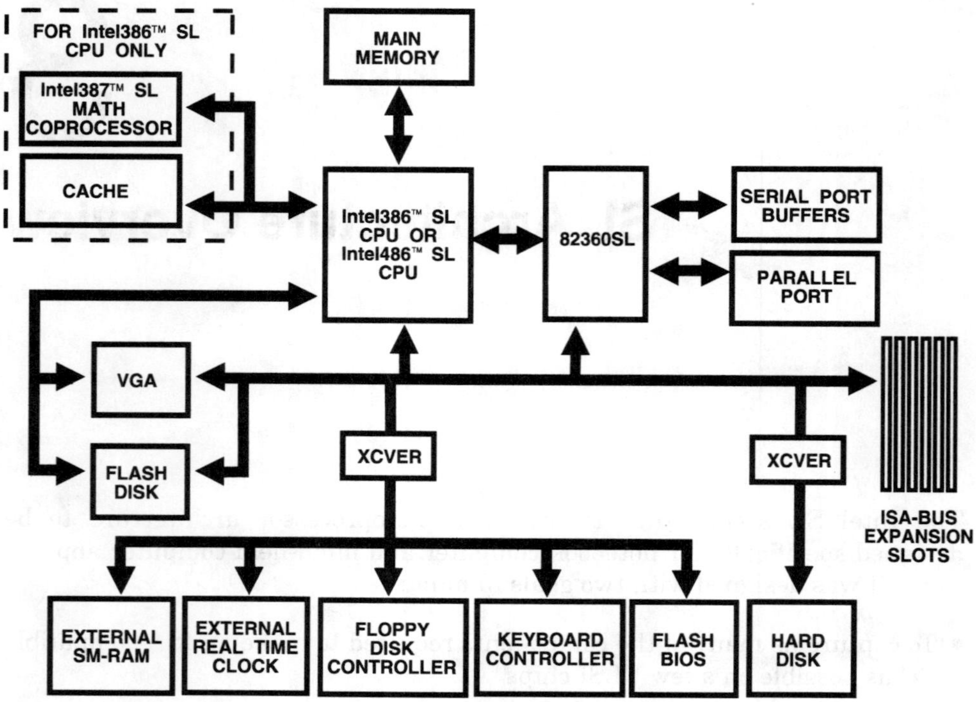

Figure 3.1 Block diagram of a portable PC based on the Intel SL architecture.

The Intel386 SL microprocessor also contains bus drivers and control circuitry for two expansion bus interfaces: Industry Standard Architecture (ISA) bus interface and Peripheral Interface (PI) bus interface. The PI-bus interface shares the same address and data buses with the ISA-bus interface but has a much higher performance control interface. Bus cycles can be programmed to be directed to either the PI-bus interface or the ISA-bus interface.

Low voltage Intel386 SL microprocessor

The low-voltage Intel386 SL microprocessor with "flexible voltage" operation combines a selectable 3.3- or 5-volt peripheral interface with a 3.3-volt static CPU and a 3.3-volt memory interface. The selectable voltage feature allows for pin-for-pin compatibility with both 3.3- and 5-volt peripherals, eliminating the translation logic typically necessary to connect 5-volt components to a 3.3-volt CPU. In addition, the "selectable voltage" operation is 100 percent software-compatible with the standard Intel386 SL processor.

Hardware implementation

The Intel386 SL Microprocessor SL SuperSet is manufactured using Intel's CHMOS IV process, combining the high performance of HMOS with the low power dissipation of CMOS. Double metal layers and 1.0-micron lithography allow a chip density of more than one million transistors. The Intel386 SL

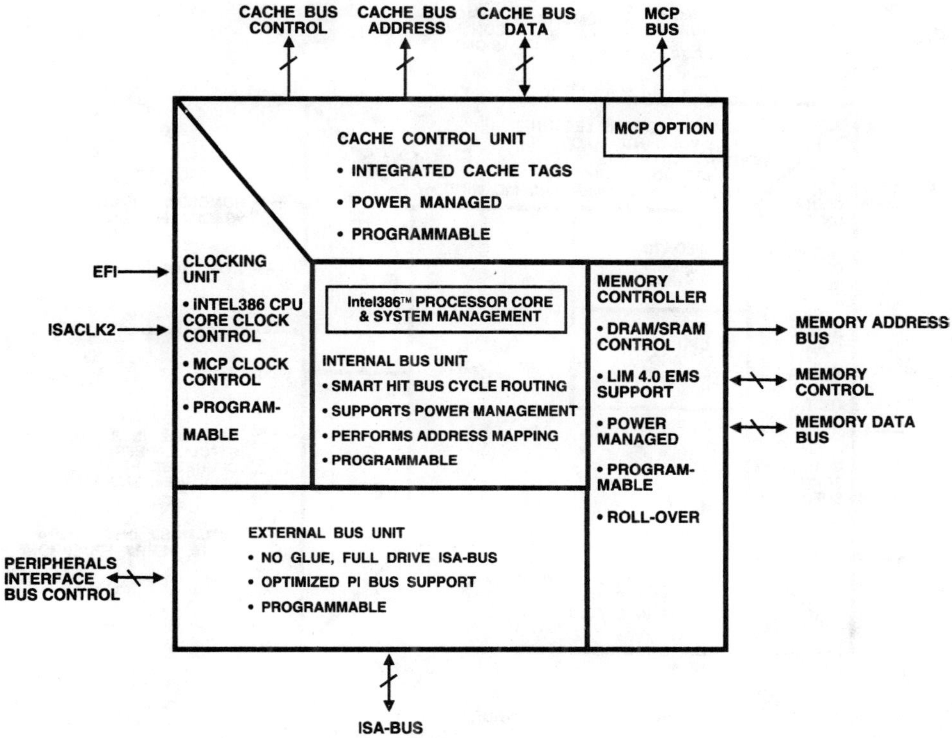

Figure 3.2 Main building blocks of the Intel386 SL microprocessor.

microprocessor is available in a 196-pin plastic Quad Flat Package (PQFP) or 227 lead ceramic Land-Grid Array (LGA) package, a package that is designed for easy upgrade. The 82360SL I/O is available in 196-pin PQFP package and 208-pin SQFP package.

Intel486 SL microprocessor

The Intel486 SL microprocessor is the newest generation of microprocessor for notebook computers, and offers the highest performance and lowest power consumption. Building on the success of the SL architecture, the Intel486 SL microprocessor offers 3.3-volt CPU core and memory interface. (See Fig. 3.3.) It is 100 percent binary compatible with the Intel386 SL microprocessor. The Intel486 SL CPU provides higher performance by virtue of the reduced clocks per instruction (CPIs) associated with the Intel486 CPU. The Intel486 SL CPU integrates a fully static Intel486 microprocessor core, cache controller with 8 Kbytes of internal cache, Floating Point Unit (FPU), on-board memory controller, and external bus controller. The higher integration allows the system designer to create a smaller notebook computer.

The Intel486 SL CPU with FPU provides both integer and floating-point performance improvements over the Intel386 SL CPU and Intel387 SL mobile math coprocessor combination. Intel486 SL CPU floating-point performance

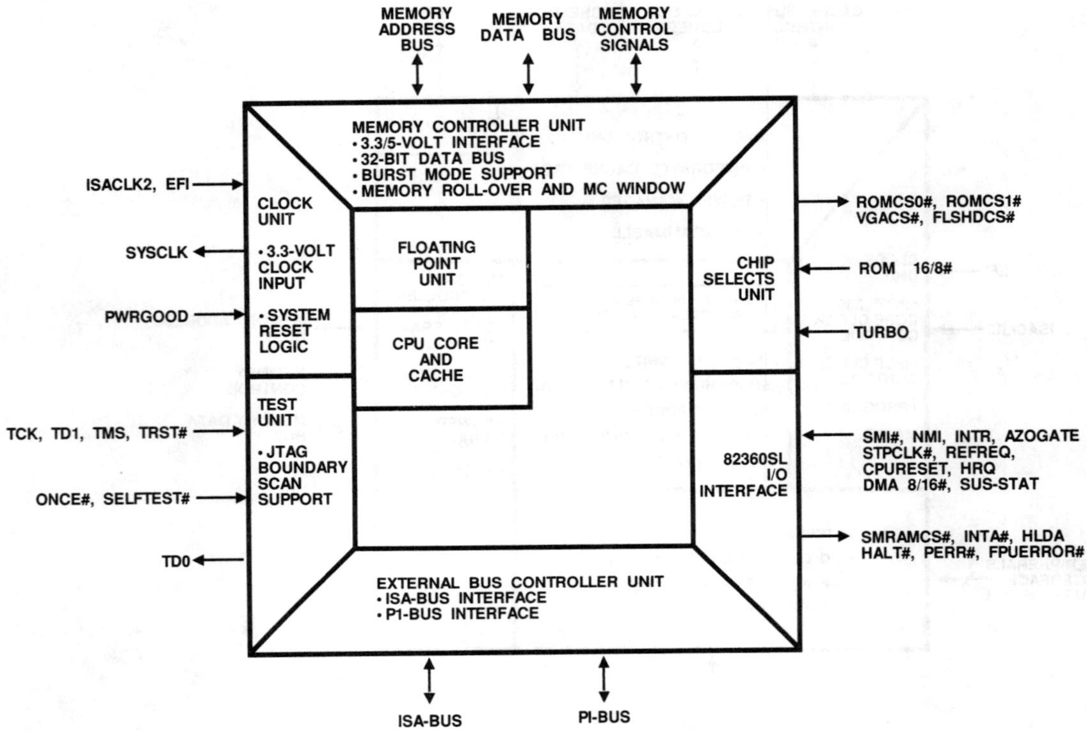

Figure 3.3 Main building blocks of the Intel486 SL microprocessor.

will offer an increase of between two to three times the performance of the Intel386 SL microprocessor and Intel387 SL mobile math coprocessor combination at equivalent clock speeds.

Power consumption is further reduced by using a lower supply voltage (3.3-volt) for the majority of the Intel486 SL CPU internal logic. The on-board DRAM buffers may be selectively powered to support either 3.3- or 5-volt DRAMs. The ISA-bus and 82360SL peripheral I/O interfaces are powered by 5-volt. The 5-volt interface to the ISA-bus and 82360SL ensures compatibility of the Intel486 SL processor with existing ISA-bus peripherals and I/O devices. The Intel486 SL processor further reduces system power by minimizing off-chip bus cycles when executing from the cache or floating-point unit.

BIOS and System Setup software written for the Intel386 SL microprocessor may be easily modified to support the new DRAM memory configurations without impacting applications software. The other existing Intel386 SL microprocessor components are supported without any required modifications. The new Intel486SL processor features are transparent to applications software running in existing Intel386 SL microprocessor systems.

Software compatibility

The Intel386 SL microprocessor is binary code compatible with all the Intel386 microprocessors. All the existing programs that are running on an Intel386

ISA PC will run on an Intel386 SL CPU-based machine without recompilation or reassembly. For programs such as power management software, the processor provides system management mode, which establishes a protected environment transparent to the operating systems and applications software. In this environment, applications software can take advantage of the transparency of system management mode without having to worry about interference from operating system and applications software that are running on the system.

Differences between the Intel386 SL microprocessor and the Intel386 SX microprocessor

The best way to describe the differences between the Intel386 SX CPU and the Intel386 SL processor is that the Intel386 SX processor is a subset of the Intel386 SL processor. The following is a list of features that are supported by the Intel386 SL CPU only.

- The Intel386 SL processor provides direct support for DRAMs and SRAMs.
- The maximum physical memory address space is 32 Mbytes on the Intel386 SL processor.
- Direct hardware support compatible with LIM EMS 4.0 is included in the Intel386 SL processor.
- Memory options such as EPROM shadowing and memory roll-over are supported by the Intel386 SL processor.
- System management mode is supported by the Intel386 SL processor.
- A cache controller is embedded inside the Intel386 SL processor which can support 16, 32, and 64 Kbytes of cache.
- ISA-bus and PI-bus peripherals can interface directly to the Intel386 SL processor.
- The Intel386 SL CPU is fully static and the clock can be stopped whenever the HLT instruction is executed or *after an I/O read to the* STP_CLK *register.*
- The Intel386 SL CPU supports suspend operation.
- In addition to the component ID, a signature register is available for software to identify CPU type and stepping information.

Differences between the Intel486 SL CPU and the Intel386 SL CPU

The Intel486 SL CPU and the Intel386 SL CPU were designed to provide the highest level of integration and performance at the lowest possible level of power consumption. The following are the more important features of the CPU:

- It has an integrated memory controller. The Intel386 SL CPU's on-chip memory management unit supports DRAMs and SRAMs directly and provides a maximum physical address space of 32 Mbytes. The Intel486 SL CPU's on-chip memory controller supports up to 64 Mbytes of physical memory. (SRAM is not supported.)

- Support for LIM EMS 4.0 is provided in the Intel386 SL CPU (not in the Intel486 SL CPU).
- The SMM is provided to allow execution of power management and other system management software to be isolated from the operating system and application programs.
- The memory controller supports EPROM shadowing and memory roll-over.
- An embedded cache controller supports a 16-, 32-, and 64-Kbyte-cache (but not in the Intel486 SL CPU, where the cache is internal to the CPU and is fixed at 8 Kbytes).
- ISA bus and PI bus (unique to the SL CPU) provide a direct interface between the CPU and peripherals.
- Suspend/resume operation is supported (allowing the system to be powered down and powered up again without losing the state of the machine).
- The SL CPUs are fully static, allowing software to stop the CPU clock without losing the state of the machine.

In addition to the core CPU, the SL CPU consists of five main building blocks: the internal bus unit, the on-board memory controller unit, the external bus unit, the cache unit (not in the Intel486 core CPU), and the clock unit.

Core CPU

The core CPU of the Intel486 SL processor is based on the core CPU of the Intel486 SX processor, and the core CPU of the Intel386 SL is based on the core of the Intel386 SX processor. The Intel486 SL CPU and the Intel386 SL CPU provide the same register set and instruction set as in the stand-alone Intel486 SX CPU and Intel386 SX CPU. Like the Intel486 SX CPU, the Intel486 SL CPU also has 8 Kbytes of internal cache. Any program that runs on the Intel486 SX CPU will run on the Intel486 SL CPU and likewise for the Intel386 SX CPU and Intel386 SL CPU.

Internal bus unit

The internal bus unit is the router between the CPU core and the other four CPU units. It directs bus cycles to the external bus unit, the cache unit, and the on-board memory controller unit. It uses configuration registers to determine where to send each cycle. These registers control roll-over of memory, the on-board memory limit, the disabling of memory in 64-Kbyte segments in the bottom 1-Mbyte memory address space, BIOS shadowing, and caching of memory-mapped I/O address space.

Normally the internal bus controller sends a bus cycle either to the external bus unit (ISA-bus or PI-bus) or the on-board memory controller unit (for on-board memory), and determines whether the cycle should be cached. All cycles to on-board memory are directed to the on-board memory controller. The internal bus unit determines the size of the on-board memory space by inspecting the OMLCR register. This register specifies the on-board memory limit in 512-

Kbyte blocks (the minimum block of memory that can be addressed in a single bank by the on-board memory controller unit). A value of zero for the limit indicates that accesses above 512 Kbytes are to off-board memory.

Clock unit

The clock unit provides clock signals and clock control for the CPU. The clock source for the clock units comes from two oscillator inputs: the External Frequency Input (EFI) and the ISA clock (ISACLK2). The EFI provides the basis for the CPU clock (CPUCLK). This clock has a maximum rate of EFI/2, but can be programmed for slower speeds or stopped. When the clock is stopped, the static design of the CPU allows it to maintain its state without being refreshed. The programmable MCP clock (NPXCLK) is derived from the CPUCLK.

The ISACLK2 provides the basis for the system clock (SYSCLK) that clocks the system bus. The SYSCLK is an ISA-type clock and is required to be 8 MHz in SL CPU-based systems.

On-board memory controller unit

The on-board memory controller unit supports both DRAM and SRAM (Intel386 SL CPU only) subsystems. When configured for DRAM mode, the DRAM controller inside the memory controller unit controls how the CPU interfaces to the DRAMs. The prime functions of the DRAM controller are address and refresh generation. The refresh logic inside the memory controller provides refresh to the DRAMs during normal operation as well as during suspend. Please note that ISA-bus refresh is not performed by the memory controller.

When programmed for SRAM mode, the SRAM controller inside the Intel386 SL CPU controls the interface between the processor and the SRAMs. The SRAM controller is responsible for generating the control signals for the data transceivers and wait state to support SRAM of different speeds. The memory controller works in conjunction with the cache controller. When the cache controller is enabled, the memory controller is activated only during CPU write cycles or cache-miss read cycles to conserve power. When the cache controller is disabled, all memory accesses occur to the memory controller.

On-board memory bus

Addresses, data, and memory control signals are transmitted on the on-board memory bus. This bus supports DRAMs or SRAMs. In the Intel386 SL processor, the address bus for the DRAM interface is multiplexed. The address bus and data bus for the SRAM interface are multiplexed together. The DRAM and SRAM interfaces share the CMUX interface (CMUX[0:13]) in the Intel386SL processor. The definitions of the CMUX signals are described in Table 3.1.

Cache controller unit

The cache controller unit (Intel386 SL CPU only) consists of the cache interface module and the Intel387SL math coprocessor (MCP) interface module.

TABLE 3.1 On-Board Memory Bus Signals for Intel386 SL CPU

Signal name	DRAM mode	SRAM mode
CMUX0	CASL3#	DIR
CMUX1	CASH3#	LE
CMUX2	CASL2#	DEN3#
CMUX3	CASH2#	DEN2#
CMUX4	CASL1#	DEN1#
CMUX5	CASH1#	DEN1#
CMUX6	CASL0#	DEN0#
CMUX7	CASH0#	DEN0#
CMUX8	RAS3#	CE3#
CMUX9	RAS2#	CE2#
CMUX10	RAS1#	CE1#
CMUX11	RAS0#	CE0#
CMUX12	PARL	OLE#
CMUX13	PARH	OHE#

The cache interface module controls how the cache controller interfaces to the cache SRAM. The 8 Kbytes of cache inside the Intel486 SL CPU is part of the CPU core.

Cache memory bus

The cache memory bus is a 16-bit bus which can address up to 64 Kbytes of cache memory. The bus interface consists of data and control signals. The control signals include Cache Write Enable (CWE#), Cache Output Enable (COE#), Cache Chip Select High (CCSH#), and Cache Chip Select Low (CCSL#).

Math coprocessor (MCP) interface module

The MCP interface module provides an interface between the CPU core and the MCP. This interface includes a register that allows the CPU to slow or stop the clock to the MCP if a static MCP such as the Intel387 SL is used.

MCP bus

The MCP bus provides a direct path between the MCP and the CPU core. It shares the same address bus and data bus with the cache memory bus. Eight additional control and clock signals are provided in the MCP bus: BUSY#, ERROR#, NPXRDY#, NPXADS#, NPXW/R#, NPXRESET, NPXCLK, and PEREQ.

External bus unit

The external bus unit consists of the system bus (ISA-bus) controller, the PI-bus controller, and byte-swapping logic for the data bus. The external bus interface is programmable.

System bus

The system bus is a 16-bit parallel memory and I/O bus. It is compatible with the standard ISA bus found in ISA-compatible PCs, and conforms with the IEEE P996 standard. Unlike some implementations of the ISA bus (such as the Intel386 SL CPU), the drive capability of the system bus is programmable in the Intel486 SL CPU. The ISA-bus clock speed is fixed at 8 MHz to maintain compatibility with existing ISA-bus peripherals.

The system bus is an extension of the CPU's local processor bus, with a maximum memory address space of 16 Mbytes (24 address lines). Memory accesses above 16 Mbytes wrap around to the beginning of memory.

Three buses are derived from the system bus: the peripheral interface bus (PI bus), the X bus, and the expansion bus.

PI bus

The PI bus is a high-speed, asynchronous bus for interfacing with peripherals such as a flash disk or a high-speed VGA graphics frame memory. It is like a decoded local bus and is derived from the ISA bus. The PI bus shares address and data signals of the system bus. It also provides special support for a VGA graphics controller interface and a flash disk interface. Chapter 12 contains a thorough description of PI bus.

X bus

The X bus is a buffered version of the system bus to support devices such as the keyboard controller, floppy disk controller, flash BIOS, external real-time clock, and EPROMs. The buffers are always enabled, with the direction of data transmission controlled by the XDIR signal. The X bus provides an 8-bit data bus (16-bit for 16-bit flash BIOS) and a 17-bit address bus. High or low system bus data bytes can be directed to the X-bus data bus through byte swapping.

Expansion bus

The expansion bus is an extension of the system bus to support ISA-bus expansion slots in the system. This bus provides the complete set of signals commonly found in the ISA bus of an ISA-compatible PC. It can support any standard ISA-bus card, including memory boards, video controllers, fax/modems, and ethernet interface boards. The bus clock rate is fixed at 8 MHz by the SYSCLK signal. The 82360SL also provides a separate OSC clock signal for this bus.

System management mode (SMM)

The SL architecture introduced a new operating mode for microprocessors: the system management mode (SMM). The SMM provides a separate execution environment for system and power management routines that is transparent to the operating system and application programs. A special system management interrupt (SMI) activates the SMM. Upon receipt of an SMI, the CPU temporarily suspends execution of its current operating system or application program, enters the SMM, and begins executing SMM routines located in a dedicated System Management RAM (SMRAM) address space. When the CPU exits the SMM (with an RSM) instruction, the CPU resumes executing the operating system or application program where it left off when the SMI occurred.

The SMM is the main component in the various power management facilities that the SL CPU and 82360SL provide. It is also available to designers to handle other system management tasks when it is important to prevent conflict with the operating system or application program. The SMM is described in detail in Chap. 4.

82360SL Peripheral Controller

The 82360SL peripheral controller contains dedicated logic to interface with the Intel486 SL or Intel386 SL CPU and a complete set of standard ISA-compatible peripheral controllers, including two serial port controllers, one parallel port, two programmable interrupt timers, two interrupt controllers, and two DMA controllers. It also provides interfaces for a keyboard controller, a floppy drive controller, and an IDE hard disk. The software and hardware interfaces to the peripherals embedded inside the 82360SL are identical to those for the discrete components commonly found in an ISA system. (See Fig. 3.4.)

Power management hardware

One of the highlights of the 82360SL is its comprehensive set of power management features. The power management facilities are tightly coupled with SMM of the SL CPU to provide a robust and efficient mechanism for managing the power consumption of a battery-powered PC. The power management mechanism includes facilities for powering down idle peripheral devices, slowing or stopping the clock to system components, and suspend/resume operation. Chapters 5, 6, and 7 describe the power management features of the SL CPU in detail.

IDE interface

The IDE (Integrated Drive Electronics) interface is a simple, hard disk drive interface that consists of 40 signals. This interface allows an IDE hard disk drive to be connected to the system with a simple adapter card containing a minimum of logic. The IDE interface uses a register-based command status protocol standardized by the DOS operating system and BIOS.

The IDE interface is derived from the system bus; therefore, bus cycles for the IDE interface are the same as the system bus. For example, an 8-bit IDE access requires 6 SYSCLKS, and 16-bit IDE access requires 3 SYSCLKS. Zero wait state operation is not supported on the IDE interface. The IDE bus shares

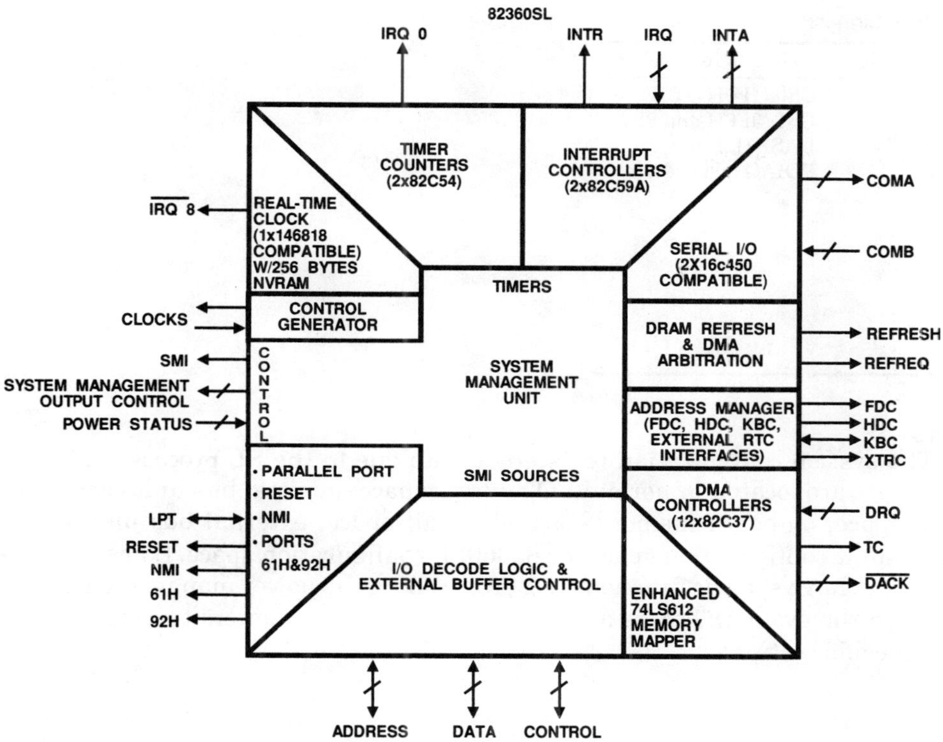

Figure 3.4 Main building blocks of the 82360 SL.

some signal lines with the system bus, plus it has several signals that are unique to it. Table 3.2 shows the IDE bus signals.

Parallel and serial ports

The 82360SL provides controllers for an ISA parallel port and two RS-232C serial ports. The parallel port provides a standard ISA parallel port interface and a second interface for an enhanced parallel port that is unique to the 82360SL. Both ISA devices and faster peripheral devices can operate at the same time on the parallel port. The enhanced parallel port is asynchronous, so it is able to handle much faster data transfers than is possible with the ISA interface. Chapter 14 describes the enhanced parallel port in detail.

Register Resources

The SL architecture offers a rich set of registers. These registers are divided into three groups: CPU registers, ISA system registers, and system configuration registers. The CPU registers include those registers normally found in a stand-alone Intel486 SX or Intel386 SX CPU. ISA-system registers provide access to the I/O ports typically found in a standard ISA system.

TABLE 3.2 IDE Bus Signals

Shared ISA-bus signals	Unique to IDE bus
Reset	CS0 (1F0H–1F7H)
IOW	CS1 (3F6H and 3F7H)
IOR	DASP (LED)
IOCHRDY	PDIAG (slave drive)
IRQ	
SA[0:2]	
SD[0:6]	
XD7	
SD[8:15]	
Ground	
IOCS16	

The system configuration registers are unique to the SL processors. These registers are located in normal I/O address space, internal bus unit configuration space, on-board memory controller unit space, external bus unit space, cache unit configuration space, or 82360SL configuration space. Some of these registers have specific functions (e.g., controlling the power management hardware in the system); others are available to system designers to control product specific features.

Summary

In this chapter we started out by looking at the SL architecture from the system level. We then looked at the internal architecture of the SL processors and the 82360SL. A good understanding of the SL architecture will be important later when we discuss how to design portable applications.

References

Quinnell, R., "Bus-Driver ICs," *EDN,* February 1992, pp. 78–86.
"ISA Bus Specification and Application Notes," Intel Corporation, January 1990.

Chapter

4

System Management Mode

For the past few years, many people have accused the PC industry of becoming stagnant and lacking innovative products. This is definitely not the case with the Intel486 SL CPU and Intel386 SL CPU and 82360SL. The creation of SMM mode offers innovative PC designers a whole new world of opportunities.

The system management mode (SMM) is a unique operating mode of the SL architecture that lets the CPU execute code transparently from the operating system and application software. Hardware, the operating system, and application software can interact directly with the SMM software. To a programmer, SMM is similar to real-address mode in the Intel x86 family of microprocessors. This chapter explains what SMM is and how to use it.

System Management Mode Architecture

The SMM is one of five operating modes in the SL architecture (real mode, protected mode, virtual mode, and ICE mode are the other four modes). As shown in Fig. 4.1, the basic components of the SMM architecture are System Management Interrupt (SMI) to invoke SMM, a unique address space for storage and execution of SMM routines, and a new instruction called RSM (opcode 0FAAh) to exit from SMM. Unlike the other four execution modes, SMM supports collaboration between system resources and the CPU. (See Fig. 4.2.) When the system hardware requires service from the SMM program, it sends

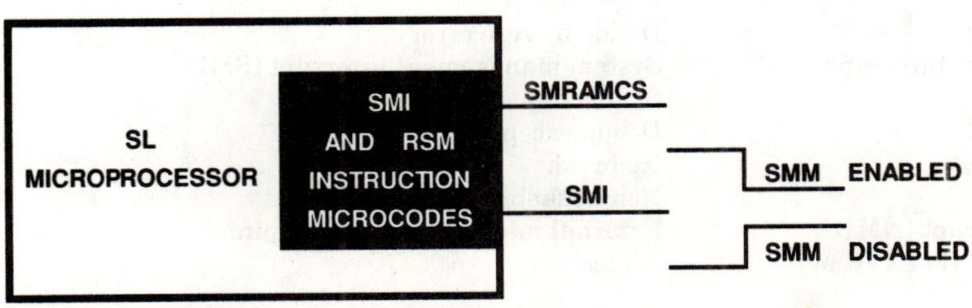

Figure 4.1 System management mode architecture.

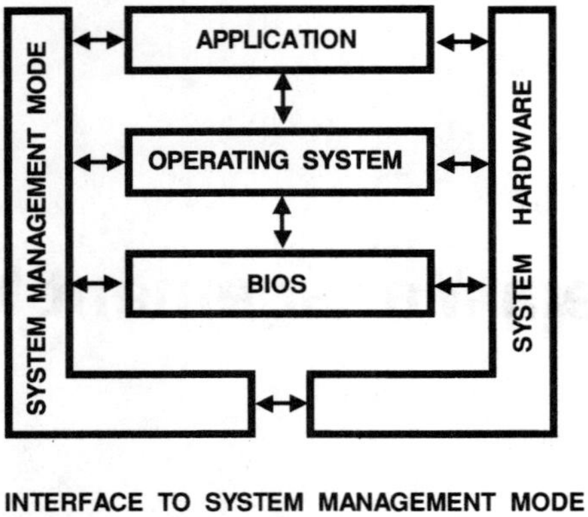

Figure 4.2 Collaboration between system management mode and system resources.

an SMI to the CPU. The CPU then enters the SMM, executes an SMM routine to service the request, and exits SMM.

The following sections describe the implementation of the SMM architecture in the SL CPU.

Entering the SMM

External or internal hardware can invoke the SMM by signaling an SMI. An SMI can be signaled directly by asserting the SMI# pin. Logic in the SL CPU and 82360SL chips also asserts the SMI# signal internally. The SMI# signal is a falling-edge-triggered signal and is recognized only on instruction execution boundaries. While in SMM, the CPU ignores all SMIs until the RSM instruction is executed.

The SL CPU assigns a priority to each type of interrupt or exception. Table 4.1 shows the priorities of the different interrupts and exceptions. The shutdown exception has the highest priority and the I/O lock has the lowest

TABLE 4.1 SL Microprocessor Interrupt and Exception Priorities

Priority	Intel486 SL CPU	Intel386 SL CPU
1	Shutdown	Shutdown
2	Double fault	Double fault
3	S_unit violation	S_unit violation
4	Page fault	Page fault
5	Divide by zero error	Divide by zero error
6	System management interrupt (SMI)	System management interrupt (SMI)
7	Stop clock	Single step
8	Single step	Debug exceptions
9	Debug exceptions	Ice break
10	Ice break	Nonmaskable interrupt (NMI)
11	Nonmaskable interrupt (NMI)	External interrupts via INTR pin
12	External interrupts via INTR pin	I/O lock
13	I/O lock	

priority. The SMI cannot preempt any interrupts or exceptions with a higher priority.

Allowing the CPU to service external interrupts while in SMM can cause the system to hang up. To protect against this problem, the CPU blocks external interrupts generated via the INTR signal after entering SMM. As a result of this action, software routines running in SMM cannot depend on interrupt-driven features. For example, a timing loop that depends on an interrupt from the real-time clock will not work inside SMM.

If the STI instruction is executed while in SMM, this protection against external interrupts is overridden, and the CPU will respond to external interrupts. To avoid hanging up the system in SMM, you should thus guard against using the STI instruction while in SMM.

System management RAM address space

The SL CPU provides a separate memory address space, called the System Management RAM (SMRAM) address space, for storage and execution of SMM software routines. The SMRAM is distinct from the physical memory address space to ensure that software running in SMM does not conflict with the operating system or application software. The SMRAM can be located in either on-board (main memory controlled by the CPU) or off-board memory (memory controlled by the SMRAMCS# signal). The size of the SMRAM can be 32 or 64 Kbytes if off-board memory is used and 64 Kbytes if on-board memory is used. After SMM is enabled, the SMRAM address space is mapped to the physical address space from 30000H to 3FFFFH (64 Kbytes) or from 38000H to 3FFFFH (32 Kbytes).

Once the CPU recognizes an SMI, it enables the SMRAM. The microcode handling the SMI saves the CPU state in the Processor State Area (PSA) in a stacklike fashion beginning with physical address 3FFFFH and ending at 3FE00H. The organization of the PSA is shown in Table 4.2.

Address formation

Unlike real-address mode, the CPU can access or jump anywhere within the 4 Gbyte logical address space in SMM. The CPU can indirectly access or perform a near jump anywhere within the 4-Gbyte logical address space. In SMM, address generation is the same as in real-address mode, without the 64-Kbyte limit. The value loaded into the selector register is shifted four bits and added to the effective address. The effective address can also be generated indirectly using a 32-bit register. The selector is limited to 16 bits. If a call is made, only 16 bits are pushed for a return.

Processor state after entering SMM

After the CPU enters the SMM and saves its state in the PSA, it sets several registers to predefined values. These values are sufficient to allow program

TABLE 4.2 Processor State Area (PSA) Map

Address	Registers
3FFFCH	CR0
3FFF8H	CR3
3FFF4H	EFLAGS
3FFF0H	EIP
3FFECH	EDI
3FFE8H	ESI
3FFE4H	EBP
3FFE0H	ESP
3FFDCH	EBX
3FFD8H	EDX
3FFD4H	ECX
3FFD0H	EAX
3FFCCH	DR6
3FFC8H	DR7
3FFC4H	TR (upper word reserved)
3FFC0H	LDTR (upper word reserved)
3FFBCH	GS (upper word reserved)
3FFB8H	FS (upper word reserved)
3FFB4H	DS (upper word reserved)
3FFB0H	SS (upper word reserved)
3FFACH	CS (upper word reserved)
3FFA8H	ES (upper word reserved)
3FFA7H-3FF04H	Reserved
3FF02H	Halt auto restart slot
3FF00H	I/O instruction restart slot
3FEFCH	SMM signature (80000H for the Intel486 SL CPU and 10000H for the Intel386 SL CPU)
3FEFBH-3FE00H	Reserved

TABLE 4.3 Predefined Register Values in SMM for SL CPU

Selector	Base	Limit
CS	30000H	4 Gbytes
DS	0H	4 Gbytes
ES	0H	4 Gbytes
FS	0H	4 Gbytes
GS	0H	4 Gbytes
SS	0H	4 Gbytes

execution, but additional initialization may be needed. Table 4.3 shows the predefined values set in the registers. In addition, the PE bit in the CR0 register and the DR7 register is cleared.

Debug registers

Upon entering SMM, the CPU automatically saves registers DR6 and DR7 in SMRAM, and these registers should not be modified. Debug registers DR[0:5] are not saved automatically, and they should be saved by power management (or SMM) software before going into suspend.

Location of first instruction

After entering SMM, the PE bit in the CR0 register is automatically cleared and CS:IP is initialized to 3000H:8000H, causing instruction execution to start at physical address 38000H. Therefore, all SMM software must be written such that the first instruction is located at 3000H:8000H when SMM is enabled.

Entering and leaving SMM

As previously mentioned, SMM is entered by asserting the SMI# signal. After an SMI is recognized, the CPU enables the SMRAM address space, saves the CPU state in the PSA, enables SMM, and starts executing instructions at system address 38000H. The SMI# pin will remain asserted until the software running in SMM exits SMM. With the SL CPU and 82360SL chips, an SMI can be generated by either hardware or software.

An SMM revision identifier, located at 3FEFCH in the SMRAM address space, indicates the SMM version and the extensions that the CPU supports. The lower word of the SMM revision identifier indicates the version of the base SMM architecture; the upper word indicates the extensions available. The I/O trap extension bit (bit 16) of the SMM identifier indicates whether or not the CPU supports the I/O trap restart mechanism. If this bit is set, the I/O trap restart mechanism is supported.

The only way to exit SMM is to execute the RSM instruction. Executing the RSM instruction restores the CPU registers to their original states using information stored in the PSA, disables the SMRAM address space, and deasserts the SMI# signal. The RSM instruction should never be executed outside SMM. Doing so will cause an invalid opcode trap.

The RSM instruction has two options associated with it, which can be enabled or disabled by writing to the PSA.

The first option enables the SMM program to return to the halt state through the use of the halt auto restart slot if the SMI occurred when the CPU was in the halt state. The halt auto restart slot is located at 03FF02H in the SMRAM address space; it is 16 bits wide. If the halt state bit (bit 0) is set prior to execution of the RSM instruction, the CPU automatically reenters the halt state; otherwise, the CPU continues execution just after the interrupted halt instruction.

The second option enables the I/O instruction that caused the SMI to be reexecuted. The I/O trap restart slot located at 3FF00H in the SMRAM address space determines if the I/O instruction is to be reexecuted. If the slot is set to 0FFH, the RSM instruction automatically executes the I/O instruction after exiting SMM; if the slot is set to 0H, the I/O instruction is not reexecuted. Upon entering SMM, the CPU automatically initializes the I/O trap restart slot to 0H. Your software should set the I/O trap restart slot to 0FFH only if the SMI was caused by an I/O trap.

Blocking CPU reset

CPU reset is one of the few interrupts that has a higher priority than the SMI. Except for CPU reset caused by shutdown and PWRGOOD, the CPU reset signal should be blocked while in SMM. Otherwise, the integrity of the system might be lost.

After entering SMM, the SMI# signal remains low (asserted) until bit 0 of the SMI_MARK register (0F9H) is cleared (normally done right before the RSM instruction is executed). The SMI# signal can be used to block the CPU reset signal.

Exit from SMM

Upon exiting SMM, program execution always returns to the program that was interrupted by the SMI. However, program execution can be passed to a program different than the interrupted program. For a program running in real mode, the CPU can be directed to go to a different program by modifying the instruction pointer in the PSA to point to the beginning of another program. Upon exiting from SMM, the CPU will then jump to the new program instead of returning to the interrupted program.

The CPU can also be directed to go into protected mode upon exit from SMM. However, before going into protected mode, the selectors for the different segment registers must be modified, or a system crash will occur. One way around this problem is to exit SMM without going back to the interrupted program. This can be done by having the SMM program generate a CPU reset prior to reenabling CPU. The CPU reset will then force the CPU to exit SMM without returning to the original application.

To differentiate the CPU reset from other CPU resets generated by the system, your SMM program can write to the shutdown byte in the CMOS RAM or a memory location in SMRAM to indicate that the CPU reset was caused by the SMM program. By examining the shutdown byte, the reset routine can redirect control to another program to enter protected mode.

Applications of SMM

One of the main reasons that Intel developed the SMM was to provide a method of executing power management software that did not interfere with the execution of the operating system or application programs. The SMM, however, is a very versatile mode that can be used for many applications. The use of the SMM for power management is described in detail in Chaps. 5, 6, and 7. The following two examples show how SMM can be used in designing new applications. The functions performed in each application are different; yet, as you will see, both applications make use of the transparent property of SMM. Software and hardware components are required in both examples.

A debugger using SMM

The SMM has proved very useful for debugging system designs based on the SL CPU. Often, when a system malfunctions, it hangs up, making it difficult to locate the cause of the problem without a logic analyzer or an in-circuit emulator (ICE). Using SMM, we can often determine the state of the CPU or a peripheral even when the system is hung.

One way to break out of a hung condition is to generate an SMI to force the CPU into SMM. You can then use a debugger program written to run in SMM to examine the registers and isolate problems in the CPU and system peripherals. Chapter 16 gives additional examples of how a debugger running in SMM can be used for system debugging.

For the debugger to run in SMM, the debugger program must be loaded in SMRAM, which can be located in main memory or external memory. One benefit of locating the SMRAM in external memory is that the debugger program can still function, even when main memory is corrupted. In addition, the external memory is backed up by battery. Thus, in the event that there is a power failure, the external memory will still be active.

The program that loads the debugger into the SMRAM must initialize the CPU before it starts loading to inform the CPU whether it is using main or external memory. Then the loader must enable SMRAM by setting bit 3 of the OMDCR register. After SMRAM is enabled, the debugger program can be copied to the 3000:0000H address space.

Once the debugger is loaded into SMRAM, any trigger (software or hardware) can theoretically be used to invoke the SMM and run the debugger. The SL CPU evaluation board provides an external SMI switch for generating SMIs. This switch is connected to the external SMI pin (EXT_SMI# on the 82360SL). Before this switch can be used to invoke the debugger, the debugger loading program must enable the external SMI pin (EXT_SMI#) as a trigger for the SMI and initialize the timer associated with the pin. Once the circuit is enabled, you can force the CPU into SMM and run the debugger anytime, merely by activating the switch (pressing the button). Figure 4.3 shows an example of this circuit.

The debugger can be a stand-alone program or it can be included as part of the system's SMM program. If the debugger is to be a stand-alone program, its first instruction must be located at 3000:8000H. To include the debugger program as part of the SMM program, the SMM program must pass control to the debugger program when a debug trigger is invoked (e.g., external SMI).

Advantages of using SMM for debugging. A debugger running in SMM offers several benefits over traditional software debuggers and ICEs, as described here:

- The debugger can be invoked in any CPU operating mode (i.e., protected, virtual, or real mode).
- You can often still use the debugger, even if the system has crashed and the CPU is hung.

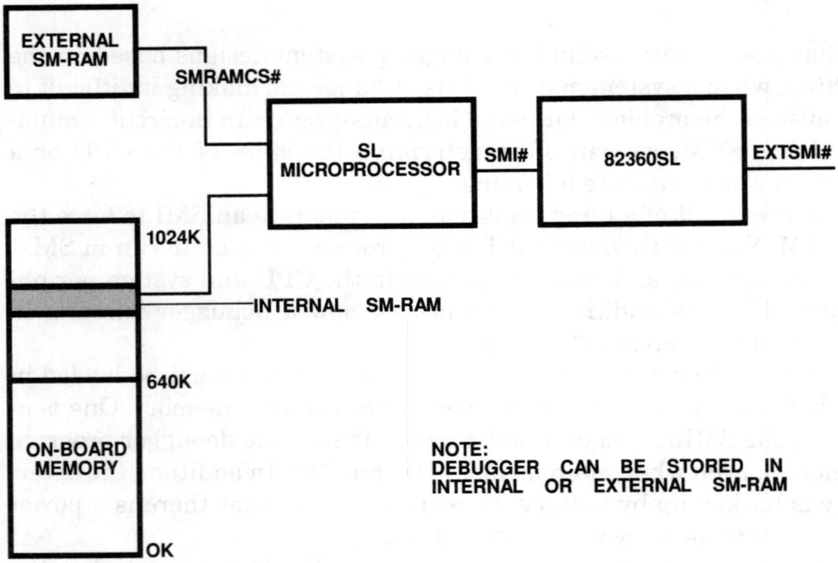

Figure 4.3 Using SMM for debugging.

- Unlike debuggers running on the same target system that will not function if the main memory is corrupted, a debugger running under SMM can still function if the program is stored in external memory.
- While in SMM, the entire memory address space appears as linear memory and the debugger can address up to 4 Gbytes of memory address space.
- With an ICE, the CPU is not running in real time. Instructions execution is done through a host system. The delay introduced by the host system can be a problem when debugging a real-time application. A debugger running in SMM runs on the same CPU in the target system and does not introduce delays in the system.
- Software timers can be set up inside the debugger to interrupt the application at a specific time.
- The debugger can be triggered by software as well as hardware. For example, the debugger can be invoked by the program that the programmer is trying to debug. Instead of inserting a breakpoint into the program, a software SMI call can be added to a program to invoke the debugger.

Features of a debugger using SMM

The following list gives the features that should be included in a debugger designed to run in SMM.

- Display registers inside an SL CPU configuration space
- Display memory contents

- Display interrupt vector locations
- Display BIOS data area
- Edit memory and register contents
- Break-point I/O and memory accesses (read or write)
- Single-step execution
- Ability of the debugger and the loading program to be stored in ROM as well as disk files

Note: The debugger can output data to either a monitor screen or a printer.

A fail-safe backup mechanism running in SMM

Losing data during a power outage can be a nightmare for a computer user who does not have an uninterruptible power supply. A cost-effective solution to this problem is to provide the computer system with a small backup battery that can keep the system active long enough for the CPU to back up all volatile data to a permanent storage device before powering down the system. After power is back to normal, the system can be powered up and the data and machine state can be restored to the state it was in prior to the power failure.

The SMM provides a convenient mechanism for running a fail-safe data backup program. A monitor circuit can be designed that generates an SMI whenever a power failure is detected. The SMI can then be used to activate the backup battery and invoke the fail-safe backup program, which runs in SMM. Figure 4.4 shows such a circuit.

The backup program might work as follows. When the monitor circuit detects a power failure, it generates a fail-safe SMI, interrupts the CPU, and runs the backup program in SMM. The backup program generates a warning beep and a message to warn the user about the power failure and to ask the user to complete processing within one minute. When one minute is over, the service routine sets the fail-safe status bit. The state of the fail-safe status bit will indicate to the CPU, upon reset, whether it is coming from a power failure or a cold boot. When system power returns, a CPU reset is generated. This CPU reset can then be used to initiate a system restore routine that uses the backup data to restore the system to its operating state before the power failure.

When developing such a backup program, one design problem you will encounter is where and how to save the machine state data. The typical memory size for a notebook computer is about 4 Mbytes, making it more practical and economical to save it on the hard disk than on another permanent memory storage device. If you choose to save the state data in a file on the hard disk, the backup program will be operating-system-dependent. In addition, saving the data to a file storage area accessible to the operating system might corrupt the data on the hard disk. This problem can be solved by reserving some tracks on the hard disk for backing up data during a power failure. Every BIOS on an ISA-compatible computer has a hard disk drive parameter table. Software interrupt 41H points to the beginning of this table. Any operating

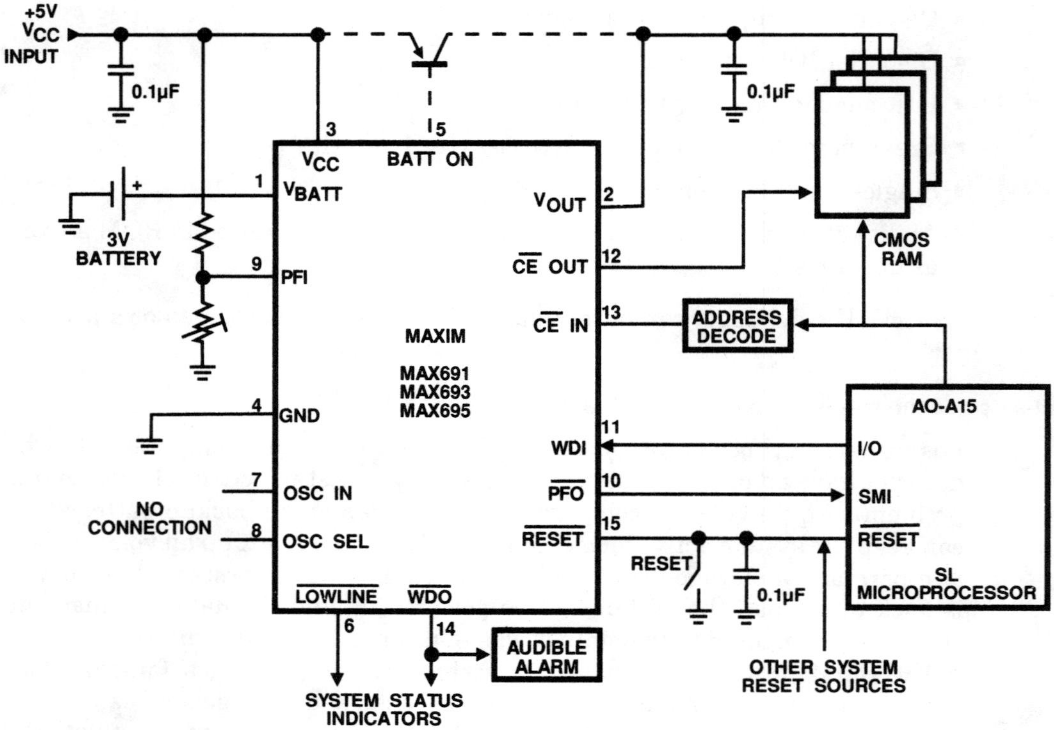

Figure 4.4 Power-fail detection circuit. (*Courtesy of Maxim Integrated Products.*)

system that runs on the system uses this table when partitioning and formatting the hard disk.

Before the hard disk is formatted by the operating system, a special hard disk format program can be used to alter the hard disk parameter table to reduce the number of tracks available to the operating system. Figure 4.5 shows a block diagram of such an arrangement. Once the hard disk parameter table has been modified, the interrupt vector for software interrupt 41H must be changed to point to a modified table.

The modified hard disk parameter table will show fewer cylinders than the hard disk actually has. After the operating system has formatted the hard disk using the modified table, the applications software and operating system will use only the cylinders indicated by the modified table. Since the operating system has no knowledge of this separate storage area on the hard disk, the backup software can save the data to the hard disk without the need to know which operating system is running on the system. Also, saving the state of the system in a separate area on the hard disk protects the rest of the data on the hard disk.

The original hard disk parameter is stored in a location known only to the program that is doing the disk saving during a 0-volt suspend (described in Chaps. 5 and 6). The disk saving program will use the original and modified

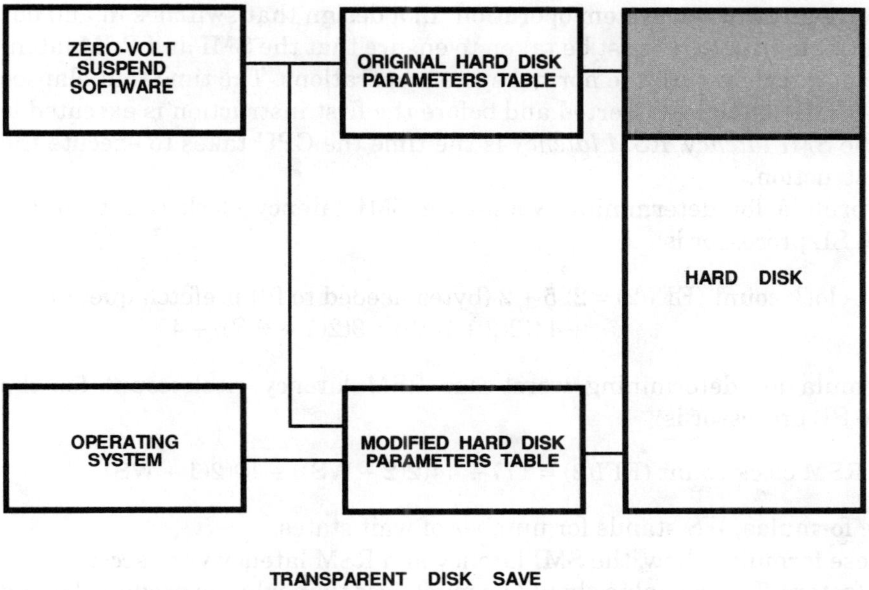

Figure 4.5 Fail-safe system backup to reserved tracks of a hard disk.

tables to determine where in the special disk partition to save the data. The disk saving program is normally included in the SMM program.

Advantages of using transparent disk save

The advantages of transparent disk save over saving data to a file are as follows:

- Data can be saved to the hard disk faster by using the transparent disk save method than by using BIOS or DOS function calls.
- Since transparent disk saves do not have to use the same format that is used by the operating system to save data, they can save more data in less space.
- Transparent disk save is independent of operating system.
- The data saved during 0-volt suspend is stored in an area separated from the operating system's file storage area. Therefore, there is no chance that there is insufficient space to save the system's state during 0-volt suspend.
- While doing a disk save to a file, something could happen to corrupt the hard disk. For example, the battery might run low before the file is completely saved to the hard disk. With transparent disk save, the hard disk will not be corrupted even if all the data has not been saved.

SMI and RSM Latency

While it is true that the SMM environment is transparent to operating systems and application software, the time the CPU takes to go in and out of SMM might have an effect on system operation. In a design that switches in and out of SMM frequently, care must be taken to ensure that the SMI and RSM latencies do not interfere with the normal system operations. The time that elapses after the SMI# signal is asserted and before the first instruction is executed is called the *SMI latency*. *RSM latency* is the time the CPU takes to execute the RSM instruction.

The formula for determining worst-case SMI latency clock count for the Intel386 SL processor is:

$$\text{SMI clock count (EFI/2)} = 225 + 2\text{ (bytes needed to fill prefetch queue)} + 44(2(2 + WS)) + 9(2(1 + WS)) + 4$$

The formula for determining worst-case RSM latency clock count for the Intel386 SL processor is:

$$\text{RSM clock count (EFI/2)} = 177 + 44(2(2 + \text{WS})) + 10(2(1 + \text{WS}))$$

In these formulas, *WS* stands for number of wait states.

As these formulas show, the SMI latency and RSM latency vary according to several factors. Typical value should be much less than what is predicted using these formulas. The SMI latency depends on the CPU clock speed, the number of memory wait states, and the number of bytes needed to fill the prefetch queue. The CPU clock speed is controlled by the EFI input and the slow CPU clock field in the CPUPWRMODE register (22h). The memory wait state is dependent on the page mode selected if DRAM is used, and the number of wait states selected in the MCSRAMWS register (303h, OMCU) if SRAM is used. The number of bytes needed to fill the prefetch queue varies from 1 to 12. Table 4.4 shows examples of SMI latency according to the page mode and CPU clock rate.

The formula for determining latency clock count for the Intel486 SL CPU is:

SMI latency clock count = (number of clocks to execute microcode)
+ (number of clocks to fill prefetch queue)
+ (number of double word memory write cycles
* number of clocks per double word memory write cycle) = 200 + (one 3-2-2-2 burst cycle) + (59 * 2)
= 200 + 9 + 118 = 327 CPU clocks

TABLE 4.4 SMI Latency Measured under Different DRAM Page Modes and CPU Clock Rates for the Intel386 SL CPU

	CPU clock rate	
	25 MHz	20 MHz
Page mode	SMI latency in microseconds	
High-speed	15	18
Fast	16	19.50
Normal	18	23.50

This calculation assumes no wait state. It also assumes that the processor is at an instruction boundary so an SMI can start immediately. There are 59 double word writes and 9 two-byte writes to memory during an SMI.

The formula for determining the clock count of an RSM instruction that has been prefetched and decoded by the Intel486 SL CPU is:

```
RSM clock count = (number of clocks to execute microcode)
                  + (number of double word memory read cycles
                  * number of clocks per double word memory read cycle)
                  + (number of word memory write cycles
                  * number of clocks per word memory write cycle)
                = 262 + (57 * 2) + (2 * 2)
                = 380
```

This formula assumes no wait state.

Writing an SMM Program

One of the best ways to learn about SMM programming is to create a simple program. In this chapter is a step-by-step guide for the development of an SMM program called "Hello." Hello displays the message 'Hello, SMM!' while another program is running.

Building an SMM program

An SMM program can be stored in a binary file or an optional ROM. In either case, a program or a routine is needed to load the SMM program into the SMRAM. Since not everyone has access to an EPROM programmer, the SMM program described here is written as a binary file.

The programming language used here is Microsoft Assembler. The same program can be written in C language.

Steps in creating an SMM program

Figure 4.6 shows the process of creating an SMM program. As you can see, the SMM program consists of three parts: the loader program (INIT.ASM), which loads the SMM program into the SMRAM; the kernel (KERNAL.ASM), which directs the SMI requests to the individual SMI service routines; and the SMI routines (in this example, SUSPEND.ASM, GSTDBY.ASM, LSTDBY.ASM, LTRP.ASM, AND MISC.ASM), which service the SMI requests.

Loading the SMM program

The INIT.ASM program reads the SMM program binary file and stores the file in the SMRAM. The program also initializes the SMM hardware. Even though the SMRAM address space is between 30000H and 3FFFFH, the SMM entry

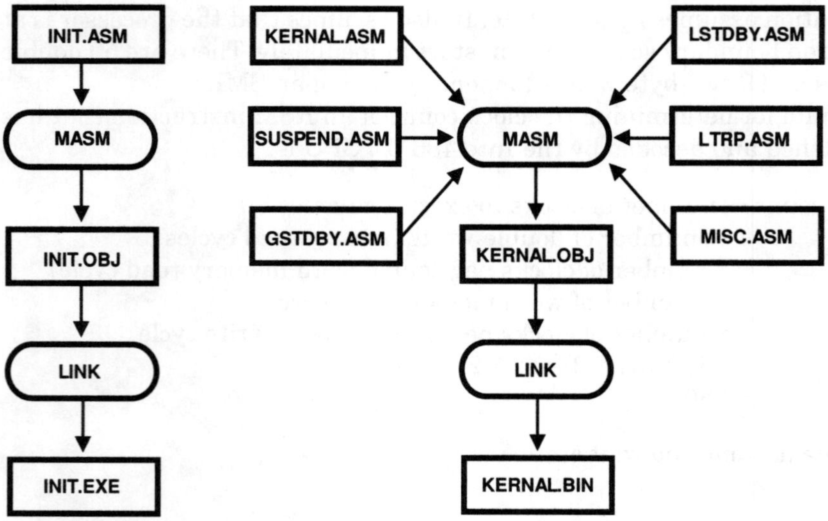

Figure 4.6 Building an SMM program.

point is always at 38000H. Therefore, the entry point of the SMM program must also start at 38000H.

Initialization

The SMM hardware must be initialized before the SL CPU can accept any SMI requests. The global power management enable bit must be enabled for any SMI to take effect. Listing 4.1 shows code to activate external SMI.

Listing 4.1 Code in INIT.ASM Program to Activate the External SMI Mechanism

```
code    SEGMENT
        ASSUME  CS:code, DS:code
        ORG  100H
include superset.inc
EXTRN open_omcu:near, close_386sl:near, open_360sl:near, write_360sl:near
EXTRN close_360sl:near, open_ibu:near,close_cpupwrmode:near
EXTRN read_360sl:near
; Open SM file
entry:
        mov     ah, 3Dh             ;open file function
        mov     al, 00H             ;read only
        mov     dx, offset SmFile
        Int     21h
        jnc     open_smmprog        ;if no error, then we are done here!
        jmp     abort
;Read the SM file, and close it
open_smmprog:
```

```
        mov  Handle, ax          ;save the handle
        push    ax
        push    bx
        push    cx
        push    dx
        mov     dx, offset version
        mov     ah, 09h
        int     21h
; Mark SmSeg as write-only memory
        call    open_ibu
        mov     ax, 30Ah
        mov     dx, ax
        mov     ax, 0FFFFH
        out     dx, ax
        call    close_386sl
; read in system management file
        mov     ax, SmSeg
        mov     ds, ax
        xor     dx, dx              ;ds:dx = SM memory buffer
        mov     cx, 8000H           ;read half of SM image
        mov     bx, cs:Handle       ;file handle
        mov     ah, 3FH                 ;read file
        Int     21h
        jc      rd_sm_exit          ;error occurred, exit
        sub     ax, 8000H           ;test for complete read
        jc      rd_sm_exit          ;error occurred, exit
; Mark SmSeg as read-only memory
        call    open_ibu
        mov     ax, 30Ah
        mov     dx, ax
        mov     ax, 05555h
        out     dx, ax
        call    close_386sl
; verify file read
        xor     dx, dx
        mov     cx, 1               ;read one byte to verify full file read
        mov     ah, 3FH                 ;read file
        int     21h
        cmp     ax, 0
        jne     bad_sm_exit
        clc
        jmp     rd_sm_exit
bad_sm_exit:
        stc
        mov     dx, offset filerr
        mov     ah, 09h
        int     21h
rd_sm_exit:
        pushf
```

```
        mov     ax, cs
        mov     ds, ax          ;restore ds
        mov     bx, Handle
        mov     ah, 3Eh                 ;close file function
        int     21h
        popf
        pop     dx
        pop     cx
        pop     bx
        pop     ax
        call    open_omcu       ; select SmSeg as the on-board
        mov     ax, MCSMRAM     ; memory segment
        mov     dx, ax
        mov     al, 06h
        out     dx, al
        call    close_386sl
; System management hardware initialization
        call    open_360sl
        mov     bl, SM_REQ_CNTRL        ; enable external SMI
        call    read_360sl
        or      al, 0c0H
        mov     bh, al
        call    write_360sl
        call    close_360sl
exit:
        mov     ax, 4C00H               ; terminate program
        int     21H
;-------------------------------------------------------------------
; OPTIONAL STACK - CAUTION - MUST USE FUNCTION 4CH IF LOCAL STACK
; IS USED
;
Handle dw  ?
SmFile db  'kernel.bin',0
filerr  db      'Error: Cannot open file "KERNEL.BIN"',cr,lf,'$'
version db      cr,lf
        db      'System Management Kernel Version 0.01',cr,lf
        db      'System Management Kernel Installed.',cr,lf
        db      cr,lf,'$'
SmSeg EQU  0E800H
;
;-------------------------------------------------------------------
code  ENDS                      ; end code segment
      END  entry
```

Creating the kernel

The kernel is basically a traffic director. It filters out the SMI requests and passes them on to the appropriate SMI service routines. When an SMI service

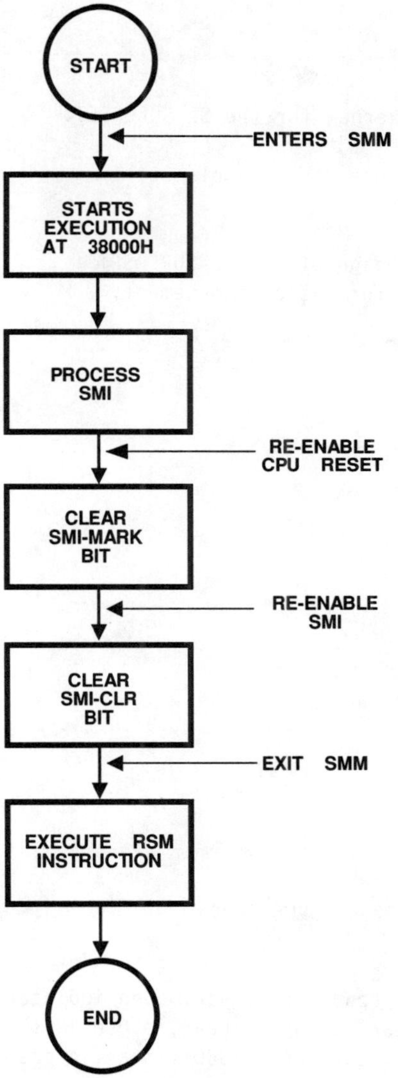

Figure 4.7 SMI processing flow diagram.

routine is complete, program control is passed back to the kernel. After all the SMI requests are serviced, the kernel executes a routine and passes program control back to the application program that was interrupted. Figure 4.7 shows how the kernel services an SMI request.

The example SMM program in Listing 4.2 displays the 'Hello, SMM!' message on the screen whenever the external SMI button on the SL evaluation board is pushed. When the external SMI triggers an SMI, program control goes to the kernel, which is executing in SMM. After verifying that the SMI was indeed caused by the external SMI button, the kernel calls the external SMI service routine.

Listing 4.2 Simple Kernel Program

```
;--------------------------------------------------------------
;
; KERNEL.ASM: System management kernel for the SL SUPERSET.
;
; This file contains the source code for a sample SL
; SUPERSET system management software.
;
; This handler demonstrates the usage of the SL SUPERSET
; system management capabilities for system management.
;
;--------------------------------------------------------------
;
;           Include files
;
;--------------------------------------------------------------
Include superset.inc
code    segment      byte  PUBLIC   'code'
        assume       cs:code
        ORG  0
ORIGIN       EQU     $
start:
      jmp    kernel
       db    "System Management Kernel", 00
;--------------------------------------------------------------
;
;           Equates
;
;--------------------------------------------------------------
IFDEF DEBUG
cr     EQU  0AH       ; used in debugging messages
If     EQU  0DH
ENDIF
EXTRN open_cpupwrmode:near, close_cpupwrmode:near, open_ibu:near
EXTRN open_omcu:near, open_ebu:near, open_ccu:near, close_386sl:near
EXTRN open_360sl:near, read_360sl:near, write_360sl:near, close_360sl:near
Stack       dw  800  dup (?)
Topofstack dw  ?
scrnbuff   dw  2000 DUP (0)
hello      db  'H',7,'e',7,'l',7,'l',7,'o',7,',',7,'S',7,'M',7,'M',7,'!',7
videobuff  equ 0b000H
;--------------------------------------------------------------
;--------------------------------------------------------------
;
;           Request processing jump table
;
;--------------------------------------------------------------
REQTAB        LABEL WORD
INIT   dw  0     ; 0 - initialization
;--------------------------------------------------------------
```

```
;
;              SM-RAM Entry Point
;
;-----------------------------------------------------------------
;-----------------------------------------------------------------
;
;       Kernel Routine
;
;       Algorithm: Determine what caused the SMI by reading
;       the status registers and pass control to the system
;       management request handler
;
;-----------------------------------------------------------------
kernel:
;determines what caused an SMI
        mov    al, MASK_NMI ; disable NMI
        out    CMOS_INDEX, al
        mov    ax, cs
        mov    ds, ax
        mov    es, ax
        mov    ss, ax
        mov    sp, Topofstack
        call   open_360sl
        mov    bl, SM_REQ_STS
        call   read_360sl   ; read SM request reg
        call   close_360sl
        shl    al, 1        ; is SMI caused by external SMI
        shl    al, 1
        jnc    exit_smi
        call   exec_ext_SMI
exit_smi:
;terminate SMI service routine
        call   open_360sl
        xor    bh, bh
        mov    bl, SMI_CLR
        call   write_360sl ; re-enable SMI
        mov    bl, SMI_MARK
        call   write_360sl ; re-enable CPU reset
        call   close_360sl

        mov    al, UNMASK_NMI ; re-enable NMI
        out    CMOS_INDEX, al
        db     0FH, 0AAh   ; execute RSM instr
;-----------------------------------------------------------------
;
;       System Management Request Handler
;
;-----------------------------------------------------------------
exec_ext_smi proc near    ; external smi request
        call   open_360sl
        mov    bl, SM_REQ_STS ; clear extsmi request bit
```

```
        call   read_360sl
        and    al, 0bfh
        mov    bh, al
        call   write_360sl
        call   close_360sl
        call   scrn_mes     ; display the 'Hello, SMM' message
        mov    al, 0eeh     ; post code to diag card
        out    80H, al
        ret
exec_ext_smi endp
scrn_mes proc near
.386
        pushad
        cld
;save video memory into temporary buffer
        lea    di, scrnbuff
        mov    ax, 3800H
        mov    es, ax
        xor    si, si
        mov    ax, videobuff
        mov    ds, ax
        mov    cx, 7D0H
        rep    movsw
; clear screen
        mov    ax, videobuff
        mov    es, ax
        xor    di, di
        mov    cx, 7D0H
        xor    ax, ax
cls:
        mov    es:[di], ax
        inc    di
        inc    di
        loop   cls
; move message into screen
        mov    ax, videobuff
        mov    es, ax
        xor    di, di
        mov    ax, 3800H
        mov    ds, ax
        mov    si, offset hello
        mov    cx, 10
        rep    movsw
; 3 seconds delay
        mov    bx, 010H
delay:
        mov    cx, 0ffffh
delay1:
        aad
```

```
        loop  delay1
        sub   bx, 1
        cmp   bx, 0
        jnz   delay
; restore video screen
        mov   ax, 3800H
        mov   ds, ax
        lea   si, scrnbuff
        mov   ax, videobuff
        mov   es, ax
        xor   di, di
        mov   cx, 7D0H
        rep   movsw
        popad
        ret
scrn_mes endp
;-------------------------------------------------------------------
;
;       END OF POWER MANAGEMENT HANDLER
;
;-------------------------------------------------------------------
code  ends
      end
```

SMI service routines

Each SMI service routine is responsible for servicing a particular SMI request. Upon completion of a service routine, program control is returned to the kernel. Listing 4.2 has only a single external SMI service routine, because the external SMI is the only SMI enabled. This service routine performs the following functions:

1. The current screen is saved into a temporary buffer and the screen is cleared.
2. The message 'Hello, SMM!' is displayed at the top left corner of the screen.
3. After a 3-second pause, the screen is restored to its original display.
4. The external SMI request status bit is cleared. (Please note that the system will remain in SMM if any status bit is not cleared when exiting SMM.)
5. Program control returns to the kernel.

Exit from SMM

Before executing the RSM instruction to exit SMM, the SMM kernel must perform several tasks. SMI and CPU reset are disabled while inside SMM. They must be reenabled before exit from SMM. SMI is reenabled by doing a dummy write to the SMI_CLR register (0BDH, INDEX) and CPURESET is reenabled by clearing the SMI_MARK bit (bit 0) of the SMI_MARK register (0F9H, INDEX). The SMI_MARK bit should be set before doing a dummy I/O read to the SMI_CLR register. If the order is reversed, another SMI can come in before the RSM instruction is complete.

Generating the SMM program

Listing 4.3 Shows MAKE Files for Assembling the INIT.ASM and KERNEL.ASM Programs.

```
;-------------------------------------------------------------------
init.obj: init.asm superset.inc
  masm init;
cfgspace.obj: cfgspace.asm superset.inc
  masm cfgspace;
init.exe: init.obj cfgspace.obj
  link init + cfgspace,,init/map,;
  del init.com
  exe2bin init init.com
;-------------------------------------------------------------------
kernel.obj: kernel.asm superset.inc
  masm kernel;
cfgspace.obj: cfgspace.asm superset.inc
  masm cfgspace;
kernel.exe: kernel.obj cfgspace.obj
  link kernel + cfgspace,,kernel/map,;
  del kernel.bin
  exe2bin kernel kernel.bin
;-------------------------------------------------------------------
```

Programming guidelines

To ensure complete transparency with application software, your SMM program should not:

- Rely on system BIOS function calls
- Rely on operating system function calls
- Write data outside the SMRAM area
- Execute any software interrupts
- Leave external interrupt requests disabled for a long time
- Enable interrupts by executing an "STI" instruction

Time slicing

While inside SMM, all the interrupt requests are blocked. If the system remains in SMM for a long time and the interrupt requests are not serviced, problems can occur. Therefore, the time it takes to process an SMI request must be minimized to prevent SMM from interfering with normal system operations.

One way to limit the latency in servicing an SMI request is to break down a large task into several smaller jobs and execute them one at a time at programmed intervals. For example, instead of sending a large block of data to a device at one time, the large block of data can be broken into several smaller blocks and output to the device over a period of time.

When an SMI request occurs, the routine servicing the request can break up the task into several smaller jobs. The jobs can be spooled in the main memory or a mass storage device such as hard disk. The software SMI timer can then be programmed to generate software SMI at regular intervals. Once programmed, the software SMI timer will generate a software SMI request whenever the timer expires. Upon detecting the software SMI request (by examining the SM_REQ_STS register), the software SMI request routine will retrieve the first job in the queue, execute the job, and exit from SMM. The process will continue until all the jobs are executed. After all the jobs are complete, the software SMI timer is disabled.

Currently, there is only one software SMI timer in the 82360SL available for time slicing. In the case of multiple SMI requests, the tasks must be spooled first and serviced on a first-come first-serve basis. The kernel in the SMRAM will service each task as previously described. Upon completion, the kernel will look for tasks waiting in the queue.

Summary

The earliest power management architectures were plagued by compatibility problems. System management mode solved the problem by isolating power management from the rest of the system. As SMM is now a universal requirement for power management on notebook computers, we should be looking at new ways to take advantage of the transparent property of SMM. The discussion in this chapter provides a good foundation for how to use SMM. Combined with your creativeness, I have no doubt that SMM will find its way into many different applications.

Chapter

5

Introduction to Power Management

In portable computer design, *power management* refers to the techniques and mechanisms used in a product to conserve power for the purpose of extending battery life. Power management is not a new subject. It is commonly employed in embedded applications. But, until a couple of years ago, the term *power management* was almost unheard of in the computer industry. The emergence of laptop computers brought power management to the forefront of PC design because the efficient use of power is critical in products such as laptop, notebook, and palmtop computers where battery capacity is limited.

This chapter and the next two chapters ("Power Management Software" and "Power Management Techniques") describe the power management facilities available with the SL architecture, and show ways to exploit these features to maximize battery life in portable computers. The concepts and techniques discussed in these chapters can be used in either Intel486 SL CPU- or Intel386 SL CPU-based products.

History of Power Management in Personal Computers

Before beginning a detailed discussion of the SL power management facilities, an historic perspective of power management in PCs will help in understanding the reasoning behind the SL power management architecture.

First-generation power management

As with any kind of evolution, the first generation of power management in PCs was primitive. Efforts to conserve power were generally limited to CPU clock control and a switch to power everything off. The power management hardware on these machines produced little power saving and had many problems.

The software controlling the first-generation power management hardware often conflicted with the operating system and application programs, leading to system crashes and data corruption. The root of this problem was in the implementation of the power management hardware. The nonmaskable interrupt (NMI) was used to perform functions like servicing a standby button, turning off power to a peripheral, and slowing or stopping the CPU clock. This mechanism saves power, but causes compatibility problems, because the software servicing the NMI is not isolated from the operating system and applications software. After it finishes servicing a power management request, the NMI handler might restore the system to its previous state incorrectly and cause the system to crash or allow the application to access a powered-down device and cause the application to crash. Those kinds of problems often limited the OEMs (Original Equipment Manufacturers) of these portable computers to a single proprietary operating system and left users frustrated. OEMs are also forced to develop many versions of power management drivers to accommodate different operating environments.

Second-generation power management

The introduction of the SL architecture's system management mode (SMM), first implemented in the Intel386 SL CPU, ushered in a new, advanced generation of power management technology that permits battery life in portable computers to be extended without interfering with the operating system and applications software. As discussed in Chap. 3, the SMM is transparent to the operating system and applications software and requires no special software drivers.

The SMM offers several useful power management facilities, including:

- A transparent system management interrupt (SMI) to the system to invoke power management service routines
- A unique address space for storing and executing power management service routines
- An RSM instruction to restore the system to the state it was in prior to entering SMM

To complement the SMM, the SL CPU and the 82360SL peripheral controller offer additional power management mechanisms that allow a system to:

- Detect idle I/O devices and power them down; then power them up again when they are needed
- Shut down power to all the system devices and turn off the clock to the CPU and 82360SL; then restore the clock and power without losing the machine state when the system is needed again
- Save the state of the system in nonvolatile memory and turn off power to all system devices, including the CPU and 82360SL; then restore the power, clock, and machine state when the system is needed again

These powerful resources give you a great deal of flexibility in designing your power management system. The power management software can be written independent of BIOS and operating systems. Software can dynamically control the CPU clock speed and the distribution of power to different parts of the system (memory, peripherals, etc.) based on a particular system profile. Using this second-generation power management technology, you can now build a new class of portable computers that allow users to work longer and more productively on a single battery charge.

Overview of the SL Power Management Support

The power management support provided with the SL CPU and 80360SL is available at five different levels of operation:

- Full on
- Local standby
- Global standby
- 5-volt (or 3.3-volt) suspend
- 0-volt suspend

Figure 5.1 shows the relationship between these operating levels and how they affect the system power consumption and battery life.

Even at the *full on* operating level with the CPU operating at full clock speed and most of the peripheral devices active, the SL CPU and 82360SL offer much more efficient use of power than is found in standard desktop components. For example, the memory controller in the CPU has been optimized for low power consumption in the following ways:

- Separate RAS# and CAS# signals for each byte of each DRAM bank are activated only when they are accessed.

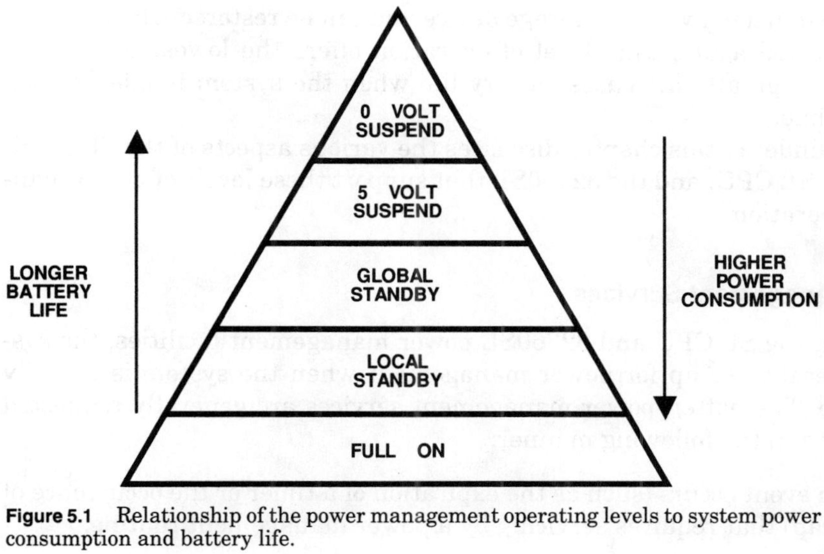

Figure 5.1 Relationship of the power management operating levels to system power consumption and battery life.

- Three DRAM page modes are supported to eliminate unnecessary clock cycles.
- The refresh rate can be programmed to take advantage of DRAMs that support extended refresh for further power saving.
- An on-chip cache controller reduces accesses to the DRAMs.

Also, the functional partitioning of the SL CPU reduces system pin count to minimize TTL buffers and power consumption. The tight coupling of the SL CPU and 82360SL reduces the number of off-chip communications and the extra power they require.

The *local standby* level of operation uses timers and I/O monitors in the 82360SL to monitor the operation of I/O peripherals and to power down devices that remain idle for preselected periods of time. Peripherals that are seldom used (such as the floppy disk drive) can thus be powered down most of the time to conserve the power they would ordinarily use even when they are in an idle state.

In the *global standby* level of operation, the clock to the CPU is stopped and, optionally, all the I/O devices are powered down. The main system components are still powered on, however, and can be returned to normal operation by normal system events. This operating state is possible because all the Intel SL components are fully static devices, meaning that the clocks for the CPU core, math coprocessor, DMA controller, and keyboard controller can be stopped without disrupting the machine state.

In the *5-volt and 3.3-volt suspend* level of operation, all the I/O devices, including the oscillators, are powered down, with only the CPU and 82360SL remaining powered on. The Intel486 SL microprocessor and the low voltage Intel386 SL microprocessor have a 3.3-volt suspend mode, because they can run at 3.3 volts Vcc during suspend.

In *0-volt suspend* operation, all devices in the system are powered off except the real-time clock and the resume logic in the 82360SL. Here, the system state is saved in a nonvolatile storage device and can be restored when the system is activated again. This level of operation offers the lowest power consumption and greatly increases battery life when the system is idle for long periods of time.

The remainder of this chapter discusses the various aspects of the SL architecture, the SL CPU, and the 82360SL that support these levels of power management operation.

Initiation of Power Management Services

When using the SL CPU and 82360SL power management facilities, the system is generally set up for power management when the system is initially powered up. Thereafter, power management services are generally requested and executed in the following manner:

1. A system event occurs (such as the expiration of a timer or the occurrence of an I/O trap) that requires servicing by a power management routine.

2. An SMI is sent to the CPU.
3. The CPU suspends execution of the current operating system or applications software function and goes into the SMM.
4. The CPU performs the selected power management routine.
5. At the end of the power management routine, an RSM instruction is executed and the CPU resumes execution of the operating system or applications software function where it left off.

Generally the occurrence of the system event and the generation of the SMI happens within the 82360SL and is invisible to the rest of the system hardware and software. However, system hardware and software can explicitly generate SMIs for the purpose of executing a power management routine.

System hardware can generate an SMI in either of the following ways:

- When the SRBTN# and BATTLOW# pins are pulled low, an SMI is generated within 128 to 256 ms.
- When the EXTSMI# pin is pulled low, an SMI is generated within 1 to 2.1 ms. The EXTSMI# pin must be held low for at least 2 SYSCLKS for the SMI to be recognized.

Software can explicitly generate an SMI in the following ways:

- An SMI is generated by setting the software SMI enable bit (bit 0) in to the SM_REQ_CNTRL register. Then, when the software SMI timer expires, an SMI is generated.
- Whenever an automatic SMI (ASMI) port is written to, an SMI is generated immediately (within 2 to 3 SYSCLKS). The ASMI control and status ports can be defined to reside anywhere within the 64 Kbytes I/O address space.

A software-generated SMI can be used for time slicing. An ASMI offers a useful interface between operating systems and application software and the system hardware.

Note: Because of internal arbitration, a minimum of 18 SYSCLKs are inserted between successive SMIs. No SMI is generated if CPURESET signal is active. The falling edge of the SMI signal triggers an SMI.

Local Standby Operation

In a typical system, not all the devices are utilized 100 percent of the time. For example, a system generally makes heavy use of its hard disk, but rarely uses the floppy drive. When a device is idle, it still consumes power. Thus, it makes sense to turn idle devices off to conserve power when they are not being used.

The 82360SL contains programmable hardware to power off I/O devices when they are idle and power them on again when they are needed. In this local standby mode of operation, the 82360SL can monitor up to six I/O devices

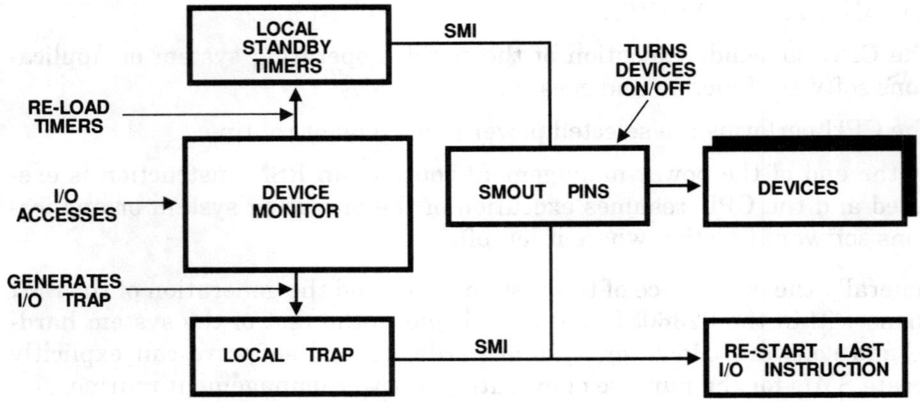

Figure 5.2 Local standby hardware.

at a time. Figure 5.2 shows a block diagram of the 82360SL hardware to support local standby.

Local standby works as follows:

1. The 82360SL is set to trap the I/O addresses used to access an I/O device.
2. Each time an I/O access is made to the device, a countdown timer is reloaded.
3. If the timer expires before another I/O access occurs, an SMI is generated and the expired timer is noted in an 82360SL register.
4. The CPU switches to SMM and executes a power management routine to determine which device is idle. It then asserts one of the SMOUT pins on the 82360SL to turn off power to the I/O device.
5. The next time an I/O access to the device is trapped, the 82360SL sends another SMI to the CPU.
6. The power management software then deasserts the SMOUT pin to turn the device on again and performs the necessary actions to restore the device's registers and service the I/O request.

The details of the mechanism are described in the following sections.

I/O access detection

Each I/O device has a set of I/O ports for interfacing with the system. I/O accesses to the device are monitored by setting the base address and address range of the I/O ports in a pair of trap address registers. The 82360SL provides six pairs of trap address registers for monitoring access to six I/O devices. The low byte of the base address is stored in the TRP_ADRL_DEVx register and the high byte of the base address is stored in the TRP_ADRH_DEVx register (where x is 0 . . . 5). An I/O trap is enabled by setting the DEVx_TRP_EN bit (bit 7) in the TRP_ADR_MSK_DEVx register. By default, only address bits SA[0:9] are used for trapping accesses to devices that use 10-bit address decoding of I/O addresses. For devices that use full 16-bit address decoding, the 16_IO_DEC bit (bit 5) in the TRP_ADR_MSK_DEVx register must be set to one. When the 16_IO_DEC bit is zero, address bits SA[10:15] are not decoded.

The I/O address range field allows trapping of addresses beyond the I/O base address programmed in the trap address registers. The I/O address range is controlled by the device I/O range mask field (bits [0–3]) in the TRP_ADR_MSK_DEVx registers. The four mask bits allow a maximum of 16 I/O addresses to be trapped.

It is a common misconception that the I/O base address and the I/O address range must be set to match the base address and address range of the device. For some devices, many of the I/O ports are not used after initialization. Therefore, these I/O addresses are not very useful for idle detection. In this case, it makes more sense to use the I/O port addresses that are always accessed by the system as trapping addresses. For best results, always select an I/O base address and I/O address range based on usage.

Idle detection timers

When a device receives no I/O requests for a preselected time period, the device is said to be idle. The inactivity period is measured by six local standby timers in the 82360SL. The count for these timers is programmed by the LSTDBY_TMR_DEVx registers. The time-out period is dependent on the type of device being monitored, software, and user profile. Each count in the timer equals to 4.096 seconds. Therefore, the maximum time-out period is about 17 minutes. Typically, the time-out period ranges from 1 to 5 minutes.

Sometimes an application requires that all I/O devices be active. To force all the I/O devices to be active if any one device is active, set the DEVx_ACTIVE bit (bit 7) in the TRP_ADR_MSK_DEVx register to one. After setting this bit, any access to the corresponding I/O device causes all the local standby timers to be reloaded with their respective count.

Power control

When a local standby timer expires, an SMI is generated. At the same time, the LSTDBY_REQ bit (bit 3) of the SM_REQ_STS register (0B7H, INDEX) is set and one of the six DEVx_STDBYREQ bits in the LSTDBY_STS register (0BAH, INDEX) is set. Once the power management software determines which timer caused the SMI, the corresponding I/O device is powered off. The 82360SL provides six SMOUTx control pins for powering devices on and off.

Save and restore

If an I/O device is to be powered off, software might be required to save the state of the device prior to switching the power off. The state of a device is normally saved by reading the contents of its I/O ports and saving it in the memory. However, not all the device registers are readable and writable. For example, some registers in the interrupt controller are write-only and some registers in the serial port controllers are read-only.

To solve this problem, the 82360SL provides 53 shadow registers which contain the last value written to some of the write-only registers in the system. These registers can be used to restore some of the I/O device registers during power on.

Some devices have their own mechanism for saving and restoring state information. The Intel387 SL mobile math coprocessor, for instance, has instructions for saving and restoring its state prior to being powered down. This kind of mechanism makes saving and restoring a device's state much more efficient and can save you a lot of programming effort.

I/O trapping

After powering off an idle device, the power management software enables the trap for the device to detect an I/O access to the device. When an access is detected, another SMI is generated. The power management software then determines which device received the I/O request and powers on the device again (deasserts the SMOUT pin or sends a software command to the device to put it in an active state). The power management software may also restore the state of write-only registers in the device at this time.

When an I/O access is trapped, the processor still executes the I/O instruction that caused the trap. However, writing to or reading from a powered-down device can cause the application or system to crash. To alleviate this problem, the SL CPU provides a feature called "auto restart of I/O instruction" which allows reexecution of the last I/O instruction after the device has been powered on again. The auto restart feature is enabled by writing 0FFH to the auto restart I/O instruction slot inside the SM-RAM. When the auto restart feature is selected, the RSM instruction's microcode will reexecute the last I/O instruction before passing control back to the application software.

Alternate methods of powering down I/O devices

Many new devices have built-in power management mechanisms, which are normally invoked by issuing a software command to the device. In some cases, it will be more efficient to use the built-in power management support provided by the device than to power down the device using the local standby mechanism. For example, it might make sense to power down the hard disk during 5-volt suspend, but not during local standby or global standby.

Returning a hard disk from its power-down state to its active state consumes a lot of power. Most of the power is consumed by the motor when it is spinning up. In an active system (CPU is still running), the hard disk will be placed in and out of local standby frequently. Therefore, the most efficient way to save power during local standby is to put the hard disk in a low-power state without having to spin up the hard disk each time a disk access request is made. However, the hard disk will not be accessed during suspend, so powering off the hard disk at this time will yield maximum power saving.

Power Management at the System Level

Power management through local standby deals with the power requirements of individual I/O devices, but it does not address the power management of the core system components. To support power management for these core system components, the SL architecture provides three power management levels: global standby, 5- or 3.3-volt suspend, and 0-volt suspend. The differences between the three levels of support lie in the amount of power saved and the time it takes to move between the different levels. (3.3-volt suspend is supported by the Intel486 SL CPU and the Low Voltage Intel386 SL CPU.)

Table 5.1 compares the system operation for the various levels of power management. The sections following describe these power management levels in greater detail.

Global Standby

At the global standby level of power management support, the 82360SL uses a set of programmable system events to detect system idleness. These system events include such things as the receipt of an interrupt, a parity error, a modem ring, or activity on an I/O channel. The system events are enabled by setting the SYS_EVNT_EN bit (bit 0) of the SYS_EVNT_CFG2 register (0B5H, INDEX). The global standby timer is then tied into these system events. Figure 5.3 shows the relationship between the system events and the global standby mechanism.

When a system event occurs, the global standby timer is reloaded automatically. If there is no system activity (as defined by the system events), the global standby timer will time out. When the global standby timer expires, the 82360SL generates an SMI and sets the GSTDBY_REQ bit (bit 2) in the SM_REQ_STS register (0B7H, INDEX). After the power management software determines that the SMI was generated by a global standby request, the software sets the SYS_IN_STDBY bit in the SM_REQ_STS register (which allows the power management software to find out if the system was in global standby during resume), enables stop break events, and stops the CPU clock. Individual devices can be powered off or put into a low-power state.

TABLE 5.1 Comparison between the Different Levels of Power Management Support

	Global standby	5-volt suspend (or 3.3-volt)	0-volt suspend
CPU clock	stopped	off	off
EFI	on	off	off
CPU	on	on	off
Transition time	fast	medium	slow
Power saving	low	medium	high

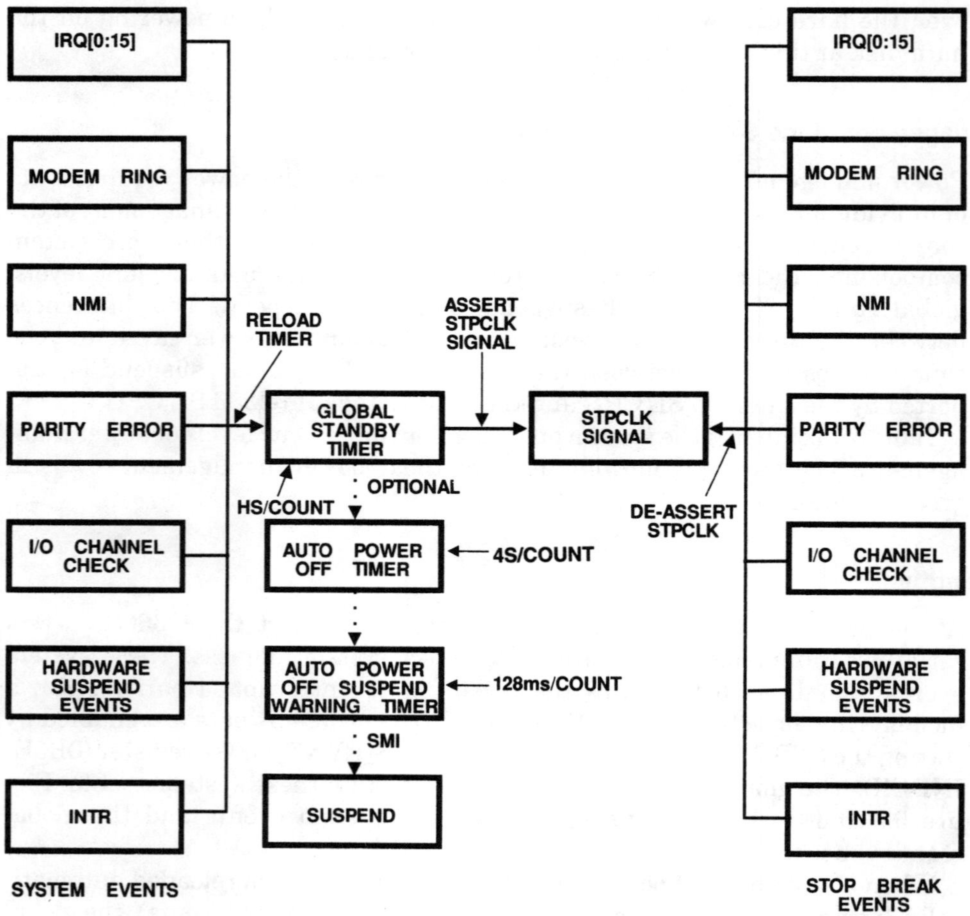

Figure 5.3 Global standby mechanism.

The system is put into global standby mode by doing a dummy I/O read to the STPCLK register (0FDH, INDEX). A dummy read to the STPCLK register causes the STPCLK pin to be asserted to stop the CPU clock inside the SL CPU. Unlike the HLT instruction, the STPCLK register allows the software to resume execution with the next instruction after the I/O read instruction.

Note: The CPU clock is automatically stopped upon detection of a halt bus cycle.

When the SYS_IN_STDBY bit is set to one, the system is in global standby mode and all local standby requests, suspend requests, and further global standby requests (the global standby timer will continue to reload and count down) are blocked. If the auto power off feature is enabled, setting the SYS_IN_STDBY bit will also enable the auto power-off timer and the auto power-off suspend warning timer. *Also, while in global standby, the CPU remains in SMM.*

System and stop break events selection

To determine when to bring the system out of global standby, the 82360SL detects stop-break events. System events and stop-break events are the same set of events; however, the 82360SL uses them differently. System events are used to detect system idleness. The stop-break events are used to take the system out of global standby. Stop-break events are enabled only after the global standby timer expires. System events and stop-break events are positive edge triggered.

The three types of suspend requests are ORed together to generate the HW_SUSRQ system event and stop-break event.

Exit from global standby

When a stop-break event occurs, the 82360SL exits global standby automatically. Upon exit from global standby, instruction execution starts at the instruction right after the I/O read to the STPCLK register and *no SMI is generated.* Returning control to the power management software (which is executing in SMM) after exiting from global standby ensures that no interrupt can occur to access a powered-down device.

A commonly asked question is, "Should the devices be returned to the states they were in before global standby or be put back to active state." Architecturally, it is logical to put the devices back to the states they were in before global standby. However, no harm can be done by putting the device back to full on state.

In some cases, it might be beneficial to put the devices back to full on state. A good example is the LCD panel. Assume that the LCD panel was off before going into global standby and the user hit a key on the keyboard to bring the system out of global standby. If the LCD panel remains in the off state, the user cannot tell if the system is already out of global standby.

Suspend Operation

Suspend, as the name suggests, means everything in the system is placed on hold for a period of time. If a system is going to be inactive for along time, putting everything inside the system in a low-power state can extend the battery life even longer. The 82360SL offers two mechanisms for extending battery life when the system is going to be inactive for a long time: 5-volt suspend (or 3.3-volt suspend for Intel486 SL CPU-based systems) and 0-volt suspend. The major difference between 5-volt suspend and 0-volt suspend is that the Vcc to the SL CPU and 82360SL is off during 0-volt suspend. Figure 5.4 shows the relationship of events in the two suspend levels of power management.

Suspend Requests

Suspend can be generated automatically or by the user through one of these mechanisms: auto power off, the suspend/resume button, the battery-low pin,

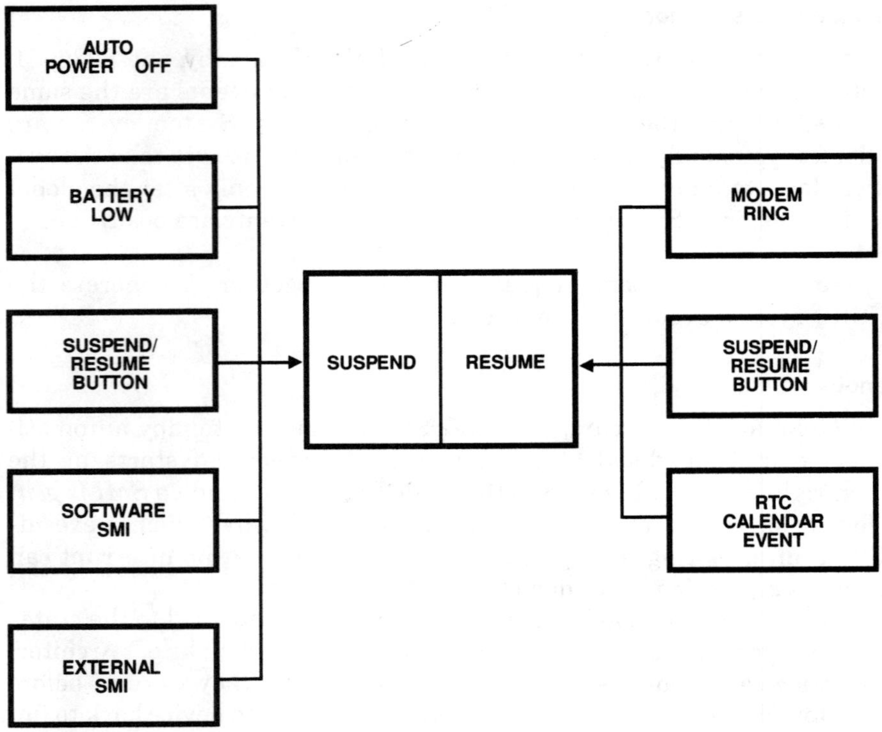

Figure 5.4 Suspend/resume events.

a software-generated SMI, or an externally generated SMI. We will discuss these five sources of suspend requests first and then examine 5-volt and 0-volt suspend states.

Auto power off

The auto power-off feature ties in with global standby. After the system is in global standby for a long period of time, the auto power-off mechanism allows the system automatically to go into a suspend state for further power conservation.

As mentioned earlier in this chapter, the auto power-off timer and the auto power-off suspend warning timer are enabled when the SYS_IN_STDBY bit is set to one. Also at this time, the auto power-off timer is loaded and starts counting. (The timer count for the auto power-off timer is stored in the auto power-off timer registers, APWR_TMRL (0F1H, INDEX) and APWR_TMRH (0F2H, INDEX), and the timer count for the auto power-off suspend warning timer is stored in the auto power-off suspend warning timer register, SUS_WRN_TMR_APWR (0F4H, INDEX).) Each count in the auto power-off timer represents 4.096 seconds and each count in the auto power-off suspend warning timer represents 128 ms.

The auto power-off suspend warning timer will be loaded when the auto power-off timer expires. If a system event occurs while either the auto power-off timer or the auto power-off suspend warning timer is running, both timers are loaded with their initial count and stopped. When the auto power-off suspend warning timer expires, an SMI is generated and the HW_SUSREQ bit (bit 1) in the SM_REQ_STS register (0B7H, INDEX) and the APWR_OFF_SUSREQ bit (bit 0) in the SPND_STS register (0B8H, INDEX) are set to one. The power management software will then put the system in a suspend state.

Suspend/resume button

The suspend/resume button input to the 82360SL is intended for user-initiated suspend requests. It is not required that the suspend/resume button input be connected to a button. The suspend/resume button input can also be driven by a lid-closing switch or the keyboard controller. A falling edge on the suspend/resume button input triggers a suspend request. Asserting the suspend/resume button pin causes the suspend/resume button suspend warning timer to load its initial count and start counting. When the timer expires, an SMI is generated, the HW_SUSREQ bit (bit 1) in the SM_REQ_STS register (0B7H, INDEX) and the SRBTN_SUSREQ bit (bit 2) in the SPND_STS register (0B8H, INDEX) are set to one. The power management software then puts the system in a suspend state.

An internal flip-flop is set after the suspend/resume button pin is asserted. The flip-flop will continue to generate SMIs unless it is cleared. The flip-flop is cleared by setting the HW_SUSREQ_EN bit (bit 1) in the SM_REQ_CNTRL register (0B6H, INDEX) to zero. To avoid getting an extra SMI, the HW_SUSREQ_EN bit must be cleared before going into suspend.

Battery low

A battery-low signal is provided for the 82360SL to detect a battery-low condition. If the BATT_LOW_MSK is not set, assertion of the BATTLOW# signal in the 82360SL will cause the battery-low suspend warning timer to load its initial count and start counting. When the timer expires, an SMI is generated, the HW_SUSREQ bit (bit 1) in the SM_REQ_STS register (0B7H, INDEX) and the BATT_LOW_SUSREQ bit (bit 1) in the SPND_STS register are set. Again, the generation of the SMI causes the power management software to place the system in a suspend state.

Software and external SMIs

Since the power management software is used to actually place the system in a suspend state, a software-generated SMI or an externally generated SMI can also be used to initiate placing the system in a suspend state. Suspend warning timers are also provided for types of suspend requests.

Warning Timers

The 82360SL provides five suspend warning timers, which you can look at as delay timers. Instead of putting the system in suspend right away, these timers allow the system to complete its current operation before a suspend is carried out. For example, the system might be writing data to the floppy disk when the user pushes the suspend/resume button. Optionally, a warning beep can also be generated to warn the user that the system is going to suspend operation.

Each timer count represents 128 ms, except for software and external SMI suspend warning timers where each count represents 1 ms. If a system event occurs while a warning timer is counting down, the warning timer is reloaded.

Enabling Suspend

Suspend can be enabled in either of these ways:

- If suspend refresh is enabled, suspend is also enabled.
- If suspend refresh is not used, suspend can be enabled by setting the SUS_STAT bit in the SPND_STS register. Setting the SUS_STAT bit will also change the state of the SUS_STAT# pin to low. Any device whose power plane is connected to the SUS_STAT# pin will get switched off.

5-volt and 3.3-volt suspend

The term *5-volt suspend* is derived from the fact that the 5-volt Vcc input for the Intel386 SL CPU and the 82360SL remains powered during suspend. With a DRAM system, extra power saving can be achieved using the suspend refresh feature provided by the Intel386 SL CPU. When suspend refresh is enabled, 5-volt suspend is automatically enabled. After suspend refresh is enabled, memory is not accessible until normal refresh is reenabled. For suspend refresh, the refresh request is generated by the real-time clock.

During 5-volt suspend, the Intel386 SL CPU and the 82360SL are placed in a low-power state to conserve power. This low-power state is achieved by stopping the clock to the devices. Because these devices are static devices, their registers maintain their states even though they are not being clocked.

With the Intel486 SL CPU and the Low Voltage Intel386 SL CPU, 3.3-volt suspend is used, because the Vcc during suspend for these devices is 3.3-volt. The operation of 3.3-volt suspend is similar to 5-volt suspend.

0-volt suspend

0-volt suspend is similar to 5- or 3.3-volt suspend except that the Vcc to the SL CPU and 82360SL is turned off. Since the processor and the 82360SL are powered off, suspend refresh cannot be supported. Therefore, the state of the CPU and the 82360SL, along with the main memory (DRAM system only), must be saved. A nonvolatile storage device with storage space big enough to save the main memory plus all the registers is required. Normally, the hard disk is used to save the state of the machine. Enabling and disabling of 0-volt suspend is essentially the same as with 5- or 3.3-volt suspend.

The SUS_STAT#, COMARI#, and COMBRI# buffers in the 82360SL are isolated from the 5-volt Vcc during suspend to prevent current drain from the real-time clock battery. When the 0V_SUS_EN bit (bit 2) is set to one in the

STP_BRK_CFG2 register, the 3-volt well signals and pull-up resistors will be enabled during suspend.

Resume

Exiting out of a suspend state is called a *resume*. Note that resume is different from the RSM instruction. Resume is a process which brings the system out of suspend state. RSM is an instruction which is executed by the SMM program to restore the system to its original state before going into SMM. Three mechanisms are supported to bring the system out of suspend: suspend/resume button, modem ring, and real-time clock's calendar event.

During suspend, the resume state machine is clocked by the real-time clock. Thus, the pulse width for the SRBTN# and COM[A:B]RI signals have to be at least 1 RTCCLK for it to be recognized. The system cannot resume if the battery-low pin remains active (i.e., battery is still low).

A resume event causes the CPURESET and RESETDRV signals to be asserted. To allow enough time for the devices to power on and reset properly, the CPURESET signal is extended to 120 ms during resume. Except for the CPURESET, SMOUTx, and REFREQ signals, all output buffers are isolated until the CPURESET signal goes inactive.

After the reset vector routine in the BIOS determines that the CPU reset was caused by a resume event, a software SMI is generated to enter the SMM. The power management software then restores the system to the state it was in before the suspend. The SL CPU and the 82360SL are reset by the PWR-GOOD signal upon a resume from 0-volt suspend.

Battery Monitoring

BATTLOW# is an input signal to the 82360SL indicating that the battery is low. During normal operation, assertion of the BATTLOW# will activate the battery-low suspend warning timer. When the timer expires, an SMI is generated and the SMM software puts the system in suspend state. The battery should be recharged during suspend. If the BATTLOW# remains active during suspend, the system is prevented from resuming.

Setting the BATT_LOW_MSK bit (bit 0) in the RESUME_MASK register (0BCH, INDEX) allows the system to resume even if the BATTLOW# signal is active. For the BATT_LOW_MSK bit to take effect, it must be set to one before the BATTLOW# signal goes active. However, allowing a system to resume when the battery is low might cause the system to crash.

The BATTDEAD# signal is like the battery-dead signal for the real-time clock. When replacing the battery, this BATTDEAD# signal will reset the real-time clock and the resume logic. This signal has nothing to do with battery monitoring.

Advanced Power Management

Even though the SL architecture has taken a giant step toward providing facilities for highly efficient power management in portable computers, several problems still exist. For example, it is sometimes difficult to determine if the CPU is idle without the help of the operating system. This is particularly true when the CPU is performing extensive computation and user interaction is not required.

Also, in a PC system, the operating system keeps track of the system time by updating the system time data area whenever the real-time clock generates an interrupt. If system operation is suspended, the system cannot update the system time every time a real-time clock interrupt occurs. After the system is in suspend for a long time, the system time will be inaccurate. This situation is sometimes called *time warp*.

Another difficult problem with power management is how to handle add-on hardware which does not come with the system. After you power down the add-on hardware, how do you restore it to its original state later on?

To help solve these types of power management problems, Intel and Microsoft jointly developed the Advanced Power Management (APM) interface to provide a convenient interface between the operating system and the power management hardware. The purpose of the interface is to maximize power saving by using the operating system in conjunction with the Intel386 2SL processor's power management hardware to detect idle conditions in the system. It also performs other power management tasks such as updating the system time when the system is suspended and handling power management for add-on hardware.

Chapter 5 describes how SL power management software can communicate with the operating system through the APM interface.

Summary

Welcome to the world of power management. In the next two chapters, we will look at how to design software and hardware to use the power management features described in this chapter.

Chapter

6

Power Management Software

As described in Chap. 5, the Intel SL architecture offers a rich set of power management facilities that solve many problems encountered when designing a power management system for a portable computer. At first glance, writing power management software to run on the SL architecture might seem complex, but in fact it is no more difficult than writing control software for any peripheral controller. One simplifying factor is that the system management mode (SMM) of the SL architecture allows power management software to execute independently from the operating system. This software independence not only eliminates the need to have a separate driver for each operating system that runs on the system, but also cuts down on the cost of developing power management software.

This chapter describes the rudiments of writing power management software for SL CPU-based products. It also includes several examples of power management routines.

How the SL architecture solves the problem of power management software*

The concept behind power management is to turn off devices when not in use, yet still provide instant on capability when the device is required. This tends to gain power; for example, even the simplest device like a COM port can use up to 15 minutes' worth of power over the life of the battery.

The SL architecture provides universal device power management by having built-in timers which monitor a device and automatically generate an SMI when the device isn't busy. The SMI handler can then turn off the device and set another SMI when the device is ready to activate. Another feature of the SL that has become standard is the suspend feature. Suspend allows the user to return to the application from a power-off condition. The SL architecture is well thought out to do suspend. The architecture doesn't just deal with the CPU, but also has provision to save the state of the system with the help of the shadow registers. This gives the

* Contributed by Bill Rallis of SystemSoft.

machine the ability to turn power off completely (complete battery drain) and yet still recover after power has restored.

Power Management Hardware Initialization

Upon initial power up, the power management hardware in the SL CPU and 82360SL chips is disabled. Before you can use the power management hardware, you must enable and initialize it as follows:

1. Initialize each of the power management features individually. Which feature should be enabled is a system-dependent issue. Some systems use up all six of the local standby timers and some need only four. Figure 6.1 shows how the power management hardware in the SL CPU and 82360SL is initialized.
2. Set the global power management enable bit to enable the power management facilities.

Once the power management hardware has been enabled and initialized, it operates without further software control until it is disabled. Please refer to the program disk included with the book for a typical routine for enabling and initializing the power management hardware in the SL CPU and 82360SL. The actual design of the power management hardware initialization routine depends on the design of the computer system.

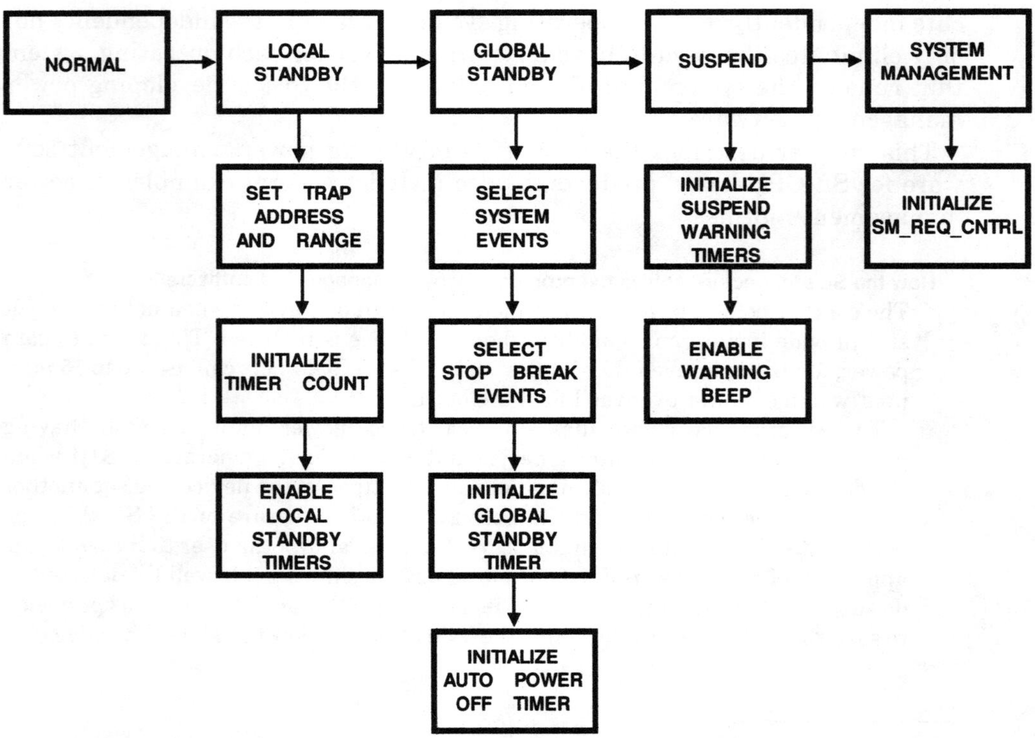

Figure 6.1 Power management hardware initialization.

Power Management Software Architecture

Even though the power management hardware in the SL architecture is well defined, it has a lot of room for flexibility for software. There are many ways to write software to work with the power management hardware inside the SL architecture. Much of it will depend on programming preferences and the hardware platform. Figure 6.2 shows the structure of a typical power management software.

No matter how your power management software is written, there are some design considerations you should be concerned with. Your code should be optimized in such a way that many low-level calls can be used for several high-level functions. For example, many of the routines in the local standby module can also be used by the global standby and suspend functions. Not only is your code size reduced, but your code will also be easier to debug and will run faster.

Many power management features in the SL architecture are programmable. Therefore, how the power management software is written can affect the power consumption of the system. For example, the clocks to the DMA controllers can be programmed to stop. You should always be on the lookout for software-controlled power management features that can further reduce the power consumption in your system.

In the following sections, we will look at some of the design issues in writing power management software.

Power Management Timers

The 82360SL contains 13 timers that the power management hardware uses to determine when to check if the system as a whole and the individual I/O devices are idle. These timers include six local standby timers (LSTDBY_TMR_DEV[0 . . . 5]); the global standby timer (GSTDBY_TMR); the auto power-off timer (APWR_TMR); and the five suspend warning timers for the suspend/resume button (SUS_WRN_TMR_SRBTN), battery-low detec-

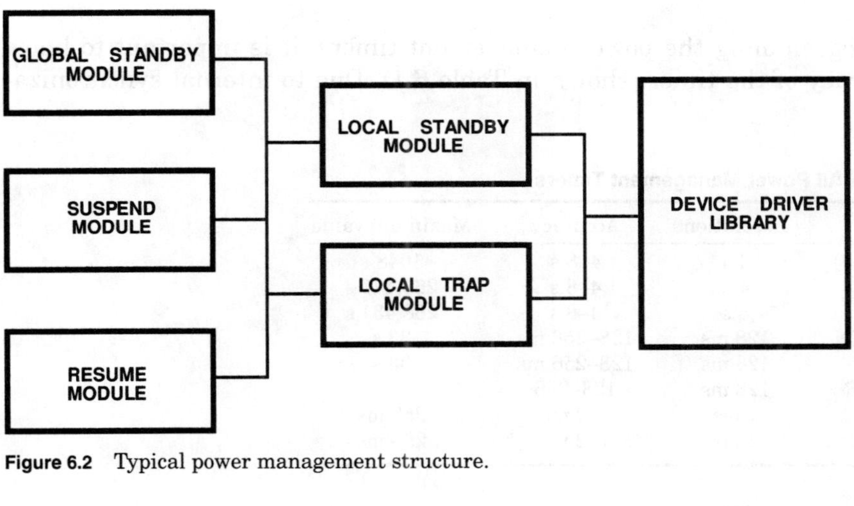

Figure 6.2 Typical power management structure.

tion (SUS_WRN_TMR_BAT), auto power-off (SUS_WRN_TMR_APWR), the software SMI (SUS_WRN_TMR_SSMI), and the external SMI (SUS_WRN_TMR_ESMI). Table 6.1 lists these timers and gives their individual resolution, accuracy, and maximum value. All these timers generate an SMI when they expire.

Initializing the six local standby timers requires three steps:

1. Load the timer count for each timer into its corresponding local standby timer register.
2. Load the I/O base address and address range for I/O access trapping into the address trap registers.
3. Set the timer enable bits in the STDBY_TMR_CNTRL register to enable the timers.

Initializing the global standby timer requires only the loading of the timer count into the global standby timer registers, GSTDBY_TMRL and GSTDBY_TMRH. Whenever a system event occurs, the global standby timer gets reloaded. If the auto power-off option is selected, the APWR_TMRL and APWR_TMRH registers should be loaded with the correct timer count.

The five suspend warning timers behave like buffers to provide sufficient time for the I/O operations to complete before initiating a suspend operation. To initialize the suspend warning timers, you merely load the timer count into the corresponding suspend warning timer register.

The warning beep option can be enabled if desired by setting the HWBTWRNBP_EN bit (bit 5) in the SM_REQ_CNTRL register to one. The warning beep option causes a warning tone to be generated every two seconds as the suspend warning timer counts down. The warning tone is generated by counter 2 in timer controller 2. The suspend warning timers are reloaded every time a system event occurs.

Timer resolution

When programming the power management timers, it is important to know the accuracy of the timer (shown in Table 6.1). Due to internal synchroniza-

TABLE 6.1 Summary of All Power Management Timers

Timer	Resolution	Accuracy	Maximum value
LSTDBY_TMR_DEV[0..5]	4 s	4–8 s	1048 s
GSTDBY_TMR	4 s	4–8 s	268,431 s
APWR_TMR	4 s	4–8 s	268,431 s
SUS_WRN_TMR_SRBTN	128 ms	128–256 ms	33 s
SUS_WRN_TMR_BAT	128 ms	128–256 ms	33 s
SUS_WRN_TMR_APWR	128 ms	128–256	33 s
SUS_WRN_TMR_SSMI	1 ms	1–2 ms	255 ms
SUS_WRN_TMR_ESMI	1 ms	1–2 ms	255 ms

tion, an SMI is not generated when the SMI# pin is asserted until an extra count has elapsed after the timer has expired.

Hardware control of I/O devices for power management

Power to an I/O device can be controlled through hardware or software commands. For hardware control, the 82360SL provides six SMOUT[0 . . . 5] pins. The 82360SL drives these pins high to initiate a power down of a device and low to reactivate the device. Listing 6.1 demonstrates how to change the state of the SMOUT pins. When reactivating a device with an SMOUT pin, you should allow time for the powered down device to get ready before making an I/O access.

Listing 6.1 Routine for Changing the State of SMOUT Pins

```
;------------------------------------------------------------
;
;
;  NAME SMOUT.ASM. Program to set the state of a
;       smout pin.
;
;  Usage SMOUT STATE PIN #
;
;------------------------------------------------------------
PAGE 60, 70
Include superset.inc
blank EQU  20H  ; space
code  SEGMENT
      ASSUME cs:code, ds:code
EXTRN open_360sl:near, close_360sl:near, read_360sl:near,
write_360sl:near;
      ORG  5DH
param1 LABEL BYTE  ; first parameter
      ORG  6DH
param2 LABEL BYTE  ; second parameter
      ORG  100H
start:
; get first parameter
      MOV    al, [param1]
      CMP    al, blank   ; anything?
      JZ     help
      CMP    al, '0'   ; low?
      JA     up
      MOV    FLAG, 0
      MOV    bx, offset ZERO
      JMP    pin
up:   MOV    bx, offset ONE
      MOV    FLAG, 1
      JMP    pin
help: MOV    ah, 09H
```

```
        PUSH   ds
        PUSH   ss
        POP    ds
        MOV    dx, OFFSET HELP_MES
        INT    21H
        POP    ds
        JMP    done
; get second parameter
pin:    MOV    al, [param2]
        CMP    al, blank     ; anything?
        JZ     help
        CMP    al, '0'      ; pin 0?
        JA     pin1
        MOV    al, ss:[bx]
        MOV    BIT_MASK, al
        JMP    send
pin1:   CMP    al, '1'      ; pin 1?
        JA     pin2
        MOV    al, ss:[BX+1]
        MOV    BIT_MASK, al
        JMP    send
pin2:   CMP    al, '2'      ; pin 2?
        JA     pin3
        MOV    al, ss:[BX+2]
        MOV    BIT_MASK, al
        JMP    send
pin3:   CMP    al, '3'      ; pin 3?
        JA     pin4
        MOV    al, ss:[BX+3]
        MOV    BIT_MASK, al
        JMP    send
pin4:   CMP    al, '4'      ; pin 4?
        JA     pin5
        MOV    al, ss:[BX+4]
        MOV    BIT_MASK, al
        JMP    send
pin5:   CMP    al, '5'      ; pin 5?
        JA     help
        MOV    al, ss:[BX+5]
        MOV    BIT_MASK, al
; set smout pin
send:
        call   open_360sl
        mov    bl, 0FEh
        call   read_360sl
        CMP    FLAG, 0
        JZ     set
        OR     al, BIT_MASK
        JMP    write
set:           AND al, BIT_MASK
write:MOV      bh, al
```

```
     mov     bl, 0FEH
     call    write_360sl
     call    close_360sl
done:
     MOV     AX, 4C00H
     INT     21H    ; terminate program
;------------------------------------------------------------
;
;          DATA AREA
;
;------------------------------------------------------------
ONE    DB  01H, 02H, 04H, 08H, 10H, 20H
ZERO    DB  0FEH, 0FDH, 0FBH, 0F7H, 0EFH, 0DFH
BIT_MASK    DB  ?
FLAG    DB  ?
HELP_MES    DB  'USAGE: SMOUT - STATE (0|1), PIN # (0..5)$'
code   ENDS
    END  start
```

Software control of I/O devices for power management

Many of the new I/O devices provide embedded power management hardware that can be activated and controlled through software. This built-in power management hardware is similar to that found in the 82360SL, and commonly supports standby and power-save modes. Typically, a device goes into a low-power or power-off state upon receiving a power-down command from the CPU or when an internal timer has expired.

Many of the new hard disk drives provide this type of power management hardware and firmware. Here, the drive can be explicitly placed in either a standby or power-save mode by issuing it a software command.

The drives also include internal countdown timers that power down the drive if accesses have not been received for a preselected period of time. The timer count for the timer is stored inside the sector count register on the hard disk. Before enabling the standby or power-save mode, the sector count register must be loaded with the desired timer count. After the timer is enabled, each disk access causes the timer to be reloaded. If the timer expires before a disk access occurs, the drive enters one of its power-savings modes.

The following listing gives an example of how to initialize the power management hardware in a hard disk drive.

```
; initialize timer count for standby mode
  mov     dx, 1F2H      ; points to sector count register
  mov     al, 3CH       ; set to 5 mins, 5 s/count
  out     dx, al
  mov     dx, 1F7H      ; points to command register
  mov     al, 0E3H      ; enable standby mode and timer
  out     dx, al
```

After power to the hard disk has been restored, the hard disk can be reinitialized by sending a software reset command to the hard disk to ensure that the hard disk is back to normal operation. The hard disk is reset automatically during resume by the RESETDRV pulse generated by the 82360SL I/O.

Serial Port

Some mouse devices use the RTS pin on the serial port as V_{cc}. A problem can occur during suspend when the serial port is powered down or three-stated. After the mouse is powered down, it will require reinitialization during resume. Since not all the mouse hardware is the same, you might have to consult the mouse's manufacturer data book to find out how to reinitialize the mouse.

System Management FILO

To aid system programmers in dealing with saving and restoring the state of a device, the SL CPU provides a System Management FILO (first in, last out register). This System Management FILO (SMFILO) is like a read-only stack that stores information about the I/O cycles executed prior to entering SMM. The SMFILO can be accessed from inside or outside SMM.

The SMFILO is 36 bits wide and consists of an address word, a data word, and a 4-bit status field. The address word contains the I/O address of the bus cycle and is always an even address (the Intel386 SL CPU has a 16-bit data bus), and the data word contains the data for the bus cycle. The status field consists of the W/R# bit (write or read cycle), the BLE# bit (even address), BHE# bit (odd address), and the Valid bit (is the information valid). The address field always contains an even address. Therefore, the BLE# bit and the BHE# bit must be used to determine if the access is for an odd or an even address.

Bus cycle information stored inside the SMFILO can be retrieved by reading (must be a 16-bit read) the SMFILO register (702H, IBU). The first access to the SMFILO register returns the I/O address; the next read returns the data; and the following read returns the status field. The SMFILO can be accessed continuously until the valid bit returned is zero (i.e., the bus cycle is not valid), which indicates that the bottom of the stack has been reached.

The listing below gives code for deciphering information from the SMFILO on the Intel386 SL processor.

```
;; example on reading information from the SMFILO
    call    open_ibu
    mov     dx, SMFILO
    in      ax, dx          ; read I/O address
    cmp     ax, 3f8H        ; is it COM1 data register
    jz      error
    in      ax, dx          ; read I/O data
    test    ax, 80H         ; is bit 8 set
    jz      error
    in      ax, dx          ; read status word
```

```
        test    ax, 01H         ; is data valid
        jz      error
        test    ax, 08H         ; was it a write cycle
        jz      error
        test    ax, 04H         ; was it the low byte
        jz      error
        jmp     exit
    error:
        stc     ; set carry flag
    exit:
        ret
        call    close_386sl
```

The SMFILO mechanism on the Intel486 SL processor is similar to the Intel386 SL processor except that 32-bit cycle must be used to access the SMFILO.

Clearing Status Bits

All the status bits have to be cleared before exiting from the SMM; otherwise, the SMI# output in the 82360SL will remain asserted. There are six status bits associated with the local standby timers in the LSTDBY_STS register. Instead of clearing them one at a time (i.e., writing a zero to the corresponding bit), it is quicker to clear them all at once after all the local standby requests have been completed.

Saving Memory Overlaid by SMRAM

While inside the SMM, the memory overlaid by SM-RAM can be accessed only by using the EMS memory mechanism. The alternative is to exit SMM and save the memory overlaid by SM-RAM. The normal way to exit SMM is to execute the RSM instruction, which causes execution control to go back to the program that was interrupted by SMI#.

The other way to exit SMM is to generate a CPU reset after the CPU RESET is reenabled. A CPU reset can be generated either by using the special feature's FASTCPURESET register (and toggling the FASTCPU RESET bit in PORT92H), or by issuing a CPURESET command to the keyboard controller. The listing below gives sample code for exiting the SMM by generating a CPURESET.

```
;; exit from SMM without returning to application that was interrupted
  xor      al, al
  mov      dx, SMI_MARK
  out      dx, al       ; clear SMI_MARK bit
;; assuming special feature set is already enabled
  mov      dx, FASTCPURESET
  in       dx, al       ; generates CPU reset
```

Global Standby

In global standby, the clock to the CPU is normally stopped and all the power-hungry devices are powered off. The SL CPU supports a stop clock feature that prevents powered down devices from being accessed after the CPU clock is re-started. If the stop break event feature is enabled, executing the HLT instruction or doing a dummy I/O read to the STP_CLK register (0FDH, INDEX) will automatically stop the CPU clock. The HLT signal is also used by shutdown. Some of the power management software implementations also wake up periodically to service system requests such as refresh and real-time clock interrupt.

Math CoProcessor

The Intel386 SL CPU supports a stop clock option that can be used to stop an Intel math coprocessor (MCP), providing that the MCP is a static type, such as the Intel387 SL mobile math coprocessor. To use this option, the power management software should detect the presence of a static math coprocessor before enabling the stop clock option. The MCPTYPE routine shown in the listing below includes a routine for detecting and identifying an MCP. Bit 8 of the device word register specifies whether the device is static (1 = Yes, 0 = No). The device word register can be read by executing the FSTDW (opcode 9B DF E1) instruction. The FSTDW instruction should be executed right after the FINIT instruction before the status word has changed. On devices without the device word, the status word (you will get 0000H) will be transferred.

```
;; determine if MCP installed is static
mcptype     proc
    finit
    fstdw   ax              ; get device word
    test    ax, 80H         ; is bit eight set
    jnz     exit
    stc                     ; mcp is non-static
exit:
    ret
mcptype     endp
```

The stop clock option is enabled by setting bit 14 in the OMDCR register (302H, IBU) and selecting the stop clock option in the idle MCP clock field (bits[11–13] in the CPUPWRMODE register. The MCP has built-in support for save-restore through the FSAVE and FRSTOR instructions. The listing below (extracted from the *Intel 80286 and 80287 Programmer's Reference Manual*) gives an example of how to use the FSAVE and FRSTOR instructions to save and restore the state of the MCP.

```
; save and restore of MCP state
save_mcp   proc
;; setup stack pointer
    cli
```

```
        push   bp
        mov    bp, sp
        mov    bp_image, bp
        sub    sp, 94
    ;; save mcp state
        fnsave [bp-94]
        fwait
        sti
        ret
    save_mcp   endp
    res_mcp    proc
        mov    bp, bp_image
        mov    byte ptr [bp-92], 0h
        frstor [bp-94]
    ;; deallocate stack
        mov    sp, bp
        pop    bp
        ret
    res_mcp    endp
```

Software should also check for the presence of an MCP in the system before doing any save and restore of the MCP; otherwise, the system will hang up. One way to find out if a math coprocessor is present is to examine the equipment list status word stored in the BIOS data area at location 40:10H. If bit 1 of the status word is set, a math coprocessor is present.

Suspend

There are two ways to enable suspend:

- Enable suspend refresh.
- Set the SUS_STAT bit in the SPND_STS register (0B8H, INDEX).

Suspend refresh mechanism is provided for enabling suspend in a DRAM system that is using 5- and 3-volt suspend facilities. The SUS_STAT bit mechanism is for enabling suspend in an SRAM system and for use with the 0-volt suspend facilities. For a description of suspend refresh enabling mechanism, please refer to Chap. 10.

On some systems, pushing the suspend/resume button when the system is not in SMM will cause the system to go into suspend immediately after SMM is enabled. To prevent this unwanted suspend operation, the SMM software should reset the SM_REQ_STS register before going into SMM.

Save-Restore

Two options are available for handling suspend and resume for the video subsystem. In the evaluation board, the video subsystem enters standby mode (remains powered) during suspend, and the RESETDRV signal to the video subsystem is blocked during resume. The second option is, if the video subsystem is to be powered off during suspend, the software needs to save all the VGA registers and the video memory before the subsystem is powered off. Many of the new video BIOS's have functions that call for saving and restoring the state of the entire VGA subsystem. The status of the keyboard shift flags is stored in system memory at address 17H in segment 40H. Software can use this status byte to save and restore the keyboard status during a suspend. The status of gate A20 should also be saved and restored for suspend/resume.

Shadow Registers

To minimize logic, many registers inside the standard peripheral controllers are write-only registers. Software cannot read back what has been written to these registers. If these peripheral controllers are powered down, the power management software cannot save the contents of these registers for restoration during resume. The SL architecture solved the problem of saving the contents of write-only registers with a unique feature called *register shadowing*. Fifty-three read-only shadow registers are provided by the 82360SL I/O to keep track of the contents of these write-only registers inside the standard ISA peripheral controllers.

Every time a write-only register is written, the corresponding shadow register is also updated. These shadow registers reside inside the 82360SL I/O space. They can be accessed like any register inside the 82360SL configuration using the CFGINDEX and CFGDATA registers. Table 6.2 is a list of these registers.

BIOS Shadowing

After a CPU reset, the first instruction fetch always goes to the ROM. If BIOS shadowing is enabled and suspend refresh is enabled during suspend, the BIOS will not be able to execute BIOS code after a resume reset because the memory is still in suspend refresh (i.e., not active; normal refresh is not running). Therefore, BIOS shadowing should be turned off before going to suspend, and reenabled before resume.

Since the power management software is stored inside the SM-RAM, it is recommended that software perform a checksum on the SM-RAM on a resume reset before executing SMI code to ensure the integrity of the SM-RAM.

After a resume reset, a software SMI should be used to reenter the SMI handler.

Multiple SMIs

To prevent further generation of SMIs during suspend/resume, software should disable all the system management features in the suspend/resume code.

APM Interface

If you are using the Intel/Microsoft Advanced Power Management (APM) interface in your design, the operating system communicates with the SL CPU by

TABLE 6.2 The 82360SL Shadow Registers

Register name	Mnemonic	Index	Default
DMA Channel 0 Base Address	SHDMA0BA	00H	XXH
DMA Channel 0 Count	SHDMA0WC	01H	XXH
DMA Channel 1 Base Address	SHDMA1BA	02H	XXH
DMA Channel 1 Count	SHDMA1WC	03H	XXH
DMA Channel 2 Base Address	SHDMA2BA	04H	XXH
DMA Channel 2 Count	SHDMA2WC	05H	XXH
DMA Channel 3 Base Address	SHDMA3BA	06H	XXH
DMA Channel 3 Count	SHDMA3WC	07H	XXH
DMA Channel 0 Mode	SHDMA0MOD	08H	XXH
DMA Channel 1 Mode	SHDMA1MOD	09H	XXH
DMA Channel 2 Mode	SHDMA2MOD	0AH	XXH
DMA Channel 3 Mode	SHDMA3MOD	0BH	XXH
DMA Controller 1 Mask Register	SHDMAMSK1	0FH	XXH
Timer 2 Counter 0 Count Low	SHT2CH0CL	10H	XXH
Timer 2 Counter 0 Count High	SHT2CH0CH	11H	XXH
Timer 2 Counter 1 Count Low	SHT2CH1CL	12H	XXH
Timer 2 Counter 1 Count High	SHT2CH1CH	13H	XXH
Timer 2 Counter 2 Count Low	SHT2CH2CL	14H	XXH
Timer 2 Counter 2 Count High	SHT2CH2CH	15H	XXH
PIC 1 ICW1	SHINT1ICW1	22H	XXH
PIC 1 ICW2	SHINT1ICW2	23H	XXH
PIC 1 ICW3	SHINT1ICW3	24H	XXH
PIC 1 ICW4	SHINT1ICW4	25H	XXH
PIC 1 OCW2	SHINT1OCW2	27H	XXH
PIC 1 OCW3	SHINT1OCW3	28H	XXH
NMI Mask and RTC Index	SHNMIMASK	2EH	XXH
Timer 1 Counter 0 Count Low	SHT1CH0CL	40H	XXH
Timer 1 Counter 0 Count High	SHT1CH0CH	41H	XXH
Timer 1 Counter 1 Count Low	SHT1CH1CL	42H	XXH
Timer 1 Counter 1 Count High	SHT1CH1CH	43H	XXH
Timer 1 Counter 2 Count Low	SHT1CH2CL	44H	XXH
Timer 1 Counter 2 Count High	SHT1CH2CH	45H	XXH
DMA Channel 4 Base Address	SHDMA4BA	90H	XXH
DMA Channel 4 Count	SHDMA4WC	91H	XXH
DMA Channel 5 Base Address	SHDMA5BA	92H	XXH
DMA Channel 5 Count	SHDMA5WC	93H	XXH
DMA Channel 6 Base Address	SHDMA6BA	94H	XXH
DMA Channel 6 Count	SHDMA6WC	95H	XXH
DMA Channel 7 Base Address	SHDMA7BA	96H	XXH
DMA Channel 7 Count	SHDMA7WC	97H	XXH
DMA Channel 4 Mode	SHDMA4MOD	98H	XXH
DMA Channel 5 Mode	SHDMA5MOD	99H	XXH
DMA Channel 6 Mode	SHDMA6MOD	9AH	XXH
DMA Channel 7 Mode	SHDMA7MOD	9BH	XXH
DMA Controller 2 Mask Register	SHDMAMSK2	9FH	XXH
PIC 2 ICW1	SHINT2ICW1	0A2H	XXH
PIC 2 ICW2	SHINT2ICW2	0A3H	XXH
PIC 2 ICW3	SHINT2ICW3	0A4H	XXH
PIC 2 ICW4	SHINT2ICW4	0A5H	XXH
PIC 2 OCW2	SHINT2OCW2	0A7H	XXH
PIC 2 OCW3	SHINT2OCW3	0A8H	XXH

means of a software SMI. A software SMI can be generated using either the automatic SMI mechanism (ASMI) or the software SMI suspend warning timer.

Using the ASMI mechanism, an SMI is generated by writing to a programmable I/O port called the *ASMI register*. The address of the ASMI register is defined by the ASMI_ADDRL (84H, INDEX) and ASMI_ADDRH (85H, INDEX) registers. The ASMI_ADDRL register contains address bits SA[1–7] of the I/O port, and ASMI_ADDRH contains address bits SA[8–15] of the I/O port. The ASMI mechanism is enabled by setting the EN_ASMI bit (bit 2) of the SYS_EVNT_CFGR2 register. Using the software SMI suspend warning timer (SUS_WRN_TMR_SMI), an SMI is generated by initializing the timer and then enabling the software SMI enable bit (bit 0) in the SM_REQ_CNTRL register (0B6H, INDEX). After the timer has expired, an SMI is generated. If the software SMI enable remains set, a software SMI will occur at regular intervals as defined by the software warning timer. This mechanism is useful in allowing the SMM program to regain control of the system.

The last 32 bytes of extended CMOS RAM inside the 82360SL I/O are reserved for use by APM. Please refer to the APM specification for a description of the usage of the CMOS RAM.

Programming Guidelines

- Interrupt requests will be serviced if an STI instruction is executed within the SMI handler. To preserve system integrity, the SMI handler should not execute any STI instructions.
- System management features (except for suspend) should be disabled during system reset and cold boot to eliminate latency due to SMIs.
- All of the system event inputs are AND'ed with their enable signals. The resulting signals are all routed into an OR gate and a "one-shot," which reloads the warning and global time-out counters. If an enable signal and system event remains high, then the one-shot input remains high and generates only a single reload pulse. If an edge-triggered interrupt is selected as a system event and is disabled by the operating system or an application program, the interrupt line is likely to go high and block all future events. The global standby timer will then expire and generate a standby request.

  An example of this situation is the hard disk interrupt request (IRQ14). In response to a power management command, the hard disk controller generates a task-complete interrupt. If this interrupt is not cleared by doing a dummy read to the fixed disk status register, it will prevent the system events logic from reloading the system management timers.

Summary

This chapter provides a good overview of how you can write your own power management software. Since it would be too much to cover all the code power management software here, sample code is provided on the disk accompanying this book to supplement this chapter.

For many of us, power management is still unfamiliar territory. The reason is that there are many different pieces of hardware out there in the PC world. We are dealing with compatibility issues—not design issues. To handle the vast domain of hardware out there, my advice is to make use of existing software modules as much as possible. For example, many component manufacturers provide sample source code to show how to enable power management on their devices. In some cases, it might require that you become familiar with the hardware by reading the data book or the user guide. It is no easy job, but it will be satisfying when it is working.

References

"APM Specification Version 1.0," Intel Corporation/Microsoft Corporation.

Chapter

7

Power Management Techniques

The techniques for lowering power consumption in a portable computer are well understood. But implementing these techniques is another matter. The SL architecture enables you to implement power management mechanisms with virtually all the components in a system—from the LCD display screen to the disk drives to active ICs. Or, you can concentrate on a few power-hungry components. The most common approach to power management is reducing clock rates and using power-down modes. This chapter describes the methodology of implementing power management and deals with problems associated with power management.

The Basics

The objective of power management is to extend battery life. There are several factors that can affect battery life besides power management—power consumption of components, efficiency of the power supply, and the type of battery used. In the following sections, we can see how careful selection of components, power supply regulator circuit, and battery will result in longer battery life.

Component Selection

Power consumption is like spending money. You can quickly empty your wallet if you spend all your money on expensive goods. Selecting the right components for a system can make a big difference in power consumption. In order to pick the right part for your system you must know how much current each component draws in a system.

Figure 7.1 shows the components of a typical portable computer and the typical power consumption of each component. This figure clearly illustrates that the LCD display is far and away the biggest power hog. However, other than using the most efficient LCD displays available and providing the ability to automatically shut off the display after a user-selected period of inactivity, you cannot do much about the LCD power drain while a user is actively using his

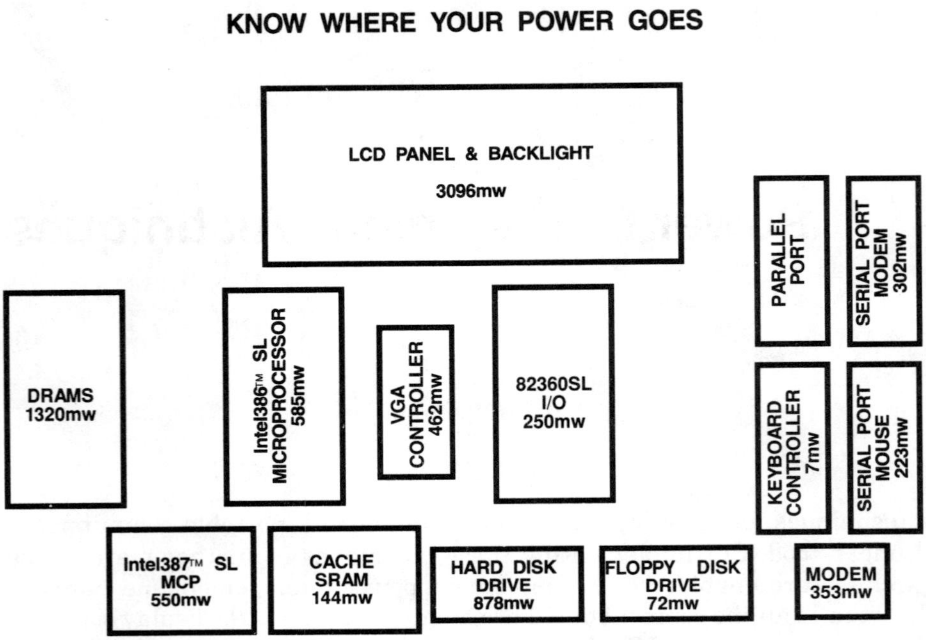

Figure 7.1 Relative power consumption of typical portable computer components (5-volt).

or her computer. Your efforts to conserve power will thus be concentrated on the other components in the system, trying to make them run as efficiently as possible when the system is actively in use.

Supplying Power

A portable computer can be powered in any of three ways: an AC adapter, a battery pack, or an automobile cigarette lighter. (See Fig. 7.2.) The AC adapter and the automobile adapter will run the machine and charge the machine at the same time. Portable computer design requires power supplies with the highest efficiencies under all operating conditions. One approach to designing an efficient power supply is to estimate the loading on the power supplies under different power modes. Ideally, the efficiency of the power supply should be held constant down to very low loads. Typically, switching regulators are used for full-on load as it can withstand power surges ranging from 20 to 40 percent above the full-on load. For low-power modes, linear regulators are used.

DC-DC converter

DC-DC converter is a switching regulator which generates stepped-up or stepped-down outputs. The efficiency of the DC-DC converter has a direct effect on battery life. The rate at which a battery is discharged depends on the load current. High-load current can shorten the battery life. Also, in a battery-operated environment, battery voltage will drop steadily over a period of time. Therefore, it is desirable to have a high-efficiency DC-DC converter that covers

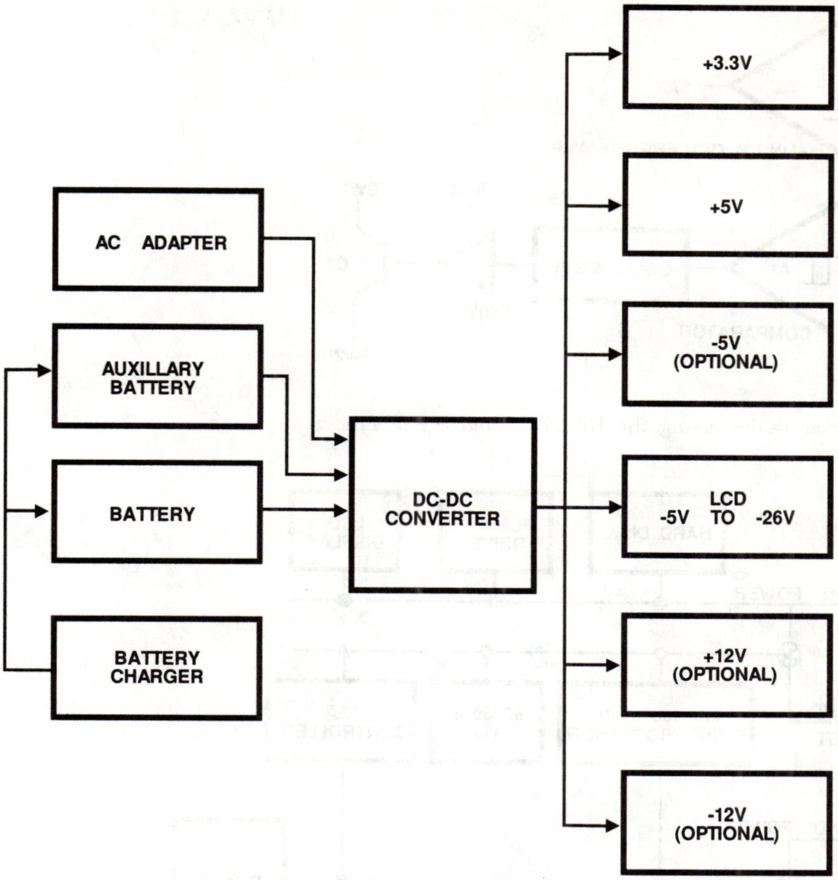

Figure 7.2 Typical power supply system for a portable computer.

a wide range of battery voltage. There are many off-the-shelf DC-DC converters from which to choose—for example, LT1073 and LT1173 from Linear Technology. Figure 7.3 shows a DC-DC converter design using the LT1073. Most DC-DC converter circuits have an efficiency of over 80 percent. Selection of a converter is usually based on load current, input voltage, quiescent current, form factor, and heat dissipation.

Power supply for flexible voltage system

The Intel486 SL CPU and low-voltage Intel386 SL processor operate with 3.3- and 5-volt. To reap full benefits of a mixed 3.3/5-volt system, power supplies must be optimized to deliver power to the system in a highly efficient manner at full-on and powered-down modes. Figure 7.4 shows a typical power supply for a mixed 3.3/5-volt system.

Sequencing of power supplies is required in a mixed 3.3/5-volt system. The 5-volt power supply must be guaranteed to reach nominal voltage at the same time or before the 3.3-volt power supply reaches nominal value. If one power

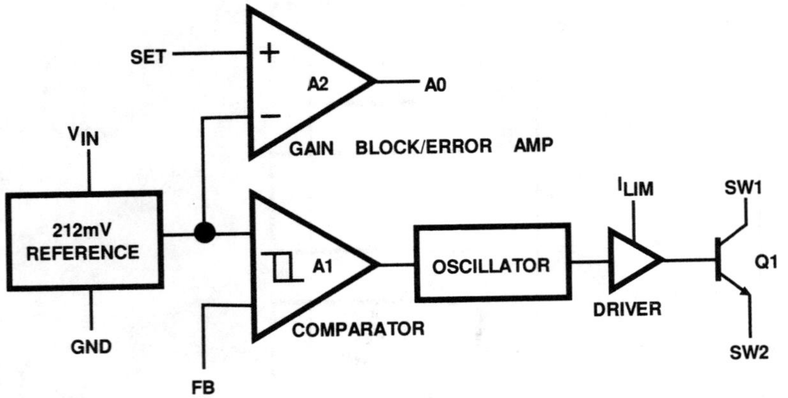

Figure 7.3 DC-DC converter design using the LT1073. (*Courtesy of Linear Technology Corporation.*)

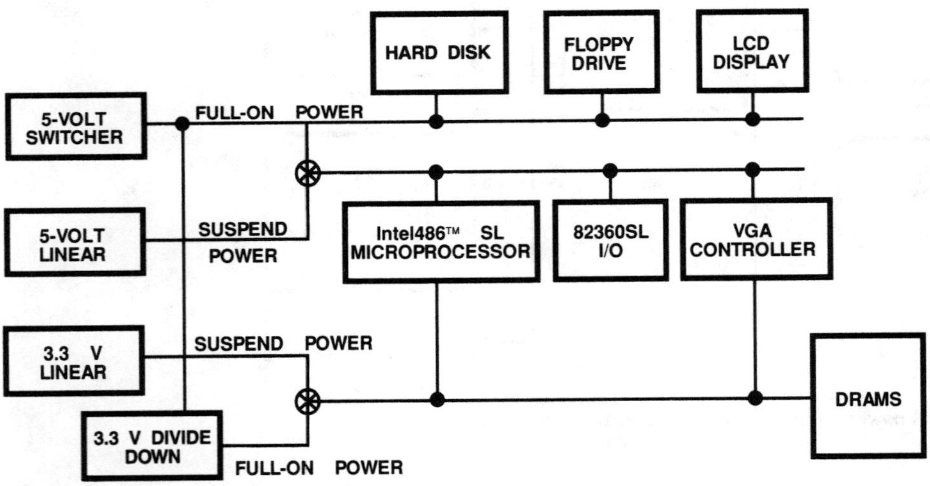

Figure 7.4 Power supply for a mixed 3.3/5-volt system.

supply experiences a delay or failure, buffers in the powered-up parts of the system can generate large amounts of leakage current into powered-down components, which will cause the power supply to overheat and components to fail.

Power sequencing

As mentioned before, sequencing of power supplies is required in a mixed 3.3/5-volt system. Power sequencing is required during power up and power down. During power up, the 5-volt power supply must reach nominal value (4.5 volts) before the 3.3-volt power supply reaches 3 volts. With power down, the sequencing order is reversed—the 3.3-volt power supply will be turned off before the 5-volt power supply is turned off. Remember the power sequencing requirement: *5-volt power supply should be turned on first and off last.* Figure 7.5 depicts the power sequencing scheme.

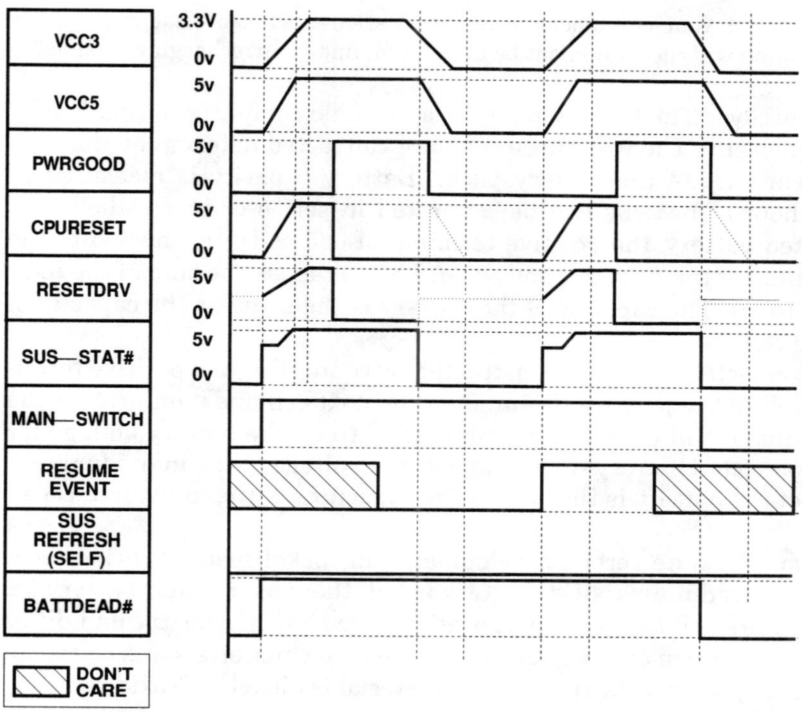

Figure 7.5 Power sequencing for a mixed 3.3/5-volt system.

Battery selection

Batteries come in a variety of shapes, sizes, and materials. Choosing the right type of battery for a portable computer design can be frustrating. A good understanding of how batteries work can help in picking the battery with the best performance and longest battery life for your application. Working closely with a battery manufacturer who provides application design assistance will also simplify the battery selection process. As a rule of thumb, you can get 15–20 watt-hours of energy for every pound of battery.

The internal resistance in a battery can have substantial impact on battery life. An electrolytic bypass capacitor can sometimes be used to reduce the effects of a battery's internal resistance.

What's the best type of battery for my application?*

Choosing a battery type means knowing something about batteries and how they'll be used in your equipment. Batteries are commonly classed as either primary or secondary. Primary cells include the disposable varieties such as carbon-zinc, alkaline, and lithium cells that can't be recharged.

Secondary cells include the varieties based on either nickel-cadmium (NiCd) or lead-acid cell chemistries, that are rechargeable several times without degradation.

---

* Contributed by Mark Dewey of Gates Energy Products.

So first, consider your equipment. Specific questions include: What is the drain rate? How often will the equipment be used? And, finally, is recharging feasible?

Voltage and capacity. The battery pack for a portable computer normally consists of multiple cells. The way these cells are connected determines the voltage and the capacity of the battery pack. (Battery capacity is measured in amperes per hour.) The cells can be connected in series or in parallel. In a series-connected battery, the positive terminal of one cell is connected to the negative terminal of the next cell and so on. The voltage is the sum of the individual cell voltages. The capacity of the battery is the same as the capacity of the individual cell.

A parallel-connected battery is constructed by connecting the positive terminal from one cell to the positive terminal on the next cell and similarly for the negative terminals. Unlike a series-connected battery, the battery voltage for the parallel-connected battery is the same as the voltage of the individual cell. The capacity of the battery is the sum of the capacities of the individual cells.

Nickel-cadmium. Despite recent developments in nickel metal hydride technology, the nickel-cadmium (NiCd) battery is still the most popular battery for portable computers. All the NiCd batteries use the same chemistry and differ primarily in construction and refinements of the active materials and electrode construction. The positive-electrode active material is nickel hydroxide and the negative-electrode active material is cadmium hydroxide. The nominal voltage for a NiCd cell is about 1.2 volts.

NiCd batteries have excellent storage time (charged or discharged). Capacity loss due to self-discharge is about one percent per day. Cell parameters for NiCd batteries can easily be modified to match application requirements. For example, the NiCd batteries can be fine-tuned for capacity, high current, high temperature performance, high temperature charging, or fast charging.

Nickel metal hydride. Nickel metal hydride (NIMH) batteries have a higher energy density than the NiCd batteries and provide a longer battery life. The disadvantage of NIMH batteries is that they take longer to recharge than the NiCd batteries. The positive-electrode active material is nickel hydroxide and the negative-electrode active material is a metal alloy matrix. Alloy choice is either nickel/rare earth mixture (i.e., LaNi) or titanium/zirconium combination.

Battery monitoring

The charging speed of NiCd batteries is dependent on the application. Normally, it will take four to five hours. Using fast charging, recharging can be done in less than two hours. Charge termination is required with fast charging. Otherwise, the batteries and the system can be damaged.

Termination of fast charging is controlled by the battery charger (typically, this is implemented with a microcontroller such as the 80C51SL.) By monitoring the time, temperature, voltage, or a combination, the battery charger can terminate fast charging at a predetermined cutoff point. The cutoff point is determined by the battery specification from the battery manufacturers. For example, if the cutoff point is set at 80° (i.e., when the temperature reaches 80°) the battery automatically terminates charging.

Battery life

A number of factors such as the user profile, depth of discharge, amount of overcharge, ambient temperature, and mechanical environment determine the battery life of a battery pack. Battery life is measured in hours. Battery life for a particular system can be calculated as follows:

$$\text{Battery life (total energy)} = (Q * V_{\text{batt}})/(V^2 * C * F)$$

where Q = battery capacity in amperes per hour
V_{batt} = battery voltage
V = V_{cc}
F = frequency
C = capacitance

Power Management Implementation

The most difficult task for any beginner in designing a portable computer is figuring out how to implement power management. We faced the same problem during the course of development of the Intel386 SL microprocessor. This is because there are many ways to implement power management. Also, different machines will have different hardware. In other words, each power mode will have a different meaning on different machine.

It is more logical and simpler to define the state of all the components under each power mode than to define a power mode for every device. Therefore, a power management table was created in the programmer's reference manual to describe the state of the hardware during different power management states. Table 7.1 shows a typical power management table similar to the programmer's reference manual.

The power management table carries important information about your system. Using this table, you can identify power-hungry devices, implement power management strategy based on system configuration selected, and calculate total power consumption and battery life based on different configurations.

Power management techniques

While the machine is fully active, your power savings is going to come largely from your choice of components. Three common techniques are normally used to further reduce power consumption of active components:

- Clock control
- Efficient memory subsystem design
- Activity monitoring

TABLE 7.1 Power Management Table

	Suspend	Global standby	Local standby
i386SL CPU CLK	off	cpu clock stopped	optional
i386SL CPU	suspended	on	on
82360SL	suspended	on	on
MCP	off	on	on
MCP CLK	off	EFI/16	EFI/16
Main memory	on	on	on
Refresh rate	sus ref	normal	normal
Cache controller	off	off	on
Cache memory	off	off	on
ROM	off	on	on
KBD ROM	on	on	on
80C51SL	powerdown mode	on	on
KBD (external)	off	on	on
CL 610/620—C	suspended	suspended	standby
Video memory ref	slow ref	slow ref	standby
Video memory	on	on	on
RAMDAC	off	idle	idle
LCD display	off	off	off
Backlight	off	off	off
CPU access 610/620	off	off	on
PCMCIA	off	on	on
Modem	off	standby	standby
Key mouse	off	on	on
External PS/2 Mouse	off	on	on
Floppy drive	off	standby	standby
82077SL	off	powerdown mode	powerdown mode
82077SL OSC	off	off	off
Hard disk	off	standby	standby
Serial port buffer	off	off	on
EFI OSC	off	on	on
ISA-bus REF	off	off	off
ISA-bus OSC	off	off	off
DMA clock	stopped	stopped	on
KBD CLK (360SL)	off	off	off
RTC CLK	on	on	on
COM[A..B] OSC	off	on	on

Clock control. The CPU is the most active component in the system. Therefore, reducing the clock speed can save a lot of power. Experiment shows that dividing the clock speed by half gives the best performance and power consumption. Finer speed control does not provide better power consumption. Reducing the clock speed for peripherals will also reduce power consumption.

Memory. Memory is frequently accessed by the system. Switching between memory banks can consume a lot of power. One technique to minimize loss of power is to use RAS as bank select. Only bank selected with RAS will be accessed; other banks are in standby. Based on experimental data, power con-

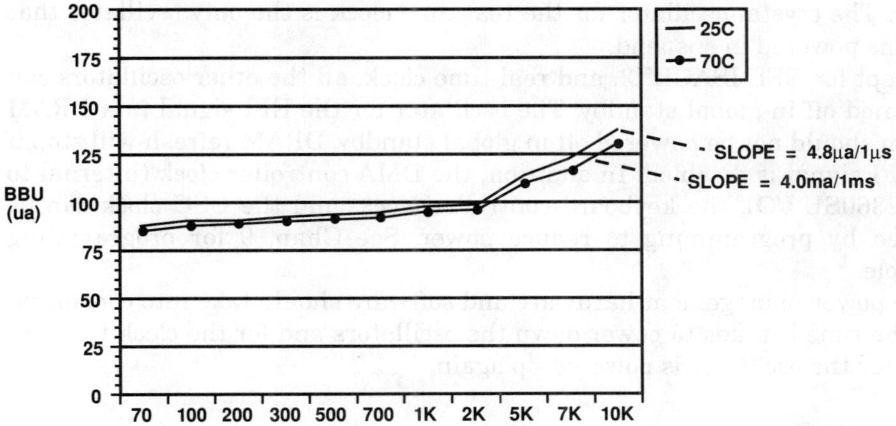

Figure 7.6 Relationship between power consumption and RAS pulse width. (*Courtesy of Micron Technology.*)

sumption increases as pulse width increases. Figure 7.6 shows how power consumption increases with RAS pulse width.

In an ISA-bus system, the DRAM subsystem has to be refreshed every 15.6 μs. DRAM refresh consumes power. The less often the DRAM controller refreshes the memory, the more power it will save. Many of the new DRAMs on the market support extend refresh and self-refresh to provide better power saving. Therefore, the DRAM controller should be programmed to take advantage these features.

Activity monitoring. Some peripherals, such as the floppy disk drive or a fax/modem board (or chip), are seldom used, even when the system is fully active. A simple way to save power is to use the local standby feature of the 82360SL to turn these components off when they are not in use. The power management hardware inside the 82360SL determines if the system or the device is idle by monitoring changes to control signals such as interrupts and trapping access to I/O or memory addresses.

Power Management Design Considerations

In the previous sections and the previous chapters, we have looked at the different techniques of conserving power.

Oscillators and clocks

The Intel386 SL processor and the 82360SL are fully static devices. Crystals and oscillators can be powered down to reduce power consumption during suspend. Typically, oscillators for the EFI, ISACLK2, ISA bus's OSC signals, and crystal for the serial controllers are powered down in suspend to conserve power. The crystal oscillator for the real-time clock is the only oscillator that remains powered in suspend.

Except for EFI, ISACLK2, and real-time clock, all the other oscillators can be turned off in global standby. The oscillator for the EFI signal in a DRAM system should not be powered off in global standby. DRAM refresh will stop if the EFI signal is disabled. In addition, the DMA controller clock (internal to the 82360SL I/O), the keyboard controller clock, and the OSC clock can be stopped by programming to reduce power. See Chap. 9 for programming example.

The power management hardware and software should take into consideration the time it takes to power down the oscillators and for the clock to stabilize after the oscillator is powered up again.

0-volt suspend consideration

As mentioned before, with a 0-volt suspend, everything is powered down except for the resume logic powered by the real-time clock's backup battery. The 82360SL differentiates between a complete power down and 0-volt suspend is through the PWRGOOD and SUS_STAT signals.

Hardware control

Table 7.2 shows the usage of the SMOUT pins in the Intel386 SL microprocessor evaluation board. The listing below shows how the SMOUT pins can be programmed to turn off power to different devices. SMOUT pins were three-stated during suspend to conserve power.

Software command

Most of the new devices in the market have built-in power management support. Some of these features are automatic and some of them are programmable. They are usually software commands that are generated by the host to put the device in different power modes.

Getting the best out of both worlds

The critical factors in determining whether to use hardware or software command to control the power consumption of a device are: actual power saving,

TABLE 7.2 SMOUT Pin Assignment

PIN	Assignment
SMOUT0	Floppy drive power
SMOUT1	COMA RS-232C buffer
SMOUT2	COMB RS-232C buffer
SMOUT3	Hard disk power
SMOUT4	Parallel port
SMOUT5	Flash Vpp control

time it takes to power a device on and off, board space, how much work it takes to save and restore a device, and cost of the device. Let's use hard disk as an example to look at the tradeoffs of hardware control versus software commands.

To decide which method to employ, you have to understand how the device functions and how it consumes power. Hard disk is a mechanical device and there is always a finite amount of time involved in bringing up the motor to access the data. In other words, you will have to wait for the motor to get ready before you can access the data after the hard disk is powered up again. And don't forget, every time the motor spins, it consumes power.

Typically, when an application is running and power management is enabled, the hard disk will go in and out of local standby quite frequently. Thus, it makes more sense to use software command to put the hard disk in a power-save mode to reduce both the wait time and the power consumed by the motor when it spins up as the hard disk wakes up. When the system is inactive for a long time (during global standby and suspend), it is more effective to use the SMOUT pin than software command since it can save more power. Powering down the hard disk completely will save more power than putting the hard disk in power-save mode using software command over a long period of time.

Hard disk

Power consumption of hard disk is very user-dependent. For example, data is always swapped in and out of the hard disk under Microsoft Windows environment. Thus, a Microsoft Windows user will use up more power than a DOS user because of the frequent access to the hard disk. If the drive is spun down frequently, overall power consumption might be higher than without power management. Tables 7.3 and 7.4 show the time it takes for the hard disk to recover from different modes and how much power is consumed.

TABLE 7.3 Recovery Time for Different Power Saving Modes (*Courtesy of Integral Corporation*)

Transition	Recovery time
Sleep mode to ready	1.5 s
Power off to ready	5 s

TABLE 7.4 Power Consumption to Exit from Different Power Modes (*Courtesy of Integral Corporation*)

Transition	Power consumption
Sleep mode to standby	35 mW
Power off to ready	1000 mW

Current Drain

As one might say, "always expect the unexpected"—and leakage current qualifies. Leakage current can cause current drain which will shorten the battery life. For the rest of this chapter we are going to talk about how to identify the source of leakage current. What we are really looking at is how current flows between the output of one component and the input of another. A component can either source current or sink it. When the output of component A is high, it supplies I_{IH} to the input of component B, which acts as resistance to ground. Thus, output of component A is acting as a source of current for component B's input. (See Fig. 7.7(a).)

In Fig. 7.7(b), the input of component B is like a resistance tied to Vcc. When output of component A goes low, current I_{IL} will flow in from the input of component B back through the output resistance of component A to ground.

Measurement techniques

A current probe or an ammeter is normally used for current measurement. A current probe clamps around the conductor carrying the current. There are

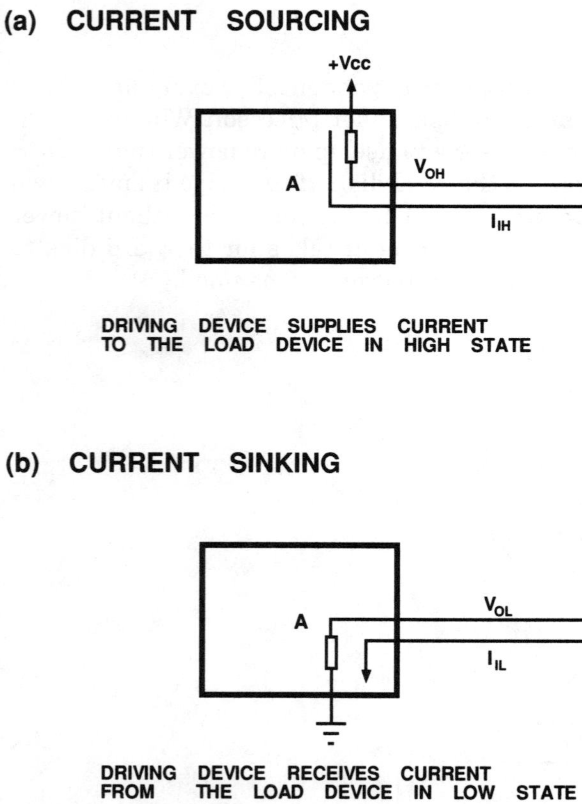

Figure 7.7 Current sourcing and sinking.

two kinds of current probes: current transformers, which measure AC current only, and Hall-Effect probes, which measure AC or DC current. The output of a current transformer is 1 mA per amp. The output of a Hall-Effect probe is 1 mV per amp, AC or DC.

Variations in voltage can have significant effect when measuring currents below 10 mA. Instead of an ammeter, a Hall probe could be used to avoid intrusive characteristics. When taking Icc measurements, be aware of any variations in the voltage of the power plane. When measuring component Icc, verify that only the current consumed by the component is measured.

When using an ammeter, a variable power supply can be connected to compensate for the voltage drop introduced by this instrument. When measuring system Icc, connect instrument directly to the battery leads to insure that all paths are included. If there are no test points for taking current measurement, break points must be created by cutting traces or unsoldering the circuit.

SL Superset Signals

Leakage current is one of the most notorious causes of excessive power drain during global standby and suspend. A good understanding of all the SL SuperSet signals can help in locating the source of leakage current. The state of all the signals in the SL SuperSet for different power states is described in the Intel486 SL CPU and Intel386 SL CPU data books.

Avoid connecting to powered-down devices. If it is necessary to connect to powered-down devices, ensure that any signals at 5 V do not overload off devices. Consider adding a buffer on the line. Whenever possible, select a low-power device with internal buffering.

Enabled input signals. During suspend, some of the signals are still active. Tables 7.6 and 7.7 show a list of signals that are active during suspend. If connected improperly, these signals can cause current drain. In general, you

TABLE 7.5 Active Output Signals during Suspend

Source	Active output signals
Intel386 SL processor	SMRAMCS#, Refresh, CMUX[0:11], MA[0:10], WHE#, WLE#
82360SL I/O	Refreq, RTCX2, SUS_STAT#, COMX2, CX2, EXTRTCRW#, EXTRTCAS, EXTRTCDS

TABLE 7.6 Enabled Signals on the Intel386 SL Processor

Termination	Signal
Pull-down	CPURESET
Pull-up	SUS_STAT#
No termination	EFI, ISACLK2, PWRGOOD, REFREQ

TABLE 7.7 Enabled Signals on the 82360SL I/O

Termination	Signal
Pull-down	IRQ8#
Pull-up	BATTDEAD#, BATTLOW#, COMARI#, COMBRI#, PWRGOOD, RTCEN#, RTCRESET#
No termination	RTCX1, SRBTN#

should avoid connecting signals that are active during suspend to powered-down devices. Signals with internal pull-downs should not be connected to an active pull-up. Signals with internal pull-ups should not be connected to ground. Signals without termination may require an external pull-down if the devices driving them are powered down.

Bushold circuitry. To avoid high current conditions caused by floating inputs to peripheral CMOS devices and to eliminate the need for pull-up/down resistors, "bus-hold" circuitry has been used on all three-state Intel386 SL microprocessor outputs. (See Fig. 7.8 for a description of the bushold circuit.)

The bushold circuit will maintain the last valid logic state if no driving source is present (i.e., an unconnected pin or a driving source which goes to a high impedance state). To overdrive the bushold circuits, an external driver must be capable of supplying the maximum "bus-hold overdrive" sink or source current at valid input voltage levels. Since this bushold circuitry is active and not a "resistive"-type element, the associated power supply current is negligible and power dissipation is significantly reduced when compared to the use of passive pull-up resistors.

During suspend, a bushold circuit is not flipped if the voltage on its line is at invalid level. To ensure that busholds flip during suspend, a sufficient path to ground must be provided. Do not connect bushold signals to planes floating above 1 volt. Avoid using pull-ups on bushold signals if the terminating device to which they are connected is off.

The following signals in Intel386 SL processor contain bushold circuitry: BALE, CA[1:15], CCSH#, CCSL#, CMUX[12:14], COE#, CWE#, HALT#, HLDS, INTA#, LA[17:23], MD[0:15], NPXADS#, NPXCLK, NPXRESET#, NPXW/R#, PCMD#, PERR#, PMI/O#, PSTART#, PW/R#, ROMCS0#, SA[0:19], SBHE#, SYSCLK, VGACS#; without refresh: CMUX[0:11], MA[0:10], WHE#, WLE#. There is no bushold circuitry in the 82360SL I/O.

Three-stated signals. Three-stated signals should not be left floating if they are connected to powered-on devices. These lines must be pulled high or low, as appropriate. Alternatively, buffers should be added to prevent signals from floating during suspend. Table 7.8 contains a list of signals that are three-stated during suspend.

Resistors. The 82360SL has pull-up resistors on some of its input pins to hold unconnected inputs at a stable level. During suspend, these pull-up resistors

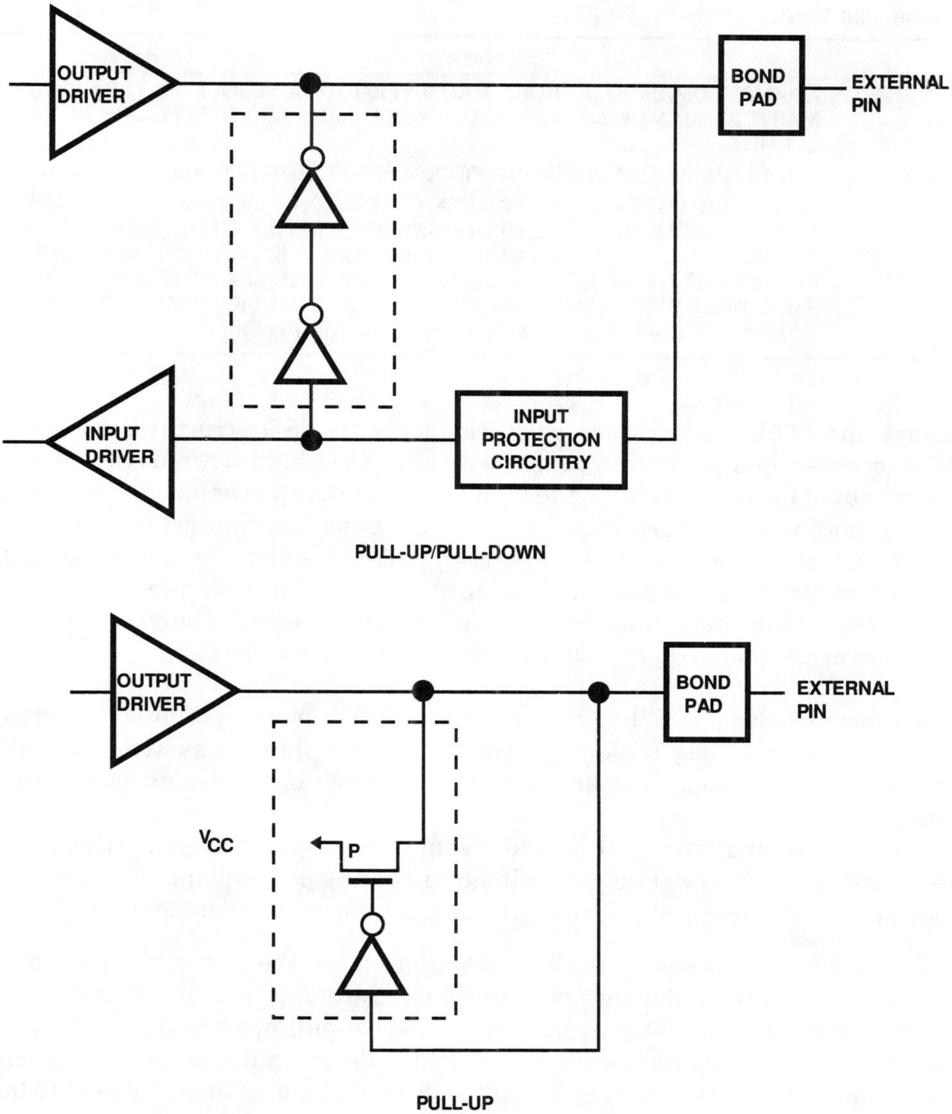

Figure 7.8 Bushold circuitries.

are isolated from the internal nodes and cause the internal nodes to float. These internal nodes will get discharged gradually and become low after a certain period of time. Upon resume, the pull-up resistors become effective again and cause a transition from low to high. False interrupts can be generated (IRQ 5, 7, 3, and 4).

To avoid pseudo-transition of signals, ensure that pull-up resistors do not provide indirect paths between a powered-on plane and an off device. Also, do not connect active pull-up resistors to bushold lines, as the resistors will prevent the bushold signals from toggling. Avoid connecting in series with a resistor to ground.

TABLE 7.8 Three-Stated Signals

Source	Three-stated signals
Common	A20GATE, DMA8/16#, ERROR#, HRQ, INTR, IOCHRDY, IOCS16#, IOR#, IOW#, MASTER#, MEMR#, MEMW#, NMI, ONCE#, SMI#, SD[0:7], STPCLK#, ZEROWS#
Intel386 SL processor	BUSY#, MEMCS16#, NPXRDY#, PEREQ, PRDY#, ROM16/8, SD[8:15], TURBO
82360SL I/O	AEN, BALE, BATTWARN#, C8042CS#, COMX1, CX1, DACK[0:3,5:7], EXTSMI#, FLPCS#, HALT#, HD7, HDCS[0:1]#, HDENH#, HDENL#, HLDA, IMUX0, INTA#, IOCHCHK#, IRQ[1,3:7,9:12,14,15], KBDA20, KBDCLK, LA[17:23], OSC, PERR# RC#, REFRESH#, RESETDRV, SA[0:16], SBHE#, SMEMR#, SMEMW#, SMOUT[0:5], SMRAMCS#, SPKR, SYSCLK, TC, TIM2CLK2, TIM2OUT2, XD7, XDEN#, XDIR, serial port signals (except COM[A:B]RI#), all parallel port signals

Diodes and LEDS. Diodes are used commonly in ESD structures. Current drain occurs when a powered device is driving a powered-down device. When the output of the driver is high, the input voltage to the power down will exceed Vcc by more than the threshold voltage causing the ESD protection structure to conduct. If a diode is used for isolation, make sure that the diode does not create unexpected paths once power planes turn off. The other alternative is to put in current-limiting resistors. The major drawbacks with current-limiting resistors are higher power dissipation and lower drive capability.

Power plane isolation. What is a power plane? A power plane is basically a power line to a host of devices. When a power plane is switched off, all the devices connected to it are turned off. Power plane design is system-dependent.

Avoid connecting active pull-ups to the input or output of a device which has been switched off. Be wary of any voltage on floating power plane. This usually indicates insufficient isolation and can prevent busholds from toggling.

Optimization of power plane. To check isolation, mark the power plane of each device and then trace the path of each signal. Carefully trace paths of signals which are used extensively in the design. Active pull-ups can be internal or external. By marking the power plane of each device, paths with alternating power plane connections can be identified. Signals used extensively tend to be those signals connected to devices with a high density of inputs and outputs (e.g., VGA and keyboard controller).

Examples

The first case has an active pull-up connected to the output of a powered-down device while the second case addresses the opposite situation. The most desirable solution is to change power plane connections such that they are homogeneous along the path. This solution usually does not require additional or specialized components. Sometimes changing power planes is not an option. In these cases, additional buffering should be considered as a solution. The second example uses a three-state buffer ('125 or '126) to resolve the power-plane isolation problem. (See Fig. 7.9.)

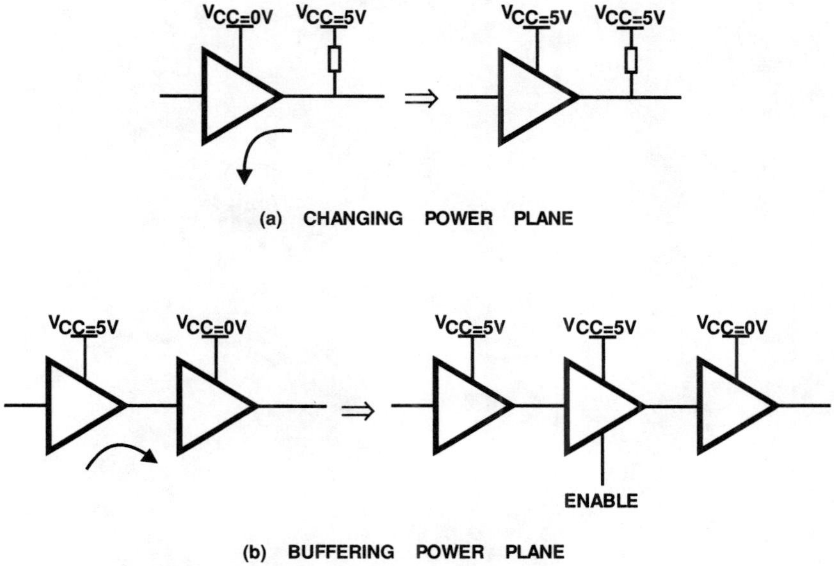

Figure 7.9 Power plane optimization.

When considering how to further isolate power planes, some compromises may be necessary. Ideally, all paths from an active power plane to a powered-down plane should be eliminated. In reality, the best isolation is achieved by eliminating the least resistive paths. Some paths which connect different power planes may be resistive enough that the power consumption is negligible compared with the target power consumption for the system.

Summary

In this chapter, we have discussed the common techniques used in power management. System power consumption can be lowered by careful selection of low-power components, elimination of current leakage paths, and battery management.

References

"The ABCs of DMMs," John Fluke Mfg. Co., Inc.

"An Introduction to Batteries," Gates Energy Products.

Buchanan, J., *CMOS/TTL Digital Systems Design* McGraw-Hill Publishing Company, Inc., 1990.

Hill, W., and P. Horowitz, *The Art of Electronics,* Cambridge University Press, 1989, pp. 917–986.

"Careful Power-Supply Design Extends Battery Life in Portable Systems," *Maxim Engineering Journal,* vol. 3.

Chapter

8

Portable Computer Design

The challenge in portable computer design is to manage the tradeoff between battery life and functionality. Although portable system designers are getting better and better at coping with the complexity of power management and system integration, portable computer users continue to ask for longer battery life, smaller form factors, higher performance, and better expansion capability. The SL architecture has solved many design problems and resulted in a new standard for portable computers that offers both increased functions and longer battery life.

This chapter describes the design and implementation of a 32-bit portable computer using the SL CPU and 82360SL peripheral controller. The goal of this design is low power consumption, high performance, and expansion capability with a small form factor. As of this writing, the Intel386 SL CPU is being used in more than 66 OEM designs for laptop, notebook, pen-based, and palmtop computers. The Intel486 SL CPU is soon to be introduced by Intel and promises to be a popular CPU for these same types of applications.

Overview of an SL CPU-based System

Figure 8.1 shows a portable computer design that uses either an Intel486 SL CPU or an Intel386 SL CPU, an 82360SL I/O, an Intel387 SL mobile math coprocessor, an 82077SL floppy drive controller, a 28F001BX flash memory, and an 82365SL PCMCIA card controller, plus memory devices and additional peripheral control devices. Using this example design, we will discuss how to design a portable computer using the SL CPU and 82360SL. For each part of the system, both hardware and software considerations will be discussed.

DRAM interface

As we have discussed in the previous chapters, the DRAM interface on the Intel486 SL CPU and Intel386 SL CPU allows DRAMs to be connected directly

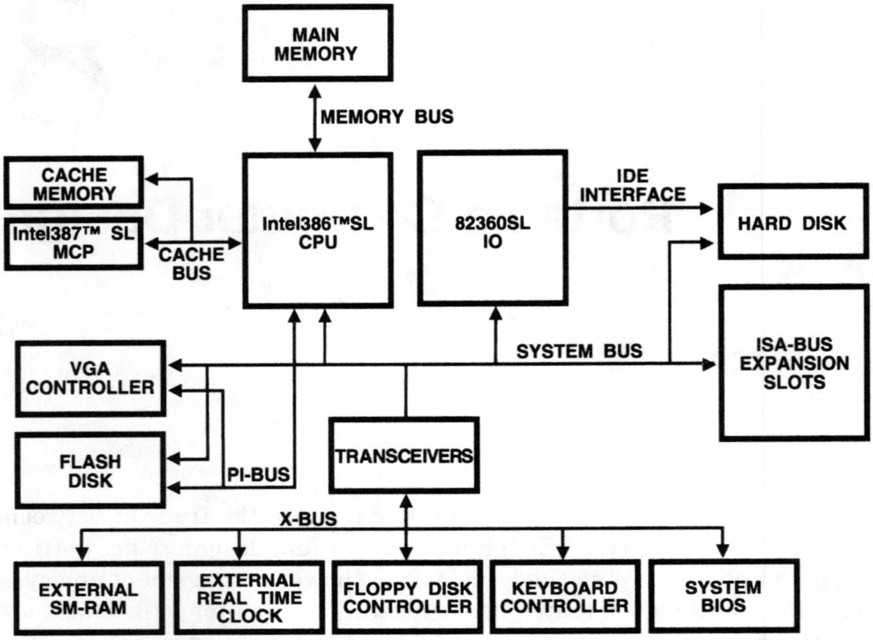

Figure 8.1 The Intel386 SL microprocessor SL superset bus architecture.

to the CPU without any additional glue logic. Configuration of the memory is completely programmable. For further information about designing a memory system, refer to Chap. 10 ("Intel386 SL CPU Memory Interfacing") and Chap. 11 ("Intel486 SL CPU Memory Interfacing").

Cache interface

To keep up with higher processor speeds, faster memory is needed. But building a system with high-speed memory is very expensive. The cache memory architecture of the Intel386 SL CPU combines the speed of expensive SRAM devices and the cost-effectiveness of slower DRAM devices. Indirectly, the cache controller also reduces the number of accesses to main memory, which in turn reduces the power consumption of main memory. (For further information about designing a cache memory, refer to Chap. 10.)

Flash BIOS

Flash memory has made it easy to upgrade firmware in portable computers. The Intel blocked flash memory further expanded the versatility offered by standard flash memory by dividing the flash memory into a hardware protected 8-Kbyte "boot block" and three separate programmable blocks: two 4-Kbyte parameter blocks and one 112-Kbyte code block. Reprogramming one block does not affect code stored in the other blocks. Thus, data integrity is ensured.

As more and more hardware is integrated into the portable computer, the size of the firmware which controls the hardware is also growing at a tremendous rate. Unlike a standard ISA system which only supports 128 Kbytes of BIOS space, the SL CPU supports up to 256 Kbytes of BIOS space. Software can use the additional 128 Kbytes to support hardware such as PCMCIA cards, a digitizer for a pen-based portable computer, or both.

Hardware considerations. Figure 8.2 shows the direct interface between the Intel 28F001BX-T flash memory and the SL CPU and 82360SL. In addition to providing the direct interface, the CPU also provides a FLASH BIOS Write Enable bit to prevent accidental write to the flash memory. When the BIOS is shadowed in the main memory for faster execution speed, the flash memory can be powered down to cut power consumption. Power-down mode is entered through low voltage on the PWD# pin.

The SL CPU supports 8-bit as well as 16-bit ROM access; the ROM8#/16 pin determines which type of access is used. ROMCS0# is asserted when the 0F0000-0FFFFFH address space is accessed through the ISA sliding window, because the decoding is done inside the EBU.

Software considerations. System configuration on an SL CPU-based system is completely under software control, thus making blocked memory particularly well suited for reconfiguring the system. The two 4-Kbyte parameter blocks of a blocked flash memory can be used to store the setup parameters, such as memory configuration, drive types, and display type.

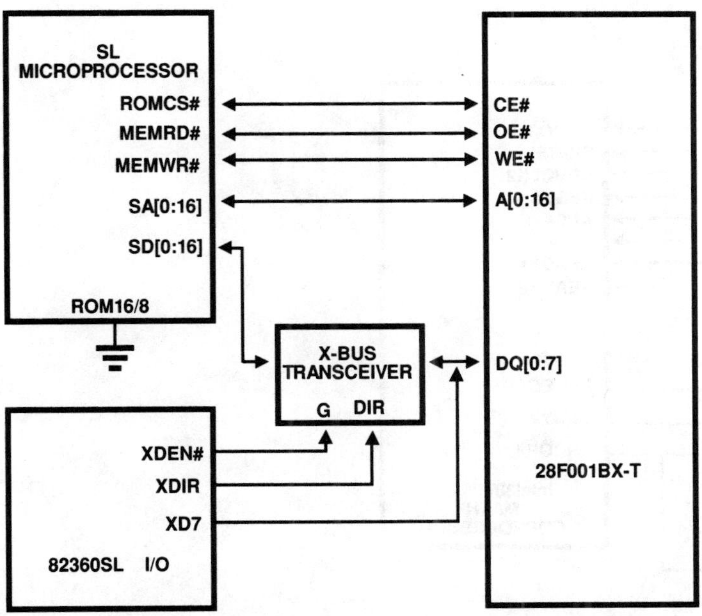

Figure 8.2 Intel 28F001BX-T flash memory interface to the SL CPU.

Intel387 SL Mobile Math Coprocessor

The Intel387 SL mobile math coprocessor (MCP) provides high performance floating point capabilities for Intel386 SL CPU-based portable systems. The Intel387 SL Mobile MCP is designed for low power and fully static operation.

Hardware considerations. Figure 8.3 shows the MCP interface to the Intel386 SL CPU. The MCP interface is fully ISA-compatible. The CPU provides the MCP clock (NPXCLK). The NPXCLK is automatically divided or stopped when the MCP is idle to conserve power. The NPXCLK input to the MCP can be tied high to minimize power consumption when it is idle.

Software considerations. The MCP can be powered off completely for maximum power saving during suspend. Typically, power to the MCP is turned off by asserting the SUS_STAT pin on the 82360SL during suspend. Two MCP instructions are also available for saving and restoring data when the MCP is powered down. The SL CPU handles MCP errors the same way it does for a standard ISA system. NPXRESET should be asserted only during power on or during resume. Therefore, a dummy write to port 0F1H does not generate NPXRESET.

Clock system

The SL CPU and 82360SL require two external oscillators and three external crystal-controlled clock generators to provide clock sources for the various sys-

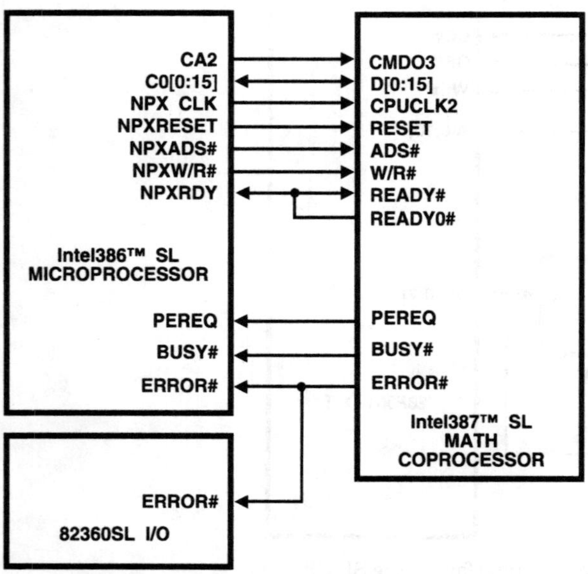

Figure 8.3 Math CoProcessor interface.

tem clocks. Chapter 9 ("Clock Control") gives a detailed discussion of the clock architecture.

Hardware considerations. Care should be taken in the design of the real-time clock (RTC) circuit, since the reliability of this clock is critical to system operation. The 82360SL provides an internal oscillator circuit to generate this clock. All you need to add is an external crystal-controlled clock source. You can also use an external oscillator circuit to provide the RTC.

The TURBO pin on the SL CPU offers a means of reducing the speed of the CPU clock (CPUCLK). You can design circuitry to assert this pin through a TURBO button or a unique key sequence.

Software considerations. The power management facilities of the SL CPU and 82360SL allow you to slow down and/or stop all of the system clocks to reduce power consumption. Control of clock speed is handled through software and internal power management facilities as described in Chap. 6 ("Power Management Software") and Chap. 9.

Power management facilities

Chapters 5 through 7 describe the wide range of power management facilities provided in the SL CPU and 82360SL. You can take advantage of a few of the power management options offered or use all of them, depending on the target market for your system. When all the power management features are used, you can design a notebook-class computer with an effective battery life of eight hours or more.

Developing an effective power management system requires smooth interaction between software and hardware. The design of a power management system is thus one area where software and hardware engineers must be in close communication. The most important decisions you will make together involve the selection of the levels of power conservation techniques you will use.

The SL CPU and 82360 offer four levels of power management: local standby (for powering down selected peripherals), global standby (for reducing power consumption in system components), 5-volt (or 3.3-volt) suspend/resume, and 0-volt suspend/resume. These power management levels are described in detail in Chap. 5 ("Introduction to Power Management").

80C51SL keyboard controller

The Intel 80C51SL is a low-power keyboard controller with a direct interface to the 82360SL. (See Fig. 8.4.)

Hardware considerations. The 82360SL provides the C8042CS and RESETDRV signals to select and reset the 80C51SL, respectively. The keyboard clock for the 80C51SL is generated by an external crystal oscillator network. Instead of using a TURBO switch, turbo mode can be implemented using the keyboard. The TURBO pin on the SL CPU can be connected to the 80C51SL. Every time

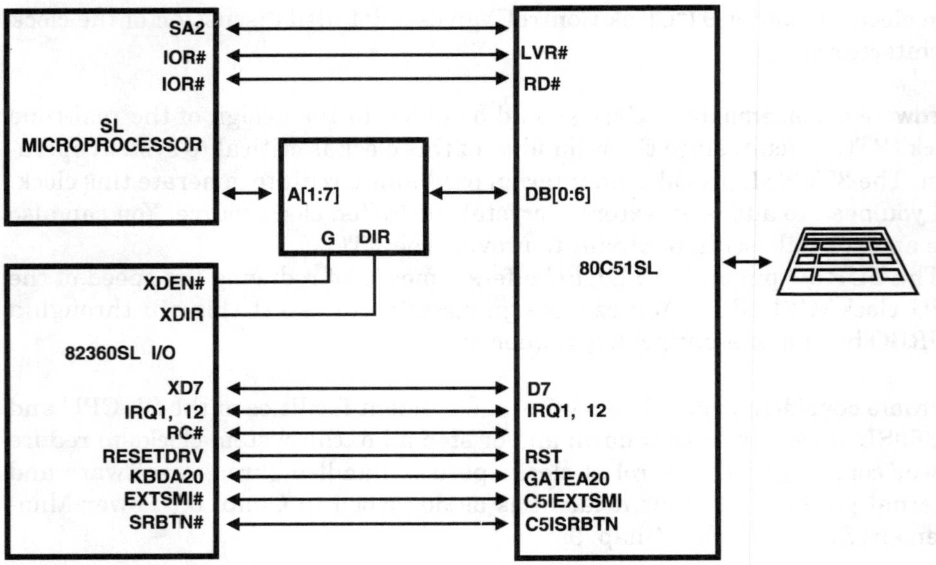

Figure 8.4 Intel 80C51SL keyboard controller interface to the 82360SL.

the 80C51SL detects a predefined key sequence, it will either assert or deassert the TURBO signal to select turbo or de-turbo mode, respectively.

Software considerations. The 80C51SL provides several power management facilities that complement those found in the SL CPU and 82360SL. For example, through software the 80C51SL can be placed in IDLE mode in between keystrokes or when the keyboard is inactive to reduce power consumption substantially. The 80C51SL also supports a POWER DOWN mode. In POWER DOWN mode, the oscillator for the 80C51SL is stopped to reduce power consumption to less than 1 percent of the normal power consumption.

VGA controller/PI bus

The example system design in Fig. 8.1 uses a Cirrus Logic CL-GD6440 high-performance, low-power LCD/CRT VGA graphics controller, which is fully compatible with ISA standard. High performance is achieved by taking advantage of the PI-bus interface.

Hardware considerations. Figure 8.5 shows how the VGA controller interfaces to the SL CPU. The CPU generates the chip select for the VGA controller internally. Thus, no external decoding logic is required.

The PI bus is based on the CPU clock which runs at a much higher rate than the ISA bus (8 MHz). The PI bus can support a very large secondary graphics frame buffer. Extra I/O addresses which can be used for compatibility reasons are provided by the PI bus. Chapter 12 ("PI-Bus Interfacing") describes the PI bus in detail and gives an example of using the PI bus to support a video-graphics frame buffer.

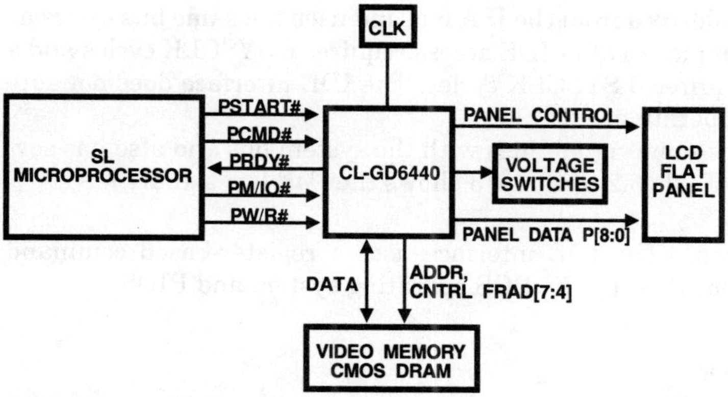

Figure 8.5 Cirrus Logic CL-GD6440 VGA controller interface to the SL CPU.

Even though the ISA address space is 16 Mbytes, the start address for the secondary graphics buffer can be set above 16 Mbytes address space. When the graphics buffer is set above the 16 Mbytes of address space, access to the buffer is wrapped around within the 16-Mbyte ISA address space.

The secondary graphics buffer cannot share the same address space with on-board memory. On-board memory must be disabled before the secondary graphics buffer can be accessed. No VGACS# signal is generated for accessing the secondary graphics buffer.

Software considerations. The CL-GD6440 uses the power management features of the 82360SL to maximize power saving, and it provides direct support for the suspend feature on the 82360SL.

The LOVGA and HIVGA bits in the ROMCS_DEC register (2FH, INDEX) are used to enable the XDIR and XDEN signals whenever there is video-ROM access. The LOVGA and HIVGA bits in the EBC1CR register are used for activating the ROMCS0# and ROMCS1# signals.

VGACS# is activated on the ISA bus when the VGA controller is located on the ISA bus. The VGACS# signal is not generated when the 0A0C00H-0BFFFFH address space is accessed through the ISA-sliding window. This is because the decoding is in the internal bus unit and not in the external bus unit.

The REFREQ signal or clock output from the real-time clock (RTC) can be used to refresh the video RAM during suspend.

IDE hard disk drive

The 82360SL provides an Integrated Drive Electronics (IDE) interface to an IDE hard disk drive controller. This interface consists of an IDE bus and control registers in the 82360SL.

Hardware considerations. The IDE interface allows a disk drive to be connected to the system with a simple adapter card that contains a minimum of logic. The IDE bus is derived from the ISA bus and uses the same bus cycles as the ISA bus. For example, an 8-bit IDE access requires 6 SYSCLK cycles and a 16-bit IDE access requires 3 SYSCLK cycles. The IDE interface does not support zero wait state operation.

The IDE bus shares some signal lines with the system bus and also has several unique signals. (Table 3.2 in Chap. 3 shows the IDE bus signals.)

Software considerations. The IDE interface uses a register-based command status protocol standardized by the DOS operating system and BIOS.

82077SL floppy drive and controller

The Intel 82077SL is a low-power floppy drive controller fully compatible with the ISA standard. This controller connects directly to the 82360SL with no need for support logic.

Hardware considerations. Figure 8.6 shows the hardware interface between the floppy drive controller and the 82360SL. The 82360SL provides all the decode logic necessary for the interface.

You can also connect the 82077SL to the SD bus or X bus. To connect the floppy drive controller to the SD bus, the decode logic and X-bus interface for the floppy drive can be disabled by software.

Software considerations. The controller supports intelligent power management. When the controller is idle, it will enter power-down mode automatically.

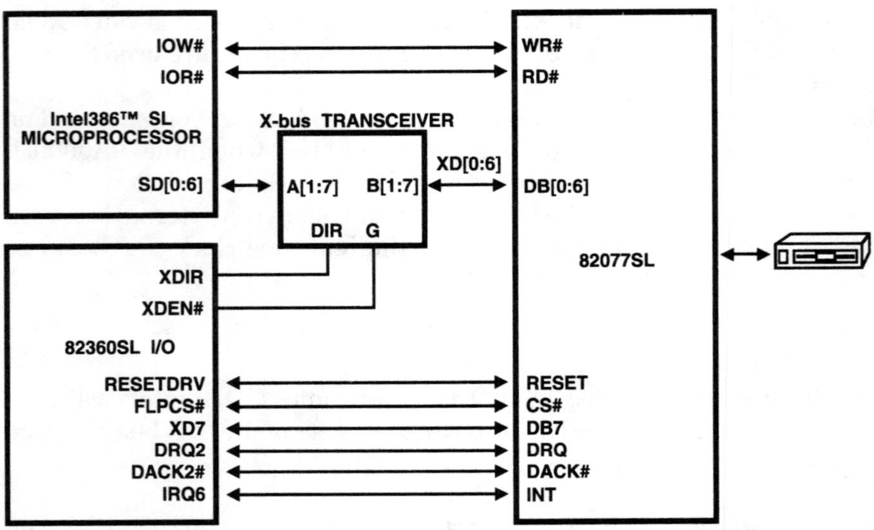

Figure 8.6 Interface to 82077SL.

When the 82360SL detects that the 82077SL is idle, it can power down the 82077SL through a software command. The PD pin on the 82077SL indicates that the 82077SL is in power-down state. If an external oscillator is used, it can be used to disable the external oscillator's output for the 82077SL.

Parallel port

The 82360SL provides a complete ISA parallel port interface. The parallel port supports three different modes of operation—standard parallel port, PS/2-compatible parallel port, and enhanced parallel port. The enhanced parallel port interface is described in Chap. 13.

Hardware considerations. The parallel port interface pins on the 82360SL can be connected directly to a standard 25-pin D-shell parallel port connector. The 82360SL provides enough drive current to support any standard ISA parallel port device.

Software considerations. The parallel port on the 82360SL defaults to standard parallel port mode after power up. PS/2-compatible mode is enabled by enabling PS/2 feature set. (See Chap. 14, "Writing an SL BIOS.")

Serial ports (RS-232C interface)

The 82360SL provides two RS-232C-style serial communication ports. They can be used for any typical RS-232C interface applications, such as a fax/modem interface, mouse port, or LAN adapter.

Hardware considerations. The serial port interface pins on the 82360SL can be connected directly to an external RS-232C port or be routed internally to a fax/modem or LAN adapter.

82365SL ExCA backplane controller chip

The Intel 82365SL is the first PCMCIA card controller that supports PCMCIA 2.0/JEIDA standards for portable computers. The 82365SL provides the expansion capability that is normally missing in a portable computer. For example, devices such as fax/modem, ethernet, and flash memory disk can be accessed through the 82365SL. It can directly support two standard 68-pin slots and is capable of supporting up to eight interchangeable slots by cascading up to four controllers. Several ExCA peripherals are currently on the market, including flash memory cards, DRAM cards, modems, LAN adapters, and hard disks. More ExCA peripherals will be available in the future.

Hardware considerations. Figure 8.7 shows the PCMCIA card controller interface to the SL CPU and the 82360SL I/O. Power management support on the 82365SL works directly with the 82360SL. The PCMCIA device can request

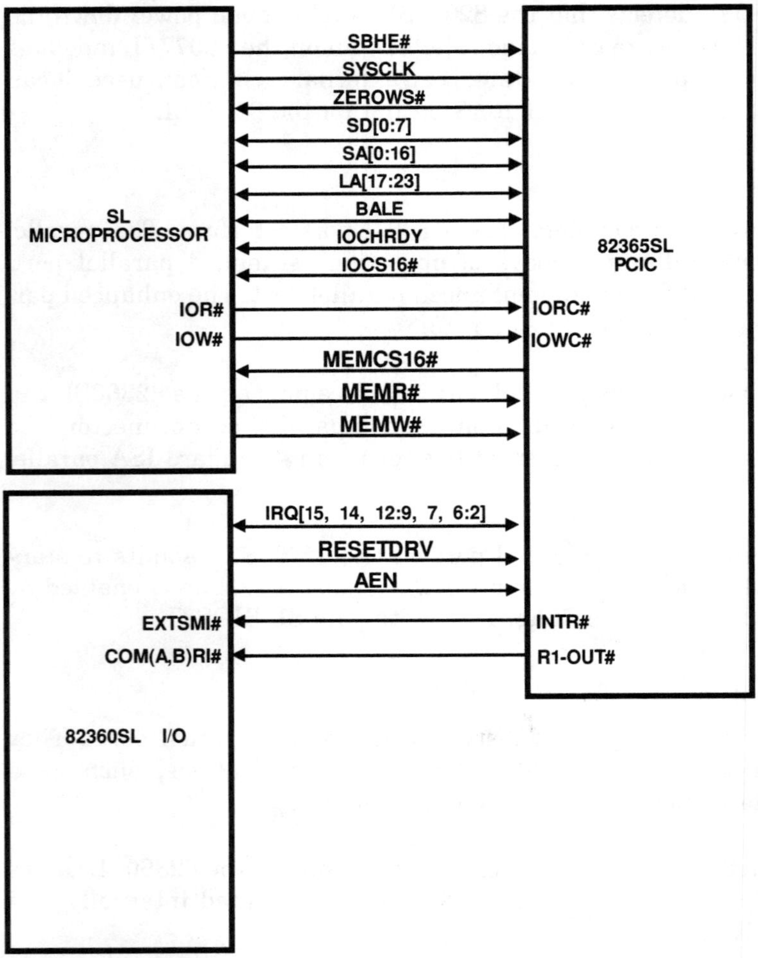

Figure 8.7 Intel 82365SL PCMCIA card controller interface to the SL CPU and 82360SL.

power management service through the INTR# pin which goes directly to the EXTSMI# pin on the 82360SL.

The 82365SL increases the memory address space of an SL CPU-based system to 64 Mbytes. It provides a mechanism to map portions of the 64-Mbyte attribute memory spaces on the PC card onto the smaller 16-Mbyte ISA system address space, making more memory available for system and application software.

SMM resources

The SMM provides a convenient mechanism for controlling system functions independently from the operating system and applications program. For example, all of the SL CPU and 82360SL power management facilities access the

SMM to execute power management routines. The SMM can also be used to control product-specific features. Chapter 4 ("System Management Mode") describes the SMM in detail.

Hardware considerations. Custom hardware in the system can initiate SMM routines by asserting the system management interrupt pin (SMI#) on the SL CPU.

Software considerations. A software SMI can also be initiated by writing to the SM_REQ_CNTRL register (0B6H, INDEX). The SMM software executes from its own address space and memory (SMRAM) and is able to access all system facilities without interfering with the operating system or application program.

Exiting from SMM is accomplished with the RSM instruction. Chapter 4 gives examples of the use of SMM for custom applications and includes code samples.

Mixed 3.3/5-volt system design

Although high integration and power management have extended battery life dramatically, lowering operating voltage to 3.3-volt promises even longer battery life. Portable computers based on the Intel486 SL CPU or the low-voltage Intel386 SL CPU will conserve more power by operating at 3.3-volt. Operating at 3.3-volt can save as much as 60 percent of the logic power. Moving to 3.3-volt also reduces heat and electric field stresses.

Since 3.3-volt components are not widely available, the designers at Intel opted for the mixed 3.3/5-volt approach. Until more 3.3-volt devices and peripherals hit the market, you will not be able to reap the full benefits of running at a lower voltage. With the hybrid approach, you can take advantage of the power saving of running at 3.3-volt immediately and migrate to a full 3.3-volt system as more 3.3-volt peripherals become available.

In the meantime, there are issues you must deal with in designing a mixed 3.3/5-volt system.

Hardware considerations. The interface between 3.3-volt and 5-volt components is a critical design issue. As shown in Fig. 8.8, when the output signal is 1.2 volts, the circuit behaves like a forward-biased diode. The 3.3-volt component generates leakage into the 5-volt component, which can damage the component, lower the guard band for noise immunity, drain more power, and heat up the component.

Buffers are required to translate signals running between 3.3- and 5-volt components to correct voltage. Adding buffers will increase cost, board space, and power consumption. To minimize the number of buffers, you must determine which signals must be translated and how many buffers are needed. In the case of the Intel486 SL CPU and the low-voltage Intel386 SL CPU, the translation buffers for the memory and ISA-bus interface are built-in, eliminating the need for glue logic in these areas.

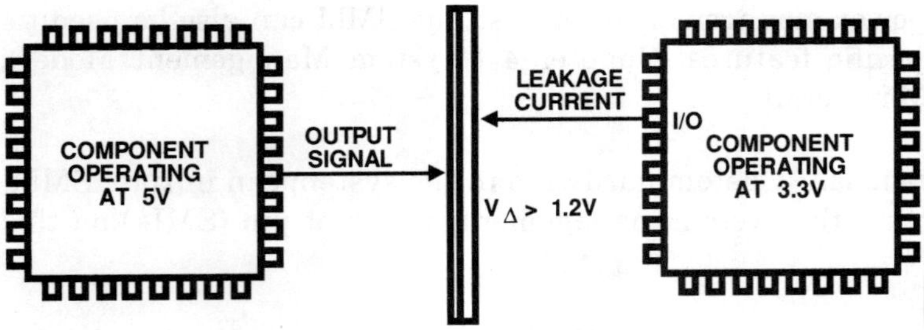

▼ CIRCUIT BEHAVIOR CAN LOOK LIKE FORWARD-BIASED DIODE
▼ HIGH DANGER OF COMPONENT DAMAGE
▼ POWER CONSUMPTION HIGHER
▼ NOISE IMMUNITY LESS

Figure 8.8 Leakage between 3.3-volt and 5-volt components. (*Courtesy of Cirrus Logic, Inc.*)

Because of the recharacterization of 5-volt components into 3.3-volt components and the timing delays introduced by translation buffers, not all 3.3-volt components meet the specification for their 5-volt counterparts. Therefore, do not assume that the AC and DC specifications are the same as those for the 5-volt components. You will need to read the specifications for all the components and ensure that they work with each other.

Putting It Together

When designing the circuitry for a portable computer, you should also consider flexible circuits, component packaging, thermal specifications, and noise control.

Flexible circuits

The lightness and bendable properties of flexible circuits make them particularly well suited for portable computers. A flexible circuit is essentially a bendable printed circuit board. It has been used extensively in portable computers for things such as connectors for the LCD panel, floppy drive, and hard disk. As portable computers get smaller and lighter, more and more electronic components will be built on flexible circuits.

Some considerations must be taken in selecting materials for building flexible circuits. As the designer, you must select material that will yield the best performance and the lowest power consumption and noise level.

Component packaging

"More in less" is the best way to sum up today's packaging technology. The growth of the portable computer market coupled with the advance in surface mount technology has driven the packaging technology to a much higher integration level. For example, many manufacturers have redesigned their products to include external components such as resistors and capacitors in their chips. At the same time, they also shrink their products into a much smaller footprint. Through a careful selection of components, a substantial saving in space can be achieved. Therefore, you should always find out what packaging options are available when looking at component data sheets.

Thermal specifications

Heat levels are critical for correct operation of any system, especially portable computers where space is limited. Portable computers usually do not have a fan. Therefore, it is important that the ambient temperature does not exceed the manufacturer's maximum rating. Ambient temperature is the temperature of the air surrounding the component. For the SL CPU and the 82360SL I/O, the ambient temperature can be determined by using the values of thermal resistance between the junction and case, Θ_{jc}, and the thermal resistance between junction and ambient Θ_{ja} in the following equations:

$$T_j = T_c + P * \Theta_{jc}$$

$$T_a = T_j - P * \Theta_{ja}$$

$$T_c = T_a + P*[\Theta_{ja} - \Theta_{jc}]$$

where
T_a = Ambient temperature in degrees Celsius
T_c = Case temperature in degrees Celsius
Θ_{jc} = Package thermal resistance between junction and case
Θ_{ja} = Package thermal resistance between junction and ambient
T_j = Junction temperature (heat at the surface of the component)
P = Power consumption in watts

Values for Θ_{ja} and Θ_{jc} are given in Table 8.1 for the 196-lead PQFP Intel386 SL CPU and the 82360SL I/O.

Noise control

Electromagnetic interference (EMI) is a common problem in portable computer design because of the use of high-impact plastic enclosures. Design for low EMI should begin early in the development process so that circuit design, PCB layout, and shielding can be designed all along the way for reduced noise. These design considerations are particularly critical when you are attempting to design an FCC Class B level of system.

TABLE 8.1 Thermal Resistances (C/W) Θ_{jc} and Θ_{ja}

		Θ_{ja} (C/W) versus airflow—ft/min (m/sec)			
		0	200	400	600
Package	Θ_{jc} C/W	(0)	(1.01)	(2.03)	(3.04)
196L PQFP	6	23	19	16	13.5

Design Considerations

The following are some additional design considerations you should note when designing a portable computer:

- When designing a multilayer motherboard, the more layers you use, the smaller the motherboard can be. Debugging a multilayer motherboard, however, is more difficult. You will not be able to get to all the signals below the first layer.
- Unless cost is an issue, keeping the chip count to a minimum will reduce board size and heat dissipation. Always use LSI to reduce chip count.
- Use CMOS devices whenever possible to reduce power consumption and heat dissipation.
- Check power requirements of components to ensure that the power supply does not get overloaded.
- When laying out the motherboard, make sure all the signals are properly grounded. Thermal relief should be added to provide good electrical contact.
- Use the thinnest and smallest package whenever possible to reduce board space and provide more vertical clearance.
- Include spare chip locations for adding workarounds.
- Test points and status displays are always helpful in debugging.
- Do not have more than one or two 74LS loads per bus signal.
- Include one bypass capacitor of 0.01 to 0.1 microfarad for every one to four chips. Capacitors should be electrically close to the IC.

Summary

Power consumption or battery life has always been the major focus of portable computer design. Very often, design issues such as performance, expansion capability, and form factors are not getting enough attention. This chapter discusses the importance of these design considerations and how to design a portable computer with these issues in mind.

There are many ways to design a portable computer and the key to designing it is integration. As a system designer, you must ensure that the hardware and software work with each other seamlessly. The materials covered in this chapter might not cover everything you need to know about designing a portable computer; however, there should be enough information to get you started.

References

Ginsberg, L., *Printed Circuits Design,* McGraw-Hill, Inc., 1990.

Intel386 SL Microprocessor SuperSet Data Sheet, Intel Corporation (order no. 240814-003).

Intel386 SL Microprocessor SuperSet Programmer's Reference Manual, Intel Corporation (order no. 240815-003).

Intel386 SL Microprocessor SuperSet System Design Guide, Intel Corporation (order no. 240816-003).

"Intel386 SL Microprocessor SuperSet Family Product Brief," Intel Corporation (order no. 240851-002).

"Pseudo-Static RAM Application Note," Toshiba America Electronic Components, Inc.

"Cache Tutorial," Intel Corporation (order no. 296543-002).

"82077SL Data Sheet," Intel Corporation (order no. 290410-001).

Dipert, B., and D. Verner, "Designing an Updatable BIOS Using Flash Memory," Intel Corporation (order no. 292077-002).

"82365SL Data Sheet," Intel Corporation (order no. 290423-001).

Chapter

9

Clock Control

Most of the power used by the CPU, coprocessors, and other integrated circuit components in a computer system is AC power (clock sensitive), as opposed to DC power. The amount of power that these components use is directly related to the clock speed at which the components are operating. For example, running the Intel486 SL CPU at a 20-MHz clock speed requires twice as much power as it does to run it at 10 MHz. To design a portable computer with extended battery life, part of your power management system design should thus include mechanisms to reduce clock speed or even stop the clock to system components when the system is idle.

This chapter examines the clock-system architecture of the Intel486 SL CPU, Intel386 SL CPU, and 82360SL I/O and shows how this architecture can be used to reduce system power consumption. Design considerations for clock-generating circuitry are also examined.

The SL Clock System

The Intel486 SL CPU, Intel386 SL CPU, and 82360SL require five input clock signals and generate four output clock signals. Figure 9.1 shows a block diagram of these clock inputs and outputs.

The function of each input clock signal is as follows:

- *External frequency input (EFI).* Clocks the core of the Intel486 SL CPU and Intel386 SL CPU. It is two times the CPU clock rate (50-MHz EFI for 25-MHz CPU operation).
- *ISA clock (ISACLK2).* Clocks the ISA-bus interface. It is two times the ISA-bus clock rate (16-MHz ISACLK2 for an 8-MHz ISA-bus clock).
- *Crystal oscillator input (CX1) and output (CX2).* Provides clock source for generation of the ISA-bus OSC signal.
- *Communications crystal oscillator input (COMX1) and output (COMX2).* Provides clock source for internal 82360SL oscillator that generates clock for serial communications port.

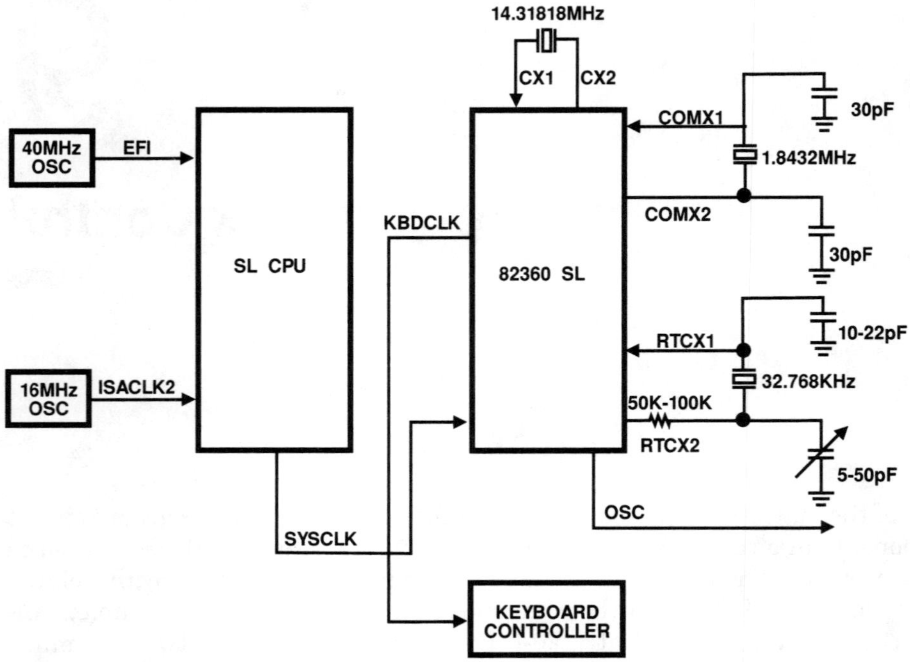

Figure 9.1 Block diagram of SL CPU and 82360SL clocks.

- *Real-time clock crystal oscillator input (RTCX1) and output (RTCX2).* Provides clock source for internal 82360SL oscillator that generates clocks for the real-time clock and the power management state machines.

The functions of the output clocks are as follows:

- *System clock (SYSCLK).* This SL CPU output clock is the ISA-bus system clock. It is one half the frequency of the ISACLK2 clock.
- *Math coprocessor clock (NPXCLK).* This Intel386 SL CPU output clock is the input clock to the math coprocessor (MCP). The frequency of this clock can be varied under program control.
- *Oscillator (OSC).* This 82360SL output clock is the ISA-bus oscillator clock. It is derived from an internal oscillator that is controlled by the CX1 and CX2 signals.
- *Keyboard clock (KBDCLK).* The 82360SL output clock is the clock input to the keyboard controller. This clock is derived from the SYSCLK.

The use of these clocks and their configuration for power management is described in the following sections.

EFI clock

From the EFI clock, the SL CPU generates two internal clocks: the internal CPU clock (CPUCLK) and the internal processor clock (PCLK). The CPU uses these clocks to control its internal operation. Fields in the CPUPWRMODE register control the frequency of the CPUCLK; the maximum CPUCLK frequency is one-half the EFI clock rate. The PCLK is derived from the CPUCLK and is half the frequency of the CPUCLK. The PCLK determines the internal phase of the Intel386 SL processor. The NPXCLK output is also derived from the EFI (Intel386 SL CPU only).

A 20-kilohm pull-down resistor is needed for the EFI input (Intel386 SL CPU only) to maintain the voltage below the input low voltage in suspend. The EFI input is not isolated during suspend. If the oscillator is powered off during suspend, the Intel386 SL processor may drain power.

Controlling the CPUCLK for power management

To reduce the power consumed by the SL CPU when it is in an idle state, the speed of the CPUCLK can be reduced or the clock can be stopped. Because the SL CPU is a static device, it can be stopped without losing its state information. The software to change the speed of the CPU clock is generally executed in SMM as part of the suspend power management mechanism, described in Chap. 5.

The following three mechanisms can be used to control the CPUCLK speed:

- The SL CPU turbo pin
- The fast and slow CPU clock fields in the CPUPWRMODE register (22H)
- The special feature set's SLOW CPU register

These features cannot be active at the same time, so a priority scheme must be used if you are going to use more than one of these mechanisms. Table 9.1 shows the priorities of these mechanisms.

When a bus master device (e.g., DMA controller) has control of the bus, the CPU clock always follows the slow CPU clock field (bits [10-9]) in the CPUPWRMODE register. During non-bus master cycles, the SFS's SLOWCPU register, the turbo pin, and the FAST CPU clock field in the CPUPWRMODE register determine the CPUCLK speed.

The SLOWCPU register and the turbo pin control the de-turbo select bit (bit 15) of the CPUPWRMODE register. When the special feature set is enabled, any dummy write to the SLOWCPU register will place the CPU in de-turbo mode. The SLOWCPU register feature is the quickest way to slow down the CPU clock. If the SLOWCPU feature is not enabled, the CPU will go into de-

TABLE 9.1 Priorities of Mechanisms for Slowing Down CPU Clock

Mechanism	Priority
Slow CPU clock field in CPUPWRMODE register	1 (highest)
SLOW CPU register	2
Turbo pin	3
Fast CPU clock field in CPUPWRMODE register	4

turbo mode when the turbo pin is asserted low. If neither the SLOWCPU feature nor the turbo pin are active, the CPU clock follows the fast CPU clock field (bits [5-4]) in the CPUPWRMODE register.

Listing 9.1

```
;-------------------------------------------------------------
;
;
;   NAME  SPEED.ASM. Program to change the speed of the CPU.
;
;    Usage  SPEED DIVISOR
;
;-------------------------------------------------------------
PAGE
Include          superset.inc
blank  EQU  20H  ; space
FULL   EQU  00H  ; full speed
HALF   EQU  10H  ; divide by 2
FOURTH EQU  20H  ; divide by 4
EIGHTH EQU  30H  ; divide by 8
code  SEGMENT
    ASSUME cs:code, ds:code
EXTRN      open_cpupwrmode:near, close_cpupwrmode:near
    ORG  5DH
param1 LABEL BYTE  ; divisor
    ORG  100H
start:
; get divisor
         call    open_cpupwrmode
         MOV   AL, [param1]
         CMP   AL, blank    ; anything?
         JZ    help
         CMP   AL, '1'      ; divide by 1?
         JA    two
         MOV   BITMASK, FULL
         JMP   set
two:     CMP   AL, '2'      ; divide by 2?
         JA    three
         MOV   BITMASK, HALF
         JMP   set
three:   CMP   AL, '4'      ; divide by 4?
         JA    four
         MOV   BITMASK, FOURTH
         JMP   set
four:    CMP   AL, '8'      ; divide by 8?
         JA    help
```

```
        MOV   BITMASK, EIGHTH
set:    IN    AL, 22H
        OR    AL, BITMASK
        OUT   22H, AL
        JMP   done
help:   MOV   AH, 09H
        PUSH  DS
        PUSH  SS
        POP   DS
        MOV   DX, OFFSET HELP_MES
        INT   21H
        POP   DS
done:
        call  close_cpupwrmode
        MOV   AX, 4C00H
        INT   21H     ; terminate program

;---------------------------------------------------------------
;
;          DATA AREA
;
;---------------------------------------------------------------

HELP_MES    DB  'USAGE: SPEED - DIVISOR (1/2/4/8)$'
BITMASK     DB  ?

code  ENDS
    END  start
```

Stop clock

The CPU clock can also be stopped automatically by executing an HLT instruction or doing a dummy I/O read to the STP_CLK register (0FDH, INDEX) when the stop-break event feature is enabled. The stop-break event feature is enabled by setting bit 0 of the STP_BRK_CFG2 register (0B2H, INDEX).

NPXCLK output

The NPXCLK output drives the clock input of the Intel387 SL mobile math coprocessor. During access to the MCP, the NPXCLK runs at the same speed as the CPUCLK. When the MCP is idle, the NPXCLK output can be slowed down or stopped automatically to conserve power. Please note that when the MCP is active, its operating frequency is the same as the CPU operating frequency.

The MCP idle field (bits [13-11]) inside the CPUPWRMODE register control the MCP clock when it is idling. The idle MCP clock can be programmed to EFI/2, EFI/4, EFI/8, EFI/16, or stopped. If the stop clock is selected, the MCP stop clock enable bit (bit 14) in the OMDCR register must be set to one for it to take effect. Otherwise, the idle MCP clock will default to EFI/16 instead. The stop clock option should not be enabled unless a static MCP (such as the Intel387 SL Mobile MCP) is installed. Listing 9.2 gives an example of how the MCP idle clock feature can be programmed.

Listing 9.2 Controlling the MCP Idle Clock

```
;-------------------------------------------------------------
;
;
;    MCPSPEED.ASM: Program to change the speed of the CPU.
;
;    Usage MCPSPEED DIVISOR
;
;-------------------------------------------------------------

blank   EQU  20H  ; space
FULL    EQU  00H  ; full speed
HALF    EQU  10H  ; divide by 2
FOURTH  EQU  20H  ; divide by 4
EIGHTH  EQU  30H  ; divide by 8

code SEGMENT
    ASSUME cs:code, ds:code

    ORG  5Dh
param1 LABEL  BYTE  ; divisor

    ORG  100h

start:

; enable MCP stop clock feature

    call  open_ibu
    mov   ax, OMDCR
    mov   dx, ax
    in    ax, dx
    or    ax, 4000h
    out   dx, ax
    call  close_386sl

; set mcp clock to full speed

    call  open_cpupwrmode ; open CPUPWRMODE register
    in    al, 23h
    and   al, 0c7h

; get divisor

        push  ax
        mov   al, [param1]
        cmp   al, blank  ; anything?
        jz    help
        cmp   al, '0'    ; stop cpu clock
        ja    one
        pop   ax
        or    al, 0FFh
        jmp   set
one:    cmp   al, '1'    ; divide by 1?
        ja    two
        pop   ax
```

```
        jmp   set
two:    cmp   al, '2'     ; divide by 2?
        ja    four
        pop   ax
        or    al, 0CFh
        jmp   set
four:   cmp   al, '4'     ; divide by 4?
        ja    six
        pop   ax
        or    al, 0D7h
        jmp   set
six:    cmp   al, '6'     ; divide by 16?
        ja    eight
        pop   ax
        or    al, 0E7h
        jmp   set
eight:  cmp   al, '8'     ; divide by 8?
        ja    help
        pop   ax
        or    al, 0DFh
        jmp   set
set:
        out   23h, al
        jmp   done
help:   mov   ah, 09H
        mov   dx, OFFSET HELP_MES
        int   21h
done:
        call  close_cpupwrmode          ; close CPUPWRMODE register
        mov   ax, 4C00h
        int   21h        ; terminate program

;------------------------------------------------------------
;
;        DATA AREA
;
;------------------------------------------------------------

HELP_MES    DB  'USAGE: SPEED - DIVISOR (0/1/2/4/6/8)$'
BITMASK     DB  ?

code ENDS
    END  start
```

A new instruction called FSTSG AX has been added to the Intel387 SL for stepping identification. After executing the FSTSG AX instruction, the signature register for the i387 SL Mobile will be stored in the AX register. This instruction can also be used to detect the presence of the i387 SL. The FSTSG instruction should be executed right after an FINIT instruction, *before* the status word has been changed. If the status word in the i387 SX has been changed, random data will appear in the status word. A i387 SX will return the status word 0000H, whereas the i387SL will return the signature register 23XX.

ISACLK2 input

The SL CPU uses the ISACLK2 (16 MHz) input to derive the SYSCLK (8 MHz) and to synchronize the ISA-BUS generation logic. The ISACLK2 must have a 60/40 duty cycle or better.

To maintain a synchronized state between the internal clocks of the CPU, the clock frequency ratio between the EFI and ISACLK2 inputs must be maintained at a minimum ratio of 2 to 1 (Intel386 SL CPU only). The ratio can be greater than 2 to 1 but cannot be less. For example, if the EFI input frequency is 50 MHz, then the ISACLK2 frequency must be 25 MHz or less. If the ISACLK2 frequency is set at 16 MHz (its typical rate), then the EFI input frequency must be 32 MHz or greater.

Note: The clock input for ISACLK2 should always be 16 MHz. The clock inputs for many peripherals inside the 82360SL are derived from SYSCLK, so changing the clock speed for ISACLK2 can cause the system to malfunction.

System clock

The SYSCLK clocks the ISA bus and the devices on the ISA bus, which include the DMA controllers, interrupt controllers, keyboard controller, and serial controller (when MIDI interface option is enabled). The SYSCLK also clocks internal logic in the 82360SL, including the system management interrupt generation logic, power management logic, and internal arbitration logic.

To be compatible with the standard ISA system, the SYSCLK on an SL CPU-based system is always fixed at 8 MHz. (Since the SYSCLK is one-half the ISACLK2, the ISACLK2 must be 16 MHz.) The internal logic inside the SL CPU always assumes that the SYSCLK is running at 8 MHz. Therefore, do not alter the SYSCLK speed, even though running the ISA bus at a higher clock rate will increase performance.

Keyboard controller clock

The 82360SL provides the KBDCLK signal (derived from the SYSCLK) as an interface to devices such as the 80C42 keyboard controller. The rate of the KBDCLK is controlled by the KC_CLK_SEL field in the KC_CLK_CNTRL register (0FCH, INDEX) and can be programmed to SYSCLK, SYSCLK/2, SYSCLK/4, or stopped. The keyboard is stopped automatically during suspend.

DMA controller clock

The 82360SL provides two internal DMA controllers that are clocked by an internal DMA clock. The DMA clock is derived from SYSCLK and can be programmed for a rate of SYSCLK or SYSCLK/2 through the DMASEL bit (bit 1) in the CFGR1 register (60H, INDEX). If the DMASEL bit is zero, the DMA controller clock will operate at 4 MHz (assuming an SYSCLK rate of 8 MHz).

If the DMA controller is idle, the DMA clock can be stopped to conserve power. The stop clock feature for the DMA controller is controlled by the DMA1_STP (bit 0) and the DMA2_STP bit (bit 1) of the DMA_STP_CLK register (2DH, INDEX). Table 9.2 shows the functions of these bits.

TABLE 9.2 Function of DMA1_STP and DMA2_STP Bits in DMA_STP_CLK Register

DMA1_STP	DMA2_STP	Function
X	0	Clocks for the two DMA controllers are enabled.
0	1	Clock to DMA controller 1 is disabled; clock to DMA controller 2 is enabled.
1	1	Clocks to both DMA controllers are disabled.

Real-time clock

The 82360SL provides an internal real-time clock (RTC) that duplicates the functions of a time-of-day clock and calendar. Other than the EFI and the SYSCLK, the RTC is the most important clock signal in the system. When the system is in suspend, the RTC is the only clock that is still running. During suspend, the RTC is used to generate refresh requests to the SL CPU to initiate suspend refresh of DRAMs and to clock the resume state machine to detect resume events. Figure 9.2 shows the power and clock-generation interface to the RTC.

Battery backup. Since the RTC must run continuously (even during power down or 0-volt suspend), it requires battery backup. The 82360SL provides a separate Vcc input for the RTC (RTCVCC). During normal and 5-volt suspend operation, RTCVCC should be connected to a 5-volt system power source. During 0-volt suspend or power off, RTCVCC should be connected to a 3- to 5-volt battery. The RTC can operate between 2.5 and 5 volts. When running from the battery backup source, a Schottky diode in the battery power circuit will minimize the voltage drop in the supply.

During suspend, the backup battery for the RTC is also used for powering the resume logic inside the 82360SL. The backup battery should thus be of sufficient capacity to power both RTC and the resume logic functions.

BATTDEAD# and RTCRESET#. The 82360SL provides a BATTDEAD# pin that is identical to the PS (Power Sense) signal in a standard MC146818 RTC. The BATTDEAD# signal controls the valid RAM and time (VRT) bit in Register D. A logic low at the BATTDEAD# pin resets the VRT bit. The VRT bit is normally used by BIOS to determine if data is valid after power up.

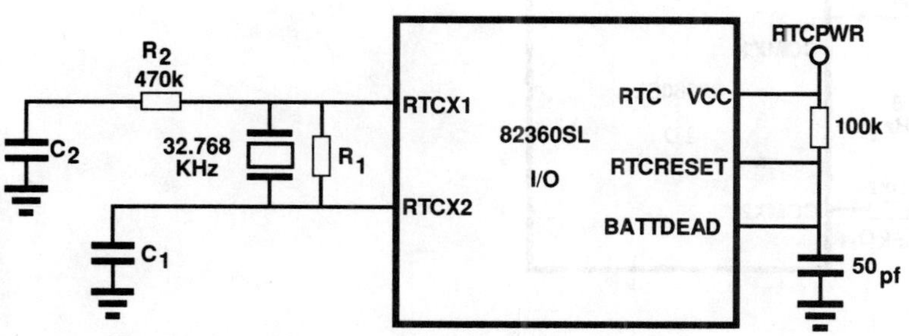

Figure 9.2 Clock interface to RTC.

The BATTDEAD and RTCRESET# pins are connected to the backup battery. Figure 9.2 shows how the RTCRESET# and BATTDEAD pins are connected together. If the battery is disconnected, the RTC (including the resume state machine) is reset and the VRT bit is set to zero. These signals are not affected by power off. The RTCRESET# pin should be tied to the RTCVCC signal to prevent current drain.

Extended CMOS RAM. The RTC also provides 128 bytes of standard CMOS RAM and another 128 bytes of extended CMOS RAM. Unlike the standard CMOS RAM which requires setting the index address for every access, the extended CMOS RAM has an internal latch that allows data to be accessed any time after the index address is set.

The I/O ports for accessing the standard and extended CMOS RAM are also different. The standard CMOS RAM is accessed using I/O port addresses 70H and 71H, and extended CMOS RAM is accessed through I/O ports 74H and 76H.

Serial controller clock

The COMX1 and COMX2 clock inputs to the 82360SL provide a 1.8432-MHz clock source for an internal oscillator. This oscillator generates a clock for the 82360SL's internal serial controllers. Figure 9.3 shows a typical circuit to drive the COMX1 and COMX2 pins. The resistor and capacitor values shown in this figure are typical for a 1.8432-MHz operation. The typical input capacitance of the clock inputs are 15 pF and the output capacitance is 20 pF.

The serial controller can be programmed to operate at 2 MHz to support an MIDI interface. When the MIDI interface option is enabled, the clock is generated by the SYSCLK rather than COMX1 and COMX2 pins. A maximum baud rate of 56,000 can be achieved with the MIDI interface option.

OSC clock

The CX1 and CX2 inputs to the 82360SL provide a 14.31818-MHz clock source for an internal oscillator. Figure 9.4 shows a typical circuit to drive the CX1

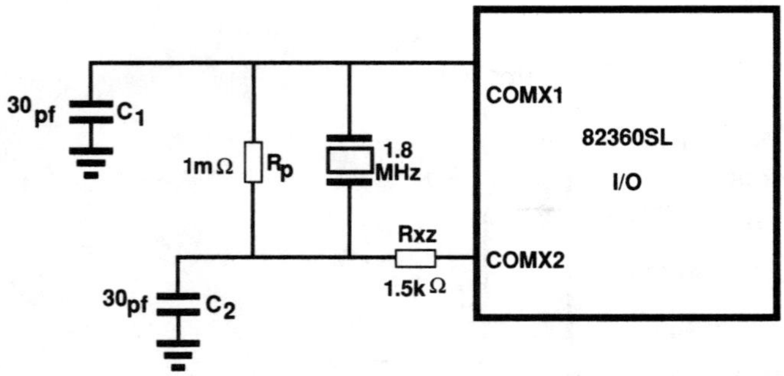

Figure 9.3 Crystal oscillator network for the serial controller clock.

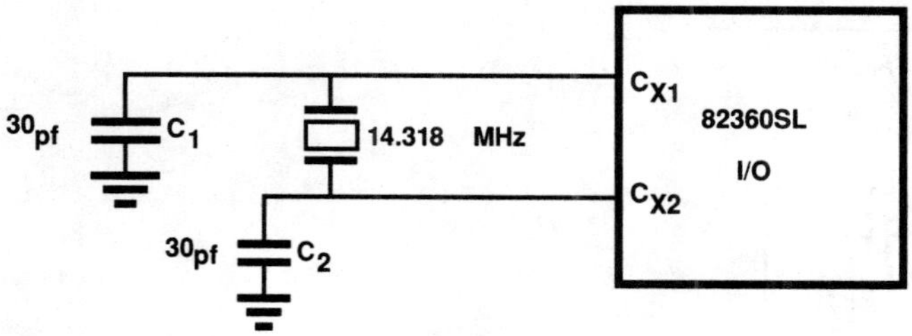

Figure 9.4 Crystal oscillator network for the OSC clock.

and CX2 pins. This clock source is divided by 12 and fed into the internal 82C54 timers.

The CX1 clock source is also used to produce the ISA-bus clock (OSC). OSC is the same frequency as the CX1 input with approximately a 50 percent duty cycle. The OSC clock is not synchronous with either the SYSCLK or any other signals on the ISA bus, so it must not be used in applications which require synchronization to the bus. This particular frequency was chosen because it allows a low-cost crystal from the color television industry to be used in the clock generation circuitry.

Oscillator Design Considerations

The preceding description of the SL clock architecture shows the clock requirements for an SL CPU-based system. The following sections give some guidelines for selecting crystals and designing clock source circuitry for the on-chip oscillators in the 82360SL.

On-chip oscillators

The RTC, serial controller clocks, and OSC clock are all generated from internal oscillators in the 82360SL. These oscillators all need a clock source that is generally provided by a crystal- (or ceramic resonator-) controlled circuit that is connected to clock source pins on the 82360SL. Figures 9.2 through 9.4 show the suggested circuits to generate these clock sources.

Crystal selection

Typically, crystal selection is based on stability, operating temperature, size, and price. When designing a low-power portable computer, you should also take input voltage, current consumption, output type (TTL level or CMOS), and packaging into consideration. Some manufacturers provide custom service if you cannot find an off-the-shelf oscillator or crystal that meets your needs.

Table 9.3 shows the specifications for the crystals required for the clock source circuits in Figs. 9.2 through 9.4. The parameters given in this table refer to the equivalent circuit shown in Figure 9.5. The R_1-L_1-C_1 branch is

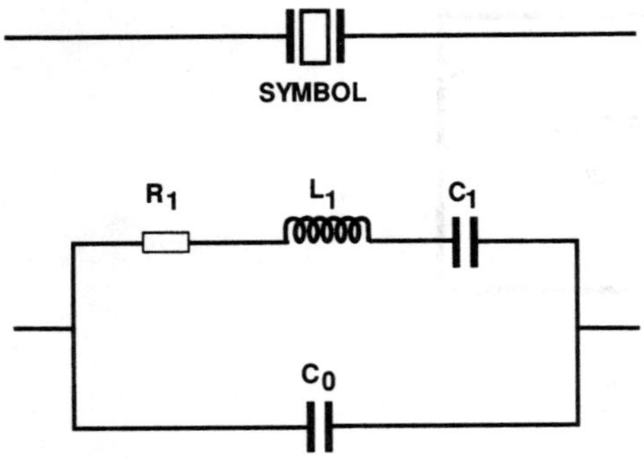

Figure 9.5 Equivalent circuit for a crystal.

called the motivational arm of the crystal. The values given in Table 9.3 are for parallel resonant crystals. The shunt capacitance of the crystal is called C_0.

Crystal specifications

Unless the frequency is critical, any fundamental-mode crystal of medium or better quality can be used. The crystal resistance can affect the start-up time and amplitude of the clock output. Therefore, the crystal resistance must be minimized. Alternatively, using the right values for the capacitors in the clock generation circuit can generally offset the effects of the crystal resistance. Generally, specifications of load capacitance and shunt capacitance are not important, unless your frequency tolerance is tighter than about 0.1 percent.

Oscillator frequency

The oscillation frequency is determined 99.5 percent by the crystal and up to about 0.5 percent by the circuit external to the crystal. The on-chip amplifier has little effect on the frequency, which is as it should be, since the amplifier parameters are temperature- and process-dependent.

The influence of the on-chip amplifier on the frequency is by means of its input and output (pin-to-ground) capacitances, which parallel oscillator capacitors CX1 and CX2, and the crystal lead (XTAL1 and XTAL2) pin-to-pin capacitance, which parallels the crystal. The input and pin-to-pin capacitances are about 7 pF each. Internal phase deviations from the nominal 180 degrees can be modeled as an output capacitance of 25 to 30 pF. These deviations from the ideal have less effect in the positive reactance oscillator (with the inverting amplifier) than in a comparable series resonant oscillator (with the noninvert-

TABLE 9.3 Crystal Specifications for RTC, Serial Controller Clock, and OSC Clock

Frequency	R_1 ohms	C_1 pF	L_1 mH	C_0 pF	Q k	C_L pF
32.768 KHz (RTC)	50	.003	8245.5	1.7	30	10–20
1.8432 MHz (COM[A:B])	100	.012	.65	4	70	15–40
14.31818 MHz (OSC)	12	.028	4.4	7	35	15–30

ing amplifier) for two reasons: first, the effect of the output capacitance is lessened, if not swamped, by the off-chip capacitor; second, the positive reactance oscillator is less sensitive, frequency-wise, to such phase errors.

Selection of CX1 and CX2

Normally, the capacitances for CX1 and CX2 are selected based on the type of crystal used, start-up time, and frequency tolerance. In a notebook environment in which the oscillator is powered up and down frequently, the start-up time is more critical than frequency stability. The accuracy of the oscillator frequency is also important. For example, the real-time clock is used for keeping track of time, generation of suspend refresh, and clock for the resume logic. Therefore, your oscillator design should have a short start-up time and a stable frequency.

Fine-tuning of both start-up time and frequency stability can be achieved by adjusting the values for Cx1 and Cx2 (which are typically equal and at least 20 pF). Increasing the capacitances improves frequency stability, but also increases the start-up time. The capacitances should not be too high. Otherwise, the oscillator will not start up at all.

Capacitances between 20 and 100 pF is generally sufficient if the on-chip amplifier is a simple inverter. To prevent the oscillator from running in a relaxation mode, smaller values of Cx1 must be used (5 to 30pF) if the on-chip amplifier is a Schmitt Trigger.

RTC oscillator

The RTC requires a 32.768-KHz clock input. An external oscillator or a parallel resonant crystal can be used as a clock source. Figure 9.2 shows a typical crystal oscillator connection. The circuit consists of a 32.768-KHz crystal (case temp spec—90 C), two resistors, and two capacitors.

Resistor R1 (470 kilohms) is a bias resistor which guarantees linear operation of the on-chip inverter. Resistor R2 and capacitor C2 (47 pF) form a voltage divider to prevent the crystal from being overdriven. Internal phase deviation is introduced by capacitor C2.

This oscillator is very sensitive to the resistance of resistor R2. A voltage increase due to a decrease in value of R2 can cause frequency instability. The change in frequency can cause symptoms such as real-time clock running twice as fast.

RTCX1 and RTCX2 can be driven together or RTCX1 can be grounded and RTCX2 driven alone. For the second method, the driving source must be capable of sinking some current when RTCX2 is being driven low.

To minimize board space and power consumption in a notebook computer, it is desirable to use the on-chip oscillator to clock other chips in the system—for example, to supply the clock for video DRAM refresh. A buffer is generally required at the clock output which clocks other chips. Using a TTL buffer puts too much load on the on-chip amplifier for reliable start-up. A fast, TTL-level-compatible CMOS buffer (such as the 74HC04) is preferred over the TTL buffer.

TABLE 9.4 Timing Specifications for External Oscillators

Clock	tr (max)/ns	tf (max)/ns	thi (min)/ns	tlo (min)/ns
RTC	20	20	1200	1200
COM[A:B]	20	20	200	200
OSC	10	10	20	20

External oscillator specification

External oscillators can be used in place of any of the three 82360SL on-chip oscillators. When an external oscillator is used, the timing specification in Table 9.4 must be observed. Please note that the logic levels are not TTL-compatible.

Placement of components

At a high frequency, crosstalk can occur through capacitive coupling between the oscillator components and PCB traces carrying digital signals with fast transition times, which can cause a miscount in the internal clock-generating circuitry. Crosstalk can be minimized by placing the oscillator components close to the chip with short traces to the XTAL1, XTAL2, and VSS pins.

Troubleshooting oscillator problems

Most of the time, oscillator problems are caused by the PCB layout. For example, long PCB traces and placing the oscillator components in an area where there is a lot of signal transitions can cause capacitive coupling and inductive coupling between the oscillator circuitry and other signals. Capacitive coupling can be reduced by surrounding the oscillator components with "quiet" traces (e.g., VCC and ground). Minimizing the areas of the loops formed by the oscillator components in the PCB layout can alleviate inductive coupling.

Summary

As explained in this chapter, clock control plays an important role in system design as well as in power management. If the clock input circuit is designed improperly, many problems can arise. The discussion in this chapter should provide enough information to allow you to manage the different clocks efficiently on an SL CPU-based system to increase performance and reduce power consumption.

References

Williamson, Tom, "Oscillators for Microcontrollers," Intel Corporation, 1983.

Svatek, Patrick, "User Consideration For MC146818 Real Time Clock Applications," Motorola Semiconductor Inc., 1990.

"MC146818 Real-Time Clock Plus RAM Data Sheet," Motorola Semiconductor Inc.

"NS16450 Universal Asynchronous Receiver/Transmitter with FIFOs Data Sheet," National Semiconductor Corporation.

Chapter

10

Intel386 SL CPU Memory Interfacing

The Intel386 SL CPU offers a very flexible memory architecture. The built-in memory controller supports a dynamic RAM (DRAM) or a static RAM (SRAM) memory system. Coupled with the internal cache controller, an Intel386 SL CPU-based system provides maximum memory performance at a reasonable cost. The memory controller architecture has been designed for maximum power saving without sacrificing any performance. It supports common memory options such as shadowing and memory roll-over. Also, on-chip hardware implements a LIM 4.0-compatible expanded memory system (EMS).

Designing a DRAM Memory System

The DRAM interface on the Intel386 SL CPU is the simplest. DRAMs can be connected directly to the processor without any additional glue logic. Figure 10.1 shows the direct interface between the Intel386 SL CPU and a 4-Mbyte two-bank DRAM card. The processor supports standard SIMM memory upgrades as well as user-installable DRAM cards. Built-in hardware supports LIM 4.0 EMS standard using on-board memory.

Typically, the performance and power consumption of a DRAM memory system is determined by the following memory options: interleaving, page mode, memory refresh, DRAM type, and bank size. Most of these options are programmable on the Intel386 SL CPU, making it easy to design a memory system that offers high performance and low power consumption. In the following sections, we are going to look at how each of these options can affect performance and power consumption of a DRAM memory system.

Page mode

DRAM access time is controlled by row access and column access. With page mode, memory access within the same page can happen very quickly because the row address strobe (RAS#) maintains the same row address from the previous memory access.

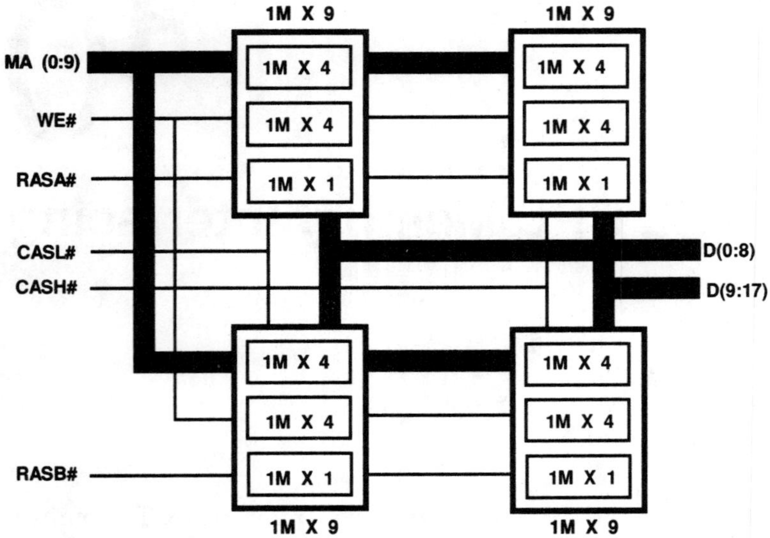

Figure 10.1 Direct interface between a 4-Mbyte double bank DRAM card and the Intel386 SL CPU.

The Intel386 SL CPU supports three page modes: normal (P1 mode), fast (F2 mode), and high-speed (F1 mode). The differences between these three modes are in the number of CPU clocks that the RAS and CAS signals keep active. All 1- and 4-Mbyte DRAMs have a latched address buffer and support fast page mode. Table 10.1 shows a comparison of the different page modes. The operating current of the DRAMs under different page modes is about the same.

The DRAM controller differs from most standard DRAM controllers in that each RAS# of each bank is kept in an inactive state so that DRAM banks are in stand-by power mode when not in use. If the bank changes or the CPU goes into idle, the currently selected bank will become inactive. RASx# and CASx# signals are generated only for memory banks that are populated.

The RAS# for each bank is kept in an inactive state so that DRAM banks are in stand-by power mode when not in use. RASx# and CASx# signals are generated only for memory banks that are populated.

Wait states

Wait states for the different types of DRAM cycles are generated by delaying generation of RAS after RAS address is valid. Table 10.3 shows the number of wait states for the different types of DRAM accesses for each DRAM mode. The first number is the number of wait states inserted for pipelined cycles and the

TABLE 10.1 Comparison of Three Page Modes in Intel386 SL CPU

Page mode	Normal	Fast	High-speed
Performance (MIPS)	3.229	3.572	4.116

TABLE 10.2 Page Sizes Commonly Used for Different DRAM Sizes

DRAM size	Page size
256 Kbytes	0.5 Kbyte
512 Kbytes	1 Kbyte
1 Mbyte	2 Kbytes
4 Mbytes	8 Kbytes

TABLE 10.3 Wait States Inserted for Different Types of DRAM Cycles for Each DRAM Mode

Mode	Bank miss	Bank hit-page hit	Bank hit-page miss
High-speed, F1	0/1	0/NA	2/NA
Fast, F2	1/2	0/NA	3/NA
Normal, P1	1/2	1/NA	3/NA

second number is for non-pipeline cycles. Notation NA means that cycle combination is not possible. Number of wait states is represented in terms of CPU clocks. After an idle cycle, one wait state is required for precharge.

Memory refresh

The Intel386 SL CPU supports two types of on-board memory refresh: normal (CAS before RAS) and suspend. During normal operation, refreshing is done by doing a read operation by the CAS# falling edge before RAS# in the period defined by the internal refresh address generator. (See Fig. 10.2.) To prevent

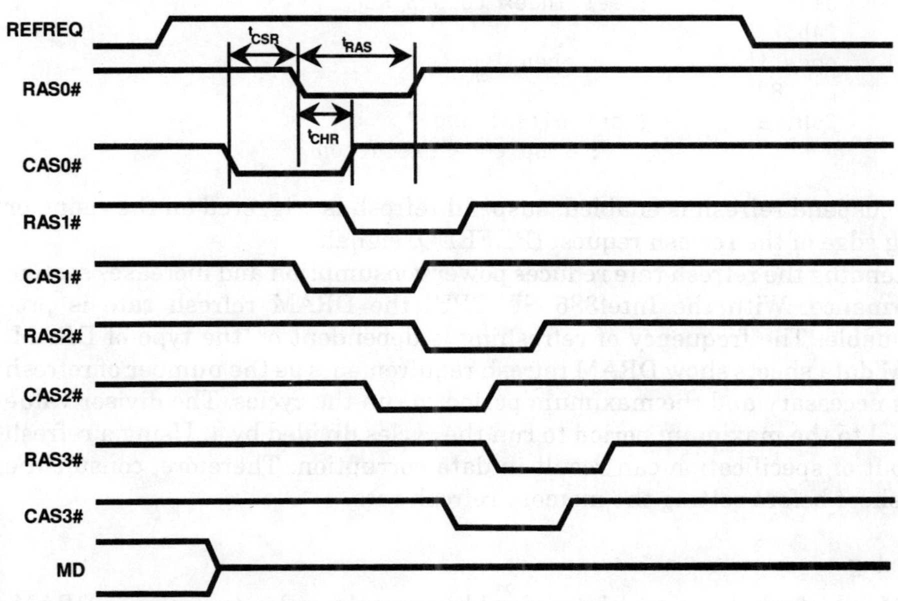

Figure 10.2 Normal refresh with staggered refresh.

current surges, multiple banks are refreshed in a staggered sequential order starting with bank 0.

Memory refresh for on-board memory is different from memory refresh on the ISA bus. On-board memory refresh is done by the Intel386 SL CPU and ISA-bus refresh is generated by the 82360SL I/O. ISA-bus refresh can be disabled by writing a one to the REFDIS bit (bit 0) of the CFGR1 register.

Suspend refresh is enabled during suspend to conserve power. The suspend refresh mechanism is similar to CAS before RAS refresh except that the CAS# signal is always active. (See Fig. 10.3.) The most common problem with suspend refresh is the enabling sequence. If suspend refresh is not enabled correctly, integrity will be lost.

The following steps are recommended for enabling suspend refresh:

1. Set the suspend rate in the MCRF register (301H, OMCU). This is normally done during system initialization.
2. Open the 82360SL configuration space and set register index to point to SUS_REF register (0FFH, INDEX).
3. Open the internal bus unit configuration space.
4. Write 82H to I/O address 25H.
5. Execute a HALT instruction immediately to stop code execution. If code execution continues after suspend refresh is enabled, memory will be corrupted.

Listing 10.1 gives sample assembly code for enabling suspend refresh.

Listing 10.1 Sample Code to Enable Suspend Refresh

```
call    open_360sl         ; open 360sl config space
mov     al, 0ffh       ; set index to SUS_REF
out     24h, al
call    open_ibu           ; open ibu space
mov     al, 82h        ;
out     25h, al        ; set bits 1 and 7
hlt                        ; stop code execution
```

After suspend refresh is enabled, suspend refresh is triggered on the rising or falling edge of the refresh request (REFREQ) signal.

Extending the refresh rate reduces power consumption and increases system performance. With the Intel386 SL CPU, the DRAM refresh rate is programmable. The frequency of refreshing is dependent on the type of DRAM. DRAM data sheets show DRAM refresh requirements as the number of refresh cycles necessary and the maximum period to run the cycles. The divisor value is equal to the maximum period to run the cycles divided by 4. Using a refresh rate out of specification can result in data corruption. Therefore, consult the data sheet before setting the memory refresh rate.

Address multiplexing

DRAM interfaces have multiplexed addressing. In order to access a DRAM, both the row and column addresses are provided on common address pins. The

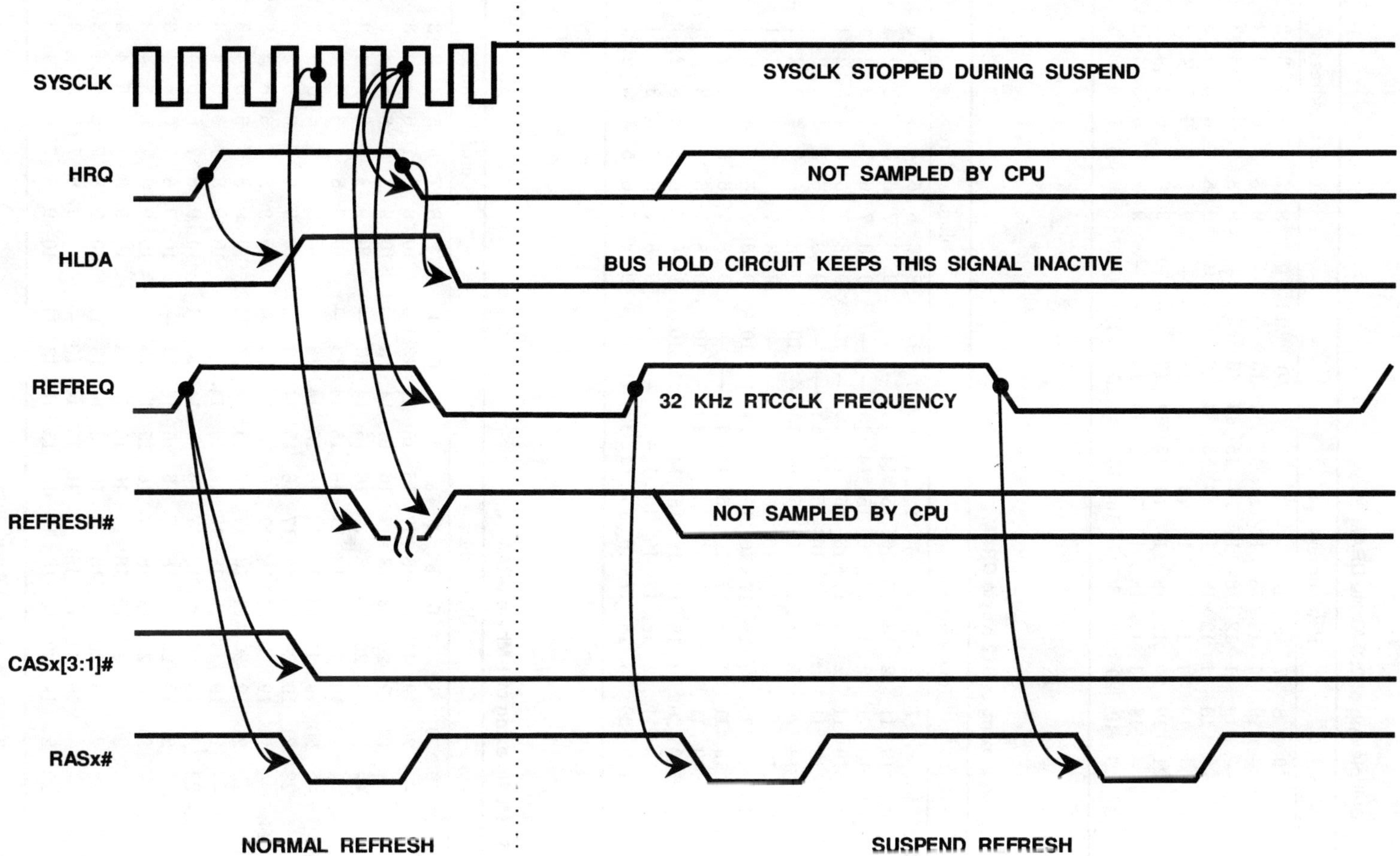

Figure 10.3 Suspend refresh cycles.

TABLE 10.4 Multiplexing of 256-Kbyte DRAM

Case*	Row address											Column address										
MA	10	9	8	7	6	5	4	3	2	1	0	10	9	8	7	6	5	4	3	2	1	0
31	—	—	19	11	12	18	17	16	15	14	13	—	—	9	8	7	6	5	4	3	2	1
32, 33	—	—	19	11	12	18	17	16	15	14	13	—	—	9	8	7	6	5	4	3	2	1
	—	20	19	11	12	18	17	16	15	14	13	—	10	9	8	7	6	5	4	3	2	1
34	—	—	19	11	12	18	17	16	15	14	13	—	—	9	8	7	6	5	4	3	2	1
	—	21	19	20	12	18	17	16	15	14	13	—	10	9	8	7	6	5	4	3	2	1
35, 36	—	—	19	11	12	18	17	16	15	14	13	—	—	9	8	7	6	5	4	3	2	1
	22	21	19	20	12	18	17	16	15	14	13	11	10	9	8	7	6	5	4	3	2	1

TABLE 10.5 Multiplexing of 512-Kbyte DRAM

Case*	Row address											Column address										
MA	10	9	8	7	6	5	4	3	2	1	0	10	9	8	7	6	5	4	3	2	1	0
1	—	20	19	11	12	18	17	16	15	14	13	—	—	9	8	7	6	5	4	3	2	1
2, 3	—	20	19	11	12	18	17	16	15	14	13	—	—	9	8	7	6	5	4	3	2	1
	—	20	19	11	12	18	17	16	15	14	13	—	10	9	8	7	6	5	4	3	2	1
4	—	20	19	11	12	18	17	16	15	14	13	—	—	9	8	7	6	5	4	3	2	1
	—	21	19	20	12	18	17	16	15	14	13	—	10	9	8	7	6	5	4	3	2	1
5, 6	—	20	19	11	12	18	17	16	15	14	13	—	—	9	8	7	6	5	4	3	2	1
	22	21	19	20	12	18	17	16	15	14	13	11	10	9	8	7	6	5	4	3	2	1
7, 8	—	20	19	11	12	18	17	16	15	14	13	—	—	9	8	7	6	5	4	3	2	1
	—	20	19	11	12	18	17	16	15	14	13	—	10	9	8	7	6	5	4	3	2	1
	22	21	19	20	12	18	17	16	15	14	13	11	10	9	8	7	6	5	4	3	2	1
9	—	20	19	11	12	18	17	16	15	14	13	—	—	9	8	7	6	5	4	3	2	1
	22	21	19	20	23	18	17	16	15	14	13	11	10	9	8	7	6	5	4	3	2	1

TABLE 10.6 Multiplexing of 1-Mbyte DRAM†

Case*	Row address											Column address										
MA	10	9	8	7	6	5	4	3	2	1	0	10	9	8	7	6	5	4	3	2	1	0
10	—	20	19	11	12	18	17	16	15	14	13	—	10	9	8	7	6	5	4	3	2	1
11, 12, 19	—	21	19	20	12	18	17	16	15	14	13	—	10	9	8	7	6	5	4	3	2	1
13, 20, 21	—	21	19	20	12	18	17	16	15	14	13	—	10	9	8	7	6	5	4	3	2	1
	—	20	19	11	12	18	17	16	15	14	13	—	10	9	8	7	6	5	4	3	2	1
14, 15, 28	—	20	19	11	12	18	17	16	15	14	13	—	—	9	8	7	6	5	4	3	2	1
	22	21	19	20	12	18	17	16	15	14	13	11	10	9	8	7	6	5	4	3	2	1
16, 17, 23, 24,	—	21	19	20	12	18	17	16	15	14	16	—	10	9	8	7	6	5	4	3	2	1
29, 30	22	21	19	20	12	18	17	16	15	14	13	11	10	9	8	7	6	5	4	3	2	1
18	—	20	19	11	12	18	17	16	15	14	13	—	10	9	8	7	6	5	4	3	2	1
	22	21	19	20	23	18	17	16	15	14	13	11	10	9	8	7	6	5	4	3	2	1
22	—	21	19	20	12	18	17	16	15	14	13	—	10	9	8	7	6	5	4	3	2	1
	—	21	19	20	12	18	17	16	15	14	13	—	10	9	8	7	6	5	4	3	2	1
25, 26	—	20	19	11	12	18	17	16	15	14	13	—	10	9	8	7	6	5	4	3	2	1
	22	21	19	20	12	18	17	16	15	14	13	11	10	9	8	7	6	5	4	3	2	1
27	—	—	19	11	12	18	17	16	15	14	13	—	—	9	8	7	6	5	4	3	2	1
	22	21	19	20	12	18	17	16	15	14	13	11	10	9	8	7	6	5	4	3	2	1

* See App. C for a complete list of DRAM configurations.

† Note: MA10 becomes A23 during autoscan, which allows access to the entire physical memory address space.

DRAM configurations determine how the addresses are multiplexed onto the memory address. Tables 10.4 through 10.6 show how the multiplexing changes with different base configurations. These tables are useful when debugging with a logic analyzer. Please note that the local address lines do not come out in ascending order on the memory address bus.

Memory autoscan

To simplify memory sizing, the Intel386 SL CPU allows memory banks to be enabled individually for memory sizing. The automatic memory-sizing mechanism is called *memory autoscan*. Memory autoscan is enabled by setting bit 0 of the Memory Auto Scan Register, MCAS (302H, OMCU). Once memory autoscan is enabled for a memory bank, the size of the corresponding memory bank can be determined by writing selective memory patterns to different boundaries and reading back the data returned from the different address boundaries. Memory banks are enabled by writing to bits [2-1] of the MCAS register.

Based on the memory configuration supported by the Intel386 SL CPU, the following algorithm can be used to determine the memory bank size. Since the maximum bank size is 8 Mbytes, the on-board memory limit should be set to anything above 8 Mbytes (16 Mbytes in this example). Before any memory sizing occurs, a simple read/write test should be run to find out if the memory bank is populated. Since the memory data bus latches data written to it, a pattern longer than a word must be written. For example, data such as "AA AA 55 55" can be written to address 0H and read back from address 0H. If the data returned is not equal to "AA AA 55 55," the memory bank is empty.

Since a memory bank can be 512 Kbytes, 1 Mbyte, 2 Mbytes, and 8 Mbytes in size, an autoscan routine can write a specific pattern to address boundaries 0H, 0200000H, and 0800000H selectively. How the data wraps around is dependent on the number of row address lines of the memory installed. Since 1 Mbyte and 2 Mbytes have the same number of RAS address lines, the column address lines should be used instead. Writing to address boundaries 0H and 0400H and reading the data returned allows the autoscan routine to determine whether the memory installed is 1 Mbyte or 2 Mbytes. Listing 10.2 shows sample code for the autoscan algorithm described previously.

Listing 10.2 Sample Code for Autosizing of Memory

```
mov     ax, 1BH
mov     es, ax
mov     fs, ax
mov     ax, 10H
mov     ds, ax
call    open_ibu
mov     dx, 301H        ; set on-board memory limit to 16 Mbytes
mov     al, 05FH
out     dx, al
call    open_omcu       use lower case
```

```
    mov     dx, 302H        ; enable autoscan for bank zero
    mov     al, 01H
    out     dx, al
    call    close_386sl
; write test pattern to memory address boundary
    mov     edi, 0H
    mov     byte ptr es:[edi], 0AH
    mov     edi, 200000H
    mov     byte ptr es:[edi], 0BH
    mov     edi, 0A00000H
    mov     byte ptr es:[edi], 0CH
; read back data from memory address boundary
    mov     edi, 0H
    mov     al, byte ptr es:[edi]
    add     al, 37H
    mov     cl,al
    mov     edi, 200000H
    mov     al, byte ptr es:[edi]
    add     al, 37H
    mov     bl,al
    mov     edi, 0A00000H
    mov     al, byte ptr es:[edi]
    add     al, 37H
; output test results to screen
    mov     edi, 0B8000H
    mov     byte ptr es:[edi], cl
    add     edi, 2
    mov     byte ptr es:[edi],''
    add     edi, 2
    mov     byte ptr es:[edi], bl
    add     edi, 2
    mov     byte ptr es:[edi],''
    add     edi, 2
    mov     byte ptr es:[edi], al
    add     edi, 2
    call    open_omcu
    mov     dx, 302H        ; disable autoscan
    mov     al, 00H
    out     dx, al
    call    close_386sl
```

Parity checking

Parity checking is enabled by setting the even parity checking enable bit (bit 2) in the MCMODE register (300H, OMCU) and clearing the parity check enable bit (bit 2) in port 61H. Parity checking is disabled if the even parity checking enable bit in MCMODE register is zero or the parity check enable bit in port 61H is one. The memory address that caused the parity error can be located by reading the MCPELA and MCPELB registers. Do not enable parity checking if memory does not support parity checking. Doing so will cause the system to malfunction.

DRAM selection

The selection of DRAM devices for a memory system is a very important design decision. Careful selection of DRAM devices can result in better performance and lower power consumption. The following factors should be considered when selecting DRAMs: speed, chip organization, power consumption, type of refresh, and operating voltage.

Faster DRAMs are required at higher frequency and for the high-speed page mode. Speed is especially important in a cacheless machine. Picking the right chip organization can increase performance and reduce board space. As wide-word parts (x8, x9, x16, and x18 DRAMs) become more available, it makes sense to use them in place of x1 DRAMs. For example, a single-chip main memory system can be built using one 4Mx16 DRAM chip.

A DRAM's power consumption is affected by the mode of operation, refresh time, and operating voltage. The standby current has a big impact on battery life when the system is in standby mode. In standby mode, most of the system current is consumed by refresh cycles. Therefore, using DRAMs with extended-refresh or self-refresh support (such as the LPDRAM offered by Micron Technology) can reduce power drain substantially. More drastic reduction in power consumption can be achieved by lowering the operating voltage to 3.3 volts.

Table 10.7 shows how power consumption varies with DRAM density.

Design guidelines

- Ringing is a common problem in DRAM memory systems. It can be solved by using damping resistors.
- Use correct values of bypass capacitors to eliminate noise.
- CAS# and RAS# signals are only generated for populated banks.
- All DRAM cycles are the same irrespective of the CPU clock. DRAM speed is irrelevant in slow clock mode.
- The WLE# and WHE# signals are independently controlled for high and low bytes.

Programming the DRAM interface

The DRAM interface must be initialized correctly before it can be used for storing data. The first initialization step is to set the memory controller mode to DRAM. If the DRAM supports parity checking, even parity checking should be

TABLE 10.7 Current Consumed in Relation to DRAM Density

DRAM type	Fast page mode	Random
1 Mbyte X1, X4	45 mA	65 mA
4 Mbytes X1, X4	50 mA	100 mA
1 Mbyte X16	70 mA	85 mA

enabled. Next, DRAM refresh should be selected. Finally, select a page mode that will give the best performance for your design.

After the memory controller is initialized for DRAM, memory sizing should then be done to determine the individual bank size and total amount of on-board memory. When autoscan is complete, the memory controller bank size register, MCBS (306H, OMCU) and the on-board memory limit register, OMLCR (301H, IBU) should be written to set the bank size and on-board memory limit. Access above the on-board memory limit where no on-board memory exists will wrap around to ISA bus. Listing 10.3 gives sample code for initialization of a DRAM interface.

Listing 10.3 Code for Initialization of a DRAM Interface

```
;; initialization of the DRAM interface
   call    open_ibu
   mov     ax, mem_size    ; set on-board memory limit
   mov     dx, OMLCR
   out     dx, al
   call    open_omcu
   mov     dx, MCBS        ; set bank size
   mov     ax, bank_size
   out     dx, ax
   mov     al, 01H         ; set page mode to high speed page mode
   mov     dx, MCDRAMMD
   out     dx, al
   mov     dx, MCRF        ; set normal and suspend refresh rate
   mov     al, 22H
   out     dx, al
   mov     dx, MCMODE      ; enable DRAM mode and even parity checking
   mov     al, 05H
   out     dx, al
   call    close_386sl
```

Designing an SRAM Memory System

The Intel386 SL CPU can also be programmed to support SRAM. Unlike DRAM, SRAM does not require refreshing and address multiplexing. Thus SRAM offers higher performance and lower power consumption than DRAM. On the other hand, SRAM costs more and takes up more board space than DRAM. Table 10.8 compares the performance of a SRAM and DRAM memory system.

TABLE 10.8 Comparison of SRAM and DRAM Memory Systems

Memory mode	SRAM (4 Mbytes)	DRAM (4 Mbytes)
Performance (MIPS)	3.836	4.213

When configured for SRAMs, the controller supports a very low power memory subsystem. When the cache controller is enabled, the SRAM memory subsystem provides performance equivalent to that of a DRAM system with a cache, but the SRAM system uses only half the power of the DRAM/cache system and one-third the power of the DRAM-only solution.

Up to four banks of SRAM are supported, but capacitive loading restrictions may require the use of additional buffers and transceivers depending on the size and type of memory used. The memory controller provides support for up to four data transceivers when used in the SRAM mode. Some SRAM control signals might also require buffering. Table 10.9 shows the address multiplexing for an SRAM memory system.

SRAM wait states

To guarantee the address access time for SRAMs of slower speed, several wait states can be inserted. Wait state generation is controlled by bits [0-1] of the memory controller SRAM wait state register, MCSRAMWS (303H, OMCU). Table 10.10 shows the effect of wait state on performance and power consumption.

Programming the SRAM interface

The initialization of the SRAM interface is almost the same as the DRAM interface except for the memory controller initialization. The memory controller mode must set to SRAM mode to enable the SRAM interface. Once SRAM mode is selected, the number of SRAM wait states can then be set. It is recommended that you use a high number of wait states when bringing up a SRAM system. After the system is fully debugged, you can reduce the number of wait states to improve system performance. The rest of the initialization is

TABLE 10.9 SRAM Address Multiplexing

Case	Row address											Column address										
MA	10	9	8	7	6	5	4	3	2	1	0	10	9	8	7	6	5	4	3	2	1	0
256 Kbytes	—	—	—	11	12	18	17	16	15	14	13	—	10	9	8	7	6	5	4	3	2	1
512 Kbytes	—	—	—	11	12	18	17	16	15	14	13	—	10	9	8	7	6	5	4	3	2	1
1 Mbyte	—	—	19	11	12	18	17	16	15	14	13	—	10	9	8	7	6	5	4	3	2	1
2 Mbytes	—	20	19	11	12	18	17	16	15	14	13	—	10	9	8	7	6	5	4	3	2	1
4 Mbytes	—	21	19	20	12	18	17	16	15	14	13	11	10	9	8	7	6	5	4	3	2	1
8 Mbytes	22	21	19	20	12	18	17	16	15	14	13	11	10	9	8	7	6	5	4	3	2	1
SCAN	23	21	19	20	12	18	17	16	15	14	13											

TABLE 10.10 Effect of Wait States in an SRAM System

Wait state	SRAM (2 WS)	SRAM (3 WS)
Performance	3.836	3.670

the same as the DRAM interface. Listing 10.4 gives sample code for enabling the SRAM interface.

Listing 10.4 Sample Code for Enabling SRAM Interface

```
;; initialize and enable SRAM interface
    call    open_ibu            ; open IBU space
    mov     ax, mem_size; set on-board memory limit
    mov     dx, OMLCR
    out     dx, al
    call    open_omcu           ; open OMCU space
    mov     ax, bank_size       ; set bank size
    mov     dx, MCBS
    out     dx, ax
    mov     al, 01      ; set # of wait state to 3
    mov     dx, MCSRAMWS
    out     dx, al
    xor     al, al      ; enable SRAM mode
    mov     dx, MCMODE
    out     dx, al
    call    close_386sl         ; close all SL configuration spaces
```

Designing a PSRAM memory system

SRAM consumes less power than DRAM but costs more and is not available in as high a density as DRAM. A less expensive alternative to SRAM is pseudo-static RAM (PSRAM). PSRAM uses the DRAM cell structure and has a built-in refresh control circuit. Only a refresh request is required at appropriate intervals.

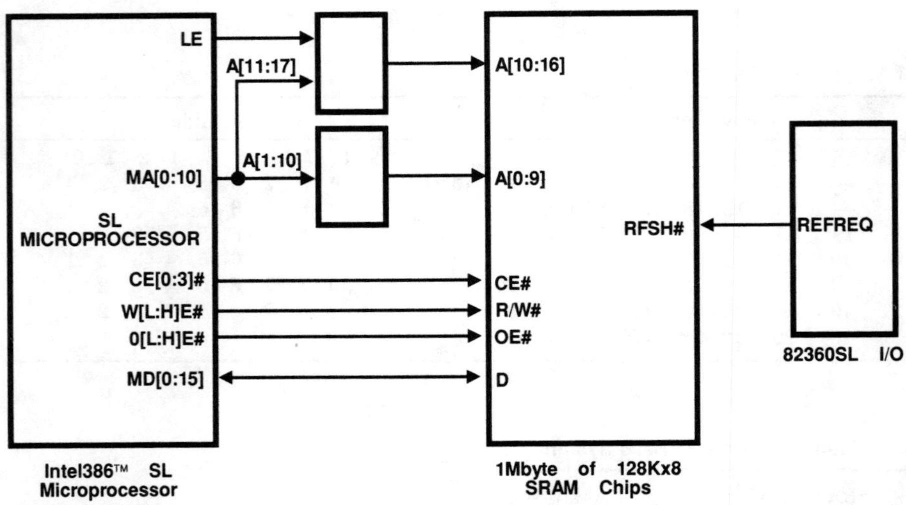

Figure 10.4 Interface to PSRAM.

Figure 10.4 shows a PSRAM interface for the Intel386 SL CPU. Unlike DRAM, SRAM does not require refreshing and address multiplexing. The interface to PSRAM is identical to SRAM. The 82360SL provides the refresh request (REFREQ), which eliminates the need for extra logic.

External SMRAM Interface

The system management mode (SMM) executes code from a dedicated memory (SMRAM) to isolate SMM routines from the operating system or application programs. If external SMRAM is used, the SMRAM interface uses MEMW#, MEMR#, and SMRAMCS# for control signals, XD bus for data, and SA bus for address. Figure 10.5 shows a design for an external SMRAM. The external SMRAM can be 32 Kbytes or 64 Kbytes. SMRAM is not cached to avoid cache coherency problems.

Memory Options

The Intel386 SL CPU interfaces directly to either DRAM or SRAM memory devices with total capacity from 512 Kbytes to 32 Mbytes. The main memory can be configured for shadowing, EMS memory, roll-over memory, and system management RAM.

When enabled, the memory controller allows the user to take advantage of several features: BIOS shadowing, roll-over address mapping, and hardware support for the LIM 4.0 EMS expanded memory specification. These options give the flexibility of remapping normally unused memory into areas that provide the user with additional performance or application memory.

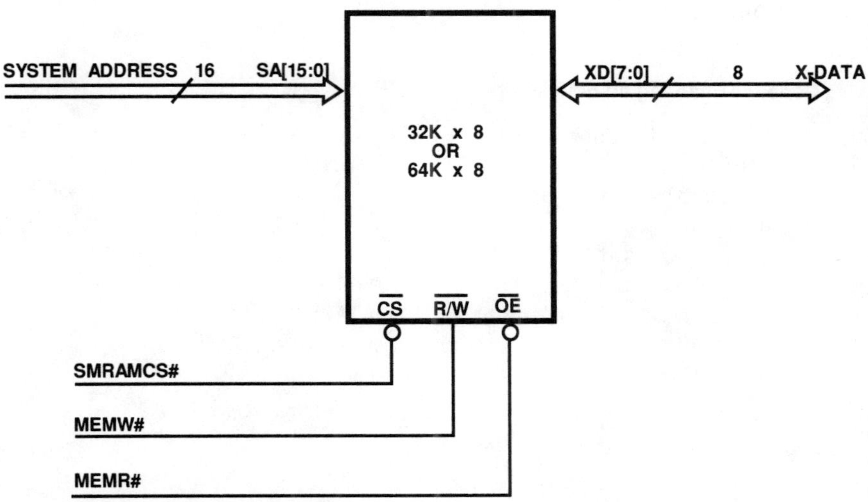

Figure 10.5 External SMRAM interface.

Memory roll-over

Typically, off-board memory such as flash BIOS (from 0E0000H or 0F0000H-0FFFFFH), graphics/user ROM (from C0000H-DFFFFH) and video memory reside between 640 Kbytes to 1 Mbyte. These off-board memory locations create inaccessible regions of local on-board DRAM memory, thereby wasting some physical DRAM.

The memory roll-over option in the Intel386 SL CPU allows the system to reclaim on-board memory that is mapped out by off-board memory residing in the same memory address space. The memory roll-over feature takes on-board memory residing on 64 Kbyte aligned addresses between 0A0000H-0FFFFFH and makes it accessible "on top" of the physical memory on a 512 Kbyte aligned address. If the system has 64 Mbytes of physical on-board DRAM, the roll-over memory is addressed above 64 Mbytes. When a block of memory is marked as "rolled" up, accesses directed to the area originally occupied in that address range will be directed off-board to the ISA bus. Noncontiguous blocks of memory that are "rolled" will appear as contiguous memory to the programmer. The OMRBCR register (300H, IBU) specifies which 64 Kbyte segment of on-board memory within the address range between 640 Kbytes and 1 Mbyte is remapped to the roll-over base address (top of physical memory) specified by the OMBRCR register.

EMS memory

High-performance hardware LIM 4.0 EMS support is built in to the Intel386 SL CPU. The EMS hardware must be enabled by exercising an unlocking sequence. Listing 10.5 gives sample code for enabling the EMS mapper. The programming interface is compatible with the LIM 4.0 EMS specification. For programming information on expanded memory, please refer to the LIM 4.0 EMS specification.

Listing 10.5 Code for Enabling an EMS Mapper

```
The EMSBASE address is configurable.
;; enabling EMS Mapper
   cli     ; disable interrupts
   mov     dx, 30h
   mov     al, 2Ah ; set index to 64
   out     dx, al
   mov     dx, 2Ch      ; points to EMS DATA register
   mov     al, 4Ah
   out     dx, al
   mov     al, 69h
   out     dx, al
   mov     al, 6Dh
   out     dx, al
   sti     ; enable interrupts
```

Cache Controller

The cache memory architecture combines the speed of expensive SRAM and the cost-effectiveness of slower DRAM. The cache controller supports memory sizes of 16, 32, and 64 Kbytes. Three types of memory caching are supported: direct-mapped, two-way associative, and four-way associative. The cache controller employs a write-through cache in which every memory write causes the system to write to main memory, whether or not the addressed location is stored in the cache.

When the cache is full, new entries have to replace the old ones. The cache controller uses the LRU (Least Recently Used) replacement algorithm to determine which entry to remove. This algorithm picks the cache entry that has been least used by the CPU. All cache cycles require two CPU clock (CPUCLK) cycles.

Cache memory interface

If the cache memory option is not used, the address and data signals on the cache memory bus can be treated as no-connect signals. Do not use pull-up resistors on the CCSH# and CCSL# signals. Figure 10.6 shows the interface between the Intel386 SL CPU and the cache RAM.

Configuring the cache controller

The cache size and mapping should be set in the CCR register (300H, CCU) before enabling the cache controller. The cache controller is enabled by setting bit 7 of the OMLCR register (301H, IBU).

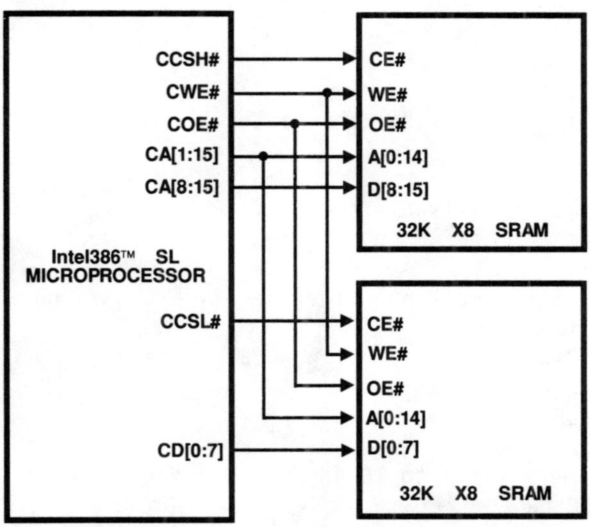

Figure 10.6 Interface to cache RAM.

Cache autosizing

The cache size in a system can be determined by performing selective writes to different address boundaries and reading data back from these locations. Listing 10.6 gives example code that determines the cache size automatically.

Listing 10.6 Code for Autosizing the Cache

```
;--------------------------------------------------------------------
;
; EXAMPLE.ASM: This file contains routines for cache
; auto-sizing on the Intel386 SL CPU.
;
;--------------------------------------------------------------------
include superset.inc
;
;-------------- INITIALIZATION --------------------------------------
code  SEGMENT
ASSUME cs:code, ds:code, es:code, ss:code
;
;
 ORG 100H
EXTRN open_ibu:near, open_ccu:near, close_386sl:near
start:
; disable all interrupts
    cli       ;disable hardware interrupts
    mov       ax, 008fh    ;turn off NMI, clear shutdown byte
    out       70h, al
  jmp      $+2
  jmp      $+2
    xchg      ah, al
    out       71h, al
    jmp       $+2
  jmp      $+2
    mov       al, OFFh
    out       21h, al      ;disable the master PIC
    jmp       $+2
  jmp      $+2
    out       41h, al      ;disable the slave PIC
    jmp       $+2
  jmp      $+2
; except for 512K-576K, mark all other memory areas as non-cacheable
  call       open_ibu
  mov        ax, NCACR    ; 0-640k as non-cacheable
  mov        dx, ax
  mov        ax, 02FFH
  out        dx, ax
; set on-board memory limit to 1024K
  mov        ax, OMLCR
  mov        dx, ax
  mov        al, 41H
```

```
  out      dx, al
 ; mark 576K to 1024K as non-cacheable
  mov        ax, NCBCR    ; a to d segments
  mov        dx, ax
  mov     ax, 0FFF0H
  out     dx, ax
  mov     ax, NCCCR       ; e to f segments
  mov     dx, ax
  mov     al, 0FFH
  out     dx, al
  call    close_386sl
 ; setup cache controller for 64K and direct mapping
  call    open_ccu
  mov     dx, CCR
  mov     al,0
  out     dx, al
   call   close_386sl
 ; disable cache controller
  call    open_ibu
  mov     dx, OMLCR
  in      al, dx
  and     al, 07FH
  out     dx, al
   call   close_386sl
 ; enable cache controller
  call    open_ibu
  mov     dx, OMLCR
  in      al, dx
  or      al, 080H
  out     dx, al
   call   close_386sl
 ; setup for cache autosizing
  mov     ax, 08000H
  mov     es, ax
.386
  mov     esi, 0010H
  mov     al, 06h
  out     80h, al
 ; test for 16K of cache
  mov     ax, 05555H     ; dummy cache cycles
  mov     es:[esi], ax
  mov     ax, 0F00FH
  mov     es:[esi+2],ax
  mov     ax, 05555H ; write to address boundary
  mov     es:[esi], ax
  mov     ax, 0F00FH
  mov     es:[esi+2],ax
  cmp     es:[esi], 05555H
  jne     nocache
chk32k:
```

```
 mov     al, 07h
 out     80h, al
; test for 32K of cache
 mov     ax, 0AAAAH
 mov     es:[esi+1000H], ax
 mov     ax, 0F00FH
 mov     es:[esi+1002H], ax
 cmp     es:[esi+1000H], 0AAAAH
 je      is16
is16:    cmp          es:[esi], 0AAAAH
 je      K16
; test for 64K of cache
 mov     ax, 0A5A5H
 mov     es:[esi+2000H], ax
 mov     ax, 0F00FH
 mov     es:[esi+2002H], ax
 cmp     es:[esi+2000H], 0A5A5H
 je      is32
is32:    cmp    es:[esi], 0A5A5H
 je      K32
K64:
 call    en_int
 mov     dx, offset kbyte64
 mov     ah, 09h
 int     21h
 jmp     exit
K32:
 call    en_int
 mov     dx, offset kbyte32
 mov     ah, 09h
 int     21h
 jmp     exit
K16:
 call    en_int
 mov     dx, offset kbyte16
 mov     ah, 09h
 int     21h
 jmp     exit
nocache:
 call    en_int
 mov     dx, offset cacheless
 mov     ah, 09h
 int     21h
exit:
 mov     ax, 4C00H      ; terminate program
 int     21H
en_int proc near
;re-enable interrupts
 push    ax
   mov   ax, 000fh      ;turn on NMI, clear shutdown byte
   out   70h, al
```

```
    jmp     $+2
    jmp     $+2
      xchg  ah, al
      out     71h, al
    jmp     $+2
    jmp     $+2
      mov     al, 00h ;enable keyboard and timer at master PIC
      out     21h, al
      pop     ax
    sti
    ret
  en_int endp
  ;-------------------------------------------------------------------
  ;
  ;  Data Area
  ;
  ;-------------------------------------------------------------------
  Kbyte64     DB    '64 Kbyte of cache installed', '$'
  Kbyte32     DB    '32 Kbyte of cache installed', '$'
  Kbyte16     DB    '16 Kbyte of cache installed', '$'
  cacheless   DB    'no cache present$'
  code  ENDS                                          ; end code segment
        END   start
```

Cache coherency during simultaneous memory writes

In a write-through cache system, like that used in the Intel386 SL CPU, *cache coherency* refers to the state in which the contents of the cache match the contents of main memory. Loss of cache coherency can result in program failure and erroneous results.

A potential threat to cache coherency is the occurrence of simultaneous memory writes. For example, a system can be performing DMA transfers or bus master writes to memory while the CPU continues to execute code.

The cache controller actually detects when a DMA transfer occurs and checks each address written to determine if it is in the cache. If found in the cache, the controller invalidates that location only, not the entire contents of the cache.

Cacheability

The following registers affect the cacheability of the on-board memory: OMLCR, ISAWINDOW, OMS[A:f]CR, OMRBCR, OMBRCR, NC[A:G]CR, GAACR, and GABCR. ISA-bus memory can also be cached.

Cache flushing

Cache flushing refers to the process of clearing the entire contents of the cache to maintain cache coherency. With the Intel386 SL CPU, the following actions can cause a cache flush:

- Toggling the cache enable bit in the OMLCR register
- Any write to the EMS_CNTRL_REG register
- Writing to any EMS page registers

Even if all the EMS windows are set as noncacheable, any write to the EMS control register or page registers still flushes the cache tags. Cache tags are always flushed on a resume reset.

Summary

We have looked at the various memory options provided by the Intel386 SL processor and the different parameters that can affect the performance as well as the power consumption of the system. The memory controller inside the Intel386 SL CPU is highly optimized and the memory interface requires no glue logic. The only thing you have to watch for is making the right selection of memory devices.

References

Armbrust, S., and T. Forgeon, "Memory in the Hot Seat," *PC TECH Journal,* February 1988, pp. 84–95.

Hennessy, J. L., and D. A. Patterson, *Computer Architecture: A Quantitative Approach,* Morgan Kaufmann Publishers, Inc., 1990.

Wilson, R., "DRAM Vendors Address Increasing Specialization," *Computer Design,* December 1991, pp. 63–70.

"Cache Tutorial," Intel Corporation (order no. 296543-002).

Smith, A., "Bibliography and Readings on CPU Cache Memories and Related Topics," *Computer Architecture News* 14, January 1986.

Chapter

11

Intel486 SL CPU Memory Interfacing

Except for a few programming features, the memory controller in the Intel486 SL CPU is a completely new design from that in the Intel386 SL CPU. This new design allows the Intel486 SL CPU's memory controller to take full advantage of the performance of the Intel486 CPU core, while offering extremely low power consumption. The memory interface supports a 32-bit wide data bus and burst-mode accesses for maximum performance. It also supports 3.3-volt DRAMs (as well as 5-volt DRAMs) to further reduce power consumption.

The Intel486 SL CPU's memory controller offers more flexibility in configuring memory than does the Intel386 SL CPU's memory controller. With the Intel486 SL CPU, DRAM bank size, speed, and configuration can be programmed independently, allowing linear upgrades of memory. The Intel486 SL CPU's memory controller also offers the following features that differ from those in the Intel386 SL CPU:

- Early address/status and internal address pipelining are provided to decode "on-board" versus "off-board" bus cycles earlier for enhanced performance.
- The output buffer strength for DRAM and the ISA bus is programmable.
- 3.3- or 5-volt selectable buffers are provided to support both 5-volt DRAMs and the newer 3.3-volt DRAMs in the same machine.
- Hardware EMS, SRAM mode, or memory interleaving are not supported.
- The ISA-bus memory is noncacheable.
- Shadow registers control cacheability of memory between 0 and 1 Mbyte.

Because of this new design, memory configuration and control software designed for the Intel386 SL CPU are not compatible with the Intel486 SL CPU. This chapter describes the Intel486 SL CPU's memory controller facilities and gives guidelines for designing a memory subsystem. (Refer to Chap. 10 for memory interfacing information for the Intel386 SL CPU.)

Memory Controller

Figure 11.1 shows a functional diagram of the Intel486 SL memory controller. The memory controller is responsible for the following functions: output control (generation of row address strobe RASx# and column address strobe CAS# signals), parity generation, address multiplexing, address mapping (memory roll-over, SMRAM, and bank decoding), refresh, and configuration registers.

Designing a DRAM Memory System

The Intel486 SL CPU's memory controller supports a total of 64 Mbytes of DRAM without any buffering. A maximum of five memory banks can be installed, with each memory bank supporting up to 64 Mbytes of DRAM. Within each of these memory banks, the memory controller can support many DRAM configurations, including memory cards. Given that so many different memory configurations are possible, it is difficult to describe each of them here.

Since 4-Mbyte DRAMs are becoming popular, we will use the 4-Mbyte configuration as an example. Figure 11.2 shows how to connect 4-Mbyte × 4 DRAMs to the Intel486 SL CPU. The DRAMs are connected directly to the CPU. (Damping resistors may be required on some of the memory signals in some designs.)

The Intel486 SL CPU provides five RAS# signals (one for each 32-bit bank), each of which is equivalent to a bank select: RAS0# is for physical bank 0, RAS1# is for physical bank 1, RAS2# is for physical bank 2, RAS3# is for physical bank 3, and RAS4# is for physical bank 4. The CPU provides 20 CAS# sig-

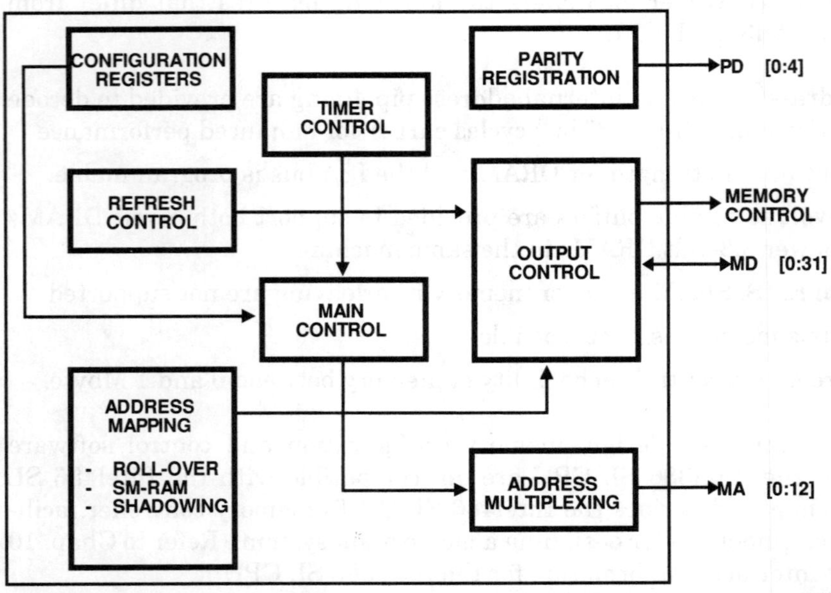

Figure 11.1 Functional block diagram of the Intel486 SL CPU's memory controller.

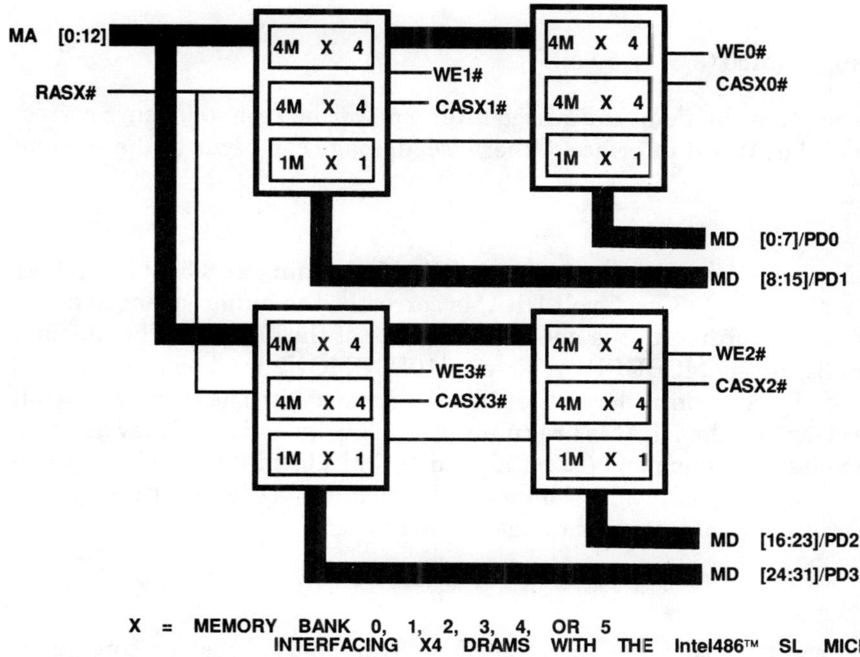

Figure 11.2 Interfacing 4-Mbyte × 4 DRAMs.

nals, four each for each of the five banks. CASx0# corresponds to MD[0:7], CASx1# corresponds to D[8:15], CASx2# corresponds to MD[16:23], and CASx3# corresponds to MD[24:31] (where x = 0 to 4).

Four write enables WE[3:0]# are mapped to each byte in the same manner as the CAS# signals. The additional WEC# is used by some DRAM SIMMs and JEIDA/JEDEC DRAM memory cards. The CAS# and WE# signals can be equated to the internal Intel486 CPU core's byte enables (BE[0-3]#). A physical DRAM bank is mapped to a physical bank by connecting the DRAM bank signals to the appropriate RAS# and CAS# signals.

Memory controller initialization

The memory controller in the Intel486 SL CPU is highly programmable, allowing it to support almost any type of DRAM. The following DRAM parameters are programmable in the Intel486 SL CPU:

- Buffer strength for memory output signals
- Type of burst mode
- Refresh rate for normal and suspend refreshes
- RAS and CAS timings
- Type of address multiplexing
- CAS, RAS, or WE 'OR'ing options

- Bank size
- Operating voltage (3.3- or 5-volt)

These parameters should be initialized after a power-on reset to ensure correct operation of the DRAM interface. Otherwise, damage can occur to the system.

3.3-volt or 5-volt

The DRAM controller can interface with DRAMs running at 3.3 or 5 volts. To interface with either 3.3- or 5-volt DRAMs correctly, the buffer strength needs to be adjusted according to the operating voltage of the DRAMs. The memory Vcc bit (bit 31) in the MCBUFFA register (710H, OMCU) must be programmed to inform the DRAM controller of the DRAM voltage type. The memory Vcc bit should be cleared if the DRAMs are running at 3.3 volts and set if they are running at 5 volts. The memory Vcc bit should be initialized after power-up and cannot be changed dynamically. Changing the memory Vcc bit after the system has been booted up may cause damage to the system.

DRAM configuration

Each memory bank that the Intel486 SL CPU supports must be configured individually. Associated with each bank is a 32-bit configuration register called the MCBANKx register. The MCBANK configuration registers are divided into six fields. The programming of MCBANK0 corresponds to physical DRAM bank 0, that of MCBANK1 to DRAM bank 1, and so forth. The functions of the register fields are as follows:

- The first field (bits [0:7]) of each register specifies the DRAM bank size in 1 Mbyte increments.
- The second field (bits [8-15]) specifies the DRAM bank CAS timing parameters.
- The third field (bits [16:19]) specifies the DRAM bank RAS timing parameters.
- The fourth field specifies the row/column address multiplexing to accommodate different DRAM densities and addressing modes.
- The fifth field (bits [20-23]) control the CAS and WE multiplexing to support different DRAM internal organizations.
- The sixth field (bit 24) enables a battery backup self-refresh mode on a per bank basis.

Memory bank size

Each of the five DRAM banks can support from 1 to 64 Mbytes in 1-Mbyte increments. The DRAM bank size is individually programmable, allowing any mix of banks without restrictions on mixing DRAM size or physical location. Physical DRAM banks can be totally or partially disabled, allowing logical DRAM banks to be mapped to physical DRAM banks on a "per bank" basis.

The bank size is controlled by an 8-bit field consisting of the Top of Bank (TOB) bits[5:0] and the boundary field enable/disable (bit 7). Physical banks of memory can be "mapped out or disabled" using the boundary field enable/disable bit. When bit 7 of any MCBANK register is zero, any access to the associated physical DRAM bank is inhibited. The TOB bits of the next sequential DRAM bank that is populated are programmed with bit 7 set to one.

RAS and CAS control

To support a wide variety of DRAMs, the RAS precharge, RAS to CAS delay, and CAS pulse-width timing are programmable on a "per bank" basis to support DRAM access times from 50 to 100 ns. *RAS precharge time* is the time it takes for the DRAMs to recharge its internal amplifiers and reset its internal machines to prepare for the next cycle. *RAS to CAS delay* is the time it takes for the CAS to go active after RAS is active. (See Fig. 11.3.) Slower DRAM banks do not penalize the performance of faster DRAM banks since each bank's timing is individually programmable.

The RAS and CAS timing parameter field is subdivided into four smaller fields: CAS pulse width (bits 8 and 9), burst mow (bits 10 and 11), RAS to CAS delay (bits 12 and 13), and RAS precharge time (bits 14 and 15). Table 11.1 shows the timing selected for the various settings of the timing parameter fields.

The CAS access time field dictates the number of CPU clock cycles (CPUCLK) for which the CAS will remain active for a valid read or write. The burst-mode field selects the burst mode supported by the memory controller. RAS to CAS access time specifies the RAS to CAS delay in CPUCLK cycle increments. The RAS precharge timer defines the number of CPUCLK cycles that RAS must remain inactive before it is allowed to be driven active. Table 11.2 shows some sample settings of these fields for various DRAM speeds.

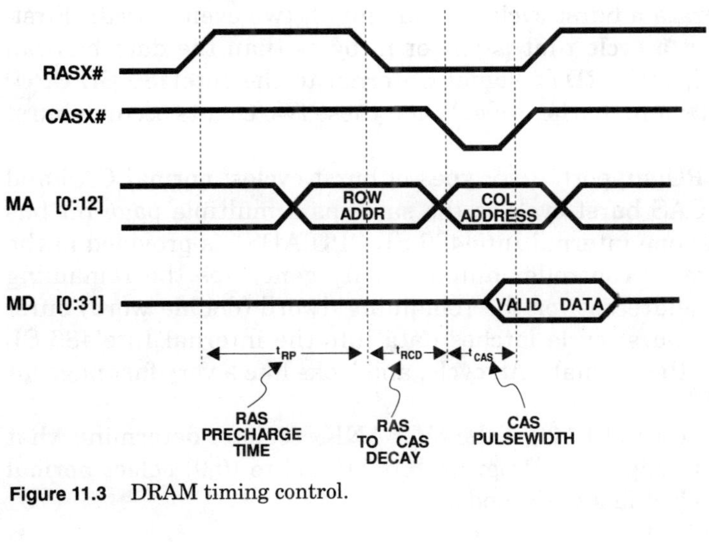

Figure 11.3 DRAM timing control.

TABLE 11.1 RAS and CAS Timing Parameter Fields

Bits	CAS pulse width bits [8–9]	Burst mode bits [10–11]	RAS to CAS delay bits [12–13]	RAS precharge time bits [14–15]
0, 0	1 CPU clock	Normal CAS	1 CPU clock	1 CPU clock
0, 1	2 CPU clocks	N/A	2 CPU clocks	2 CPU clocks
1, 0	3 CPU clocks	Fast CAS	3 CPU clocks	3 CPU clocks
1, 1	4 CPU clocks	N/A	4 CPU clocks	4 CPU clocks

TABLE 11.2 Sample RAS/CAS Timing Parameter Field Configurations

DRAM speed	CAS pulse width	Burst mode	RAS to CAS delay	RAS precharge time
50 ns	1 CPU clock	Fast CAS	1 CPU clock	2 CPU clocks
60 ns	1 CPU clock	Normal CAS	2 CPU clocks	2 CPU clocks
70 ns	1 CPU clock	Normal CAS	2 CPU clocks	2 CPU clocks
80 ns	1 CPU clock	Normal CAS	2 CPU clocks	2 CPU clocks
100 ns	1 CPU clock	N/A	2 CPU clocks	2 CPU clocks

Note: The timing of the RAS and CAS signals is dependent on the CPUCLK speed. For example, one CPUCLK cycle is 40 ns for a 25-MHz CPUCLK and 50 ns for a 20-MHz CPUCLK. You should refer to the DRAM manufacturer's data sheet to ensure that whatever is programmed into the RAS and CAS timing field meets the DRAM specification. *For fast burst mode, the CAS pulse width parameter is ignored by the memory controller.*

The burst cycle

Like the Intel486 SX CPU, the Intel486 SL CPU also supports burst bus cycle features with a new type of memory transfer cycle called *burst mode.* During burst mode transfer, the Intel486 SL CPU can shift data in or out every clock rather than every other clock. The fastest burst cycle requires two clocks for the first data transfer and one clock for subsequent data transfers.

The CPU can generate a burst cycle if, and only if, two events occur. First, the CPU must request a cycle that is longer in bytes than the data bus can accommodate. Second, the BRDY# signal (internal to the Intel486 SL CPU) must be activated to terminate the cycle. When these two events occur, a burst cycle takes place.

The Intel486 SL CPU supports two types of burst cycles: normal CAS and fast CAS. A normal CAS burst cycle is the same as a multiple page hit bus cycle, except that only one internal Intel486 SL CPU ADS# is provided in the first access. The memory controller automatically generates the remaining multiplexed memory addresses for the remaining dword (double word) burst transfers. A fast CAS burst cycle latches data into the internal Intel486 SL CPU earlier than does the normal CAS cycle, and looks like a very fast page hit on the memory bus.

The burst mode bits (bits [10-11]) of the MCBANKx register determine what type of burst mode is supported. Program bits [10,11] to (0,0) select normal CAS mode and (1,0) select fast CAS mode.

Address multiplexing

The row address multiplex control field (bits [16-19]) of the MCBANKx register controls the Intel486 SL CPU's internal address mapping. This field specifies the number of row address and column address bits for the DRAMs installed. Table 11.3 shows the decoding of the row address multiplexer control field.

Some DRAM cards require OR'ing of the WEx# and CASx# signals. The write enable OR'ing control field (bits [20-21]) of the MCBANKx register controls the OR'ing of the WE[0:3]# and WEC# signals. The decoding of this field is shown in Table 11.4.

The CAS OR'ing control bit (bit 22) controls the OR'ing of the CAS signals. When this bit is zero, one CAS per byte is driven. When this bit is one, CASx0# and CASx1# are internally OR'ed and only CASx0# is driven for 16-bit (16 asymmetric DRAM) lower word write accesses, and CASx2# and CASx3# are OR'ed and only CASx2# is driven for 16-bit (16 asymmetric DRAM) upper word write accesses.

Row and column address mapping

Table 11.5 shows how the row addresses are mapped to the memory address bus. The bold numbers indicate that the address line is driven but is not used by the DRAM. Note that the local address lines do not come out in ascending order on the memory address bus.

TABLE 11.3 Decoding of the Row Address Multiplex Control Field

Row address × column address	Bits [16–18]
9 × 9 10 × 9	00H
10 × 10 11 × 10 12 × 10	01H
11 × 11 12 × 11 13 × 11	03H
12 × 12	07H
12 × 8	08H

TABLE 11.4 Decoding of the Write Enable OR'ing Control Field

Bits (21, 20)	Function
0, 0	WE0# driven for MD[0–7], WE1# for MD[8–15], WE2# for MD[16–23], WE3# for MD[24–31], WEC# disabled
0, 1	WE0# driven for MD[0–15], WE2# for MD[16–23], WE1#, WE3#, and WEC# disabled
1, 0	WEC# driven for MD[0–31], WE0#, WE1#, WE2#, and WE3# disabled
1, 1	Reserved

TABLE 11.5 Row Address Mapping

		Row address												
DRAM depth	Row/column	12	11	10	9	8	7	6	5	4	3	2	1	0
256 Kbytes	9 × 9	**25**	**23**	**22**	**20**	19	18	17	16	15	14	13	12	11
512 Kbytes	10 × 9	**25**	**23**	**22**	20	19	18	17	16	15	14	13	12	11
1 Mbyte	12 × 8	**25**	21	10	20	19	18	17	16	15	14	13	12	11
1 Mbyte	10 × 10	**25**	**23**	22	20	19	18	17	16	15	14	13	12	21
2 Mbytes	11 × 10	**25**	23	22	20	19	18	17	16	15	14	13	12	21
4 Mbytes	12 × 10	**25**	24	22	20	19	18	17	16	15	14	13	12	21
4 Mbytes	11 × 11	**25**	24	22	20	19	18	17	16	15	14	13	23	21
8 Mbytes	12 × 11	**25**	**24**	22	20	19	18	17	16	15	14	13	23	21
16 Mbytes	13 × 11	25	24	22	20	19	18	17	16	15	14	13	23	21
16 Mbytes	12 × 12	**25**	24	22	20	19	18	17	16	15	16	25	23	21

Table 11.6 shows how a column address is mapped to the memory address bus. The bold numbers are address lines not used by the DRAM. Note that the local address lines do not come out in ascending order on the memory address bus.

Refresh modes

The Intel486 SL CPU's memory controller supports three types of refresh modes: normal refresh, suspend refresh, and self-refresh. Normal refresh is for use during normal system operation. Suspend refresh is for use during a 3.3- or 5-volt suspend, when the clock is stopped to the CPU and 82360SL but they remain powered. Self-refresh is for use during 3.3- or 5-volt suspend with low-power DRAMs that support self-refresh.

Normal refresh. With normal refresh, The 82360SL furnishes the DRAM refresh request (REFREQ). The REFREQ occurs at a programmed interval determined by the 82C54 programmable interval timer in the 82360SL (typically 15.6 ms). A REFREQ has a higher priority than a DMA or a BUS MASTER request. For each REFREQ, the Intel486 SL CPU's memory controller performs a CAS before RAS refresh.

TABLE 11.6 Column Address Mapping

		Column address												
DRAM depth	Row/column	12	11	10	9	8	7	6	5	4	3	2	1	0
256 Kbytes	9 × 9		**13**	**12**	**11**	10	9	8	7	6	5	4	3	2
512 Kbytes	10 × 9		**13**	**12**	**11**	10	9	8	7	6	5	4	3	2
1 Mbyte	12 × 8		**13**	**12**	**11**	10	9	8	7	6	5	4	3	2
1 Mbyte	10 × 10		**13**	**12**	11	10	9	8	7	6	5	4	3	2
2 Mbytes	11 × 10		**13**	**12**	11	10	9	8	7	6	5	4	3	2
4 Mbytes	12 × 10		**13**	**12**	11	10	9	8	7	6	5	4	3	2
4 Mbytes	11 × 11		**13**	12	11	10	9	8	7	6	5	4	3	2
8 Mbytes	12 × 11		**13**	12	11	10	9	8	7	6	5	4	3	2
16 Mbytes	13 × 11		**13**	12	11	10	9	8	7	6	5	4	3	2
16 Mbytes	12 × 12		**13**	12	11	10	9	8	7	6	5	4	3	2

To support DRAMs with longer refresh times, the Intel486 SL CPU provides programmable refresh rate. The refresh rate is controlled by the normal refresh rate field (bits [7-4]) of the memory controller refresh configuration register, MCRF (704H, OMCU). Table 10.7 shows the bit encoding for the normal refresh rate field. The Intel486 SL CPU's memory controller uses the MCRF register to determine when a REFREQ should or should not result in a refresh cycle being performed.

The Intel486 SL CPU ignores a REFREQ based on the normal refresh rate field in the MCRF register. The REFREQ generates a hold request in the Intel486 SL CPU. The CPU then returns an HLDA to the 82360SL to acknowledge the REFREQ. The Intel486 SL CPU provides an internal ready immediately after a HOLD/HLDA bus cycle if the refresh request is to be ignored.

Suspend refresh. The suspend refresh mechanism for the Intel486 SL CPU is similar to that of the Intel386 SL CPU. The only difference is that the Intel486 SL CPU supports a refresh rate of ISA-bus refresh rate divided by 128. The enabling mechanism is the same as with the Intel386 SL CPU (as described in Chap. 10).

Self-refresh. Most newer DRAMs support a lower-power refresh mode called self-refresh. Self-refresh is a special case of CAS before RAS refresh in which the DRAMs are capable of generating their own refresh request and refresh address. The battery backed-up (BBU) self-refresh DRAMs must provide their own battery power. The Intel486 SL CPU supports self-refresh during 5-volt suspend.

Entering self-refresh appears as an extended CAS before RAS refresh. WE# is HIGH when CAS# is first driven LOW. WE# must be high to prevent the DRAM from entering a test mode. If CAS# and RAS# are both held low for a predetermined time period (typically greater than 16 ms), DRAMs supporting BBU self-refresh will begin generating their own refresh requests and refresh addresses.

Once a DRAM enters self-refresh mode, the Intel486 SL CPU's memory controller can ignore refresh requests. When in self-refresh mode, the CAS# and

TABLE 11.7 Encoding of the Normal Refresh Rate Field in the MCRF Register

Bits [7,6,5,4]	Normal refresh rate
0,0,0,0	ISA-bus refresh rate divided by 1
0,0,0,1	ISA-bus refresh rate divided by 2
0,0,1,0	ISA-bus refresh rate divided by 4
0,0,1,1	ISA-bus refresh rate divided by 8
0,1,0,0	ISA-bus refresh rate divided by 16
0,1,0,1	ISA-bus refresh rate divided by 32
0,1,1,0	ISA-bus refresh rate divided by 64
0,1,1,1	ISA-bus refresh rate divided by 128
1,x,x,x	Reserved

RAS# must remain low (CAS# is held low with a pull-down), WE# and OE# are high and the MA lines are three-stated. The DRAM automatically exits self-refresh mode when CAS# and RAS# go high.

The self-refresh enabling mechanism is the same as suspend refresh except that the self-refresh enable bit (bit 24) in the MCBANKx registers has to be set to one before enabling suspend refresh. The suspend refresh rate has no effect on self-refresh. Self-refresh is automatically disabled after a resume reset. The REFNORM bit (bit 0) of the MCRF register (704H, OMCU) should be examined before accessing the DRAMs to find out if the DRAM is out of self-refresh mode.

Memory sizing and enabling

An autoscan algorithm can be used to determine the amount of on-board memory present on a per bank basis. Before doing any memory sizing, enable the protected mode so that the program can test all the row address bits. Also, memory options such as cache, memory roll-over, BIOS shadowing, and SMRAM must be disabled.

The first step in the autoscan algorithm is to set the on-board memory limit to 64 Mbytes by programming the TOB bits in the corresponding MCBANKx and OMLCR registers, and then enabling the memory bank. Before performing the address aliasing test, the autoscan routine must determine whether CAS OR'ing or WE OR'ing are required and determine the RAS/CAS timing for the DRAMs being used. Typically, this information is stored inside a BIOS parameter table or the BIOS setup program.

The next step is to verify if physical memory is present. To do this, the autoscan routine writes a double word test pattern to absolute address 0H and a different double word test pattern to absolute address 04H. It then reads back from address 0H to determine if a memory bank is populated. If populated, the data returned from a double word read to address 0H should be the same as that written to that address.

If physical memory is present, the autoscan routine can start sizing the memory. The autoscan algorithm determines the bank size by detecting the number of row and column address bits present. Table 11.8 shows the different multiplexing configurations supported by the Intel486 SL CPU and the corresponding bank size for each configuration.

The row address testing starts with the largest possible number of row address bits, working from left to right on the row address. In each test, a multiplexing configuration is chosen such that the leftmost bit to be tested does not appear anywhere else in the map. A simple 32-bit read/write test can be performed on absolute address 0H at the location which toggles the leftmost row address bit. If the DRAM installed does not have that many row address bits, it will alias to absolute address 0H. If the write to the location that toggles the leftmost row address bit does not alias, then the row size is determined. Otherwise, it selects another multiplexing configuration and performs the same test.

TABLE 11.8 Multiplexing and Bank Size Configurations

DRAM density	Row/column addresses	Mux cntrl field	TOB field
256 Kbytes	9 × 9	00H	1H
512 Kbytes	10 × 9		2H
1 Mbyte	12 × 8		4H
1 Mbyte	10 × 10	01H	4H
2 Mbytes	11 × 10		8H
4 Mbytes	12 × 10		10H
4 Mbytes	11 × 11	03H	10H
8 Mbytes	12 × 11		20H
16 Mbytes	13 × 11	07H	40H
16 Mbytes	12 × 12	08H	40H

A multiplexing configuration is then chosen to test the column address bits. The location chosen for a column address test must be such that the address does not appear in the row map (i.e., the row address bits are all zeros). Then, by doing the same kind 32-bit read/write test to toggle the leftmost bit of the column address, the number of column address bits can be determined.

Listing 11.1 gives an example of an autoscan algorithm for memory sizing. Note that this algorithm is merely one way of doing memory sizing. Other algorithms can also be used.

Listing 11.1 Example of How to Autoscan Memory

```
;;disable cache, memory roll-over, BIOS shadowing, and SM-RAM
;;set bank size to 64 Mbytes and enable memory bank
write 7FH to OMLCR register
write 3FH to the TOB field
;; test for presence of physical memory
do a read/write test at location 0H and 04H
if data read back from 0H equals to data written
  physical memory is present
;; enable protected mode and selects the multiplexing configuration
with the largest number of row address bits
write 03H to bits[16:18] of the MCBANKx register
write double word test patterns to 0H and 800000H
if there is no alias # of row address bits equals to 13 bits
else
  write double word test patterns to 0H and 400000H
  if there is no alias # of row address bits equals to 12 bits
  else
    write double word test patterns to 0H and 200000H
    if there is no alias # of row address bits equals to 11 bits
write 00H to bits[16:18] of the MCBANKx register
write double word test patterns to 0H and 100000H
if there is no alias # of row address bits equals to 10 bits
else
```

```
  # of row address bits equals to 9 bits
;; selectsawhe multiplexing configuration with the largest number of
column address bits and has the same number of row address bit found
in the row address test
if # of row address bits equals to 13
  column address must equal to 11 bits
if # of row address bits equals to 12  ;column address could be 12,
11, 10, or 8
write 08H to bits[16-18]
write double word test patterns to 0 H and 800H
if there is no alias # of column address bits equals to 12
else
  write 03H to bits[16-18]
  write double word test patterns to 0H and 400H if there is no
alias # of column address bits equals to 11
  else
    write 01H to bits [16-18]
    write double word test patterns to 0H and 200H
if there is no alias # of column address bits equals to 10
else
# of column address bits equals to 8
if # of row address bits equals to 11
  ;column address could be 11 or 10
write 03H to bits[16-18]
write double word test patterns to 0H and 400H
if there is no alias # of column address bits equals to 11
else
  # of column address bits equals to 10
if # of row address bits equals to 10  ; column address could be
10, or 9
write 01H to bits[16-18]
if there is no alias # of column address bits equals to 10
else
  # of column address bits equals to 9
if # of row address bits equals to 9    ; column address must be 9
  # of column address bits equals to 9
;; set bank size and mux configuration based on number of row and
column address bits found
```

Memory controller output buffer control

For maximum power-saving, the drive capability (the maximum capacitive loads which the buffer can directly drive in picofarads) of the memory interface is programmable. If the buffer drive is too weak, it cannot drive the data into the memory chips. On the other hand, if the buffer strength is too strong, it will cause transient current (overshoot and undershoot can cause excessive current drain) during power up. The memory buffer strength can also affect the rise and fall time of the memory signals.

The output strength of the memory interface is controlled by either a 2- or a 3-bit field in the MCBUFF[A:B] registers. MCBUFFA (710H, OMCU) is a 32-bit register and MCBUFFB (714H, OMCU) is an 8-bit register. The memory buffers are divided into five different groups: CAS# for each bank, memory address, common write enable, RAS for each bank, and memory data and parity. The decoding of the CAS # buffer strength field is shown in Table 11.9. Each load in this table equals 34 picofarads (pF).

The CAS# buffer field (bit [0-9]) in the MCBUFFA register controls the buffer strength of the CAS[0:4] signals. Each of the five pairs of 2-bit fields corresponds to one bank of memory. The default buffer strength for the CAS signals is 5 loads.

The MA buffer strength field (bits [10-12]) of the MCBUFFA register is a 3-bit field which controls the buffer strength of the on-board memory address bus. The default buffer strength for the MA signals is 3 loads. Buffer strength for the WECxx signals is controlled by the WEC buffer strength field (bits [13:15]) of the MCBUFFA register. The default buffer strength for the WECxx signals is 3 loads.

The RAS# buffer field (bit [16-25]) in the MCBUFFA register controls the buffer strength of the RAS[0:4] signals. Each of the five pairs of 2-bit fields corresponds to one bank of memory. The default buffer strength for the RAS signals is 5 loads.

The buffer strength for the memory and parity data bits is determined by the MD/PD buffer strength field (bits[28-30]) in the MCBUFFA register. The default buffer strength for the MD/PD signals is 3 loads.

The buffer strength for the MA[0:12] signals is controlled by the memory address buffer strength field (bits [10-12]) of the MCBUFFA register. The decoding of this field is the same as the CAS buffer field.

Normally, the write enable common (WEC#) is a buffered signal on DRAM cards. In the case where the WEC# signal is not buffered, the write enable common buffer strength field (bits [13-15]) can be used. The decoding of this field is the same as CAS buffer field.

The buffer strength for the WEx# signals is controlled by the write enable buffer strength field (bits [5-7]) of the MCBUFF register. The decoding of this field is the same as CAS buffer field.

TABLE 11.9 Decoding of CAS# Buffer Strength Field

Buffer strength	Bits (7,6,5)	MSB, LSB
1 load	0,0,0	0,0
Three-state	0,0,1	
2 loads	0,1,0	0,1
3 loads	0,1,1	
4 loads	1,0,0	1,0
5 loads	1,0,1	
6 loads	1,1,0	1,1
7 loads	1,1,1	

Note: The buffer strengths for 3.3- and 5-volt DRAMs are different. The MCBUFF[A:B] registers must be programmed according to the operating voltage to ensure correct operation.

Parity checking

The Intel486 SL CPU's memory controller provides even parity support for DRAMs. Parity support features include identification of high and low bytes and automatic even parity generation/checking. Any time a parity error is detected, the memory controller latches and stores the bank number and byte or bytes of the faulty memory location. The address for parity error can be determined by a memory test. Parity checking is enabled by setting the even parity checking enable bit (bit 15) of the MCPARITY register (708H, OMCU).

A 16-bit register, the Memory Controller Parity Control Configuration register MCPARITY (708H, OMCU), is used to locate the memory address that generated the parity error. When a parity error occurs, this register contains the parity status. This parity status is kept until it is explicitly cleared, by first resetting and then setting the even parity enable bit. With the Intel486 SL CPU, any memory bank can be disabled and mapped out. If the BIOS detects a parity error on a given bank, the corresponding bank may be disabled and mapped out. Parity checking should be disabled if the DRAMs installed do not support parity checking.

Memory roll-over

Memory roll-over is controlled by the MCROLL register (700H, OMCU), which is equivalent to the OMBRCR and OMRBCR registers. The MCROLL register is a 16-bit register in the Intel486 SL CPU's memory controller I/O space. It is divided into two fields: the memory rollover block field and memory rollover base field. The first field (MCROLL bits [0-6]) is a 7-bit field that is functionally equivalent to the OMRBCR register, and the second field (MCROLL bits [8-13]) is functionally equivalent to the OMBRCR register. One bit in both fields of the MCROLL register must be set for roll-over to be enabled. The memory rollover block field specifies which on-board memory in the range of 640–1024 Kbytes is to be remapped to the address specified by the memory roll-over base field.

System management RAM

The Intel486 SL CPU provides a flexible mechanism for allocating of on-board memory for system management RAM (SMRAM). Any 64-Kbyte memory segment within the first 1 Mbyte of address space can be designated for SMRAM. Writing a one to a bit in the MCSMRAM register enables the corresponding 64-K-byte segment as on-board SMRAM.

On-board memory-sliding window

With the Intel386 SL CPU, extended memory above 1 Mbyte can be accessed in real mode using the built-in LIM 4.0 EMS hardware. EMS is not supported in Intel486 SL CPU. Instead, a mechanism called a *memory controller window* is provided to allow access to memory above 1 Mbyte in real mode. The operation of the memory controller window is similar to EMS mapping. Any 64-Kbyte segment in the first 1 Mbyte of address space can be selected as the window to map into memory above 1 Mbyte.

The on-board memory-sliding window is also available in protected mode. The access mechanism to the on-board memory-sliding window is identical to the EMS mechanism. When this window is enabled, any 64-Kbyte memory block above 1 Mbyte can be accessed through one of the sixteen 64-Kbyte windows located below 1 Mbyte, according to the base address and window field in the MCWINDOW register (70EH, OMCU). The base address field (bits [0-9]) contains the upper address bits for the 64-Kbyte memory block above 1 Mbyte that is remapped to one of the sixteen 64 Kbyte windows. Table 11.10 shows the encoding of this base address field. The window field (bits [11-14]) specifies which of the sixteen 64-Kbyte memory space windows is to be used to access the 64 Kbytes of memory above 1 Mbyte.

Highest priority is given to the onboard SMRAM area. If SMRAM is enabled, then the Intel486 SL CPU automatically directs CPU accesses within the address range of the SMRAM window (30000H-3FFFFH) to the SMRAM (on-board or off-board). When SMRAM is enabled by an SMI or by setting bit 3 of the OMDCR register, any DMA or external bus master accesses to the 30000H-3FFFFH memory address range are automatically directed to the correct on-board system memory locations.

Memory mapping priority

The memory controller does not provide arbitration for memory allocation. In other words, a segment assigned for memory roll-over can be reassigned for BIOS shadowing. Therefore, it is possible to create a conflict in memory mapping if the memory controller is programmed incorrectly. The memory controller does provide a memory mapping priority scheme, however, which assigns priorities to the roll-over, shadowing, and memory mapped I/O features. Table 11.11 shows the priorities of these features, with 1 being the highest priority.

Highest priority is given to the on-board SMRAM area. If SMRAM is enabled, the Intel486 SL CPU automatically directs CPU accesses within the address range of the SMRAM window (30000H-3FFFFH) to the SMRAM (on-

TABLE 11.10 Encoding of the Base Address Field of the MCWINDOW Register

Bit 0	Bit 1	Bit 2	Bit 3	Bit 4	Bit 5	Bit 6	Bit 7	Bit 8	Bit 9A16
A16	A17	A18	A19	A20	A21	A22	A23	A24	A25

TABLE 11.11 Priorities Assigned to Memory Options

Priority	Memory option
1 (highest)	On-board SMRAM area
2	Memory mapped I/O
3	Shadowing
4	Roll-over

board or off-board). When SMRAM is enabled by an SMI or by setting bit 3 of the OMDCR register, any DMA or external bus master accesses to the 30000H-3FFFFH memory address range are automatically directed to the correct on-board system memory locations.

Memory mapped I/O has the next highest priority. When a section of memory is enabled as memory mapped I/O, the internal bus controller always sends accesses to that memory to the external bus controller. Such accesses are then redirected to the PI bus or the ISA bus. Roll-over has the next highest priority, and shadowing has the lowest priority. Conflicts arising from incorrect programming of memory control hardware are resolved based on this priority scheme. These priorities apply to memory cycles that qualify for more than one simultaneous mapping. They do not apply to accessing the same memory block on different memory cycles. For example, if a memory block is used for shadowing and is also programmed for memory roll-over, the memory block will still be accessible separately through either type of cycle.

DRAM selection

Some considerations must be given in selecting 3.3-volt DRAMs to match the CPU requirements. The voltage limits for the 3.3-volt Vcc in the Intel486 SL CPU is ±0.3 volts. Most DRAMs will support voltage limits between ±5 and ±1 percent. Care must be taken to ensure that the DRAM interface operates within the operating voltage limits. Since 3.3-volt DRAM is still relatively new, the availability of 3.3-volt DRAM is still limited. Some of the 3.3-volt DRAMs are actually 5-volt DRAMs recharacterized to run at 3.3 volts. These DRAMs will only work at a lower speed. Running at a lower DRAM speed will cause a drop in system performance. For DRAMs that are recharacterized to work at 3.3 volts, the noise immunity guardbands will be reduced. Figure 11.4 shows the difference in power consumption between 3.3- and 5-volt DRAMs.

To assist you in DRAM selection, an application note written by Scott Schaefer of Micron Technology, an expert in memory devices, is included at the end of the chapter.

Cache Controller

Like the Intel486 DX CPU, the Intel486 SL CPU supports an 8-Kbyte internal cache. A second-level cache is not supported. The internal cache is enabled by setting bit 7 of the OMLCR register (301H, IBU) and writing a zero to the CD and NW bits of the CR0 register.

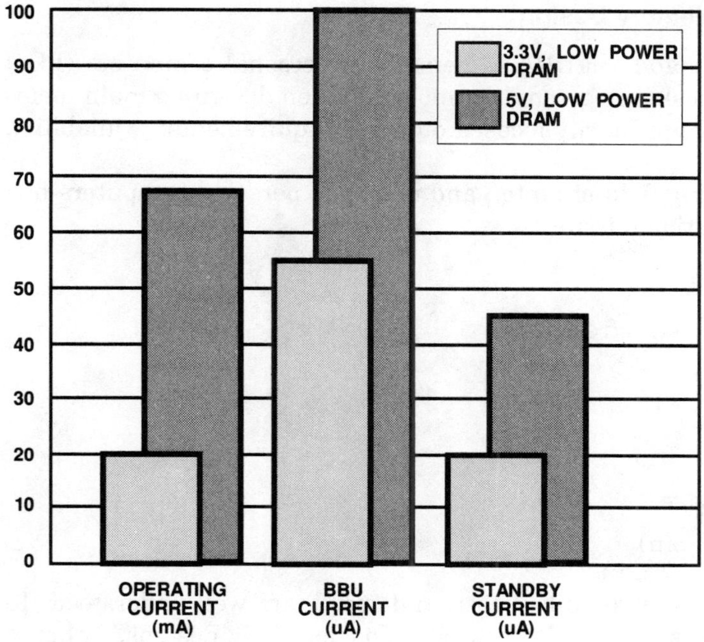

Figure 11.4 DRAM power consumption comparison. (*Courtesy of Micron Technology, Inc.*)

Cacheability

Except for the cache write-protect feature provided by the BIOS shadowing registers, cacheability control in the Intel486 SL CPU is quite different from that in the Intel386 SL CPU. With the Intel486 SL CPU, cacheability is controlled by the OMS[A:F]CR, OMDCR, OMLCR, C[A:D]CR, MCROLL, GAACR, GABCR, ISAWINDOW, and MIO[A:D]CR registers. After power up, the entire Intel486 SL CPU's physical address space is noncacheable. The ten 64-Kbyte memory segments in the address space between 0 and 640 Kbytes can be made noncacheable by disabling the corresponding memory segment through programming of the OMDCR. Memory between 640 Kbytes and 1 Mbyte can be disabled by programming the OMS[A:F]CR registers.

Four memory mapped I/O configuration registers (MIO[A:D]CR) are provided to maintain cache coherency with memory mapped I/O devices. Each register can define a 4-, 8-, 16-, or 32-Kbyte block of a memory segment within the 16-Mbyte ISA-address space as noncacheable.

Cache flushing

Cache is flushed as the result of any of the following actions:

- Toggling the cache enable bit in the OMLCR register
- Setting both the CD and NW bits in the CR0 register
- Executing either an INVD or a WBINVD instruction

DRAM Considerations for PC Memory Design*

Introduction. The demand for DRAM memory in personal computers (PCs) has been mainly for desktop personal computers. When designing main memory, PC designers have primarily focused on three requirements: availability, cost, and speed.

The new and growing field of laptop and notebook personal computers has introduced seven additional issues:

- Parity
- Lower power (extended refresh)
- Self-refresh
- Package size
- Operating current
- 3.3V operating voltage
- IC DRAM cards (88-pin)

The first three issues (availability, cost, and speed) are well understood. To help memory designers choose the best solution for their designs, either a portable or a desktop system, this paper discusses these additional issues.

Offerings. To design main memory, four basic offerings of DRAM are available or will be available in the near future:

1. 256K × 4 (plus 256K × 1 for parity)
2. 1 Meg × 4 (plus 1 Meg × 1 for parity)
3. 512K × 8 (512K × 9 for parity)
4. 256K × 16 (256K × 18 for parity)

The first two offerings are referred to as "standard DRAM," and the second two are referred to as "wide DRAM." Generally, standard DRAMs are more readily available and have more sources. Wide DRAM development is usually a generation behind standard DRAM and is not expected to catch up until third-generation 16-Meg DRAMs and first-generation 64 Meg DRAMs.

Parity (or no parity). There is a growing trend to build laptop, notebook, and low-end desktop PCs without parity. Within a few years, all parity-based systems may switch to either nonparity-based systems (as in most PCs) or to error detection and correction (EDAC) based systems (high-end PCs).

---

* Contributed by Scott Schaefer, Marketing Applications Engineer for Micron Technology.

Some of the reasons for this trend away from parity are listed below:

1. Parity does not significantly improve reliability.
2. DRAMs from a quality manufacturer now have very low soft error rates (SERs).
3. Parity increases memory costs 10 to 15 percent.
4. Some chipsets allow turning off the parity bit.
5. Parity requires extra board space as well as previous generation devices or less available parity chips.
6. Some software does not use parity.

The most important of these factors is the memory system's reliability. In the early days of semiconductor DRAM memories, the high SER of 4K and 16K DRAMs, coupled with the high cost of implementing EDAC (8-bit buses), made implementing parity critical. DRAM manufacturers, however, have significantly improved SER during the last five generations (Fig. 11.6). For example, the SER on a 16K DRAM was approximately 1 to 5 FITs per bit, whereas the SER on a 4 Meg DRAM is closer to 0.0002 to 0.0004 FITs per bit—a 10,000x improvement! (FIT is a Failure in Time where time is 1 billion device hours.)

Taking these industry SER averages and applying them to a 2MB, 16-bit-wide memory system, meaningful benchmarks for PCs can be obtained. Most systems measure errors in mean time between failures (MTBF). Applying the SER numbers from the previous figure, the improvement in MTBF for a typical 2MB, 16-bit-wide memory system can be demonstrated (Fig. 11.7).

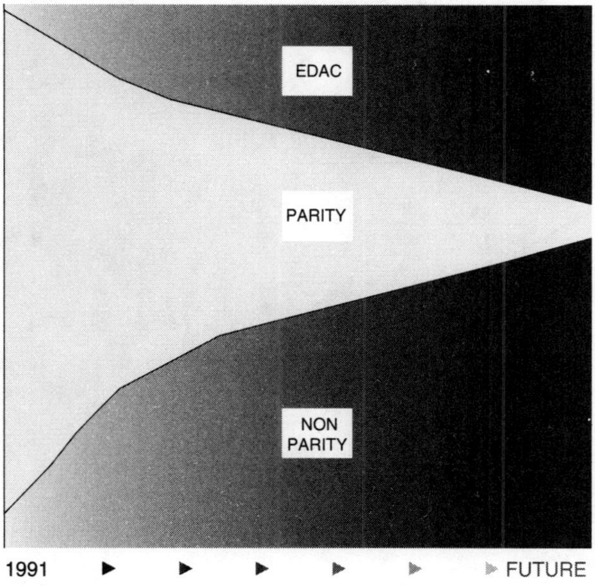

Figure 11.5 Trend away from parity.

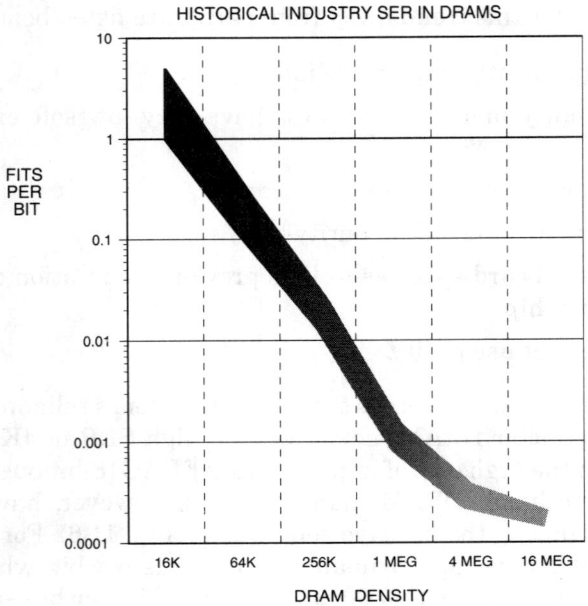

Figure 11.6 Historical DRAM SER.

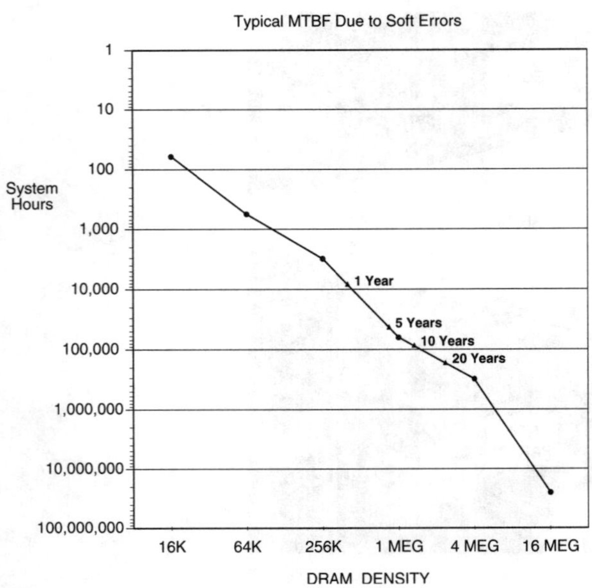

Figure 11.7 MTBF for 2-Mbyte memory system.

It is obvious why parity was instituted in the 16K DRAM days. A memory system made up from 16K DRAMs would experience a SER hit every 60 to 70 hours! Because of this, it has been standard operating procedure to design in parity. But changes are ahead. System designers are starting to ask, "Why?" Using today's high-quality 4 Meg DRAMs rather than yesterday's 16K DRAMs extends the MTBF from around 60 hours to an MTBF of 30 to 35 years on a 2MB by 16-bit-wide memory system.

Another way to look at this same data is to calculate the number of SER hits a user would see after 10 years of continuous use (Fig. 11.8). As expected, the SER is negligible after 10 years of continuous use when using today's high-quality DRAMs.

It is important to note that the SER and MTBF must be carefully calculated for any given system and its application. The DRAM's SER is dependent on V_{cc} (power supply voltage), operating speed (cycle rate), and memory configuration. For example, taking the previous 2MB example and doubling it to 4MB, the SER will either increase slightly or double. If the width of the memory system is increased to 32 bits, the SER would double since all DRAM bits are active. If, on the other hand, the memory is interleaved and the bus remains 16 bits wide, the SER increases only slightly. This is because the bank not being accessed is in standby mode and is much less susceptible to SER hits (the faster the cycle rate, the more susceptible a DRAM is to SER).

Although the need for parity would appear to be greater for wider buses, the additional cost to implement EDAC, rather than parity, decreases substantially as the bus width increases. In fact, the DRAM memory cost is the same for a 64-bit-wide bus (Table 11.12). Besides detecting two errors for a given word, EDAC will also correct any single-bit error.

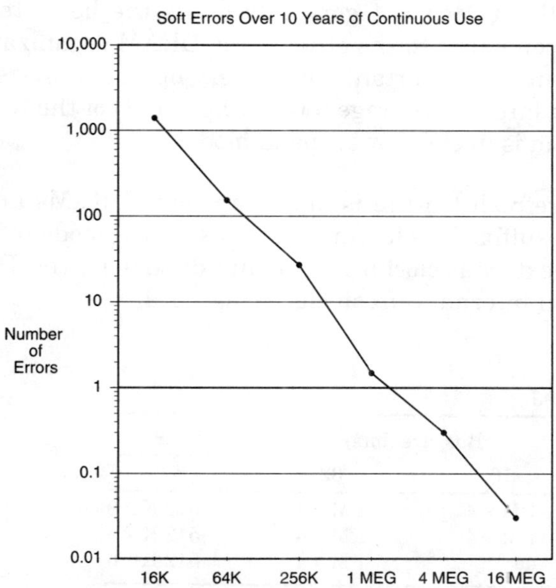

Figure 11.8 2-Mbyte memory system SER.

TABLE 11.12 Parity and EDAC Overhead

	Extra bits required		Bus width increase	
Bus size (bits)	Parity	EDAC	Parity	EDAC
8	1	5	12.5%	62.5%
16	2	6	12.5%	37.5%
32	4	8	12.5%	25%
64	8	8	12.5%	12.5%

Most applications with buses no more than 32 bits wide do not require parity, whereas applications using bus widths of 64 bits or more, and some 32-bit, generally require some kind of bit-checking for errors. The choice is usually EDAC rather than parity.

Table 11.13 summarizes which DRAM would be the optimum choice, considering price, performance, and space. It takes into account the typical PC which ships with a minimum of 4MB of memory. A 256K × 16 or 512K × 8 DRAM could be a better alternative than a 1 Meg × 4 DRAM, should the memory system's depth be equal to or less than 512K deep. This is typically the case with wider buses. The 64-bit bus choice of 512K × 8 DRAMs would change to 1 Meg × 4 should the total memory size increase from 4MB to 8MB.

Low power, extended refresh. A low-power, extended refresh DRAM (LP-DRAM) has a reduced CMOS standby current limit (typically from 1 mA to 200 μA) and an 8x longer refresh interval (from 15 μs per row to 125 μs per row). The extended refresh offers a Battery Backup (BBU) mode, which is a low current, data retention cycle. Each of the four DRAM options in the technical note have low power, extended refresh versions available.

On a per-bit basis, the 1 Meg × 4 generally offers the best standby and refresh power savings compared to the other three DRAM organizations. The DRAM standby current is important in battery-operated systems since DRAMs usually draw a large percentage (50 to 70 percent) of the total system current when the system is in sleep or suspend mode.

Self-refresh. The self-refresh feature is built into some DRAMs and usually indicated by an LL or S suffix. This feature performs a BBU mode refresh, with the exception that no external clocking is required; that is, the DRAM will refresh itself via its own internal refresh clock (Fig. 11.9).

TABLE 11.13 Selection for Error Checking

	Bus size (bits)			
Error checking	8	16	32	64
Non-parity	1 M × 4	1 M × 4	1 M × 4	512 K × 8
Parity	512K × 9	1 M × 4	1 M × 4	512 K × 8
EDAC	na	na	1 M × 4	512 K × 8

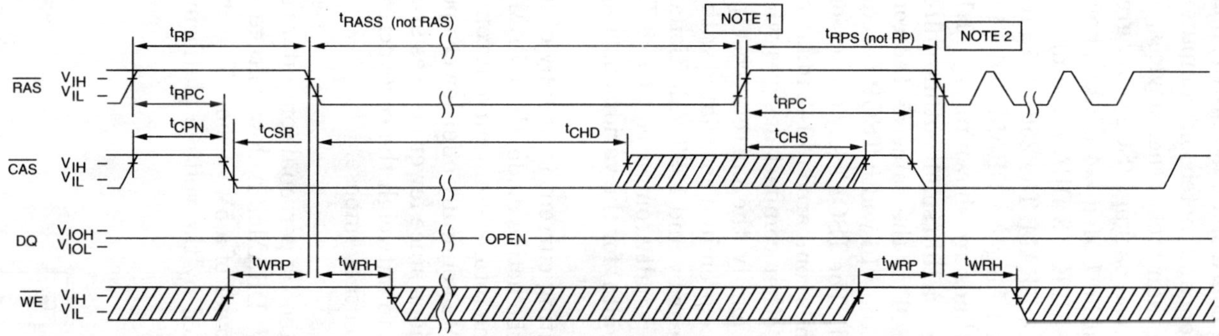

NOTES:
1. Once $t_{RASSmin}$ is met and RAS remains LOW, the DRAM will enter SELF REFRESH mode.
2. Once t_{RPS} is satisfied, a complete burst refresh of all rows should be executed, although providing distributed refreshes at the specified refresh rate is acceptable, provided CBR refreshes are utilized.

Figure 11.9 Self-refresh operation.

Control of self-refresh is defined by JEDEC and de facto standard timing specifications: $^tRASS = 100\ \mu s$, $^tRPS \approx 200$ ns and $^tCHS \approx -70$ ns. Some DRAMs include ^tCHD, which is 600 μs.

Package size. Conserving board space is always an important design consideration, especially for laptop and notebook computers. Functionally, DRAMs require more board space than most other devices. The size between the four options in small outline J-lead package (SOJ) vary greatly. The 256K × 4 DRAM uses the same package as the 1 Meg × 4 DRAM; however, four times as many devices are required. The 512K × 8 DRAM requires approximately 50 percent more area than a 1 Meg × 4 DRAM. The 256K × 16 requires approximately 110 percent more area than a 1 Meg × 4 DRAM and 44 percent more area than a 512K × 8. Actual sized outlines are shown in Fig. 11.10 for comparison.

These are also available in a thin small outline gull-lead package (TSOP). The length and width of a TSOP is the same as the corresponding SOJ package (same board area) except the ×16 width TSOP is reduced because of a smaller lead pitch (50 mil to 32 mil). The TSOP's key attraction is that it is one-third the thickness of the SOJ (47 mils compared to 142 mils), as illustrated in Fig. 11.11.

Laptop, notebooks and other compact designs which have height or layout restrictions can usually justify the current cost premium required to use TSOPs. However, any price premium associated with TSOPs will be short lived and is expected to disappear by mid 1993. Additionally, in TSOP, the ×16 does not impose a board space penalty compared to a ×8 TSOP. Table 11.14 lists the dimensions (length and width) for the various packages.

Operating current. Operating current is usually of less importance in system design. When a PC is in the active mode, the DRAM's portion of current draw is minimal compared to the total system current consumption, typically from 4 to 6 percent. Wider DRAMs generally offer lower operating currents (10 to 20 percent) in most applications since fewer devices are active for a given access, but generally not enough to outweigh the cost increase, board space increase, and performance reduction they impose.

3.3 volts. Laptop and notebook personal computers and BBU systems are also starting to employ 3.3V DRAMs. A low-voltage (3.3V) DRAM consumes approximately half the power of a 5V version. The choice of whether to use 5V or 3.3V DRAMs is dictated by the voltage platform selected, which is deter-

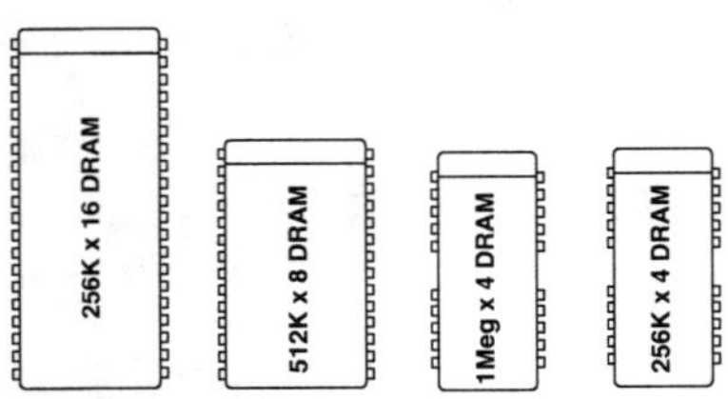

Figure 11.10 Package-size comparisons.

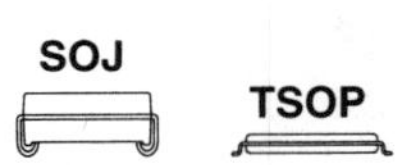

Figure 11.11 Thickness comparison.

TABLE 11.14 Package Dimensions (in mils)

	SOJ		TSOP	
Device type	Width	Length	Width	Length
1 Meg × 4	340	679	367	677
512 K × 8	445	729	467	727
256 K × 16	445	1029	467	727

mined by the CPU and chipset specifications. Once the voltage range is selected, the considerations discussed in this technical note apply for either 5V or 3.3V DRAMs.

IC DRAM card. The 88-pin IC DRAM card is JEDEC, JEIDA, and PCMCIA standard. Other than multichip modules, it is the most efficient form of packaging DRAM memory. With 4 Meg DRAMs, up to 8MB of memory in either ×16, ×18, ×32, ×36 or ×40 widths is obtainable in a small form factor: 3.37 × 2.13 × 0.13 inches.

The primary demand for these cards comes from laptop and notebook systems. But when the price of TSOPs matches those of the SOJ, the prudent PC designer will convert from modules and mounting to the IC DRAM card for both base and upgrade memory. Many benefits will be realized, such as reduced manufacturing costs, "sealed" systems, secondary upgrade markets and improved delivery response times.

Future features. Many new features will be available in the near future. Some of the more important features may be EDO (extended data out) and SYNC (synchronous) DRAMs. The EDO DRAM is a FAST-PAGE DRAM with the exception that the data Inputs/Outputs (DQ) are not controlled by $\overline{\text{CAS}}$ but rather by $\overline{\text{OE}}$ exclusively.

The key advantage with EDO is a faster PAGE-MODE READ cycle—up to 50 percent faster. Since $\overline{\text{CAS}}$ does not three-state the DQs, ^{t}CAS can be made a minimum and $\overline{\text{CAS}}$ precharge can occur *while* the output data is being latched. EDO is considered as a possible bridge for performance increase until SYNC DRAMs are a reality.

The SYNC DRAM is a radical change from the standard DRAM. Rather than being dependent on time delays, the SYNC DRAM's inputs will all be clocked in on the positive edge of the system clock. The SYNC DRAM is expected to

Figure 11.12 IC DRAM card.

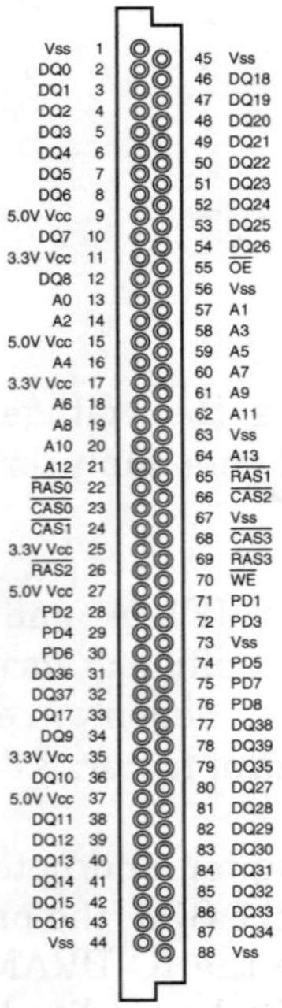

Figure 11.13 33-pin IC DRAM card connector.

provide the speed performance required for 66-, 75-, and 100-MHz systems. Future SYNC DRAM will achieve speeds beyond 100 MHz. The SYNC DRAM will most likely have internal dual banks and burst capabilities for very high speed data rates, as fast as 15 to 10 ns per access.

Summary. The 1 Meg × 4 DRAM is today's best choice for main memory in laptop, notebook and desktop personal computers. Table 11.15 summarizes and compares the issues involved in selecting DRAMs for PC memories.

TABLE 11.15 2-Meg, 16-Bit-Wide Memory

Parameters		1 Meg × 4	256K × 4	512K × 8	256K × 16	Units
Number of devices required		4	16	4	4	Devices
Availability (market volume)		20	160	2	1	Relative to
	Base price	1.0	1.0	1.15[1]	1.2[2]	1 Meg × 4
Costs	Low-power adder	5	5	5	5	% of base
	TSOP adder	10	40	10	10	% of base
Minimum speed (typical)		70	70	80	80	ns @ 5V
BBU ICC[3]	Maximum spec	1.2	4.8	1.6	1.6	mA @ 5V
	Typical	0.6	1.3	1.2	1.2	mA @ 5V
Minimum board space used		6	24	9	13	cm^2
Active ICC[3]	Maximum spec	340	260	200	140	mA @ 5V
	Typical	200	160	170	120	mA @ 5V

NOTES: 1. A parity version (×9) would be 1.3 times a 1 Meg × 4.
2. A parity version (×18) would be 1.35 times a 1 Meg × 4.
3. Parity versions (×9/×18) typically have higher currents, approximately 10 percent more.

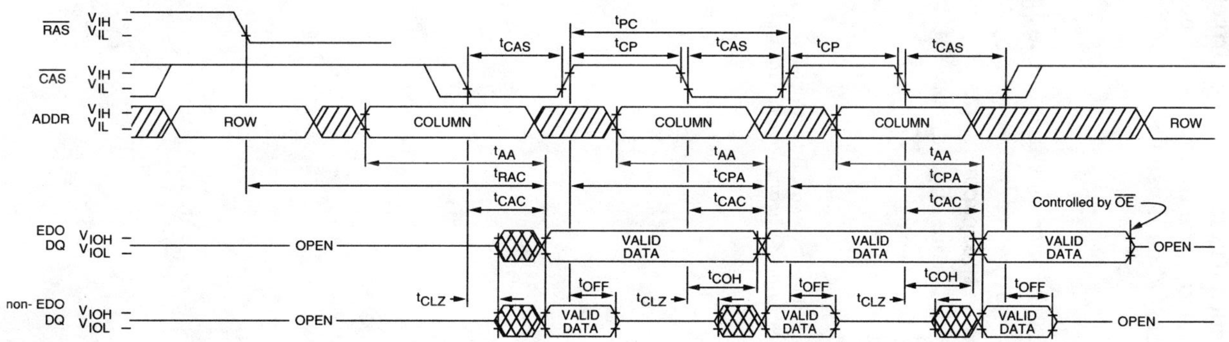

Figure 11.14 EDO versus non-EDO (fast-page mode) DRAMs.

Wider DRAMs are best suited to systems which require shallow and wide arrays. The 256K × 16 is a good choice for high-end video graphics and printer buffers requiring up to 256K deep and 16 or more bits wide. The 512K × 8 is usually a good choice for 8-bit systems requiring more than 256KB but less than 1 Meg of memory, such as high-end disk drives.

Most PC systems do not require the burden of parity when using 1 or 4 Meg DRAMs. High-end systems should use EDAC for the best reliability.

Summary

As you can see, the DRAM controller inside the Intel486 SL is highly versatile. However, you must not get carried away by the flexibility of the DRAM controller. You must assume the responsibility of programming the DRAM interface correctly. If in doubt, you should consult the DRAM manufacturer's data sheet.

References

Intel486 DX Programmer's Reference Manual, Intel Corporation.

Yuen, D., *Intel486 SL Microprocessor Software Writers Guide,* Intel Corporation, 1992.

Chapter

12

PI-Bus Interfacing

The PI bus in the SL CPU is an inexpensive yet high-performance system expansion bus. It is similar to the ISA bus. In fact, the PI bus and the ISA bus share the same address and data signals, making it easy to connect ISA-bus peripherals to the PI bus. The main benefit of the PI bus is that it runs off the CPU clock signal (CPUCLK), so it is much faster than the ISA bus (which is limited to 8 MHz in an SL CPU-based system). The PI bus also eliminates the decoding and synchronization delays associated with the ISA bus. Since the PI bus is a normally not-ready bus, fully interlocking capability (i.e., the cycle is not terminated until the device responds) is provided automatically.

Two candidates for connection to the PI bus are a flash disk and a VGA graphics frame buffer, because they can benefit from the PI bus's faster clock speed. This chapter describes the PI-bus architecture and shows how a flash disk and VGA memory can be interfaced with the PI bus.

PI-Bus Architecture

The PI bus consists of three groups of signals: address, data, and control. Figure 12.1 shows the connection of these signal lines to a PI-bus device. The PI bus and the ISA bus share the address and data signals and one of the control signals. Other control signals are specific to the PI bus.

The address signals are divided into two groups: system address and local address. The system address signals (SA[0..19]) provide 20-bit addressing on the PI bus. The local address signals (LA[17..23]) provide 24-bit addressing on the PI bus. Both groups of address signals are output during PI-bus cycles and float during external bus master cycles.

The system data signals (SD[0..15]) provide a 16-bit data path between the CPU and the peripherals connected to the PI bus. The PI bus and ISA bus share the system bus high-enable (SBHE#) control signal. This active low signal indicates data transfer on the upper byte of the data bus (SD[8:15]). Table 12.1 lists the control signals that are specific to the PI bus.

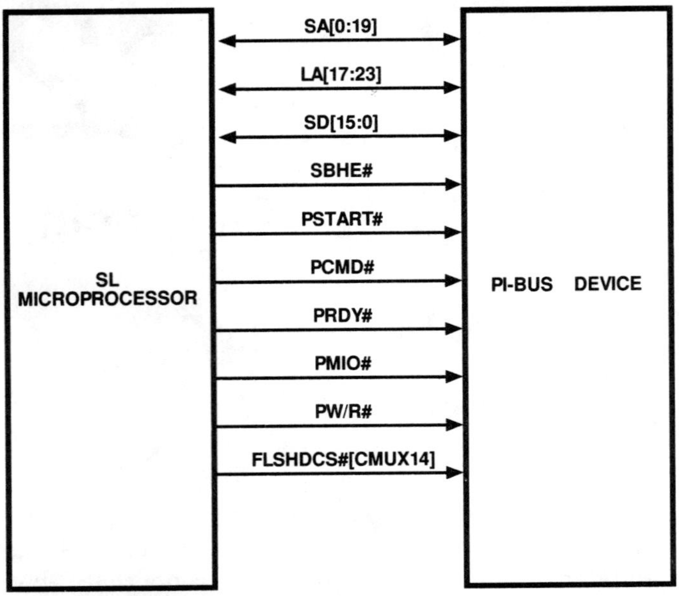

Figure 12.1 PI-bus interface to peripheral devices.

As previously mentioned, the PI bus runs off the CPU clock (CPUCLK), which can be slowed down by software or the turbo pin. Thus, the interface to the PI bus has to be synchronous.

Comparison of the PI bus and the ISA bus

The PI bus and the ISA bus are similar in that they have the same address and data signals. Figure 12.2 shows the typical applications that can be ported

TABLE 12.1 PI-Bus Control Signals

Signal	Description
PSTART#	PI-bus START is an output signal which indicates the start of a PI-bus cycle. The address bus (SA[0:19] and LA[17:23]), command signals (PM/IO# and PW/R#), and chip selects (VGACS# and FLSHDCS#) are valid.
PCMD#	PI-bus ComManD is an output signal which indicates that valid data is on the data bus (SD[0:15]) during a write cycle or that the SL CPU is ready for data during a read. This signal must be used as output enable during PI-bus read cycles. During PI-bus write cycles, the rising edge of this signal can be used to latch data in external devices.
PRDY#	PI-bus ReaDY is an input to the SL processor to terminate a PI-bus cycle. The PI bus is normally not ready and a bus cycle will continue until PRDY# is asserted low. PRDY# must be asserted until the rising edge of PCMD# to guarantee recognition and cycle termination. If PRDY# activation is not recognized within a programmed time interval, a time-out counter will terminate the cycle.
PM/IO#	PI-bus Memory or I/O is an output to indicate the type of cycle currently executing on the PI bus. A memory cycle is indicated by PM/IO# high, while an I/O cycle is indicated by PM/IO# low.
PW/R#	PI-bus Write or Read is an output which indicates the type of access currently executing on the PI bus. A high indicates a write access and a low indicates a read access.

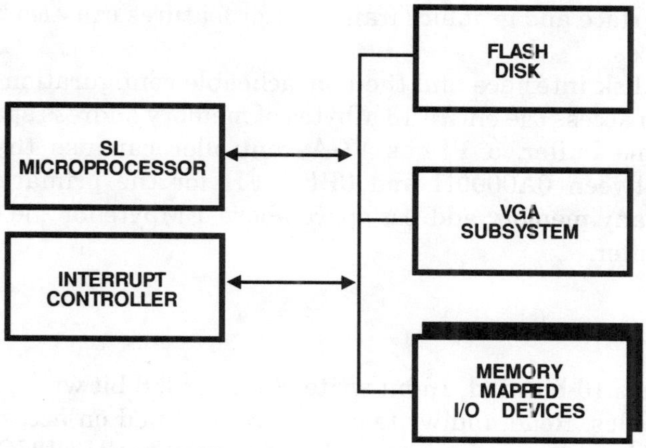

Figure 12.2 Typical applications of PI bus.

from ISA bus to PI bus. The major difference between the two buses is in the way bus cycles are decoded.

The PI bus uses a simpler cycle-decoding mechanism than the ISA bus, which requires only two signals, PM/IO# and PW/R#. These signals are equivalent to the SMEMW, MEMW, SMEMR, MEMR, IOR, and IOW signals on the ISA bus. The PSTART# signal of the PI bus is similar to the BALE signal on the ISA bus, which functions as an address latch. Unlike BALE, PSTART# occurs in every PI-bus cycle. Table 12.2 summarizes the differences between the PI-bus and ISA-bus cycle control signals and commands.

Another difference between the PI bus and the ISA bus is that the PI bus is a normally not-ready bus. A PI-bus cycle is not terminated until the PRDY# signal is asserted by the device, whereas, with an ISA-bus cycle, the IOCHRDY normally indicates ready. The shortest PI-bus cycle requires at least one wait state, which completes in three CPU clocks.

PI-bus address space

Because the PI bus shares the same memory and address bus with the ISA bus, the PI bus can access up to 16 Mbytes of memory address space and 64 Kbytes of I/O address space. In addition, a unique I/O address space from 900H-9FFH is also available for PI-bus devices. Three different mapping mechanisms control the PI-bus address space: flash disk interface, graphics frame buffer, and noncacheable configuration registers. Despite their names,

TABLE 12.2 Comparison of PI-Bus and ISA-Bus Cycle Control Signals

Signal type	PI-bus	ISA-bus
Cycle type	PM/IO#	SMEMW, MEMW, SMEMR, MEMR,
Cycle type	PW/R#	IOW, IOR
Address latch	PSTART#	BALE
Data enable	PCMD#	Commands
Wait state generation	PRDY#	IOCHRDY

the flash disk interface and graphics frame buffer features can also be used by other PI-bus devices.

With the flash disk interface and the noncacheable configuration registers, PI-bus devices can access the entire 16 Mbytes of memory address space. Using the graphics frame buffer, a PI-bus VGA controller can use the memory address space between 0A0000H and 0BFFFFH for the primary graphics frame buffer and any memory address space above 1 Mbyte for the secondary graphics frame buffer.

PI-bus operation

The PI bus supports 16-bit read, 16-bit write, 8-bit read, 8-bit write, and external bus master cycles. Read and write cycles are modified on accesses to odd addresses. The PI-bus signals are internally referenced to the CPUCLK. Since CPUCLK can be slowed down to reduce power consumption, PI-bus timing is asynchronous.

As shown in Fig. 12.3, a PI-bus cycle is initiated by asserting the PM/IO#, PW/R#, VGACS# (for VGA access), and FLSHCS# (for flash disk) signals. These signals remain active until the access is complete. The PSTART# is then asserted indicating that the address on the bus is valid and the states of the PM/IO# and PW/R# signals are valid. The bus owner then deasserts the PSTART# signal and asserts the PCMD# signal. The PCMD# signal remains active until PRDY# signal is sampled low (active).

For a write cycle, data driven onto the data bus by the bus owner remains valid until the PCMD# signal is inactive (rising edge of PCMD#). For a read cycle, the bus owner latches data from the data bus when PRDY# signal is active (low) and deasserts the PCMD# signal.

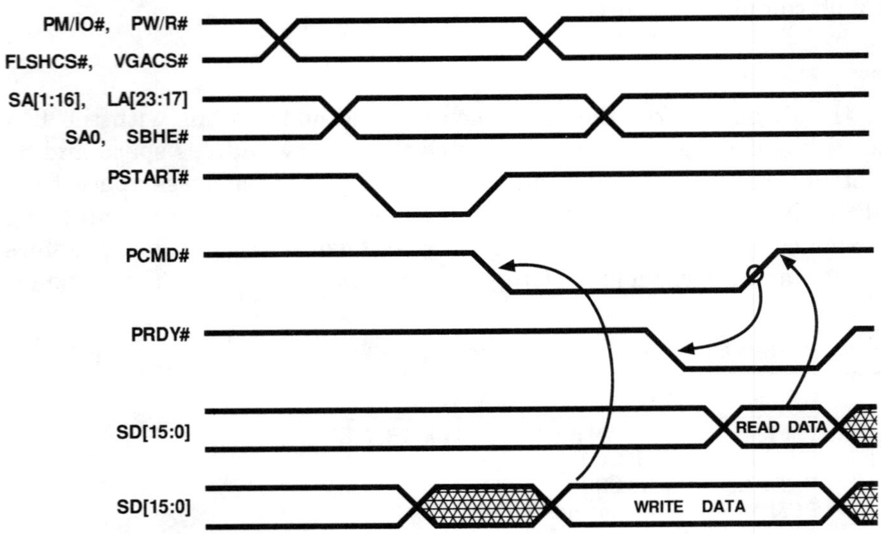

Figure 12.3 PI-bus cycle operations.

16-bit access to an 8-bit device

The SL CPU can execute either 8-bit or 16-bit PI-bus cycles. When accessing an 8-bit device, hardware in the CPU automatically swaps high bytes and low bytes. Table 12.3 summarizes this byte-swapping mechanism. In this table, *b* indicates a byte transfer and *w* indicates a word transfer. *l, m, h,* and *x* indicate low order, middle order, high order, and don't care, respectively.

PI-bus cycle termination

A PI-bus cycle is terminated either by asserting the PRDY# signal or by the expiration of the PI-bus watchdog timer. The watchdog timer runs off the CPU-CLK for bus cycles initiated by the CPU and off the SYSCLK for external bus master cycles. When the timer expires, it causes the current PI-bus cycle to terminate automatically, optionally generating an NMI.

The timer count for time-out is dependent on the number of wait states. The minimum number of timer counts required can be calculated using the formula below:

minimum number of CPU clocks to complete the memory or I/O access
+ the number of wait states added

The timer count for the watchdog timer is stored in the EBC2CR register (700H, EBU) in the Intel386 SL processor. Bits [0-13] of the EBC2CR register are used in setting up the timer count for the watchdog timer. Thus, the maximum time-out period is 2^{13}. For the Intel486 SL processor, the timer count is stored in the IBCTOUT register (708H, IBU). Bits [5-13] of the IBCTOUT register are used for programming the timer count. When the watchdog timer in the Intel486 SL CPU expires, it terminates the ISA-bus as well as PI-bus cycles.

The NMI option is enabled by setting the watchdog timer NMI enable bit (bit 15) of the EBC2CR register or the IBCTOUT register. A "1" in the watchdog timer NMI flag bit (bit 14) of the EBC2CR then causes an NMI to be generated upon expiration of the watchdog timer.

Bus master and DMA operation

A bus master cycle is initiated when a bus master addresses a section of memory-mapped I/O space that has been assigned to the PI bus. When a

TABLE 12.3 Byte-Swapping Mechanism When Accessing an 8-Bit Device

		Byte length of logical operand								
		1	2				4			
Physical byte address (low order bits)		xx	00	01	10	11	00	01	10	11
	1	b	w	lb	w	hb	lw	hb	hw	mw
Transfer cycle	2			hb		lb	hw	lb	lb	hb
	3							mw		lb

b—byte, w—word, lb—lower byte, hb—higher byte, lw—lower word, hw—higher word, mw—middle word bus master has control of the PI bus, all cycle timing is based on the SYSCLK.

During a bus master cycle, the bus master drives the PI-bus address and data lines. The SL CPU translates the MEMR# and MEMW# signals on the ISA bus into PW/R# and PM/IO# signals on the PI bus. The CPU drives IOCHRDY on the ISA bus as an inversion of the PRDY# signal on the PI bus.

DMA transfers can occur between 8-bit I/O and PI-bus memory, but DMA transfers on the PI bus between on-board memory and VGA palette memory are not supported.

Advanced decoding of ISA-bus cycles

As shown in Table 12.4, the PI bus can be used for advanced decoding of the next ISA-bus cycle. On the falling edge of BALE, PM/IO# and PW/R# can be sampled to determine the type of ISA-bus cycle that is about to occur. This information can be used to generate early ISA-bus control signals. During HALT and shutdown, the PM/IO# and PW/R# signals are held at logic-high level.

PI-Bus Applications

As described earlier in this chapter, two applications of the PI-bus are as an interface to a flash disk and as an interface to a VGA graphics frame buffer. To support these applications, the SL CPU provides enabling pins for these functions (FLSHCS# and VGACS#). These pins are not reserved for flash disk and VGA applications. They can be used by other devices connected to the PI-bus.

Flash disk interface

The SL CPU provides special hardware support to allow a flash disk device to take advantage of the PI-bus. The flash disk interface is enabled by setting the flash disk enable bit (bit 7) of the CPUPWRMODE register (22H). After the flash disk interface is enabled, any I/O accesses in the range of 900H-9FFH are directed to PI-bus. Therefore, I/O accesses to the PI-bus will not interfere with ISA-bus activity.

Memory on the flash disk is accessed through the 64-Kbyte ISA-sliding window. The ISA-sliding window is normally used for accessing extended memory above 1 Mbyte on the ISA bus. Enabling the flash disk interface overrides the ISA-sliding window. Memory accesses to memory address space 0D0000H-0DFFFFH are remapped according to the setting in the ISA-sliding window register (0B00H, EBU). FLASH DISK enable overrides ISA-sliding window.

TABLE 12.4 Decoding ISA-Bus Cycles with PI-Bus Signals

Type of ISA-bus cycle	PM/IO#	PW/R#
Memory read	1	0
Memory write	1	1
I/O read	0	0
I/O write	0	1

Figure 12.4 shows an example of how to design a simple flash disk interface using the PI bus. The access to the flash disk is controlled by four signals: FLSHCS#, PCMD#, PM/IO#, and PW/R#. The read and write commands to the flash disk are generated by decoding the PCMD#, PM/IO#, and PW/R# signals. (See PAL equation below.) The chip select to the flash disk (FLSHCS#) is controlled by a pin on the SL CPU. To minimize glue logic, the PI-bus watchdog timer can be used to terminate a flash disk access cycle. Listing 12.1 shows the steps for initializing and accessing the flash disk interface.

PAL equation for flash disk interface

```
; PINS 1 2 3 4 5 6 7 8 9 10
  /PCMD PWR NC NC NC NC NC NC GND
; PINS 11 12 13 14 15 16 17 18 19 20
  NC /WE /OE NC NC NC NC VCC
EQUATIONS
  /WE = /PCMD * PWR
  /OE = PCMD * /PWR
```

Listing 12.1 Code for Initializing and Accessing a Flash Disk through the PI Bus

```
;-------------------------------------------------------------
;
;  FLASH.ASM: Example on how to enable FLASH disk interface
;
;-------------------------------------------------------------
include superset.inc
;
;-------------- INITIALIZATION -----------------------------------
code  SEGMENT
ASSUME cs:code, ds:code, es:code, ss:code
;
  ORG  100H
EXTRN open_ebu:near, open_ibu:near, close_386sl:near
start:
;
; setup PI-bus watchdog timer
;
  cli
  call    open_ibu
  mov     dx, EBC2CR
  mov     ax, 000FH
  out     dx, ax
  call    close_386SL
; setup Flash disk interface
  call    open_ebu
  mov     dx, ISAWINDOW
  mov     ax, 8040H          ; enable ISA window, set starting address
  out     dx, ax             ; to 4 MB
  call    close_386SL
; enable Flash disk interface
  call    open_cpupwrmode
```

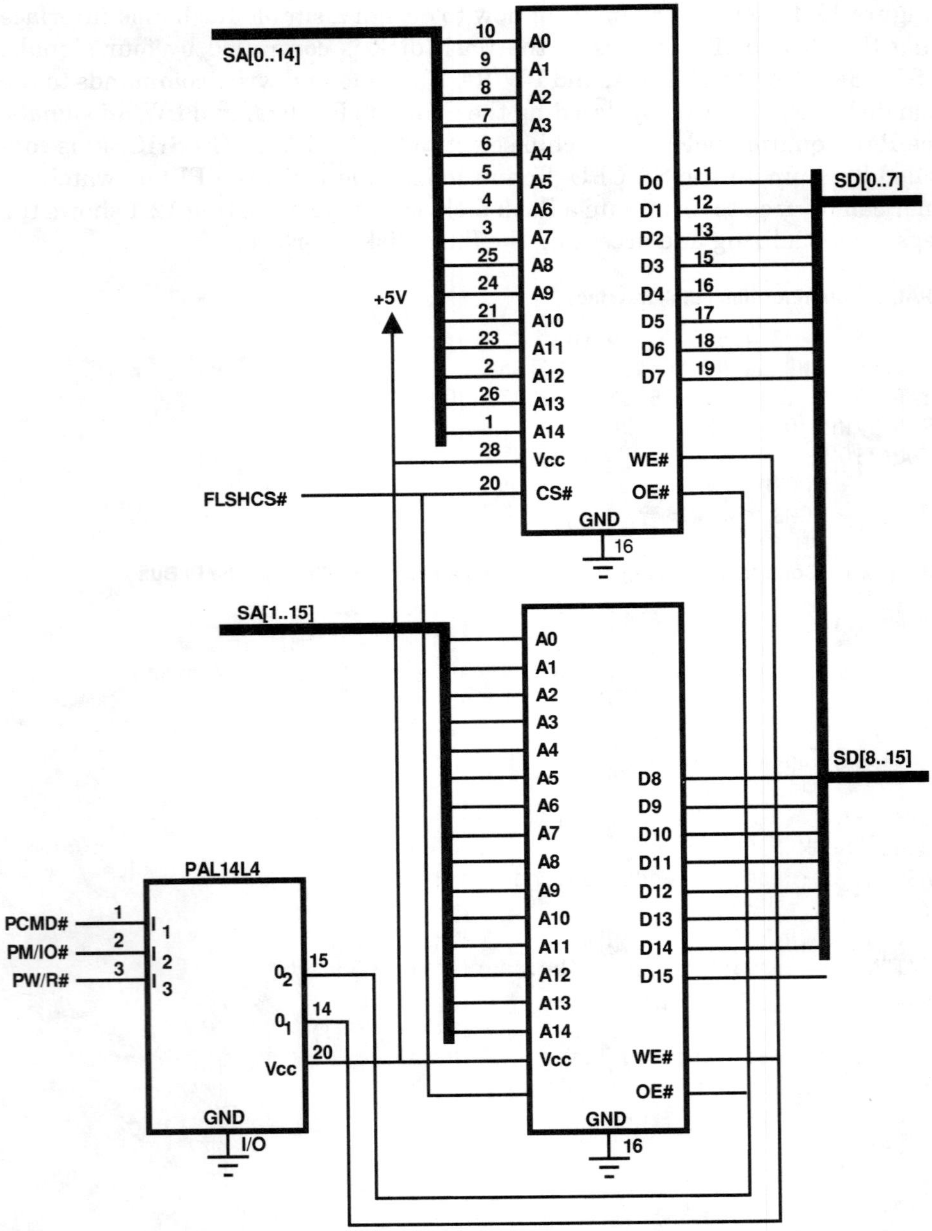

Figure 12.4 Flash disk interface to the PI bus.

```
    mov     dx, CPUPWRMODE
    in      ax, dx
    or      ax, 0008H           ; set flash disk enable bit
    out     dx, ax
    call    close_cpupwrmode
    move memory from B000 segment to A0000 segment
    push    ds
    push    es
    push    si
    push    di
    push    cx
    mov     ax, 0B800H
    mov     ds, ax
    mov     ax, 0D000H
    mov     es, ax
    xor     ax, ax
    mov     si, ax
    mov     di, ax
    mov     cx, 07FFFH
    rep     movsw
    pop     cx
    pop     di
    pop     si
    pop     es
    pop     ds
    sti
    mov     ax, 4C00H           ; termirate program
    int     21H
  code      ENDS                ; end code segment
            END                 entry
```

VGA graphics frame buffer

In a graphics-intensive environment such as Microsoft Windows, the performance of the graphics hardware is an important factor in the overall performance of the system. To help improve VGA performance in an SL CPU-based system, the SL CPU provides several hardware facilities to allow VGA graphics hardware to access a VGA graphics frame buffer through the PI bus, thus taking advantage of the PI bus's high data transfer rate.

The PI bus supports a 128-Kbyte (0A0000H-0BFFFFH) primary graphics frame buffer and a very large secondary graphics frame buffer. The GAACR register (311, IBU) assigns 16-Kbyte blocks of memory in the primary frame buffer to the ISA bus or PI bus.

The GABCR register (312H, IBU) defines a secondary graphics frame buffer. The size of the secondary graphics frame buffer is determined by the block size field (bits [6-7]) and the large block bit (bit 10) of the GABCR register. Table 12.5 shows the encoding of these size bits for the secondary graphics frame buffer.

The starting address of the secondary graphics frame buffer is programmed by the starting address field (bits [0-10]) in the GABCR register. The starting

TABLE 12.5 Size of Secondary Graphics Frame Buffer Set by Bits in Register GABCR

Bit 7	Bit 6	Bit 10	Buffer size
0	0	0	128 Kbytes
0	1	0	256 Kbytes
1	0	0	512 Kbytes
1	1	0	1 Mbyte
0	0	1	1 Mbyte
0	1	1	2 Mbytes
1	0	1	4 Mbytes
1	1	1	8 Mbytes

address must be aligned on a 1-, 2-, 4-, or 8-Mbyte boundary. When bit 8 of the GABCR register is zero, all cycles to the secondary graphics frame buffer are directed to the PI bus. If bit 15 of the GABCR register is zero, all I/O accesses to the VGA controller can be directed to the PI bus. Listing 12.2 shows how to enable PI-bus access to a VGA graphics frame buffer.

Listing 12.2 Code to Enable Access to VGA Graphics Frame Buffer through PI Bus

```
;-------------------------------------------------------------
;
;  PIBUS.ASM: Example on how to enable PI-bus access to the
;         graphics frame buffer
;
;
;------------------------------------------------------------
include superset.inc
;
;-------------- INITIALIZATION ------------------------------------
code  SEGMENT
ASSUME cs:code, ds:code, es:code, ss:code
;
  ORG  100H
EXTRN open_ebu:near, open_ibu:near, close_386sl:near
start:
;
; setup PI-bus watchdog timer
;
  cli
  call    open_ebu        ; enable watchdog timer to
  mov     dx, EBC2CR
  mov     ax, 000FH       ; terminate PI-bus cycle
  out     dx, ax
  call    close_386SL
; setup graphics frame buffer address
  call    open_ibu
  mov     dx, GAACR
  mov     al, 0FH         ; direct accesses to A000 segment to PI-bus
  out     dx, al
```

```
      call     close_386SL
    ; mov memory from B000 segment to A0000 segment
      push     ds
      push     es
      push     si
      push     di
      push     cx
      mov      ax, 0B800H
      mov      ds, ax
      mov      ax, 0A000H
      mov      es, ax
      xor      ax, ax
      mov      si, ax
      mov      di, ax
      mov      cx, 07FFFH
      rep      movsw
      pop      cx
      pop      di
      pop      si
      pop      es
      pop      ds
      sti
      mov      ax, 4C00H          ; terminate program
      int      21H
    code       ENDS               ; end code segment
               END  entry
```

Memory mapped I/O

The PI bus can also be used to access memory mapped I/O devices. The SL CPU provides four 16-bit noncacheable configuration registers (NC[D:G]CR) for use by memory mapped I/O devices on the PI bus. The four registers are identical, and each register is comprised of four programmable fields:

- Bits [0-9] store the starting address (address bits SA[15-24]) of the memory mapped I/O device.
- Bits [10-11] control the size of the block, which can be either 4, 8, 16, or 32 Kbytes.
- Bit 12 specifies which bus the memory mapped I/O device is on and must be zero for PI-bus device.
- Bit 13 enables the memory mapped I/O window when it is set to one.

Design Guidelines

The following design guidelines give additional information you should be aware of when you design a system that uses the PI-bus interface.

- PI-bus ready (PRDY) signal is floating and should not be left floating.

- During HALT and shutdown conditions, PM/IO# and PW/R# are held at a high logic level.
- PI bus and ISA bus are mutually exclusive.
- On the falling edge of the BALE signal, the PM/IO# and PM/R# signals are sampled to determine the type of ISA-bus cycle that is about to occur. These signals are not included in the timing specification.
- If the device is not fast enough to respond with valid data before the valid address, data latch is required for PI-bus interface.

As the CPU clock speed continues to double every year, the performance gap between the CPU and the I/O devices has increased. Running slow I/O devices with a high-performance CPU is a waste of CPU time. One way to improve the speed of the I/O devices is to have a faster bus.

Over the years, many new bus standards were invented to boost the speed of I/O devices. But they all suffered the same problem—incompatibility with the ISA bus. Given the large number of ISA-bus I/O devices in the market today, it will be a big loss of investment for users to switch over to a new bus standard.

The PI bus runs at the same speed as the CPU clock, and it shares the same address and data bus with the ISA bus. Therefore, PI-bus peripherals can operate in step with the CPU and coexist with ISA-bus peripherals without any conflict. Existing ISA-bus devices can be easily modified to take advantage of the high-performance of the PI bus. The discussion in this chapter serves as the foundation for designing PI-bus peripherals that take full advantage of the CPU's performance.

Summary

As the CPU clock speed continues to double every year, the performance gap between the CPU and the I/O devices has increased. Running slow I/O devices with a high-performance CPU is a waste of CPU time. One way to improve the speed of the I/O devices is to have a faster bus.

Over the years, many new bus standards were invented to boost the speed of I/O devices. But they all suffered the same problem—incompatibility with the ISA bus. Given the large number of ISA-bus I/O devices in the market today, it will be a big loss of investment for users to switch over to a new bus standard.

The PI bus runs at the same speed as the CPU clock, and it shares the same address and data bus with the ISA bus. Therefore, PI-bus peripherals can operate in step with the CPU and coexist with ISA-bus peripherals without any conflict. Existing ISA-bus devices can be easily modified to take advantage of the high performance of the PI bus. The discussion in this chapter serves as the foundation for designing PI-bus peripherals that take full advantage of the CPU's performance.

References

Ed Garcia, "Using the Intel386 SL Microprocessor PI-Bus with the CL-GD6410," Cirrus Logic, Inc., 1991.

Chapter

13

Enhanced Parallel Port

With more people today choosing notebook computers as their primary computer, users are demanding many of the same features found on the desktop computers for their notebooks. However, due to the compact nature of notebook computers, their expansion capability is limited. One way to expand a notebook computer is to connect expansion devices to the parallel port.

Virtually every notebook computer has a built-in parallel port. However, the standard ISA parallel port is slow and cannot support multiple devices. The new enhanced parallel port on the SL CPU provides a high-performance parallel port that can support multiple external devices.*

Applications of the Enhanced Parallel Port

The 82360SL parallel port interface can be programmed to support a standard ISA unidirectional parallel port, a PS/2-compatible bidirectional parallel port, or an enhanced parallel port. Because configuration of the interface is programmable, the interface can be changed automatically to accommodate several devices connected to the same parallel port connector.

The interface to the enhanced parallel port (shown in Fig. 13.1) is extremely simple. Only five control signals are required. Devices such as network cards, hard drives, and tape backup drives are ideal candidates for enhanced parallel port. Using the enhanced parallel port, the Xircom adapters achieved a tenfold increase in performance.

The fact that the parallel port is external to the machine makes it very easy for the users to hook up peripherals to the system. There are already many devices available that connect to the parallel port. These devices often run slowly only because the transfer rate of the standard ISA parallel port is slow. The high-speed capability of the enhanced parallel port will make the parallel port an even more attractive option for I/O expansion.

---

* This fast parallel port was implemented based on the enhanced parallel port specification jointly developed by Dirk Gates and Ken Kiba of Xircon and Clark Buxton and Robert Kohtz of Zenith Data Systems.

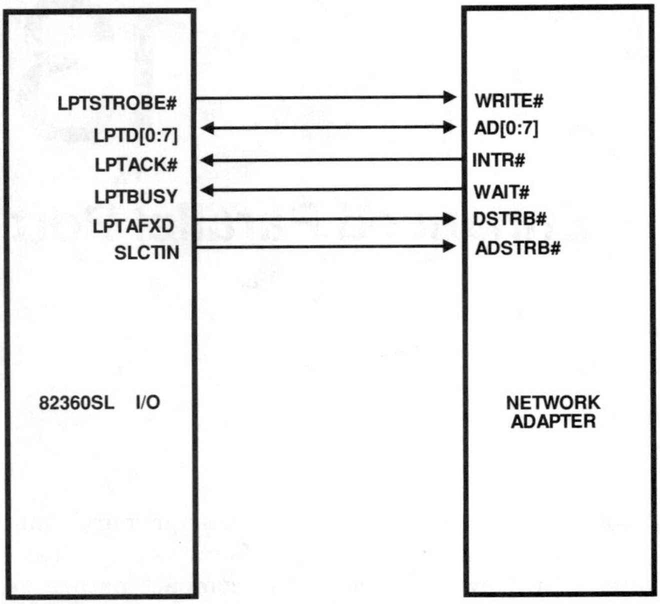

Figure 13.1 Control signals for the 82360SL Enhanced Parallel Port.

Comparison of the ISA Parallel Port and the Enhanced Parallel Port

The enhanced parallel port interface improves performance over that of the ISA parallel port by making data strobe generation automatic and by replacing open collector drivers with faster CMOS drivers. Table 13.1 summarizes these enhancements. While the standard ISA parallel port can transfer data at a maximum rate of 150 Kbytes/sec, the enhanced parallel port as implemented on the 82360SL provides data throughput of up to 2 Mbytes/s.

The enhanced parallel port employs the same 25-pin D-Type connector as does the ISA parallel port. After power up, the parallel port on the 82360SL functions like a standard ISA parallel port. When the enhanced parallel port is enabled (as described later in this chapter), five of the control pins (pins 1, 10, 11, 14, and 17) are given alternative functions. Table 13.2 shows the differences in pinout between the standard ISA-compatible parallel port and the enhanced parallel port.

TABLE 13.1 Differences Between ISA Parallel Port and Enhanced Parallel Port

Features	ISA parallel port	Enhanced parallel port
Data strobe generation	By software	Automatic
Data strobe control	By software loop	Not required
Data type	8-bit	8-bit
Driver type	Open collector	CMOS

TABLE 13.2 Pinout of a 25-pin 'D'-Type Connector

Pin	ISA parallel port	Enhanced parallel port
1	LPTSTROBE#	WRITE#
2	LPTD0	LPTD0
3	LPTD1	LPTD1
4	LPTD2	LPTD2
5	LPTD3	LPTD3
6	LPTD4	LPTD4
7	LPTD5	LPTD5
8	LPTD6	LPTD6
9	LPTD7	LPTD7
10	LPTACK#	INTR#
11	LPTBUSY	WAIT#
12	PE#	PE#
13	SLCT#	SLCT#
14	LPTAFDXT#	DSTRB#
15	ERROR	ERROR
16	INIT	INIT
17	SLCTIN	ADSTRB#
18	GND	GND
19	GND	GND
20	GND	GND
21	GND	GND
22	GND	GND
23	GND	GND
24	GND	GND
25	GND	GND

Hardware Interface

The enhanced parallel port uses the same standard 25-pin D-shell connector as is commonly used for ISA parallel port implementation. Figure 13.2 shows the enhanced parallel port signal assignments for the parallel port connector. All the interface logic is embedded inside the 82360SL. Thus, no external interface circuitry is required to use the enhanced parallel port feature. A WAIT# line is provided for asynchronous devices that may require more time to react to I/O

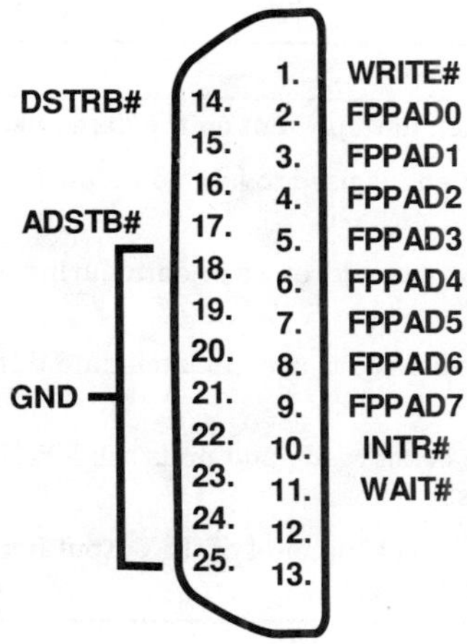

Figure 13.2 Pinout of the connector when Enhanced Parallel Port is enabled.

requests. This line pulls IOCHRDY on the ISA-bus inactive, causing the system to add wait states.

Signal descriptions

Table 13.3 describes signals on the enhanced parallel port. Care should be taken not to assert the WAIT# pin for too long, as it will prevent memory on the ISA bus from being refreshed. The INTR# pin is the same as the ACK# pin in standard ISA parallel port. A device can use the INTR# signal to request service from the host. IRQ5 or IRQ7 can be used to generate interrupt requests to the host system. The signals that are not used by the enhanced parallel port are still available when enhanced parallel port is enabled and can be used the same way as in standard ISA mode.

Read and write cycles

During a write cycle, data is transferred from the 82360SL to the device attached to the parallel port. During a read cycle, data or address is transferred from the device on the parallel port to the 82360SL. Figure 13.3 shows the bus cycle for data read. Figure 13.4 shows the bus cycle for address read.

There are two kinds of write cycles: address write and data write. Figure 13.4 shows the bus cycle for data write. Figure 13.5 shows the bus cycle for address write. An address write cycle is started by writing to the auto address strobe port on the enhanced parallel port. When the address port on the enhanced parallel port is written to, the ADSTRB# signal and WRITE# signals are asserted and the address is driven onto LPTD address and data lines. The cycle is terminated after four SYSCLKs (500 ns) if the WAIT# signal is not asserted by the external device. When the WAIT# signal is asserted, the IOCHRDY signal is pulled down to extend the I/O cycle.

TABLE 13.3 Description of the Enhanced Parallel Port Signals

Symbol	Name and function
WRITE#	WRITE is an output that signals the device to latch data present on the data bus.
DSTRB#	Data STRoBe indicates that valid data is present and is used to latch data during write cycles or enable buffers during read cycles.
LPTD[0..7]	Enhanced Parallel Port Address and Data bus outputs addresses or data during write cycles and inputs addresses or data during read cycles.
ADSTRB#	Address STRoBe indicates a valid address is present and is used to latch data during write cycles or to enable buffers during read cycles.
WAIT#	WAIT is an input which indicates that the device is not ready and pulls the IOCHRDY signal inactive on the ISA bus to lengthen I/O cycles.
INTR#	INTerrupt Request is a maskable input (enabled by setting bit 4 of the output handshake register X7AH) to generate interrupt requests on the ISA bus.

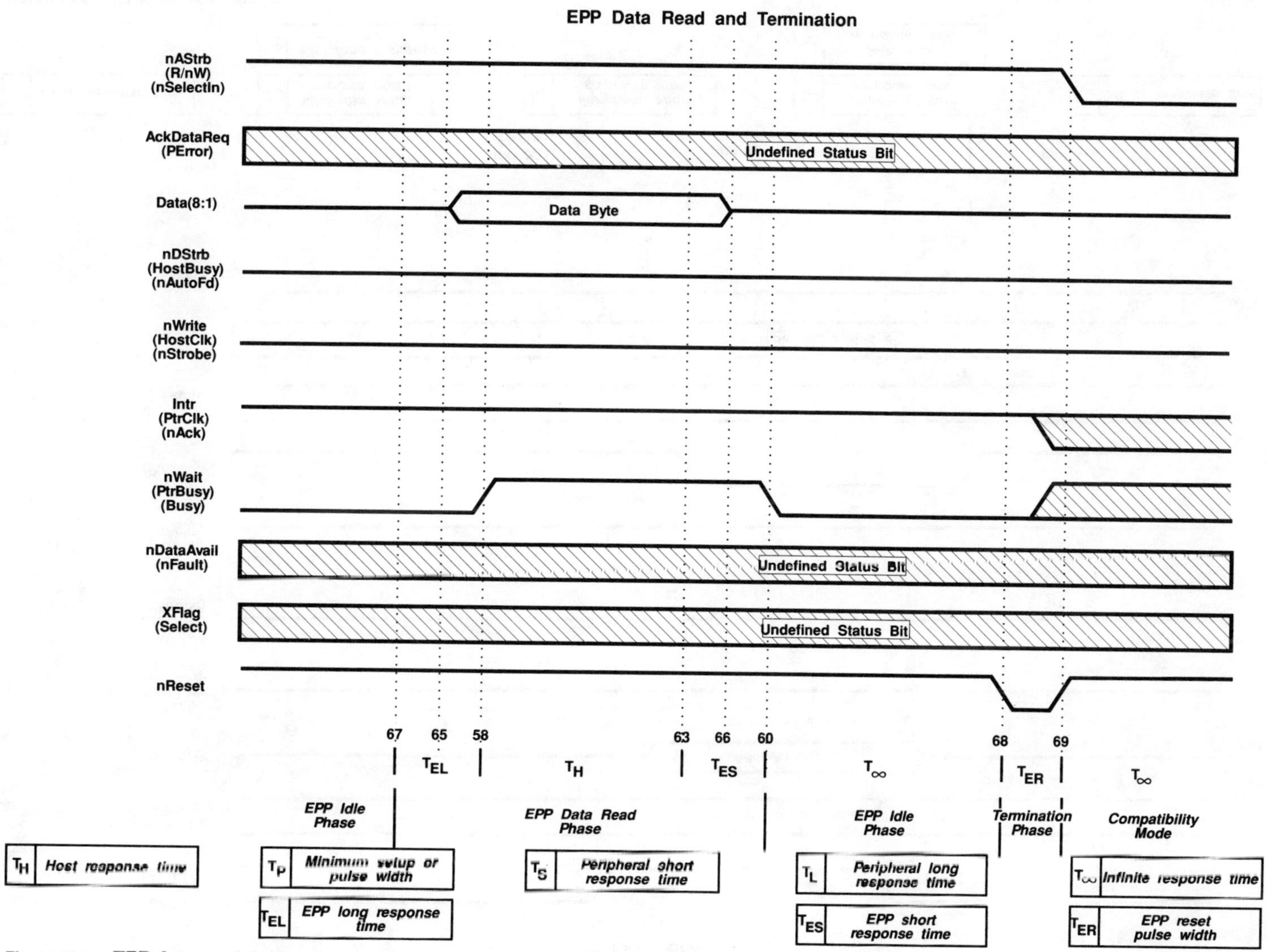

Figure 13.3 EPP data read cycle.

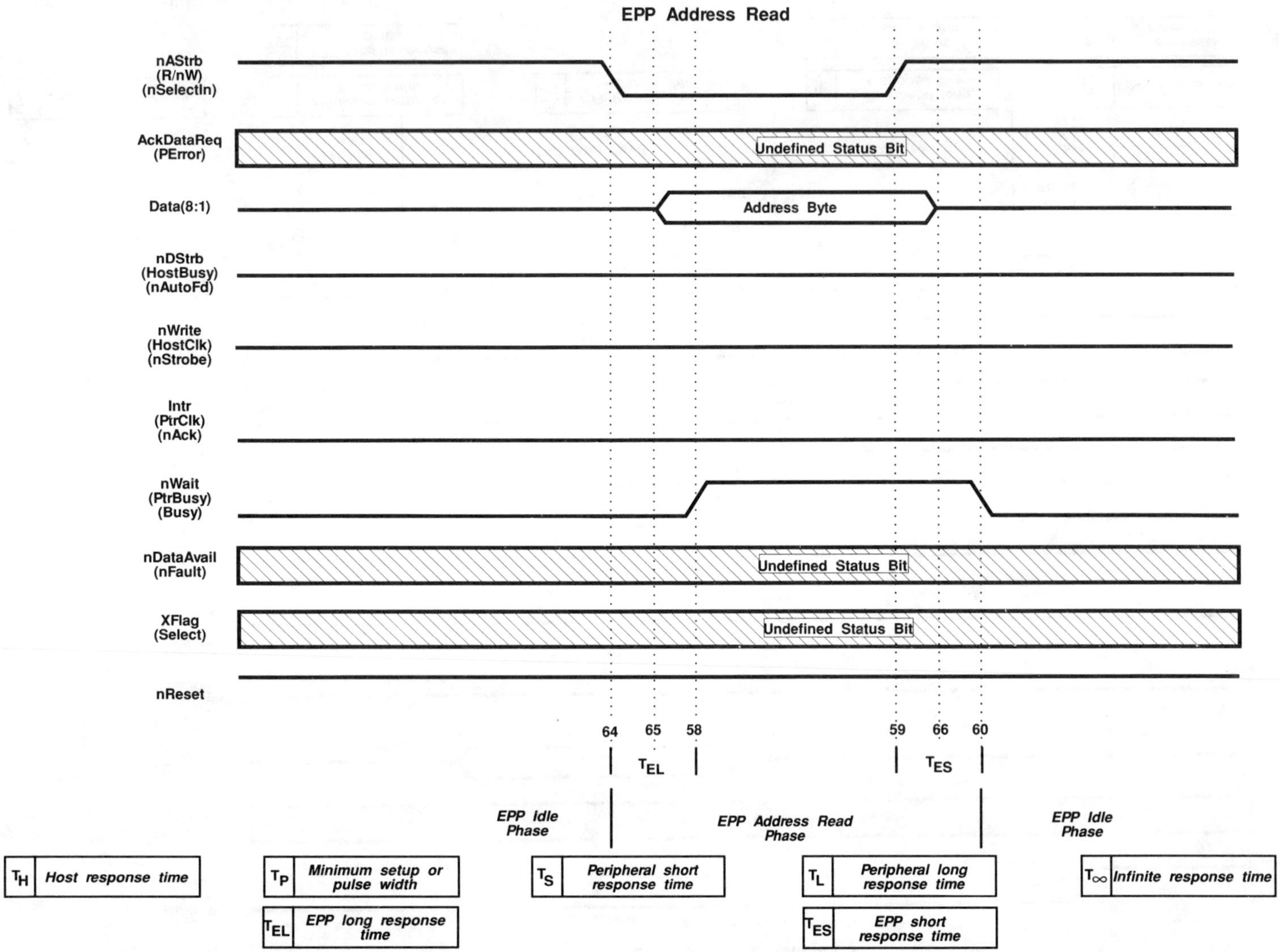

Figure 13.4 EPP address read cycle.

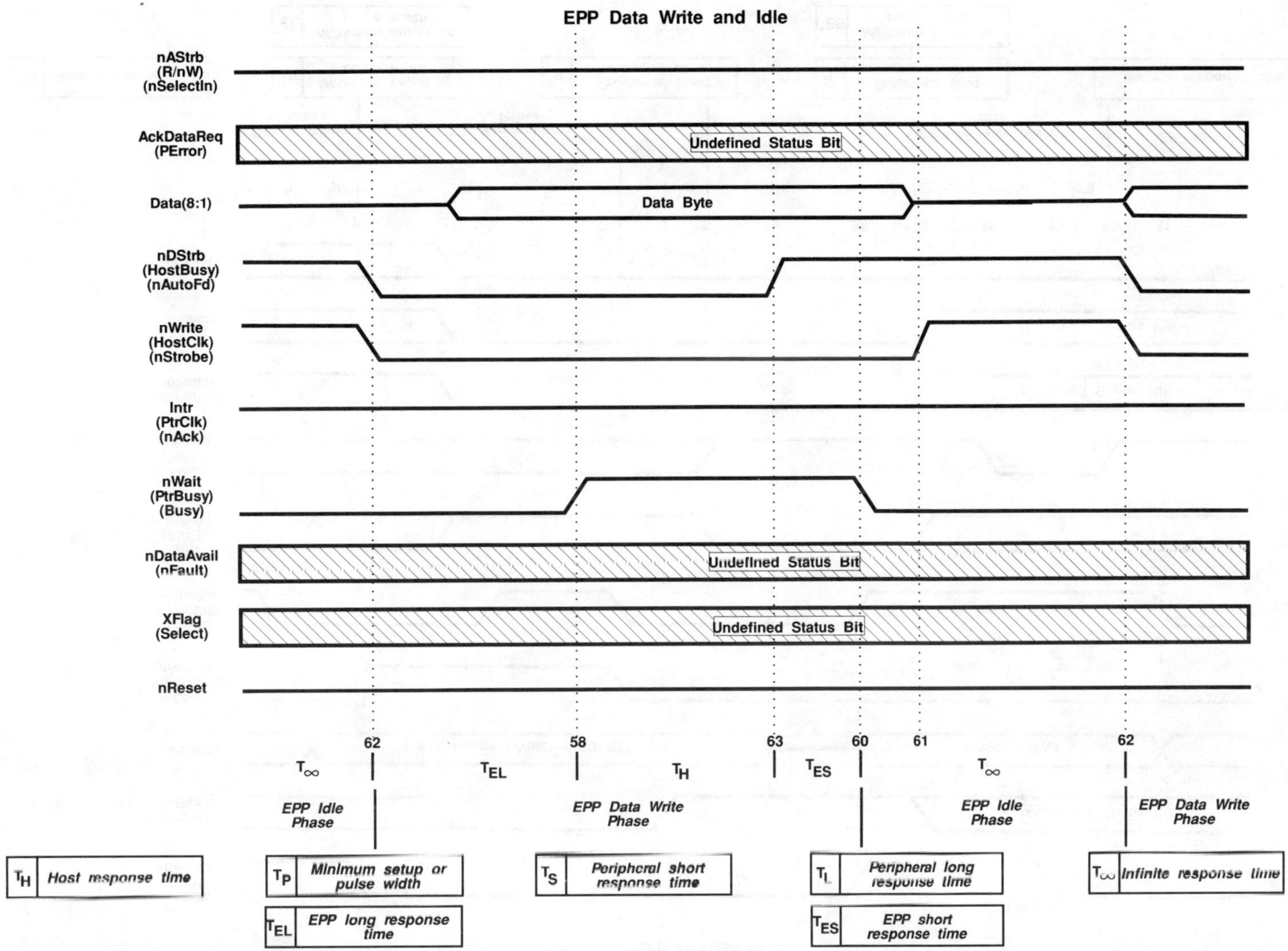

Figure 13.5 EPP data write cycle.

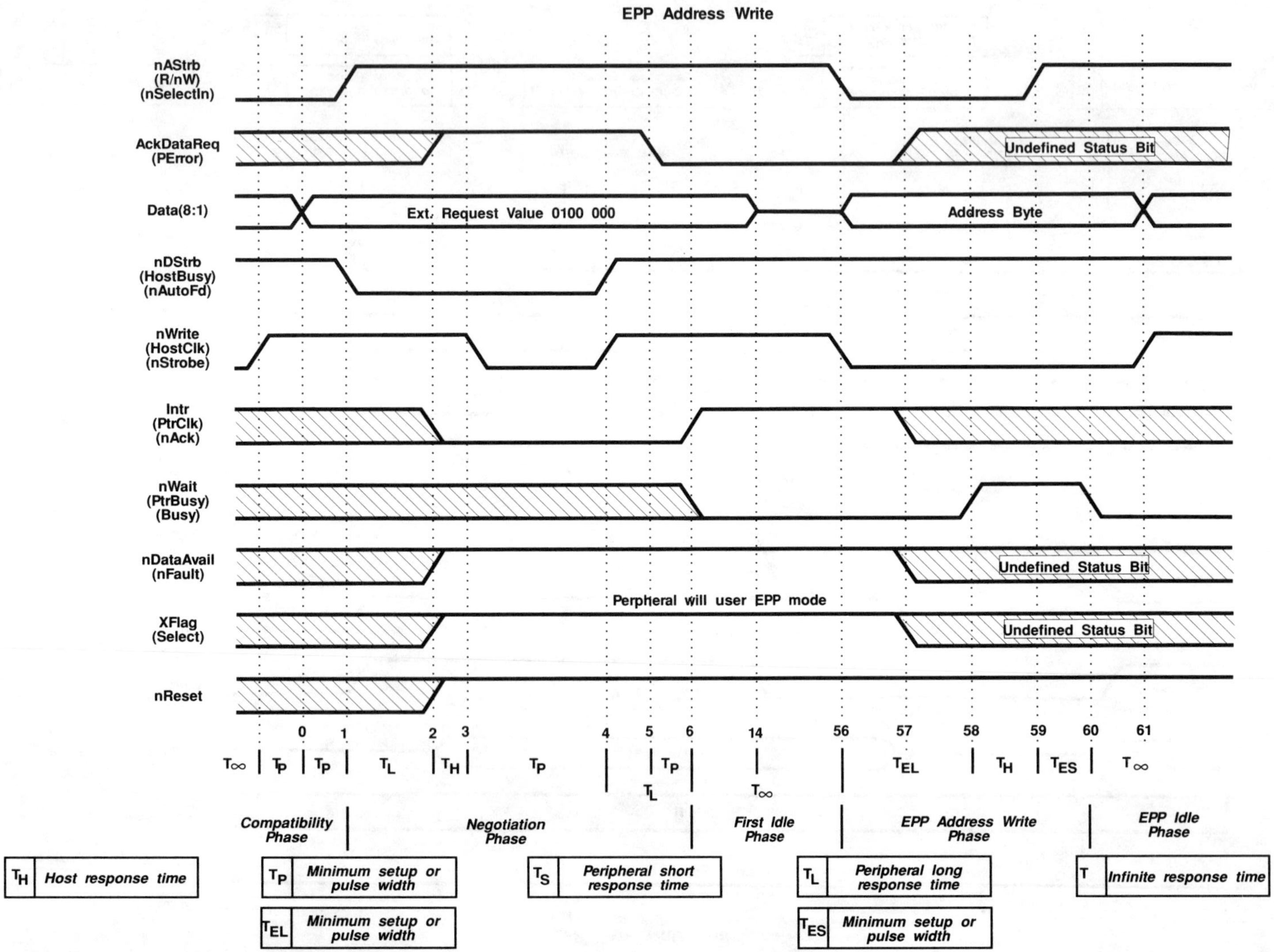

Figure 13.6 EPP address write cycle.

A data write cycle is initiated by writing to one of the four auto data strobe ports. When the data port is written to, the DSTRB# and WRITE# signals are asserted and the data is driven onto the LPTD lines. Like the address write cycle, the cycle is terminated in four SYSCLKs if the device does not assert the WAIT# signal to extend the I/O cycle.

When one of the data ports on the enhanced parallel port is read, a read cycle is started and the DSTRB# signal is asserted. When the external device recognizes that the DSTRB# signal is active and WRITE# signal is inactive, it must then place the data on the data bus. The 82360SL will latch the data from the LPTD lines after four SYSCLKs if the WAIT# signal is not active. The external device can extend the I/O cycle by asserting the WAIT# signal.

Design guidelines

- The control signals for the enhanced parallel port are CMOS drivers, but they are TTL-level-compatible.
- The address strobe signal is for generating a device ID or a user definable command.
- The INTR# pin is used by an external device to request service from the host. The INTR# input is connected to either IRQ 5 or 7 (programmable) on the ISA bus.
- Unlike the LPTBUSY pin in standard ISA parallel port, the WAIT# pin is active low. The WAIT# input is connected to the IOCHRDY signal on the ISA bus to generate wait state.

Software Interface

Software uses the following registers in the 82360SL to enable, initialize, and perform writes and reads with the enhanced parallel port:

- FPP_CNTL—enhanced parallel port configuration register
- SFS_ENABLE—special feature set enable register
- SFR—special feature register
- CFGR2—system configuration register 2
- special feature index register
- special feature set data register

Initialization

After power up, the parallel port defaults to ISA mode. The enhanced parallel port feature has to be enabled and initialized before the parallel port can be used in enhanced parallel port mode. The enhanced parallel port is part of the special feature set. The enhanced parallel port configuration register (FPP_CNTL), which is a special feature index register, is used to configure the parallel port for enhanced parallel port operation.

To enable the FPP_CNTL register, perform the following steps:

- Set the SFCPUEN bit of the SFR register and the SFIO_EN bit of the CFGR2 (61H, INDEX) register.
- Do a dummy 8-bit write to the SFS_ENABLE register (0FBH).
- Write an 02H to the special feature index register (0AEH).

Table 13.4 shows the functions of the bits in the FFP_CNTL register.

To enable the enhanced parallel port, set bit 7 of the FPP_CNTL register. Bits 4 and 5 select LPT1 or LPT2 for the port. Setting bit 6 enabled the port for bidirectional data transfers when data is read or written to the standard data port (I/O address 278H if LPT2 is selected or 378H if LPT1 is selected).

Table 13.5 shows the functions of the bits for the output handshake port (X7AH) after the enhanced parallel port is enabled.

The parallel port control register must be initialized correctly before doing any data transfer on the enhanced parallel port.

I/O address map

Table 13.6 shows the I/O address map for the enhanced parallel port. This map is the same as the one for the standard ISA parallel port except for the addition of an address port and four data ports. Any write to the address port generates an address strobe. The four data ports are similar to the parallel port data reg-

TABLE 13.4 Function of Bits in FFP_CNTL Register

Bits	Description	
Bits [3-0]	Not used	
Bits [5-4]	Bits (5,4)	Description
	0, 0	parallel port disabled
	0, 1	parallel port set to LPT1, IRQ7
	1, 0	parallel port set to LPT2, IRQ5
	1, 1	reserved
Bit 6	Set to enable extended mode	
Bit 7	Set to enable enhanced parallel port mode	

TABLE 13.5 Functions of Output Handshake Port Bits When Enhanced Parallel Port Is Enabled

Bits	Description
Bit 0	Must be set to 0 in order for the WRITE# line to function properly.
Bit 1	Must be set to 0 in order for the data strobe to function properly.
Bit 2	Will function the same as the standard port INIT line.
Bit 3	Must be set to 0 for the address strobe to function properly.
Bit 4	Will function as an active high interrupt enable the same as the standard port.
Bit 5	Will function the same as the PS/2 compatible port and isolate the standard data port buffer when set high. In order for bit 5 to function, the configuration bit must be set to extended mode by setting bit 6.
Bits [6–7]	Not used.

TABLE 13.6 I/O Address Map for the Enhanced Parallel Port

Address	Description	Mode
3(2)78H	Parallel port data register (SPP)	Write
3(2)79H	Parallel port status register (SPP)	Read
3(2)7AH	Loopback handshakes register (SPP)	Read
3(2)7AH	Output handshakes register (SPP)	Write
3(2)7BH	Auto address strobe register (EPP)	Read/write
3(2)7CH	Auto data strobe register (EPP)	Read/write
3(2)7DH	Auto data strobe register (EPP)	Read/write
3(2)7EH	Auto data strobe register (EPP)	Read/write
3(2)7FH	Auto data strobe register (EPP)	Read/write

ister. The 82360SL supports an 8-bit I/O cycle only. Any read or write to any of the data ports generates a data strobe.

After the enhanced parallel port is enabled, the parallel port can still support a standard ISA parallel port device. The pinout of the parallel port changes only when the auto address strobe and auto data strobe registers are written to it. The enabling and disabling of the enhanced parallel port can be implemented as BIOS function calls or included in a device driver. Listing 13.1 can be used as a reference for implementing these functions.

Listing 13.1 Sample Code for Enabling and Disabling Enhanced Parallel Port

```
PAGE 60, 132 ;WIDE LISTING
;-----------------------------------------------------------------
;
;  FPP.ASM: This file contains routines to demonstrate
;  the enhanced parallel port feature.
;
;  Revision History:
;
;  Copyright (©) by Intel Corporation 1991. All rights reserved
;
;-----------------------------------------------------------------
FALSE EQU  0      ;FALSE COMPARE
TRUE EQU  OFFFFH ;TRUE compare & mask
include superset.inc
;
;-------------- INITIALIZATION -----------------------------------
code  SEGMENT
ASSUME cs:code, ds:code, es:code, ss:code
;
;
  ORG  100H
EXTRN enable_sfs:near, disable_sfs:near
start:
  call    enable_fpp
  jmp     exit
enable_fpp proc near
```

```
;enable enhanced parallel port mode
  push    ax
  call    enable_sfs
  mov     al, FPP_CNTL  ; selects FPP_CNTL register
  out     SFS_INDEX, al
  mov     al, 0D0h
  out     SFS_DATA, al  ; selects lpt1, irq7, extended mode
  mov     al, 10h; initialize the control register
  mov     dx, 37ah
  out     dx, al
  pop     ax
  ret
enable_fpp endp
disable_fpp proc near
;disable enhanced parallel port mode
  push    ax
  mov     dx, SFS_INDEX  ; selects FPP_CNTL register
  mov     al, FPP_CNTL
  out     dx, al
  mov     dx, SFS_DATA  ; disable enhanced parallel port
  mov     al, 00h
  out     dx, al
  pop     ax
  ret
disable_fpp endp
exit:
  mov     ax, 4C00H     ; terminate program
  int  21H
;------------------------------------------------------------------
;
;  Data Area
;
;------------------------------------------------------------------
code  ENDS       ; end code segment
  END  start
```

Software loop comparison

Once enhanced parallel port mode is enabled, the host can start transferring data to the device. Unlike standard parallel port, data transfer with enhanced parallel port is easy. (See Table 13.7.) Data is transferred by writing or reading the data directly to or from the EPP data port. No wait loop and polling are required.

Summary

As of this writing, the enhanced parallel port has already become an industry standard; it is now part of IEEE P1284 standard. EPP is supported by many chipset manufacturers, and many companies are coming out with peripherals that will work with EPP, such as network adapters, hard disks, and tape

TABLE 13.7 Steps Performed to Transfer Data

	SPP software loop		EPP software loop
1	Output register address to data port	1	Output address to EPP address port
2	Output strobe to control port	2	Output data to EPP data port
3	Fetch register data		
4	Output register data to data port		
5	Output strobe to control port		
6	Input (device-ready) from status port		
7	loop to 3		

backup drives. As the chairman of the EPP committee, it has been a great experience for me to be directly involved in defining the EPP standard.

References

Intel386™ SL Microprocessor SuperSet Data Book, 1991 (order no. 240814-003).

Intel386™ SL Microprocessor SuperSet Programmer's Reference Manual, 1991 (order no. 240815-003).

Intel386™ SL Microprocessor SuperSet System's Design Guide, 1991 (order no. 240816-003).

Enhanced Parallel Port Specification, Xircom, Inc., January 1991.

Chapter

14

Writing an SL BIOS

What Is the SL BIOS?

The term *SL BIOS* refers to the basic I/O system (BIOS) commonly provided for an Intel486 SL CPU- or Intel386 SL CPU-based system. Ordinarily, the SL BIOS comprises the standard ISA system BIOS, VGA BIOS, and keyboard BIOS, plus the setup program and the system initialization and power management software. Figure 14.1 shows a diagram of the relationship of these BIOS modules. Depending on the hardware configuration, the SL BIOS might also include battery control, PCMCIA socket service, and penbase support software.

Notebook machines built around the Intel486 SL CPU and Intel386 SL CPU often use highly integrated designs and require the same level of integration in the SL BIOS. Because each of these machines has its own unique features, integrating all the different pieces of firmware into a compact SL BIOS is no easy task. However, by using a modular design approach, the effort required to develop an integrated SL BIOS can be minimized.

Differences in SL BIOS for Intel486 SL CPU and Intel386 SL CPU

The information in this chapter comes from our work in helping Intel customers design and write SL BIOS's for the Intel386 SL CPU. However, the principles are essentially the same for writing an SL BIOS for the Intel486 SL CPU. In fact, if you have already written an SL BIOS for the Intel386 SL CPU, it is relatively easy to modify it to run on the Intel486 SL CPU. Where appropriate, hints are given in this chapter on how to modify an SL BIOS designed for the Intel386 SL CPU so that it will run on the Intel486 SL CPU.

System BIOS

Except for system initialization, the system BIOS for the Intel486 SL CPU and Intel386 SL CPU is almost the same as for a standard Intel386 ISA system BIOS. The Intel386 SL CPU is designed so that it can be booted from a generic

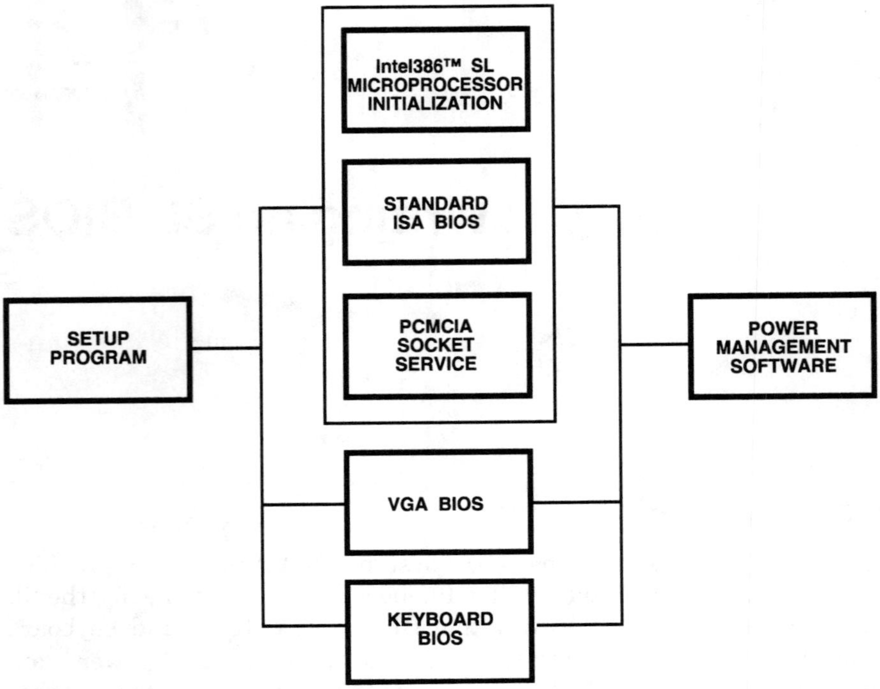

Figure 14.1 Modules in a typical SL BIOS.

Intel386 PC AT BIOS without any modification. The fastest way to create a system BIOS for an SL CPU-based system is to have the reset-handling routine in the system BIOS pass control to the system initialization program. After the initialization program has finished setting up the CPU, it then passes control to the standard ISA BIOS routines in the system BIOS. A system BIOS (not including the initialization code) written for the Intel386 SL CPU should run on the Intel486 SL CPU without modification.

To help you customize your BIOS, many of the BIOS vendors offer: a FLASH BIOS utility to allow users to upgrade their BIOS on the fly; a BIOS setup program to change system parameters dynamically; and a BIOS edit program to change the default values of the CPU and 82360SL registers during system initialization.

System initialization

A system initialization program called SYSINIT.ASM is located on the companion disk which is included with this book. This program, an example of how to initialize an Intel486 SL CPU- or Intel386 SL CPU-based system, includes the following initialization steps:

- Initialize the memory controller.
- Initialize the cache controller.

- Initialize the DMA controller.
- Initialize the keyboard controller.
- Initialize the power management hardware.
- Download the SMM program to SMRAM.

If you are writing system initialization code for a Intel486 SL CPU-based system by modifying existing code designed for Intel386 SL CPU-based system, you need to make the following changes:

- Because the memory controller for the Intel486 SL CPU and the Intel386 SL CPU are completely different, you must write all new initialization code for the Intel486 SL CPU memory controller.
- Since the Intel486 SL CPU does not support an external cache, you need to remove the external cache initialization code for the Intel486 SL CPU and add code to enable the internal cache.
- Because the cacheability mechanism for the two CPUs is completely different, you must provide a new code for the Intel486 SL CPU; this will enable caching of various sections of physical memory.
- The two 16-bit roll-over registers in the Intel386 SL CPU have been combined into a single 32-bit register, called the MCROLL register in the Intel486 SL CPU.
- The Intel486 SL CPU does not provide on-chip expanded memory system (EMS) support. If you want to use EMS in an Intel486 SL CPU-based system, you need to include a software EMS driver and modify the EMS initialization code for the Intel386 SL CPU.

The Intel486 SL CPU allows you to program the buffer strength of some of the ISA-bus signals; you can do this within the initialization code.

Setup program

Traditionally, the system setup information such as the hard disk type, floppy drive type, and amount of memory is stored in a 128-byte CMOS RAM inside the real-time clock. In an Intel SL CPU-based system, the CMOS RAM is contained in the 82360SL. Also, this CMOS RAM has been enlarged to 256 bytes to accommodate the additional setup data needed for the configuration registers in the Intel486 SL CPU, Intel386 SL CPU, and the 82360SL. (The configuration registers are discussed in the next section.)

Table 14.1 shows the typical partitioning of the CMOS RAM for an Intel486 SL CPU or Intel386 SL CPU. In addition to storing the standard setup information, it also stores setup information for setup options like the power management hardware, CPU clock speed, and DRAM page mode.

The first 128 bytes of CMOS RAM is generally referred to as standard CMOS RAM while the other 128 bytes of CMOS RAM is called the extended

TABLE 14.1 Partitioning of Setup Information in CMOS RAM

Location	Function
00H	Seconds
01H	Seconds alarm
02H	Minutes
03H	Minutes alarm
04H	Hours
05H	Hours alarm
06H	Day of week
07H	Date of month
08H	Month
09H	Year
0AH	Status register A
0BH	Status register B
0CH	Status register C
0DH	Status register D
0EH	Diagnostic byte
0FH	Shutdown byte
10H	Floppy drive type
11H	Reserved
12H	Hard disk drive type
13H	Reserved
14H	Equipment byte
15H	Base memory, low byte
16H	Base memory, high byte
17H	Expansion memory, low byte
18H	Expansion memory, high byte
19H	Hard disk drive type, drive C
1AH	Hard disk drive type, drive D
1BH-2DH	Reserved
2EH	CMOS checksum, high byte
2FH	CMOS checksum, low byte
30H	Actual memory above 1 Mbyte, low byte
31H	Actual memory above 1 Mbyte, high byte
32H	Century byte
33H	Information status flag byte
34H-3FH	Reserved
40H-7FH	OEM defined
0H-5FH (Extended CMOS RAM)	OEM defined
60H-7FH (Extended CMOS RAM)	APM

CMOS RAM. The standard CMOS RAM is accessed using the same index mechanism as on a standard ISA system through an index register (port 70H) and data register (port 71H). You must write to the index register (port 70H) first, before accessing the data register; otherwise, invalid data will be written or read. This access sequence is necessary because the contents of the index register is flushed after every access to protect CMOS data from being overwritten accidentally.

The extra 128 bytes of CMOS RAM is accessed through ports 74H and 76H. Port 74H is the address port and port 76H is the data port. This second index and data port is needed because bit 7 of I/O port 70H is used for disabling NMI generation. Therefore, there are only enough bits to address 128 bytes of

CMOS RAM. With the extended CMOS RAM, the address is latched after the index register has been written to.

Listing 14.2 gives an example of code to access setup data in standard and extended CMOS RAM.

Listing 14.2 Accessing Setup Data in CMOS RAM

```
;--------------------------------------------------------------
;
;  CMOS.ASM: Routines that access the CMOS RAM
;
;-------------------------------------------------------------------
Include Superset.inc
code  segment  public 'code'
      assume  cs:code
PUBLIC  read_xcmos, write_xcmos, read_cmos, write_cmos
;--------------------------------------------------------------
;
; read_xcmos: get extended CMOS port value
; Input : bl = index of an extended CMOS port
; Output : al = data read
;
;--------------------------------------------------------------
read_xcmos  proc near
  mov     al, MASK_NMI ; disable NMI
  out     CMOS_INDEX, al
  jmp     $+2
    jmp     $+2
  mov     al,bl   ; point to the index
  out     XCMOS_INDEX,al ;
    jmp     $+2
    jmp     $+2
  in      al,XCMOS_DATA  ; read the data
    xchg    ah, al
    jmp     $+2
    jmp     $+2
    mov     al, UNMASK_NMI      ; enable NMI
    out     CMOS_INDEX, al
    xchg    ah, al
    ret
read_xcmos  endp
;--------------------------------------------------------------
;
; write_xcmos: write new value into an extended CMOS port
;
; Input : bl = index of an extended CMOS port
;  bh = data to be written
; Output : None.
;
```

```
;----------------------------------------------------------------------

write_xcmos  proc near
    mov     al, MASK_NMI ; disable NMI
    out     CMOS_INDEX, al
    jmp     $+2
    jmp     $+2
  mov     al, bl            ; point to the index
  out     XCMOS_INDEX, al ;
    jmp     $+2
    jmp     $+2
  mov     al, bh            ; get data to be written
  out     XCMOS_DATA, al ; write to extended CMOS PORT
    jmp     $+2
    jmp     $+2
    mov     al, UNMASK_NMI       ; enable NMI
    out     CMOS_INDEX, al
    ret
write_xcmos  endp
;----------------------------------------------------------------------
;
; read_cmos: get CMOS port value
; Input : bl = index of a CMOS port
; Output : al = data read
;
;----------------------------------------------------------------------
read_cmos   proc  near
    mov     al, MASK_NMI ; disable NMI
    out     CMOS_INDEX, al
    jmp     $+2
    jmp     $+2
  mov     al, bl            ; point to the index
  out     CMOS_INDEX,al ;
    jmp     $+2
    jmp     $+2
  in      al,CMOS_DATA      ; read the data
    jmp     $+2
    jmp     $+2
    xchg    ah, al
    mov     al, UNMASK_NMI       ; enable NMI
    out     CMOS_INDEX, al
    xchg    ah, al
    ret
read_cmos endp
;----------------------------------------------------------------------
;
; write_cmos: write new value into a CMOS port
;
; Input : bl = index of a CMOS port
```

```
;  bh = data to be written
; Output : None.
;
;-------------------------------------------------------------

write_cmos        proc    near
     mov     al, MASK_NMI ; disable NMI
     out     CMOS_INDEX, al
     jmp     $+2
     jmp     $+2
   mov     al, bl             ; point to the index
   out     CMOS_INDEX, al ;
     jmp     $+2
     jmp     $+2
   mov     al, bh             ; get data to be written
   out     CMOS_DATA, al  ; write to standard CMOS PORT
     jmp     $+2
     jmp     $+2
     mov     al, UNMASK_NMI      ; enable NMI
     out     CMOS_INDEX, al
     ret

write_cmos  endp

code  ends
  end
```

For system security, the 82360SL also supports the PSx compatible password security feature, which prevents unauthorized access to the system. The PSx feature is enabled by setting bit 3 in port 92H to one. Once this bit is set, the data in the CMOS RAM from bytes 38H to 3FH is locked. A read to these CMOS locations will return the address of the byte read and not the actual contents.

Register resource

A unique, common feature of the Intel486 SL CPU, Intel386 SL CPU, and 82360SL is that they are highly programmable. Instead of requiring hundreds of jumpers on the motherboard to configure the hardware, you can configure the CPU and 82360SL by writing to the extension registers in the different configuration spaces. The extension registers also allow the system configuration to be changed on the fly.

The SL CPU and 82360SL registers are divided into three groups: CPU registers, ISA system registers, and SL extension registers. The CPU registers are those registers normally found in an Intel486 SX CPU or Intel386 SX CPU. The ISA system registers are the I/O ports normally found in a standard ISA system. The SL extension registers are configuration registers unique to the Intel486 SL CPU, Intel386 SL CPU, and 82360SL. These registers are located in normal I/O address space, internal bus unit configuration space, on-board memory controller unit space, external bus unit space, cache unit configuration space, or in the 82360SL configuration space. (Please refer to Fig. 14.2.)

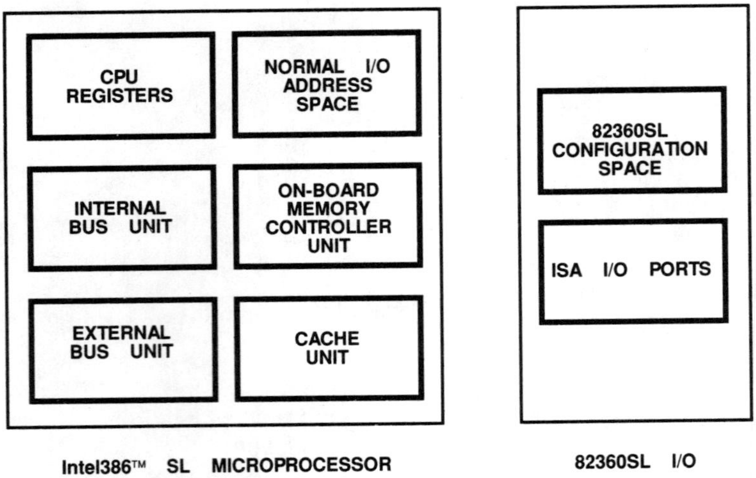

Figure 14.2 Register resources for the SL architecture.

Access to the unit configuration spaces

The Intel386 SL CPU has four unit configuration spaces and the Intel486 SL CPU has three unit configuration spaces (cache configuration space is not supported), only one of which can be active at a time. Access to these configuration spaces is controlled by the unit enable bit (bit 1) and the unit ID field (bits [2-3]) in the CPUPWRMODE register (22H).

The CPUPWRMODE register is a 16-bit register that is normally hidden. It is unlocked by executing the unlocking sequence given in Listing 14.3.

Listing 14.3 Unlocking Sequence for CPUPWRMODE Register

```
cli                 ; disable interrupts
mov     ax, 8000h
out     23h, al     ; byte write to 23h with MSB = 0
xchg    ah, al
out     22h, al     ; byte write to 22h with MSB = 1
out     22h, ax     ; word write to 22h with MSB = 0
sti                 ; re-enable interrupts
```

The unlock status bit (bit 0) of the CPUPWRMODE register will be set after the unlocking sequence is executed. After the CPUPWRMODE register is unlocked, a unit configuration space is enabled by writing the corresponding unit ID into the unit ID field and setting the unit enable bit. The unit enable bit and the unit ID field can be written simultaneously.

Note: Interrupts should be disabled before executing the unlocking sequence. If the CPU is interrupted in the middle of the unlocking sequence, the unlocking sequence will be broken.

Access to the 82360SL configuration space

The 82360SL configuration space is inside the 82360SL I/O. Access to registers inside the 82360SL configuration space is through an index addressing mechanism similar to that used to access the CMOS RAM. Before any access can be made, the 82360SL configuration space must be unlocked by executing an unlocking sequence. The unlocking sequence consists of four consecutive I/O reads to the following addresses: 0FC23H, 0F023H, 0C023H, and 0023H. Interrupts should be disabled prior to executing the unlocking sequence.

After the 82360SL configuration space is unlocked (a read to CFGSTAT register at 23H will return 7FH), registers can be accessed using the configuration index register, CFGINDEX(24H) and configuration data register, CFGDATA(25H). To access any register, the index of the register must be written to the CFGINDEX register first. Data can then be read, or written, through the CFGDATA register.

The sample code in Listing 14.4 contains function calls to access registers in the different configuration spaces. The sample code is used by other programs throughout the book.

Listing 14.4 Code for Accessing the SL Extension Registers

```
;-------------------------------------------------------------------
;  CFGSPACE.ASM: This file contains routines for accessing
;  the SL SUPERSET extension registers.
;-------------------------------------------------------------------

Include superset.inc

code segment  byte public 'code'
  assume cs:code

PUBLIC  open_cpupwrmode, close_cpupwrmode, open_ibu, open_omcu
PUBLIC  open_ebu, open_ccu, close_386sl, open_360sl
PUBLIC  read_360sl, write_360sl, close_360sl
;-------------------------------------------------------------
;
;  open_cpupwrmode: open CPUPWRMODE register
;
;  Input: None
;
;  Output: carry flag set if not opened
;
;-------------------------------------------------------------

open_cpupwrmode proc near
  push    ax
  mov     ax, 8000h  ; execute unlocking sequence
  out     23h, al
  xchg    ah, al
  out     22h, al
  out     22h, ax
```

```
  in      al, 22h    ; is it opened?
  and     al, 01
  jnz     open_cpu_exit
  stc
open_cpu_exit:
  pop     ax
  ret
open_cpupwrmode endp
;-------------------------------------------------------------
;
;  close_cpupwrmode: lock CPUPWRMODE register
;
;  Input: None
;
;  Output: None
;
;-------------------------------------------------------------
close_cpupwrmode proc near
  push    ax
  in      al, 23h
  or      al, 01h    ; set lock bit
  out     23h, al
  in      al, 22h
  and     al, 01     ; is it closed
  jz      close_cpu_exit
  stc
close_cpu_exit:
  pop     ax
  ret
close_cpupwrmode endp
;-------------------------------------------------------------
;
;  open_ibu: open IBU configuration space
;
;  Input: None
;
;  Output: None
;
;-------------------------------------------------------------
open_ibu proc near
  call    open_cpupwrmode
  push    ax
  in      al, 22h
  or      al, 0Ah    ; enable IBU
  and     al, 0FBh
  out     22h, al
  pop     ax
  call    close_cpupwrmode
  ret
open_ibu endp
```

```
;------------------------------------------------------------
;
;  open_omcu: open OMCU configuration space
;
;  Input: None
;
;  Output: None
;
;------------------------------------------------------------

open_omcu proc near
call    open_cpupwrmode
push    ax
in      al, 22h
or      al, 02h   ; enable OMCU
and     al, 0F3h
out     22h, al
pop     ax
call    close_cpupwrmode
ret

open_omcu endp

;------------------------------------------------------------
;
;  open_ebu: open EBU configuration space
;
;  Input: None
;
;  Output: None
;
;------------------------------------------------------------

open_ebu proc near
  call    open_cpupwrmode
  push    ax
  in      al, 22h
  or      al, 0Eh; enable EBU
  out     22h, al
  pop     ax
  call    close_cpupwrmode
  ret

open_ebu endp
;------------------------------------------------------------
;
;  open_ccu: open CCU configuration space
;
;  Input: None
;
;  Output: None
;
;------------------------------------------------------------
```

```
open_ccu proc near
  call    open_cpupwrmode
  push    ax
  in      al, 22h
  or      al, 06h     ; enable CCU
  and     al, 0F7h
  out     22h, al
  pop     ax
  call    close_cpupwrmode
  ret
open_ccu endp
;---------------------------------------------------------------
;
;  close_386sl: close all configuration spaces on 386SL
;
;  Input: None
;
;  Output: None
;
;---------------------------------------------------------------
close_386sl proc near
  push    ax
  in      al, 22h     ; is CPUPWRMODE unlocked
  and     al, 01h
  jnz     en
  call    open_cpupwrmode
en:       in      al, 22h
  and     al, 0FDH    ; disable all configuration
  out     22h, al     ; spaces
  call    close_cpupwrmode
  pop     ax
  ret
close_386sl endp
;---------------------------------------------------------------
;
;  open_360sl: open 360SL configuration space
;
;  Input: None
;
;  Output: None
;
;---------------------------------------------------------------
open_360sl proc near
  push    dx
  push    ax
  mov     dx, 0FC23h
  in      al, dx
  mov     dx, 0F023h
  in      al, dx
```

```
    mov     dx, 0C023h
    in      al, dx
    mov     dx, 0023h
    in      al, dx
    pop     ax
    pop     dx
    ret
open_360sl endp

;------------------------------------------------------------
;
;close_360sl: close 360SL configuration space
;
;Input: None
;
;Output: None
;
;------------------------------------------------------------

close_360sl proc near
    push    ax
    mov     al, IDXLCK
    out     CFGINDEX, al
    mov     al, 01h
    out     CFGDATA, al
    pop     ax
    ret
close_360sl endp
code ends
    end
```

Setting up a calendar event

When an Intel SL-based system is in suspend mode, it can resume prior operation by pressing the suspend/resume button, a modem ring, or a calendar event. The calendar event is generated by the real-time clock alarm. Listing 14.5 gives an example of how to set up a calendar event for resume.

Listing 14.5 Code for Setting Up a Calendar Event

```
mov     bl, 01H         ; set seconds
mov     bh, cal_sec
call    write_cmos

mov     bl, 03H         ; set minutes
mov     bh, cal_min
call    write_cmos
mov     bl, 05H         ; set hours
mov     bh, cal_hour
call    write_cmos
mov     bl, 0Bh         ; get current value in REG B
call    read_cmos
and     al, 04h         ; set alarm interrupt enable bit
```

```
mov     bh, al
call    write_cmos
in      al, 0A1h        ; read 2nd PIC
and     al, 0FEh        ; enable RTC interrupt
out     0A1h, al
```

Keyboard BIOS

The most common keyboard controllers are the 80C42 and 80C51SL. If the 80C42 is used, the keyboard BIOS should be the same as the standard keyboard BIOS used in a ISA system. Unlike the 80C42, the 80C51SL has more pins and contains an analog interface, which allows it to perform additional functions, such as battery monitoring and interfacing to the SMM control logic on the 82360SL.

A keyboard BIOS for the 80C51SL keyboard typically supports the ISA-compatible keyboard interface, a scanner interface for matrix keyboards, the turbo mode, a PSx-compatible mouse, and power management features. The features supported by the 80C51SL keyboard BIOS are largely determined by the hardware configuration. For example, the keyboard BIOS can control the CPU speed if the 80C51SL is connected to the turbo pin on the Intel486 SL CPU or on the Intel386 SL CPU.

Power management is the most interesting aspect of the 80C51SL keyboard BIOS. By putting the 80C51SL in IDLE mode between keystrokes or when the keyboard is inactive, power consumption can be reduced substantially.

The 80C51SL keyboard controller supports a POWER DOWN mode. In POWER DOWN mode, the oscillator for the 80C51SL is stopped to reduce power consumption to less than 1 percent of normal. A power down can be initiated either from the power management software running in SMM or from a keyboard BIOS routine. The 80C51SL is fully static. While in POWER DOWN mode, all the registers and signals will remain in the same state prior to entering POWER DOWN mode.

The external SMI pin on the 82360SL is a general purpose pin for hardware to enable SMM. The keyboard BIOS can access this pin through the keyboard controller to invoke the setup program stored inside SMRAM to configure the system at any time, even in a protected mode environment.

VGA BIOS

The most challenging part of the VGA BIOS is the support for LCD panels and power management. The difference between a standard VGA BIOS and a VGA BIOS for a notebook system lies in the added support for LCD display and power management.

Architectural support for VGA

The SL architecture offers several features to increase the performance and expandability of a VGA subsystem. The VGA BIOS can be relocated from the

0C0000H segment to the 0E0000H segment. The relocation of the VGA BIOS allows it to be stored in the same ROM that contains the system BIOS, which in turn reduces the chip count and board space. Listing 14.6 shows how the VGA BIOS can be relocated to 0E0000H segment.

Listing 14.6 Code for Relocating the VGA BIOS

```
; program to redirect accesses to 0C0000H-0C7FFFH to 0E0000H-0E7FFFH
  call    open_ebu        ; enable VGA remapping in SL CPU
  mov     dx, EBC1CR
  in      ax, dx
  or      ax, 030h
  out     dx, ax
  call    close_386sl
  call    open_360sl      ; enable VGA remapping in the 82360SL
  mov     bl, ROMCS_DEC
  call    read_360sl
  or      al, 03h
  mov     bh, al
  call    write_360sl
  call    close_360sl
```

Normally, the graphics frame buffer sits between 0A0000H and 0BFFFFH in the system address space. The SL architecture supports a second graphics frame buffer. The second graphics frame buffer can be as large as 8 Mbytes. The larger graphics frame buffer can be used to increase graphics resolution and to speed up graphics operations.

As discussed in Chap. 12, placing the VGA subsystem on the PI bus can dramatically improve performance.

Power management for the VGA subsystem

The VGA controller can also provide power management for the VGA subsystem. The LCD display is still the biggest power hog on any notebook system. The common approach to conserve power is to control the backlight for the LCD panel. Other power-saving measures may include extended refresh for video DRAM, and putting the VGA subsystem in low-power modes.

In standby mode, the backlight is turned off. The video memory and VGA registers are still accessible. Suspend mode is similar to standby mode, except that the video memory and VGA registers are not accessible. The most effective—and also the most difficult—method to implement suspend is to power off the entire VGA system. This requires saving the entire state of the VGA system (including video memory).

Interrupts are disabled in SMM. To work with the power management software under SMM, the VGA BIOS must be re-entrant. To make the VGA BIOS re-entrant, INT10H function calls must be written such that the address of the INT10H entry is at a fixed location.

VGA BIOS setup

The VGA BIOS setup program typically controls the LCD display and power management on the VGA subsystem. It allows the users to configure features like the timing parameters for the LCD panel, gray scales, frame buffer size, and power management timers.

SMM software

SMM software is the program that is executed by the processor when the CPU is running in SMM. Commonly, it is used for power management. While it is not necessary for the SMM software to reside in flash memory with the system and VGA BIOS's, it makes sense to do it that way for portability reasons and cost saving. With the SMM program stored inside the BIOS, there is no need to create a different driver for each different operating system in order to load the SMM program into SMRAM.

Power management support

With the SL architecture, power management software can come in many flavors, depending on the hardware configuration. Power management software normally includes power management hardware initialization, handling of power management service requests, and interfaces to the other parts of the system.

Post codes are values written to an I/O address port that are then shown on a two-digit display to assist in debugging efforts and to indicate how far the code has executed. Post codes should be used for different power management operations. If possible, use a diagnostic port different from 80H to avoid confusion with the standard post codes.

BIOS integration

The Intel486 SL CPU and Intel386 SL CPU support both 8- and 16-bit BIOS interfaces. It is generally more practical to use the 8-bit BIOS interface (in terms of cost and reduction of board space) for the following reasons. The 16-bit interface gives better performance than the 8-bit interface, but it also takes up more space and consumes more power. A 16-bit interface requires two 8-bit flash memory chips while the 8-bit interface requires only one. Furthermore, it is common practice to shadow the BIOS after system initialization to improve performance.

As more and more hardware is integrated into a portable computer, the size of the firmware also grows. On a standard ISA system, only 128 Kbytes of BIOS space are available. The system BIOS, setup program, power management software, and VGA BIOS use most of this space. Thus, there is not much room for adding other firmware.

To accommodate additional firmware, the Intel486 SL CPU and Intel386 SL CPU support up to 256 Kbytes of BIOS space. Firmware can use the extra 128 Kbytes to support a PCMCIA card and/or a digitizer for a pen-based computer.

The sample code in Listing 14.7 shows how to enable the full 256 Kbytes of BIOS space.

If the 256 Kbytes BIOS space feature is enabled, the VGA BIOS remapping mechanism will not be available. Therefore, the VGA BIOS must be located between 0C0000H and 0CFFFFH.

Listing 14.7 Example of How to Enable the Full 256 Kbytes of Flash BIOS Space

```
en_256k_BIOS proc  near
  call    open_360sl
  mov     bl, ROMCSDEC
  call    read_360SL
  or      al, 04h; set ROM256KEN bit
  mov     bh, al
  call    write_360SL
  call    close_360sl

  call    open_ebu
  mov     dx, ISAWINDOW
  in      ax, dx
  or      ax, 4000h      ; set BIOS256KEN bit
  out     dx, ax
  mov     dx, EBC1CR     ; set no of EPROM banks
  in      ax, dx
  and     ax, 0DFFFh     ; one EPROM bank
  out     dx, ax
  call    close_386sl
en_256K_BIOS endp
```

Flash BIOS programming

During the development cycle, firmware has to be updated from time to time. Using flash memory instead of EPROM makes code updates much easier and faster. Flash memory can be reprogrammed in a system even if it has been surface mounted to the motherboard. Thus, flash memory is particularly well suited for portable computers and embedded applications.

Access to flash memory

When Vpp is high, a command register controls access to the flash memory and a status register verifies that access has been obtained. Vpp need not be high to read the intelligent identifier and status register. The command register itself does not occupy an addressable memory location. This register is a latch used to store the command, address, and data needed to execute the command.

Every flash memory has a component identifier. The component identifier can be accessed by writing a read identifier command (90H) to the command register at 0H. Subsequent reads to address 0H return the manufacturer code and reads to address 01H return the device code. After the component identifier is read, the operation can be terminated by writing the read array command (0FFH) to the command register.

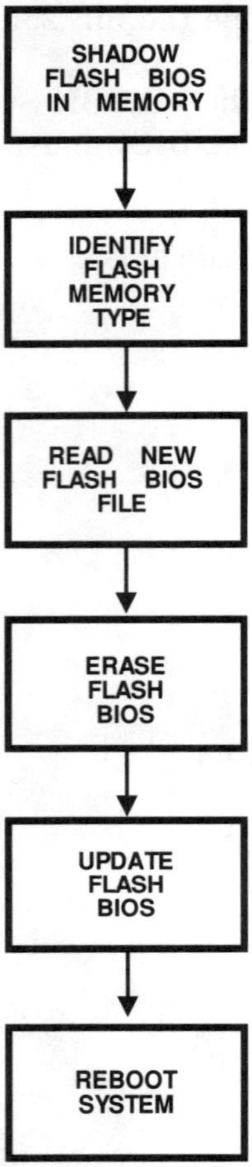

Figure 14.3 Flash BIOS update.

Flash memory update

To protect the flash BIOS from accidentally being overwritten, the flash BIOS is normally read-only in an SL CPU-based system. (See Figure 14.3.) The flash BIOS can become writable by setting the flash BIOS write enable bit (bit 14) of the EBC1CR register (300H, EBU) to one. Listing 14.8 shows how to read and write flash memory.

Listing 14.8 Reading and Writing the Flash BIOS Memory

```
write_only   proc  near
   push    ax
   push    dx
   call    open_ibu
  mov      dx, 308H
  mov      ax, 05555H   ; write cycles go to ISA-bus (ROM)
  out      dx, ax       ; read cycles go to on-board memory
  mov      dx, 30AH
```

```
    out      dx, ax
    mov      dx, 30CH
    out      dx, ax
    mov      dx, 30EH
    out      dx, ax
    call     close_386sl
    call     open_ebu      ; enable flash BIOS write
    mov      dx, 300h
    in       ax, dx
    or       ah, 40H
    out      dx, ax
    call     close_386sl
     pop     dx
     pop     ax
     ret
write_only   endp

read_only    proc  near

    push     ax
     push    dx

     call    open_ibu
    mov      dx, 308H
    mov      ax, 0AAAAH    ; write cycles to on-board memory
    out      dx, ax        ; read cycles to ISA-bus (ROM)
    mov      dx, 30AH
    out      dx, ax
    mov      dx, 30CH
    out      dx, ax
    mov      dx, 30EH
    out      dx, ax
     call    close_386sl

    call     open_ebu      ; disable flash BIOS write

    mov      dx, 300h

    in       ax, dx

    and      ah, 0BFH

    out      dx, ax

     call    close_386sl
     pop     dx
     pop     ax
     ret
read_only   endp
```

On the SL evaluation board, the SMOUT5 pin controls the Vpp pin to the flash BIOS. The routines in Listing 14.9 show how the SMOUT5 pin can be toggled to disable and enable Vpp. Please note that some time delay is inserted to allow the voltage level on the Vpp to settle down.

Listing 14.9 Code to Enable and Disable Vpp for the Flash BIOS Memory

```
vpp_on    proc   near
    push     ax
    push     bx
    push     cx
    push     dx

  cli
    call  open_360sl     ; enable Vpp
    mov   bl, SMOUT_CNTRL
  call    read_360sl
  and     al, 0DFH       ; set SMOUT5 bit to zero
  mov     bh, al
  call    write_360sl
    call  close_360sl
  sti
;wait for voltage level to stabilize

  mov     cx, 500
  call    delay ; insert 100 µs delay
  pop     dx
  pop     cx
  pop     bx
  pop     ax
  ret

vpp_on    endp

vpp_off   proc   near
    push     ax
    push     bx
    push     cx
    push     dx
  cli
    call     open_360sl
    mov      bl, SMOUT_CNTRL   ; disable SMOUT5
    call     read_360sl
  or      al, 20H              ; set SMOUT5 bit to zero
  mov     bh, al
  call    write_360sl
    call     close_360sl
  sti

; wait for power pin to settle

    mov   cx, 500
    call  delay                ; insert 100 µs delay
    pop      dx
    pop      cx
    pop      bx
    pop      ax
    ret
vpp_off  endp
```

Flash BIOS mapping

The mapping of the flash BIOS into the system memory can be confusing. As shown in Figure 14.4, the top of the flash BIOS should be mapped to segment 0F0000H of the address space; that is, the system BIOS should be located at the top of the flash memory. If a 256-Kbyte flash memory chip is used, the flash BIOS will take up the address space from 0C0000H to 0FFFFFH, and VGA BIOS relocation should be disabled.

BIOS parameters editor

The SL processor has a rich set of configuration registers that make hardware configuration extremely simple. During product development, there is often a need to modify or fine-tune the default settings of these registers. Therefore, it is useful to keep the default settings in a table inside the BIOS at a fixed location. This technique lets you use an editor to modify the parameter table without having to touch the source code. Therefore, quick experiments can be tried without the overhead in modifying the source code and recompiling.

Setup screen

Normally, the BIOS setup screen is used only to specify the type of floppy drive and hard disk being used. Things have changed with the introduction of the SL architecture. The SL architecture is designed to be highly programmable to

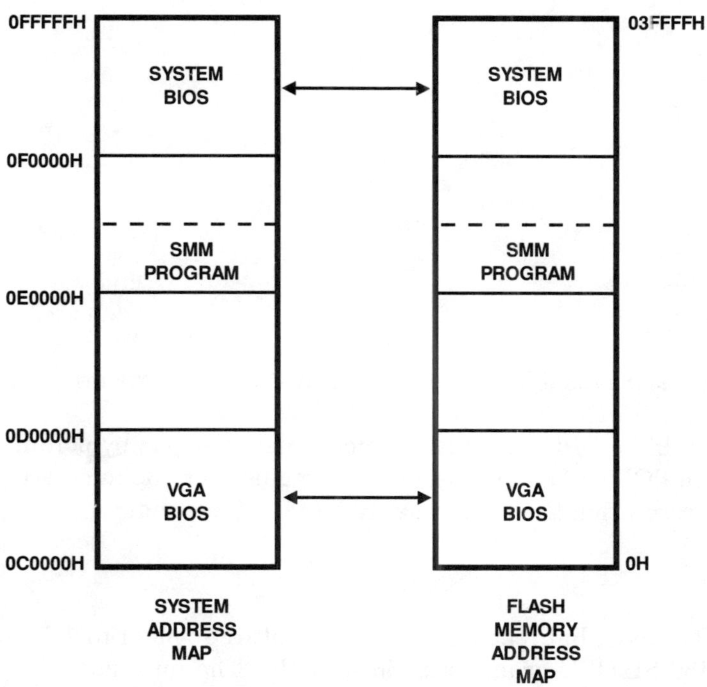

Figure 14.4 Mapping of the flash BIOS into system memory.

allow OEMs and end users to configure their systems for highest performance and lowest power consumption. The easiest and quickest way to change the system configuration without doing any programming is to go through the setup screen. The setup screen also comes in handy when you are debugging systems. Options can be provided in the setup screen to disable onboard peripherals and change I/O addresses and interrupts to isolate problems.

Software delay loop

BIOS time-of-day count provides a convenient way of regulating a timing loop. The count in this register is stored as a 32-bit number starting at 0H:046CH. On an ISA system, channel 0 of the 82C54 timer is programmed by the BIOS to increment this value about 18.2 times per second. With each timing pulse, the 82C54 generates an interrupt via INT8H to the CPU and the increments the count by 1.

A program can use the BIOS function call INT 1AH to retrieve the lower two of the four bytes and store them in the DX register. The program can later use this value to determine when a specified number of ticks has occurred. Listing 14.10 shows how a software delay loop can be implemented with this technique. This loop is not tied to the CPU's processing speed.

Listing 14.10 Code for a Software Delay Loop

```
soft_loop  PROC near
delay:
  mov      ah, 0
  int      1Ah
  add      dx, 100
  mov      cx, dx
d_loop:
  int      1Ah
  cmp      dx, cx
  jne      d_loop
  ret
soft_loop  endp
```

Since external interrupts are disabled inside SMM, this kind of software loop should not be used inside SMM.

The other way of writing a CPU speed-independent delay loop is by polling the refresh bit (bit 4) in PORT 61H. The refresh bit toggles every 30 microseconds and has a better resolution than the timer tick (45 milliseconds).

Test for presence of an Intel SL CPU

Listing 14.11 gives BIOS code that reads the CPU's signature register to determine if it is an Intel486 SL CPU or an Intel386 SL CPU. The information in this register provides CPU identification and stepping information.

Listing 14.11 Code for Identifying the CPU

```
include superset.inc
;
;-------------- INITIALIZATION -----------------------------------
code  SEGMENT
ASSUME cs:code, ds:code, es:code, ss:code
;
  ORG     100H
EXTRN     open_omcu:near, open_360sl:near, close_360sl:near,
close_386sl:near
start:
  call    open_360sl    ; execute unlock sequence for 82360SL
  mov     dx, 23h; I/O configuration space
  in      al, dx
  and     al, 01h
  jz      not_sl        ; not SL based system
  call    close_360sl
  call    open_omcu
  mov     dx, SIGNATURE  ; examine the SIGNATURE register
  in      ax, dx
  call    close_386sl
  cmp     ah, 43h
  jne     not_sl
i386sl:
  mov     dx, offset is386sl
  mov     ah, 09h
  int     21h
  jmp     exit
not_sl:
  mov     dx, offset notsl
  mov     ah, 09h
  int     21h

exit:
  mov     ax, 4C00H     ; terminate program
  int     21H

;-----------------------------------------------------------------
;
;  Data Area
;
;-----------------------------------------------------------------
is386sl   DB     'Intel386 SL microprocessor found.', '$'
notsl     DB     'SL microprocessor not found.', '$'
code  ENDS                  ; end code segment
  END  start
```

Stepping identification

An alternate way of determining the stepping of the CPU is to look at the marking on the chip. As shown in the following example, the first line indicates the type and speed of the CPU. The second line provides the lot number of the CPU, which is like a date code. The last line is the s-spec (step identification) number.

```
80386SL - 25i
i1272135-ES
iSA SXE90
```

Special Feature Set

The special feature set (SFS) is a group of unique features that allows the programmer to improve the performance of the system BIOS, as well as providing a convenient interface for operating systems and applications software. One of SFS's acknowledged attributes is that after it is enabled, the features are invoked by either a dummy I/O write or read. Doing a dummy read or write is much more efficient than reading the contents of a register, setting a bit, and then writing the data back to the register. The SFS consists of a 4-Kbyte scratchpad RAM and four registers: FASTA20GATE, FASTCPURESET, SLOWCPU, and FASTCPU.

Scratchpad RAM

The 4-Kbyte scratchpad RAM is located between 0F0000H and 0F1000H. Access to the scratchpad RAM is enabled by doing a dummy I/O write to the SFS ENABLE register (0FBH). The scratchpad RAM is disabled by doing a dummy I/O write to SFS DISABLE register (0F9H). The BIOS typically uses the scratchpad RAM for temporary storage of data. Application software should not access this area, at the risk of causing a system malfunction.

FASTA20GATE

The conventional method of toggling the A20 GATE using the keyboard is slow. This can be a problem in switching frequently between protected and real mode. The SFS contains a FASTA20GATE register to allow quick switching between protected and real mode. A20 GATE is enabled by doing an I/O write to I/O address 0EEH. An I/O read to I/O address 0EEH disables the A20 GATE.

FASTCPURESET

A fast CPU reset is generated by doing a dummy I/O read to the FASTCPURESET register at I/O port address 0EFH.

SLOWCPU and FASTCPU

A dummy write to the SLOWCPU register (0F4H) puts the CPU in de-turbo mode; a dummy write to the FASTCPU register (0F5H) puts the CPU in turbo mode. The CPU clock speed in de-turbo mode is determined by the deturbo select bit (bit 15) in the CPUPWRMODE register (22H). The CPU clock speed is EFI/2 when bit 15 is zero and EFI/4 when bit 15 is one.

Enabling and disabling the SFS

The FASTA20GATE and FASTCPURESET registers are inside the 82360SL I/O and the SLOWCPU and FASTCPU registers are inside the Intel486 SL CPU and Intel386 SL CPU. If you enable the SFS in the CPU only, you will not be able to access the FASTA20GATE and the FASTCPURESET registers.

To enable the SFS in the CPU, set the SFCPUEN bit (bit 0) in the SFR register (705H, lbu) to one. To enable the SFS in the 82360SL, set the SFIO_EN bit (bit 3) in the CFGR2 (61H, INDEX) to one. After these bits are set, the SFS ENABLE (0FBH) and SFS DISABLE (0F9H) registers become visible. A dummy write to the SFS ENABLE register will enable access to the SFS. The SFS is disabled by setting bit 0 of the SFS DISABLE register to one.

Listing 14.12 contains routines for accessing the SFS.

Listing 14.12 Code for Accessing the SFS

```
;-----------------------------------------------------------------
;  SFS.ASM: This file contains routines for accessing
;  the SFS.
;----------------------------------------------------------------

Include superset.inc
code  segment  byte  public 'code'
      assume cs:code
EXTRN  open_ibu:near, close_386sl:near, open_360sl:near,
close_360sl:near
PUBLIC  enable_sfs, disable_sfs

;------------------------------------------------------------
;
;  enable_sfs: enable special features set
;
;  Input: None
;
;  Output: carry flag set if not opened
;
;------------------------------------------------------------
enable_sfs proc near
  push    ax
  call    open_ibu
  mov     dx, SFR
  mov     al, 01h
  out     dx, al ; set SFCPUEN bit
  call    close_386sl
  call    open_360sl
  mov     al, CFGR2
  out     CFGINDEX, al
  in      al, CFGDATA
  or      al, 08h; set SFIO_EN bit
  out     CFGDATA, al
  call    close_360sl
```

```
  out     SFS_ENABLE, al    ; dummy write to enable SFS
  mov     dx, SFS_INDEX     ; read/write test to index register
  mov     al, 0DDh
  out     dx, al
  in      al, dx
  cmp     al, 0DDh
  jz      sfs_open          ; SFS is enabled
  stc
sfs_open:
  pop     ax
  ret
enable_sfs endp
;---------------------------------------------------------------
;
;  disable_sfs: disable special features set
;
;  Input: None
;
;  Output: None
;
;---------------------------------------------------------------
disable_sfs proc near
  push    ax
  out     SFS_DISABLE, al   ; dummy write to disable SFS
  mov     dx, SFS_INDEX     ; read/write test to index register
  mov     al, 0DDh
  out     dx, al
  in      al, dx
  cmp     al, 0DDh
  jnz     sfs_close         ; SFS is closed
  stc
sfs_close:
  pop     ax
  ret
disable_sfs endp
code  ends
  end
```

I/O Cycle Recovery Time

The I/O cycle recovery time is the delay that the CPU automatically inserts between back-to-back I/O cycles. This recovery time is programmable on the Intel486 SL CPU and Intel386 SL CPU. For 8-bit back-to-back I/O cycles, the I/O cycle recovery time feature is enabled by setting bit 12 of the EBC1CR register (300H, EBU); the minimum I/O cycle recovery time is programmed by the I/O cycle recovery time field (bits [9-11]) of the EBC1CR register. For 16-bit back-to-back I/O cycles, the I/O cycle recovery time feature is enabled by setting bit 8 of the EBC1CR register and bits [6-7] in the EBC1CR register control to the minimum I/O cycle recovery time.

The I/O cycle recovery time does not increase as the number of SYSCLKs in the I/O cycle recovery time field increases. The number of SYSCLKs selected is the minimum delay the CPU will insert between back-to-back I/O cycles. It does not imply that the CPU will generate this many SYSCLKs for all the back-to-back I/O cycles.

Reset

The pulse width of the CPURESET signal is programmable and the generation of the CPURESET signal can be delayed. The CPURESET pulse-width timer sets the width of the CPURESET signal. Timer counts for the pulse-width timer are stored inside the CRST_PULSE register (0F8H, INDEX). Each count represents 0.5 microsecond and the default value is 0EH (7 microsecond).

When using either the SFS or PS/2 fast CPU reset feature to generate a CPURESET signal, it is sometimes desirable to delay the generation of the CPURESET signal. The CPURESET delay timer inside the 82360SL chip generates the delay. The CRST_TMR register contains the timer count for this delay timer. The resolution of this timer is 1 microsecond and the default timer count value is 07H (7 microseconds).

To ensure that the Intel386 SL CPU is initialized properly, the CPURESET signal must be active for at least 18 CPU clocks or 80 CPU clocks (if processor self-test is enabled) after power up. The SYSCLK must be active during system reset so that the synchronous logic inside the 82360SL also gets reset.

Modular Approach

A good rule of thumb in developing firmware for Intel486 SL CPU- or Intel386 SL CPU-based machines is to adopt a modular approach. Large software modules should be broken down into smaller building blocks and all routines should be kept as short as possible.

Keep all the common modules in the same place and separate the hardware-dependent modules from the common routines. A BIOS written in modular fashion makes it easy to update the BIOS and locate problems.

What should a programmer watch for in programming the SL Architecture?*

- SMM is a powerful tool because it can interrupt any application at any time. If used incorrectly, software incompatibility can occur.
- Every time the SFS is enabled, a 4-Kbyte scratchpad RAM is opened at 0F000H of the BIOS address space. If the programmer accesses the SFS in real or SMM mode and does not close the SFS, BIOS routines overlaid by the scratchpad RAM will not be accessible, potentially causing a system crash if the BIOS needs to execute code in that area.

---

* Contributed by Bill Rallis of SystemSoft.

- The ISA-sliding window is designed to access memory in the ISA bus and cannot be used to access system memory controlled by the on-board memory controller. Pointing the ISA window to the on-board memory can cause bad data.
- When doing a software SMI to enter SMM, it is advisable to wait for the software SMI request bit to clear by polling the SM_REQ_STS register (0B7H, INDEX) to ensure the software SMI has completed before continuing into the code that may assume this software SMI is complete.

Summary

When the Intel386 SL CPU was introduced, no one had any idea about what an SL BIOS should look like or how to test it. Some designers had a difficult time designing an SL BIOS, for two major reasons: first, SMM was a new concept to most designers; and second, PC designers were used to the idea that the system BIOS, VGA BIOS, and power management BIOS are separate pieces of software—and they had difficulty integrating these elements into a single BIOS.

Designers looked to Intel for guidance. A BIOS specification was created to help the BIOS writers. This BIOS specification was designed to pack more firmware into a single ROM, and is a good reference for writing your own BIOS. The BIOS specification can be obtained from your local Intel sales office.

References

System BIOS for IBM PC/XT/AT Computers and Compatibles, Phoenix Technologies, 1989.

Dipert, D., and D. Verner, "Designing an Updatable BIOS Using Flash Memory," Intel Corporation, 1991.

Chapter

15

System Development Tools and Debugging

One of the keys to smooth, efficient product development is to make use of existing tools as much as possible. This chapter identifies all the tools you need to design and debug an Intel486 SL CPU- or Intel386 SL CPU-based portable computer. Following the discussion of tools is a series of techniques and hints that will help you to complete your design quickly.

Hardware Development Tools

There are many different motherboard design tools in the market, and they vary in price and selection of features. OrCAD is one inexpensive and popular design package that runs on a PC. OrCAD offers a complete set of schematic capture, simulation, and PCB layout tools. A set of symbols for the Intel SL components in OrCAD format is included in the disk that comes with this book. In addition, you will need equipment such as an oscilloscope, logic analyzer, logic probe, and multimeter.

Software Development Tools

To create software for the Intel486 SL CPU and Intel386 SL CPU, you can use any DOS-based application development tools you are familiar with. A program can be created using any high-level language. The most popular languages are assembly and C. With assembly language, you need an assembler. And if you prefer to use C, you need a C compiler. A good text editor, such as the Brief editor, always helps in writing programs.

After your program is compiled or assembled, you need to use a linker to produce the binary executable files. A program maintainer simplifies the task of updating and generating the programs. There are good program maintainers on the market. I find the Microsoft MAKE program sufficient for my programming needs.

Assuming your program does not always work the first time, a debugger such as SoftICE or Microsoft's CodeView will always help in code tracking. If performance is important, you should consider getting an optimization tool such as the Microsoft Profiler. The Profiler will tell you the relative amount of time it takes for your program's code segments to execute.

If you are going to develop a BIOS, you should have an EPROM programmer. If you are using flash memory for your BIOS, a BIOS update utility program can save you a lot of time in BIOS modifications.

Create Your Own Tools

Unless you really have to, you should not consider building your own tools. It is more productive to use existing tools than to create your own tools. However, there are times when you have no choice. For example, there are many new configuration registers in the Intel486 SL CPU and Intel386 SL CPU, and access to these registers requires an unlocking sequence. Therefore, tools such as a utility to edit the contents of the SL extension registers and a library that contains all the common routines for the Intel486 SL CPU and/or the Intel386 SL CPU will be very useful.

Debugging

Most of the unpleasant surprises that can delay product development occur during the debugging phase. Finding and fixing errors can be very time-consuming. The following sections discuss the techniques that I find helpful for debugging problems. One thing that always amuses me is how the subject of debugging is treated in many books. Many of them stop abruptly at the point where the system starts executing instructions out of the ROM and do not delve any further into debugging problems. This shortcoming is unfortunate, because 99 percent of all bugs occur after you begin executing code from ROM.

This is especially true for the very highly integrated notebook computer environment. Because of the high integration, debugging requires knowledge of every part of the system. I will make an attempt here to look at debugging at a more in-depth level. However, debugging is a very broad subject. Rather than trying to cover every aspect of debugging, I will concentrate on materials pertaining to the Intel486 SL CPU and Intel386 SL CPU only.

Debugging Tools

To debug a design efficiently, you need to have the right tools. Many forms of debugging tools are available for the Intel SL components. On the less expensive side, you might choose a logic probe, logic pulser, monitor ROM, ROM emulator, diagnostic card, and register monitor program. At the high end, you might choose a logic analyzer and an in-circuit emulator (ICE). Each of these tools has its own merits, depending on your needs and budget.

Logic probe and logic pulser

A logic probe and logic pulser are easy to use and can be carried around. Since we are dealing with digital electronics most of the time, a logic probe will serve most of our needs.

I have found a logic pulser especially useful in debugging SMI-related problems. For example, what should you do when you push the suspend/resume button and nothing happens? When the button is pressed, a pulse is generated at the SRBTN# input of the 82360SL, and the 82360SL in turn asserts the SMI# input on the SL CPU. What I would normally do here is use the logic pulser to inject a pulse directly at the SRBTN# input of the 82360SL and the SMI# input of the CPU to see if the system will go into SMM.

ROM emulator

A ROM emulator consists of a probe that connects to the ROM socket on the target system, a serial port to communicate with the host, and a loader program to download the ROM monitor code to the target system. Typically, a ROM emulator provides debugging features such as letting you set breakpoints on individual instructions, set data breakpoints, and single-step a program. With a ROM emulator, a new BIOS can be downloaded to the target system on the fly, making it easier to make changes in the BIOS. Also, you can use the time it would normally take to burn a ROM for other development activities.

A ROM emulator does not have all the capabilities of an ICE, but it also does not suffer from some of the limitations of an ICE. For instance, the transmission line effects of ICE cabling can slow down the execution speed of the target system. This can be a major problem in a high-speed computer system. A ROM emulator, on the other hand, resides on the target system and makes use of the processor running on the system. Therefore, the ROM emulator allows the processor to run at full speed. Some ROM emulators can even be used with source-level debuggers to provide better debugging capability.

ROM monitor

Very often, a register is modified at different locations in your code by different routines. Such occurrences can make debugging difficult. A monitor ROM comes in handy in these situations. To use the ROM monitor, you need a ROM that goes to the target system, a debug program that runs on the host system, and a null modem cable that connects the target system to the host.

The target system must be powered first, before the host can establish the connection. After power up, the ROM monitor will initialize only the interrupt controller, timer, DMA controller, and the serial port. None of the SL CPU extension registers is modified. Once the target system is running, the debugger on the host can be activated.

If you are familiar with the DOS debug program, you should have no problem using the ROM monitor debugger. As with the DOS debug program, you can use the ROM monitor debugger to edit and display memory, input and output data to the I/O ports, and dump the contents of all the CPU registers. It also contains macros for doing memory tests.

Logic analyzer

The most time-consuming part of using a logic analyzer is setting it up. Therefore, it pays to have setup files for different parts of the system. For example, setup files can be created for all the buses on the SL CPU. Having standard test points on your prototype board for hooking up to the logic analyzer is very helpful. Keep in mind that you see only HIGHs and LOWs on the logic analyzer. There are times you might need an oscilloscope to examine a waveform closely, especially when you are dealing with power-control circuitry.

The Intel SL components are CMOS parts. Therefore, be careful when making measurements of the capacitance and resistance of the logic analyzer probes. This caution applies to oscilloscope probes as well. To see how the probe can affect your measurements, think about what happens when you attach a probe to a circuit. The output resistance of the circuit forms an RC circuit with the probe's resistance and capacitance. The RC circuit will slow the rise time of any signal transitions. Thus, you should be careful in probe selection. A probe resistance of 100 kilohms is adequate for most of the CMOS circuits. For high-speed circuits where probe capacitance is critical, you might consider using a high-impedance probe.

Diagnostic card

Sometimes when the BIOS fails to initialize the system, it is helpful to find out where it is going wrong. On a standard ISA system, test codes inside the BIOS are written to I/O port 80H during system initialization and can be displayed on a diagnostic card. There are many variations of diagnostic cards out in the market. Some of them even allow you to single-step the BIOS (for example, the debug card manufactured by AMI). I prefer the ones that allow you to use a different I/O port for displaying the test codes. This is especially helpful if you are writing your own software. Using a different I/O port separates your test codes from the standard BIOS test codes and makes it easier to locate problems.

ICE486SL and ICE386SL

An Intel ICE486SL or ICE386SL offers the advantage of an integrated development environment. You can assemble your code and run it on the target CPU all from a PC or development system. The ability to plug the ICE probe into your target circuit while being able to control and monitor code execution from the host system gives you a great deal of flexibility in debugging your programs and the system.

Note: When using an ICE486SL or an ICE386SL, the ONCE pin is a no-connect signal used to disable all the input and output buffers in the SL CPU.

Isolator

An isolator is a DIP-switch device that allows isolation of IC pins quickly and easily. It eliminates the need for cuts and jumpers.

Isolating the problem

Before I move on to discuss some of the techniques I use to isolate problems, I would like to point out that doing it right in the beginning can save a lot of time in debugging. It always helps to do several design reviews with a group of people before building the prototype. Many common errors can be caught in a design review.

The hardest part of debugging is isolating problems. Sometimes the debugging of a problem becomes so difficult that you need a test plan just for that problem. For example, an Intel customer reported a global standby problem whenever the keyboard generated a system event. However, since a keyboard interrupt is not the only system event, a simple test plan was designed that called for disabling all the other system events (except for the keyboard interrupt) and rerunning the test.

For initial debugging, enable as few options as possible to make it easier to isolate problems. For example, the cache controller, IDE controller, and floppy drive controller can be disabled during initial debugging. You should try to bring up the screen as soon as possible. Once the screen is up, you can display data to the screen.

When powering up a board for the first time, I recommend running the system at a slower speed. If the system does not appear to be doing anything, you should verify that the EFI clock is running. Next, find out if the CPU is fetching instructions from the ROM. The quickest way to find out what the system is doing is to hook up the system to the ICE. If an ICE is not available, a diagnostic card or a logic analyzer can then be used to determine what the system is doing. The test code displayed on the diagnostic card can help you determine where the system is stopping. The logic analyzer can trap the opcodes coming out of the ROM. By translating the opcodes into instructions, you can figure out what the system is doing.

Keeping track of the errors can be a big help at a later date if the same problems resurface. I usually recommend that you log everything you find in a notebook or a database so that you can refer to it later.

Testing Methodology

Laying out all the steps for bringing up a system in a test plan can save you a tremendous amount of time. A test plan usually outlines all the steps required to bring up a system and also the sizes of the resources that are required. This test plan also helps you ensure that you have procured all the test equipment you will need in advance and have written all the test programs to check the hardware.

Milestones are usually included in the test plan to monitor the progress. The milestones are guidelines for bringing up the system incrementally. Below is a list of typical milestones:

1. Fetching instructions out of ROM
2. Booting DOS
3. Running Windows
4. Devices going in and out of local standby
5. System entering and exiting global standby
6. Suspending and resuming the system

During testing, it is recommended that you change one thing at a time only. Changing several things at the same time will make it difficult for you to narrow down the cause of the problem.

In terms of testing, specific test programs can be written to validate different parts of the design. However, the most robust test is to use commercial application software.

Power management testing

Designers often encounter the most problems when trying to bring up the power management system. Many of these problems boil down to how you expect power management to work. In many instances, no single rule of thumb describes how the power management system should work. Having a good power management test plan will help you to discover holes in your power management scheme.

Coming up with a power management test plan is not easy with the SL CPU, since you have many power management options at your disposal. A sample test plan for power management testing can be obtained from your local Intel sales office. Some of the tests might not be relevant to your system, but at least it gives you some idea of how to devise your own test plan.

Memory testing

The memory interface to the SL processor is very straightforward. Since the memory controller is embedded inside the processor, the address multiplexing tables in Chaps. 10 and 11 must be used to determine which address is being accessed by the CPU. Whenever there is a problem, always start with the slowest memory access.

One of the most common problems with memory interfacing is a floating data bus. A good way to find out if the memory or data bus is floating is to do continuous reads from the same location and see if the data changes. To determine whether an address or data bit got stuck at a certain level, specific pattern tests can be developed.

When doing memory tests, keep in mind that the bus-keeper on the memory bus always holds the last value written to the data bus. For instance, if you write "OAA55H" to an unpopulated memory bank, you will get "OAA55H" back. Therefore, to determine if a bank is populated, you must do a double word read/write test. Writing "OAABBCCDDH" to an unpopulated bank will return data invalid data "OXXXXCCDDH".

Test points

Most of the devices in a notebook computer are small and dense. For example, the SL CPU and the 82360SL use 196-pin packages. For debugging, it will be much easier to use test points instead of trying to connect probes directly to the components. However, board space is limited on a notebook computer, making it difficult to add test points. An alternative is to use vias. Vias are used to connect surface-mounted components to the conductor layers. The size of the via should match the aspect ratio. Vias should not be located too close to the components, in order to prevent draining of solder from the component. Another alternative is using test adapters that can mount on top of the SL CPU and the 82360SL.

Common Errors

It is always a good practice to check for common errors before diving into the problem. Learning from someone else's mistakes can save you countless hours in debugging. Common errors can be categorized into three groups:

1. Logic/conceptual errors
2. Noise, electrical, and physical errors
3. Manufacturing errors—poor soldering, layout errors, wiring errors, and faulty devices

In the following sections, we will discuss some useful concepts that will help you solve some of the most common errors.

PWRGOOD signal

The PWRGOOD signal is an active high input to the Intel486 SL, the Intel386 SL CPU, and the 82360SL. The power supply circuitry generates this signal to indicate that the power to the system is good. When the PWRGOOD signal goes low, the CPU and the 82360SL are reset globally, causing the 82360SL to generate a CPURESET and a RESETDRV to reset the system. PWRGOOD should be low for at least one EFI clock cycle to be recognized.

Floating inputs

Floating inputs can cause a device to malfunction and increase system noise levels. It is especially important not to allow unused inputs on CMOS devices to float. Open inputs on CMOS devices may cause the device to overheat and destroy the device. All unused inputs should be tied to a valid logic level.

For most TTL devices (except standard TTL and S logic families), unused inputs can be tied directly to Vcc or ground. However, a pull-down or pull-up resistor may be required in some cases. If a pull-up or pull-down resistor is needed, the resistance must be sized to ensure that input level requirements are met.

All unused inputs on a CMOS device should be pulled low or high, as required, for proper operation. For most CMOS and TTL applications, a 1-kilohm pull-up resistor is normally sufficient. With TTL and CMOS devices, logic high input current is very low (20 mA for TTL devices and 1 mA for CMOS devices). To minimize board space and component count, many unused inputs (should be limited to less than 10) can be pulled up with the same pull-up resistor.

Real-time clock

The real-time clock may be a small part on an ISA computer, but it is definitely a star in an SL CPU-based system. The suspend mechanism on CPU relies heavily on the real-time clock. It is the only clock that is running during suspend. All the logic that is active is clocked by the real-time clock oscillator.

Windows

Understanding how the application software works is always beneficial in isolating the problem. The Microsoft Windows environment is often used to verify that power management is working. Many people are intimidated by problems associated with Windows; however, understanding a few aspects of Windows operation can make it a useful test tool.

Windows is an operating environment that runs on top of a copy of MS-DOS (Version 3.0 or later). When Windows is running in enhanced mode, the Virtual DOS Machine Manager (VDMM) is loaded into extended memory. The VDMM runs in virtual 8086 mode and manages the virtual tasks created by Windows. It also emulates LIM 4.0 EMS memory using the Intel386 processor's paging capability, which eliminates the need for EMS hardware and an EMS driver. Each virtual task created by Windows is called a virtual machine.

The initial virtual machine contains a copy of the Windows program running on top of DOS. When a DOS application is started, a new virtual machine is created. After a copy of DOS, the ROM BIOS data area, and other data structures are loaded in the new virtual machine, the application can be loaded into the virtual machine.

Windows' standard mode is intended for use with 80286 machines. The 80286 microprocessor has no provision for returning to real mode from protected mode because it will defeat the protection mechanisms. To allow the Windows program to return to real mode, the Windows program writes to the shutdown byte in the CMOS RAM, sends a CPU reset command to the keyboard controller, and halts the CPU. The CPU reset command causes the keyboard controller to reset the CPU and execute the reset routine in the BIOS. The reset routine will then examine the CMOS RAM. When it sees the flag, it restores the contents of the CPU and pass control to the application program.

TABLE 15.1 Sources of a CPU Reset

Sources of CPU reset	Actions
Cold boot	Execution starts at 0FFFF0H. All POST tests and initializations are executed. All peripherals are reset by the RESETDRV signal.
Hardware reset	Execution starts at 0FFFF0H. All POST tests and initializations are executed. All peripherals are reset by the RESETDRV signal.
Warm boot	Execution starts at POST tests entry point. Except for POST test and initialization for memory above 64 Kbytes, all other POST tests and initialization are executed.
Resume	Execution starts at 0FFFF0H. System enters SMM through software SMI.

CPU reset

In an SL CPU-based system, four types of system events can generate a CPU reset: cold boot, hardware reset, warm boot, and resume. Table 15.1 shows the actions that are taken for each of these reset events. A cold boot is what we normally call power on, and the CPU reset is generated by the PWRGOOD signal. A hardware reset can be generated by a hardware switch or by a special key sequence. The entire system is initialized during a cold boot and a hardware reset. A warm boot is invoked by typing the CNTRL-ALT-DEL key sequence, and only part of the system is initialized. Resume is initiated by a resume event (suspend/resume button, modem ring, or calendar event).

In an SL CPU-based system, the 82360SL generates the CPU RESET. Generating the CPU reset signal through the 82360SL ensures that CPU reset will not occur while the CPU is in SMM.

System management interrupt

On a standard SL CPU-based system, the 82360SL acts like a traffic director for system management interrupts (SMIs). The 82360SL functions as a gate that filters all the incoming SMI requests, plus those generated inside the 82360SL, and passes them on to the CPU.

SMI generation is not instantaneous, because all SMI requests go through some sort of arbitration inside the 82360SL before they get passed on to the CPU. Table 15.2 shows the delay due to internal arbitration for the different SMI requests.

For some SMI requests, an SMI is not generated until the suspend warning timer has expired. For example, pushing the suspend/resume trigger button will not generate an SMI until the suspend warning timer for suspend/resume requests expires.

TABLE 15.2 Delays for Various Types of SMI Requests

SMI request	Minimum delay	Maximum delay
External SMI	1 ms	2.1 ms
Suspend/resume button	128 ms	256 ms
Battery low	128 ms	256 ms
ASMI	2 SYSCLKs	3 SYSCLKs

How often a register is sampled

Whenever a bit is set or cleared, the actual changing of the bit's state does not always happen immediately. Because of internal synchronization, a delay is normally inserted before the bit is actually changed. The length of this delay depends on the sampling rate, which in turn depends on the clock rate.

Signal path

When running at a fast clock rate, the length of a signal line must be limited to a point where it will cause a significant voltage drop. During layout phase, you should ensure that all signal paths are within limit.

Table 15.3 shows the maximum signal line lengths in millimeters and inches for various logic families.

Signal terminations

In a high-speed memory interface, ringing can happen if signals are not properly terminated. Table 15.4 shows the typical damping resistance requirements for the various memory control signals in an SL CPU-based system. The recommended characteristic impedance for boards is 50 ohms. Lower values are better, since higher values increase the amount of ringing.

The buffers for MEMR#, MEMW#, IOR#, and IOW# are designed to drive 240 picofarads, sink 24 milliamperes, and provide a maximum delay of 19 nanoseconds. If there are no series damping resistors, under the worst-case conditions the ringing takes 20 nanoseconds to die down, which means the pin timing will be off by a large margin. For the SYSCLK signal, the maximum amplitude is 1.2 volts under worst-case if no series damping resistor is used.

TABLE 15.3 Maximum Allowable Signal Line Lengths

Logic family	Signal line length, mm (in)
Low-power Schottky (LS)	760 (30)
Schottky (S)	280 (11)
Advanced LS (ALS)	280 (11)
Advanced Schottky TTL	200 (8)
Advanced Schottky (AS)	150 (6)
Advanced CMOS technology	200 (8)
Emitter-coupled logic (ECL)	150 (6)

TABLE 15.4 Damping Resistor Requirement for Different Memory Signals (Intel386 SL CPU)

Signals	Damping resistor
MA[10:0] and RAS [3:0]	22-ohm
MEMR#, MEMW#, IOR#, IOW#, and SYSCLK	10-ohm
IOCHRDY, IOCS16#, MEMCS16#, WLE#, WHE#, BALE, SD[15:0]	Recommended but not required

What to Do If a System Hangs Up

A lot of things can cause the system to hang up, such as getting in an infinite loop, a memory error, or a malfunctioning peripheral. The quickest way to find out if a system is still alive is to check if the NumLock key on the keyboard still toggles. To see if the system hangs up because of a memory problem, you can check the RAS#, CAS#, and refresh signals. If you suspected a peripheral is causing the problem, you can replace the peripheral with another one.

Sometimes, if an SMM program is not written correctly, it can cause the system to hang up. One way to find out if the system is hung up inside SMM is to examine the SMI# pin on the CPU. If the SMI# is low (active), the system is still in SMM.

What If Everything Else Fails?

Very often, we will run into situations where we have tried everything we can think of to solve a problem but the problem still persists. In this kind of situation, it always helps to discuss the problem with someone. My experience is that even talking to someone who doesn't know anything will help. In telling someone about your problem, what you are effectively doing is summarizing what the problem is and what you have done about it. A lot of times, people such as your colleagues can provide useful suggestions for you to try, and explanations for the problems. And sometimes, I realize what I have done wrong even before I finish describing the problem.

One thing I would recommend is to try not to spend an excessive amount of time on the problem—even when you are under the pressure of a deadline. Pushing yourself too hard can work against you. When you are tired, you tend to make more errors. It would be better to stay away from the problem for a short while and come back with a new perspective.

Development Methodology

Designing an SL CPU-based system requires a high level of integration between hardware and software. To have a better chance of success at integrating the firmware, the software design process should start in parallel with the hardware design. This will help the software engineers identify software–hardware interaction problems much earlier.

It takes time to learn how to use new tools. To make your product development time more productive, you should use the tools you are familiar with, unless you find them insufficient for the task at hand.

Summary

Many people think that debugging a system is much harder than designing a system, and there is definitely some truth to it. As portable computer designers, we often have to deal with unfamiliar hardware and software. This is especially true with power management. What is supposed to be a power-saving feature can turn out to be a problem. For example, powering off the RS232 buffers for the serial ports during suspend can save power, but doing so will also block the modem ring signal from going through the buffers to resume the system.

Debugging an SL CPU-based system does not require elegant tools. Most of the problems can be solved with a logic probe and a software debugger. However, it does require that you have a clear understanding of the SL architecture, which is what this book is about. Much of the discussion in this chapter is based on my experience in debugging SL architecture-based systems. Even though no two systems are identical, the same debugging technique can still be applied to any system.

References

Buchanan, J., *CMOS/TTL Digital Systems Design,* McGraw-Hill Publishing Company.

Dawson, P. and A. Lantz, "ROM Monitor Tips and Tricks Aid Debugging Effort," *EDN Magazine,* special software supplement, June 1991, pp. 23–29.

Duncan, R., "Microsoft Windows/386: Creating a Virtual Machine Environment," *Microsoft Systems Journal,* September 1987, pp. 1–11.

Porter, A. "Use the Analytic Approach to Avoid Errors When Probing CMOS Circuits," *EDN Magazine,* March 1992, pp. 123–128.

Seidensticker, R., *The Well-Tempered Digital Design,* Addison-Wesley Publishing Company, 1986.

Chapter

16

Performance and Potential

Introduction

The Intel486 SL CPU is based on the Intel486 SX CPU core, and the Intel386 SL CPU is based on the Intel386 SX CPU core. The SL CPUs thus offer performance similar to that of the SX versions and, in some cases, even better. This chapter contains performance data for the 16-, 20-, and 25-MHz versions of the Intel386 SL CPU. (At the time this book went to press, performance information was not available for the Intel486 SL CPU.) The performance data presented here highlights the benefits of various CPU attributes that can affect system performance. You can use this information as a general guideline for fine-tuning your portable computer designs.

The benchmark programs used in this chapter measure system performance only. Unlike CPU performance benchmarks, which show the performance of the CPU only, system performance shows the performance of the various system components working together.

As with any benchmark program, it is relatively easy to tailor a benchmark that shows one machine outperforming another. For some of the benchmark programs, using a different configuration might yield different results. In the process of collecting benchmark data for this chapter, extra effort has been made to create the same environment for every machine tested. However, due to the compact nature of notebook systems, it is difficult to do an exact "apple to apple" comparison using the same hardware configuration for all the systems benchmarked.

It is helpful to keep the following questions in mind when comparing the performance data in this chapter against results published by others: When were the benchmarks run? By whom? Using which hardware and software configuration? In addition, a good understanding of the benchmark programs can help in interpreting the results correctly. Since DOS is the operating system of choice for notebook platform, only DOS benchmark programs were used.

Common Terminology

This section discusses some terms commonly used in benchmark reports. Skip to the next section if you are familiar with these terms already.

Wait state

One thing people always tout when describing performance is the number of wait states. In the Intel386 SL CPU, it takes a minimum of two CPU clock cycles to complete a memory cycle. Any extra CPU clock cycle added is called a *wait state.*

To determine the number of wait states that a system is using, testers normally measure the time it takes to perform a fixed number of memory cycles and subtract it from the time it takes if no wait state is inserted. They then divide this number by the number of cycles. Below is a formula for calculating the number of wait states:

((time to perform a fixed number of memory cycles)
– (# of CPU clock cycles* (1/CPU clock speed))
÷ number of cycles performed

Since not every memory cycle incurs a wait state, the number of wait states is not always an even number.

Turbo mode

The term *turbo mode* is often used when describing the various levels of performance a machine might offer. With the SL CPU, turbo mode refers to a state in which the CPU is running at full speed. *De-turbo mode* means running at less than full CPU clock speed. As explained in Chap. 9, the CPU clock speed is controlled through hardware and software, and can be slowed or stopped to reduce power consumption.

Battery life

Battery life is a reference to the power-saving capability of a system. It is generally given as the number of hours the machine can operate on a single battery charge. This number is normally obtained by running a program on the machine continuously. *Battery life* of the system is the number of hours it takes to discharge the battery to below the level needed to operate the system.

The power consumption of the system is measured in watts per hour.

$$\text{Power} = V^2 * \text{K}$$

where V is voltage and K is a constant (K = capacitance * frequency).

Power consumption can be measured with a current probe or a multimeter, and is highly dependent on the operating state of the system. For example, the clock speed or the number of disk accesses required can greatly affect the power consumption of a system.

Intel386 SL CPU Performance Summary

The high level of function integration in the Intel386 SL CPU allows a cache controller and a memory controller to be included on the chip. These controllers help the Intel386 SL CPU achieve its high performance levels. Programmable options are also provided on the Intel386 SL CPU for fine-tuning system performance. The following are programmable options that can affect performance: cache size, cache mapping, DRAM page mode, DRAM refresh rate, flash BIOS wait states, and SRAM wait states. These options allow the OEMs to balance the tradeoff between cost and performance.

Test results show that notebooks using the Intel386 SL CPU deliver higher performance than other notebook PCs in the market. The 25-MHz Intel386 SL CPU delivers the highest performance among all the systems tested. The relative performance of the 25-MHz Intel386 SL CPU is about half that of the Intel486 DX CPU at the same clock speed. The 20-MHz Intel386 SL CPU is about 20 percent slower than its 25-MHz counterpart. There is a dramatic difference in performance between the standard part and a cacheless part at the same clock speed. The difference can be as much as 40 percent.

In a comparison of a 20-MHz Intel386 SX-based machine (without a cache) and the 20-MHz Intel386 SL CPU-based evaluation board (with cache), the controller disabled showed that the performance of the Intel386 SL CPU-based system is about 10 percent higher.

Most DOS benchmark programs are small. Thus, a system with a small cache, such as a machine with only 4 Kbytes of cache, can produce results as good as an SL evaluation board with a large cache. A larger cache should improve system performance measurement when running large benchmark programs such as the SPEC benchmark or the Unix benchmark, and real-life applications like Microsoft Windows and EXCEL.

Impact of System Attributes on Performance

To get a good understanding of how some of the system attributes can affect performance, the SL evaluation board was tested using several different system configurations. The configuration of the memory system is a critical factor in the overall system performance. The cache controller and memory controller inside the Intel386 SL CPU have been designed to offer the highest possible performance with maximum flexibility.

The on-chip cache controller supports three different cache sizes: 16-, 32-, and 64-Kbyte. You might expect that large caches offer greater performance than small caches. However, as mentioned earlier in this chapter, due to the small size of the DOS benchmark programs, a large cache often does not result in better benchmark performance. Also, adding a 16-Kbyte cache offers a dramatic improvement in performance over a system with no cache.

The cache controller supports three different cache mapping mechanisms: direct, two-way, and four-way. Again, due to the small size of the benchmark programs, the impact of cache mapping on performance is minor. The cache controller has a write poster which will post up to three words before the CPU stops processing. However, only local memory or ISA-bus memory write cycles during hold acknowledge are posted. If the write poster is disabled, the overall performance drops by about 5 percent.

Memory paging is a technique to improve system memory performance, and the Intel386 SL CPU offers three DRAM page modes. With the cache controller enabled, the difference in performance between the different page modes is about 2 percent. Thus, designers can use slower and cheaper DRAMs with the Intel386 SL CPU and still have a high system throughput. On the other hand, the DRAM page mode makes a big difference for cacheless systems. When the cache controller is not used, the difference in performance between the different page modes is about 13 percent.

The normal refresh rate and suspend refresh rate on the Intel386 SL CPU are programmable to support DRAMs with extended refresh rates. However, changing the refresh rate does not affect the performance of the system. This is also true for interleaving. The performance of the system is the same with or without interleaving. Changing the refresh rate and using interleaving does, however, have a big effect on battery life.

The memory controller supports a DRAM as well as an SRAM interface. Using the smallest number of wait states (two), the performance of a SRAM system is about 7 percent slower than a DRAM system using the high-speed page mode. Adding one wait state to an SRAM system has a 4 percent performance penalty.

Flash BIOS wait states can be implemented to support slower flash memory devices. Using wait states for the flash BIOS affects code execution speed whenever code is executed out of the flash BIOS (e.g., an application makes a BIOS function call). Test results show, however, that adding wait states to the flash BIOS have little impact on performance.

Overall, the Intel386 SL CPU delivers the highest performance with maximum flexibility to accommodate factors such as cost, power consumption, product differentiation, and product size.

Low on high performance

A high-performance processor can be slowed down to a crawl by slow I/O traffic. The key to high system performance is sustained throughput. System performance in an Intel486 SL CPU- or an Intel386 SL CPU-based system can be improved dramatically through effective use of the I/O support mechanism provided in the CPU and 82360SL, and through careful selection of peripherals.

CPU clock speed

Table 16.1 contains benchmark results for different CPU clock speeds, using a 20-MHz Intel386 SL CPU-based evaluation system with a 64-Kbyte cache. As you can see, CPU performance is directly proportional to clock speed. However, CPU performance does not always correlate directly to system performance.

De-turbo mode was provided not only for power management, but also to maintain compatibility with older software. Newer software designs, however,

TABLE 16.1 Power Meter V1.5 Benchmark Results under Different Clock Speeds

Test	EFI/2	EFI/4	EFI/8
Aggregate (PMU)	210.66	105.08	52.35
Clock (MHz)	10.77	6.20	3.83
MIPs	1.986	.997	.499
Dhrystone (K/s)	2.547	1.278	.639
Whetstone (K/s)	385.39	202	104.97
Sieve (s)	1.634	3.283	6.619
Video Agg (PMU)	1786.3	894	487.1
Video Char (s)	1.8	3.516	6.382

generally do not restrict system operation at high CPU speeds. Therefore, you rarely need to slow down the CPU to get software to work.

Listing 9.1 in Chap. 9 gives a short program that changes the clock speed of the CPU under software control.

Math coprocessor

For numeric-intensive programs such as spreadsheets or CAD programs, a math coprocessor (MCP) such as the Intel387 SL mobile math coprocessor can improve performance by as much as five times. An MCP is useful only when a program is doing a lot of number crunching of real numbers (floating-point numbers). For some of the AutoCAD benchmarks, you can see a performance increase ranging from 30 percent to 100 percent.

Peripherals

Have you ever wondered why machines with the same motherboard often get different performance reviews using the same set of benchmark programs? One reason for these performance differences is that different peripherals are used in the systems. Your choice of peripherals has a strong impact on overall system performance. For example, a hard disk drive with a fast access time can improve the system performance by as much as 10 percent (over systems that use slower drives) in some benchmarks.

Careful selection of peripherals is thus important in designing a high-performance system. On the other hand, data throughput for some of the devices can be increased by the addition of external hardware. For instance, a disk cache can significantly improve the data access time for a hard disk drive.

Sometimes, even minor changes can improve performance. An example (Listing 16.2) gives a few simple lines of code for changing the step rate of a floppy drive to improve the disk access time.

Listing 16.2 Code to Change the Step Rate of a Floppy Drive

```
xor    ax, ax
mov    ds, ax                ; set data segment at 0
mov    bx, 522               ; offset of the disk parameter table
mov    byte ptr [bx], 0EFh   ; change step rate to 4 ms
```

DMA clock speed

The DMA controllers are typically used for ISA-bus memory refresh and by the floppy drive and network adapters. On a standard ISA-bus system, the clock speed for the DMA controller is 4 MHz, which is very slow. With the 82360SL, the DMA controller clock can be set to 8 MHz to improve data throughput. Increasing the DMA clock speed is done by setting the DMASEL bit (bit 1) in the CFGR1 register (63H, INDEX) to 1.

ISA bus

To remain compatible with the industry standard ISA-bus architecture, the ISA-bus clock speed is restricted to 8 MHz only. Wait states are normally inserted in memory and I/O cycles (one wait state for memory cycles and four wait states for I/O cycles). Higher performance can be achieved if wait states are eliminated (that is, using zero wait states for both memory and I/O cycles). When you have to access the ISA bus, use it efficiently (e.g., always use zero wait state transfer and I/O string instructions for data transfers).

PI bus

If you wish to use one or more peripheral devices that have performance greater than is possible with ISA-bus devices but you do not want to abandon the ISA bus completely, you should definitely consider using the PI bus. Except for a few control signals, the PI-bus interface is essentially the same as the ISA-bus interface, except that the PI bus runs at the CPU clock speed. In an SL CPU-based system, PI-bus peripherals can coexist with ISA-bus peripherals.

You can achieve significant improvement in performance at a very small cost by modifying key peripherals that affect performance of the system to run on the PI bus. For example, the performance of the VGA graphics controller is critical in graphics-intensive applications such as Microsoft Windows. A VGA controller using the PI bus can run anywhere from 30 to 100 percent faster than on the ISA bus.

Impact of Power Management on Performance

The power management system of an SL CPU-based system does have some impact on system performance. Some of this impact is by design. For instance, slowing the clock speed of the CPU reduces power consumption at the expense of CPU throughput. Running power management software affects performance because it uses CPU cycles (even though it is running in SMM). The effect of your power management system on overall system performance is thus highly dependent on how it is implemented and which benchmarks are being used to measure performance.

Most of the power management operations (e.g., disabling of the serial port buffers) take less than a millisecond to execute, so they will have minimal impact on performance when the system is working intensely at full CPU speed. You probably will not see the difference in performance when running standard DOS benchmark programs, since they tend to exercise the entire machine. With a multitasking environment benchmark, you will probably see some difference, but the overall impact on performance will still be small.

Performance and Cost

People often say that if you want the best you have to pay more. The question is, how much you are willing to pay? In any design, you must evaluate the tradeoffs between cost and performance. For example, with the Intel386 SL CPU's built-in cache controller, you can use slower and less expensive DRAMs; however, the savings in using cheaper DRAMs might be offset by the cost of implementing the cache. But, then again, this cost might be justified by the overall performance gain from the cache.

With portable computers, you also have to balance tradeoffs between power consumption and cost. For instance, using SRAMs for main memory can lower power consumption. However, SRAMs are more expensive than DRAMs and not available in high-density packages. For a typical portable machine with 4 Mbytes of base memory, SRAMs are ordinarily too expensive. But for a hand-held computer with a small amount of base memory, SRAMs might be a better choice than DRAMs, since power consumption is more critical in hand-held products.

Power Consumption Benchmarks

Power consumption benchmarks are relative new and not well understood. Due to a misunderstanding of how power management is supposed to extend battery life, many battery-life benchmarks ignore the built-in power management capabilities of a system.

Typically, power consumption benchmarks are obtained by exercising the system continuously until the battery goes dead. A more refined power consumption benchmark might use a test script with a typical user profile. For example, users always pause when they are typing. During pauses, sophisticated power management systems often slow or stop the CPU clock. Using scripts that force periodic pauses in processing are thus better able to measure the effectiveness of a power management system.

Benchmarks can also be created to check out a specific part of a system. For example, running Microsoft Windows in enhanced mode is very CPU-intensive. Therefore, it can be used as a benchmark for CPU power efficiency. Again, a special test script using a typical user profile can be developed to benchmark the display system.

Knowing the relative power consumption efficiency of all the components in the system can help you design power consumption benchmarks and understand the results of other benchmarks. For example, the SL CPU can be made to operate in several different low-power modes. However, if you look at the power consumption of all the peripherals in a system, you will realize that the power consumed by the CPU is negligible compared with that of the hard disk and LCD panel.

Interpreting Benchmark Results

Power consumption benchmark results are often quoted without giving background information. Therefore, they can be very misleading, especially for the end users. When looking at any power consumption benchmark, you should always ask yourself these questions: What functions does the benchmark program perform? What is the system configuration of the machines tested? What type of battery is used, and what is the capacity of the battery?

How the benchmark program is written can affect the battery life. For example, two different benchmark programs often yield different battery-life numbers. Also, since not all the machines are identical, it makes no sense to compare a fully loaded machine to a machine with minimal configuration. If a machine has two battery packs, it will likely have a longer battery life than other machines, regardless of how efficient its power management system is.

Benchmark Collection Methodology

The benchmark data quoted in this chapter was obtained on an Intel386 SL CPU-based evaluation board. The evaluation board was used for benchmarking because it is easy to configure. Since the evaluation board is strictly a vehicle for evaluation, no optimization was done to achieve the highest performance possible. The performance data obtained on the SL evaluation board thus provides typical data. It is possible to obtain better performance by changing hardware or software configuration. Also, some benchmark programs depend on video graphics controller and hard disk performance.

DOS environments

All benchmarks were executed under DOS 3.3, DOS 4.01, or DOS 5.0 with the same config.sys file, the contents of which are as follows:

```
FILES = 30
BUFFERS = 20
DEVICE = HIMEM.SYS
DEVICE = SMARTDRV.SYS 2048 512
```

Except for the SL system, all the machines tested came with proprietary DOS operating systems. Installing a different version of DOS might cause the system to malfunction. Therefore, no attempt was made to use the same version of DOS on all the systems tested.

System configurations

The Intel386 SL CPU evaluation board used for benchmarking has the following configuration:

Intel386 SL CPU—B0 stepping

16/20/25 MHz

4 Mbytes of main memory (2 banks, interleaved)

64-Kbyte write through cache

16-bit VGA card

28-ms Prairie 240 IDE drive

(no MCP installed)

Except as indicated, all benchmarks were executed with the following BIOS configurations: system and video BIOS shadowed, cache configured for four-way mapping, and DRAM mode set to high-speed page mode.

Summary

Beauty is in the eyes of the beholder and so are benchmark programs. Different benchmark programs will give different performance results. There is no rigid rule or guideline for interpreting benchmark data. A lot of it is common sense. As long as you compare the results to the actual user environment, you can always gain a good grasp of what to expect.

Chapter

17

The Future

We cannot predict precisely how portable computers will evolve. However, we can foresee the general direction. Ever since I started working on the Intel386 SL processor, I have seen an analogy between the evolution of portable computers and the evolution of calculators. It may have something to do with the fact that the first microprocessor was used in the calculator. In their early days, calculators were bulky and expensive. As time went by, both the demand for calculators and advances in technology drove manufacturers to produce calculators that were cheaper, lighter, and faster. Now, we are acknowledging that same trend in the portable computer market. Portable computers are getting cheaper, lighter, and more powerful. The future of portable computers will definitely bear a close resemblance to the evolution of calculators.

What Next?

3.3-volt and 5-volt hybrid system

Power is equal to V^2/R. So, lowering the operating voltage (V_{cc}) will reduce power consumption and in turn extend battery life. Currently, manufacturers and Intel are moving toward 3.3-volt technology for components. However, the conversion from 5 to 3.3 volts will not happen overnight. Many issues remain to be resolved.

Two of the major problems facing designers of 3.3-volt systems are the lack of standardization and the availability of 3.3-volt components. Even though the JEDEC standard is available, it does not cover areas such as interfacing to a 3.3-volt ISA bus. The lack of standardization has made it hard for chip designers to design and test their components, slowing the development of 3.3-volt components.

Even though the CPU and memory manufacturers have taken the lead in supplying 3.3-volt components, the availability of 3.3-volt parts to build a complete 3.3-volt system is still very limited. To speed up the conversion process, most manufacturers have recharacterized 5-volt parts to run at 3.3-volts. The only drawback to this practice is the degradation of performance. After recharacterization, the 5-volt parts will run at a slower speed.

In the absence of standardization and availability, it is better to take an incremental approach. The first and most logical step in migrating to a complete 3.3-volt system is to run everything at 3.3 volts except for the ISA-bus peripherals. And this is exactly how the Intel486 SL CPU is designed, as you learned in Chap. 16.

A complete 3.3-volt system

The Intel486 SL CPU has certainly paved the way toward a complete 3.3-volt system. The knowledge which you gained in building a hybrid system using the Intel486 SL CPU will definitely help you in moving one step closer to a complete 3.3-volt system. Based on the rate at which manufacturers are currently creating 3.3-volt components, we will see many complete 3.3-volt systems toward the end of 1993.

How low is low? If lowering operating voltage from 5 volts to 3.3 volts can save substantial power, reducing operating voltage further will save even more power. The question is, how low can we go? As we push for higher speed and lower power consumption, there is no doubt that the operating voltage will decrease again. People have already started talking about moving all the way down to 1 volt—which will probably not happen for several years.

However, we can prepare for yet another voltage migration even though we don't know when it is coming. For example, whatever standards are formulated for 3.3-volt components should be flexible enough to be easily extended to 1-volt components.

LCD display

The LCD display market is moving in two directions. As more and more portable computer manufacturers are using color LCD panels, they will find the means to improve the color display technology as well as to reduce the cost of production. On a different front, LCD panel manufacturers are looking for ways to reduce power consumption.

The LCD panel is the most power-hungry device in a system consisting of liquid crystal display, LCD driver chips, and the backlight. In an average system, the LCD display consumes 30 to 40 percent of the total power.

Battery technology

Since I have been working with the SL CPU, I have been looking forward to the day when portable computers are solar powered (like calculators). With a solar powered system, users never have to bother recharging the battery. I do not expect solar power to become a feasible source of power for portable computers for many years to come.

What technology improvements, if any, have occurred that we should be aware of, and is there anything better available on the horizon?*

NiCd manufacturers are continuously seeking to improve product capabilities and quality. Increased capacity means longer run times. For many years, battery makers have boosted capacity by over 10 percent a year, driving research into new electrochemical couples. Rechargeable lithium and Ni-metal hydride cells are prominent contenders, with significant increases in energy density over NiCd cells.

Metal hydride is progressing steadily, and is also equivalent in voltage to NiCd cells. Broad acceptance of metal hydride depends on its ability to be successfully used in several environments.

Pen-based computers

Will pen-based computers universally replace computers with keyboards? Probably not anytime soon. The technology is still in its infancy. Pen-based computers are still limited to vertical markets such as specific industrial and business applications.

Software collaboration

With the introduction of Advanced Power Management Specification for DOS and Windows, we should expect other operating systems such as UNIX and OS/2 to become power aware.

User psychology

Is it necessarily true that the lightest portable with the longest battery life is the best portable computer? Not always. Frequently, portable computer designers have neglected the importance of understanding user needs and psychology. For example, just look at the ergonomics of the track ball in some portable computers. Many manufacturers placed the track ball in a location that is hard for users to reach. User-friendly features are becoming increasingly important in today's PC market, where there is little differentiation between machines.

Another logical question is, of course, who are the users? Have you ever asked a friend, "Would you buy a portable computer for your own use?" Probably 90 percent of respondents to this question would say, "No." Most of the people who are buying portable computers are business users, most of whom travel frequently. They buy portable computers so that they can work while they travel.

Frequently, portable computers are designed to serve the needs of these people. For example, many portable computers have built-in fax modems or offer them as an option. These options allow you to communicate easily with your office while you are traveling. Some portable computers even offer a connector to hook up with a cellular phone.

---

* Contributed by Mark Dewey of Gates Energy Products.

So, how do you determine users' needs so that you can design appropriate features into your future products? The best way to find out is to become a user yourself. The other way is to do some research by reading magazines, market research reports, and consumer reports.

Mainstream computing

Will portable computers replace desktop computers in the next few years? The answer to this question hinges on cost and ease of use. If the price points for portable and desktop computers converge, and portable computers become as powerful as desktop computers, more people will switch over to portable computers.

Does that mean desktop computers will become history? That is unlikely. Instead, we will see many PC manufacturers applying portable computer technologies to desktop computers, to conserve energy. For example, a few desktop computer manufacturers are already experimenting with using Intel SL CPUs and other SL components to reduce power usage in desktop machines.

Appendix A

List of Vendors

Manufacturers of DRAMs

Electronic Designs Inc.
42 South St.
Hopkinton, MA 01748
(508) 435-6302
Fax (508) 435-6302

Fujitsu Microelectronics Inc.
Integrated Circuits Division
3545, N. First St.
San Jose, CA 95134
(800) 642-7616
in CA, (408) 922-9000
Fax (408) 432-9044

Goldstar Electron America
3003 N. First St.
San Jose, CA 95134
(408) 432-1331
Fax (408) 432-6067

Hitachi America Ltd.
Semiconductor and IC Division
2000, Sierra Point Pkwy.
Brisbane, CA 94005
(415) 589-8300
Fax (415) 583-4207

Hyundai Electronics America
166, Baypointe Pkwy.
San Jose, CA 95134
(408) 473-9200
Fax (408) 493-9567

Micron Technology
2805, E. Columbia Rd.
Boise, ID 83706
(208) 368-3900
Fax (208) 368-4617

Mitsubishi Electronics America Inc.
Electronic Devices Group
1050 E. Arques Ave.
Sunnyvale, CA 94086
(408) 730-5900
Fax (408) 749-0453

Motorola Inc.
3501 Ed Bluestein Blvd.
MS K13
Box 6000
Austin, TX 78762
(512) 928-6700
Fax (512) 928-6809

NMB Technologies
9730 Independence Ave.
Chatsworth, CA 91311
(818) 341-3355
Fax (818) 341-8207

Oki Semiconductor
785 N. Mary
Sunnyvale, CA 94086
(408) 770-1900

Panasonic Industrial Co.
1616, McCandless Dr.
Milpitas, CA 95035
(408) 945-5650
Fax (408) 946-9063

Samsung Semiconductor
3725 N. First St.
San Jose, CA 95134
(408) 954-7229
Fax (408) 954-7873

Sharp Electronics Corp.
5700 NW Pacific Rim Blvd.
Camas, WA 98607
(206) 834-8700
Fax (206) 834-8611

Texas Instruments Inc.
Semiconductor Group
Box 809066
Dallas, TX 75380
(800) 366-5236, Ext. 700
In Texas (214) 995-6611 Ext. 700

Toshiba America
Electronic Components Inc.
9775 Toledo Bay
Irvine, CA 92718
(714) 455-2000
Fax (714) 859-3963

Vitelic Semiconductor Corp.
3910 N. First St.
San Jose, CA 95134
(408) 433-6000
Fax (408) 433-0185

Manufacturers of LCD Display

Cherry Corp.
3600 Sunset Ave.
Waukegan, IL 60087
(708) 360-3513
Fax (708) 360-3566

Epson America Inc.
20770 Madrona Ave.
Torrance, CA 90503
(310) 787-6300
Fax (310) 782-5350

Fujitsu Microelectronics
Electronic Components Div.
3545 North First St.
San Jose, CA 95134
(408) 922-8933
Fax (408) 428-0640

Hitachi America, Ltd.
3850 Holcomb Bridge Rd.
Suite 300
Norcross, GA 30092
(404) 409-3000
Fax (404) 409-3028

Optrex/Satori
3830 De Amo Blvd.
Suite 101
Torrance, CA 90503
(310) 214-1791
Fax (310) 214-8228

Planar Systems, Inc.
1400 North West Compton Dr.
Beaverton, OR 97006
(503) 690-1100
Fax (503) 690-1244

Plasmaco Inc.
180 South St.
Highland, NY 12528
(914) 883-6800
Fax (914) 883-6867

Manufacturers of Power Supplies

Astec Standard Power
401 Jones Rd.
Ocean Side, CA 92054
(619) 757-1880
Fax (619) 439-4243

Coutant-Lambda
Kingsley-Ave.
Ilfracombe EX34 8ES, UK
(271) 863781
Fax (271) 864894

Deltron
Box 1369
North Wales, PA 19454
(215) 699-9261
Fax (619) 699-2310

Philips Industrial
Box 218, 5600 MD Eindhoven,
The Netherlands
(40) 786280
Fax (40) 785968

Power-One
740 Calle Plano
Camarillo, CA 93012
(805) 987-8741
Fax (805) 388-0476

Qualidyne Systems
3055 Del Sol Blvd.
San Diego, CA 92154
(619) 575-1100
Fax (619) 429-1011

Unipower
2981 Gateway Dr.
Pompano Beach, FL 33069
(305) 974-2442
Fax (305) 971-1837

Vicor
23 Frontage Rd.
Andover, MA 01810
(508) 470-2900
Fax (508) 475-6715

Manufacturers of Hard Disk Drives

Areal Technology
2075 Zanker Rd.
San Jose, CA 95131
(408) 436-6844
Fax (408) 436-6844

Conner Peripherals Inc.
3081 Zanker Rd.
San Jose, CA 95134
(408) 456-4500
Fax (408) 456-4501

Fujitsu America Inc.
3055, Orchard Dr.
San Jose, CA 95134
(408) 432-1300
Fax (408) 432-1318

Hewlett-Packard Co.
Disk Mechanisms Div.
11413 Chinden Blvd.
Boise, ID 83714
(208) 323-2332
Fax (208) 323-3991

Hitachi America Ltd.
Computer Div.
2000 Sierra Point Pkwy.
Brisbane, CA 94005
(415) 589-8300
Fax (415) 583-4207

IBM Corp.
3605, Highway 52 N
Rochester, MN 55901
(507) 253-1897

JVC Companies of America
19900 Beach Blvd., Suite I
Huntington Beach, CA 92648
(714) 965-2610
Fax (714) 968-9071

Kalor Corp.
1289 Anvilwood Ave.
Sunnyvale, CA 94089
(408) 747-1315
Fax (408) 747-1319

Kyocera Electronics Inc.
Memory Products Div.
100 Randolph Rd.
Somerset, NJ 08875
(201) 563-4333
Fax (201) 560-8380

Maxtor Corp.
211 River Oaks Pkwy.
San Jose, CA 95134
(408) 432-1700
Fax (408) 433-0457

Microscience International Corp.
90 Headquarters Dr.
San Jose, CA 95134
(408) 433-9898
Fax (408) 954-0989

NCL America Computer Products Inc.
1221 Innsbruck Dr.
Sunnyvale, CA 94089
(408) 734-1006
Fax (408) 744-0709

NEC Technologies
1414 Massachusetts Ave.
Boxborough, MA 01719
(508) 264-8000
Fax (508) 264-8673

Quantum Corp.
1804 McCarthy Blvd.
Milpitas, CA 95035
(408) 432-1100
Fax (408) 943-0689

Rodime Inc.
901 Broken Sound Pkwy. NW
Boca Raton, FL 33487
(407) 994-6200
Fax (407) 997-9390

Seagate Technology Inc.
920 Disc Dr.
Scotts Valley, CA 95066
(408) 438-6550
Fax (408) 429-6356

Teac America Inc.
Data Storage Products Div.
7733 Telegraph Rd.
Montebello, CA 90640
(213) 726-0303
Fax (213) 727-7621

Toshiba America Information Systems Inc.
Disk Products Div.
9740 Irvine Blvd.
Irvine, CA 92713
(714) 583-3109
Fax (714) 583-3133

Western Digital Corp.
8105 Irvine Center Dr.
Irvine, CA 92718
(714) 932-5000
Fax (714) 932-7502

Manufacturers of Crystal Oscillators

AT&T Microelectronics
555 Union Blvd.
Allentown, PA 18103
(215) 439-6011

Bliley Electric Co.
Box 3428
Erie, PA 16508
(814) 838-3571
Fax (814) 833-2712

Connor-Winfield Corp.
1865 Selmarten Rd.
Aurora, IL 60505
(708) 851-4722
Fax (708) 851-5040

Hybrids International Ltd.
311 N. Lindenwood Dr.
Olathe, KS 66062
(913) 764-6400
Fax (913) 764-6409

IC Designs
12020 113th Ave. NE
Kirkland, WA 98034
(206) 821-9202
Fax (206) 823-8898

K&L Oscillatek
620 N. Lindenwood Dr.
Olathe, KS 66062
(913) 829-1777
Fax (913) 829-3505

KDS America
10901 Granada Ln.
Overland Park, KS 66211
(913) 491-6825
Fax (913) 491-6812

MF Electronics Corp.
10 Commerce Dr.
New Rochelle, NY 10801
(914) 576-6570
Fax (914) 491-6812

M-tron Industries Inc.
Box 630
Yanton, SD 57078
(605) 665-9321
Fax (605) 665-1709

Murata Erie NA
1900 W. College Ave.
State College, PA 16801
(814) 237-1431
Fax (814) 238-0490

NEL Frequencies Controls Inc.
357 Beloit St.
Burlington, WI 53105
(414) 763-3591
Fax (414) 763-2881

Piezo Technology Inc.
Box 547859
Orlando, FL 32854
(407) 298-2000
Fax (407) 293-2979

Pletronics Inc.
9026 Roosevelt Way NE
Seattle, WA 98115
(206) 523-9395
Fax (206) 525-2350

Vectron Laboratories Inc.
166 Glover Ave.
Norwalk, CT 06850
(203) 853-4433
Fax (203) 849-1423

Manufacturers of Bus-Driver ICs

Harris Semiconductor
Box 883
Melbourne, FL 32902
(407) 724-3978
Fax (407) 724-3111

Hitachi America Ltd.
Semiconductor and IC Div.
2000 Sierra Pt. Pkwy.
Brisbane, CA 94005
(800) 448-2244

Integrated Device Technology
Box 58015
Santa Clara, CA 95052
(408) 492-8675
Fax (408) 492-8362

Motorola Inc.
Logic IC Div.
2200 W. Broadway Rd.
Mesa, AZ 85202
(602) 962-2908
Fax (602) 898-5020

National Semiconductor Corp.
333 Western Ave.
South Portland, ME 04016
(207) 775-8305
Fax (207) 775-8745

Philips Components/Signetics
Box 3409
Sunnyvale, CA 94088
(408) 991-2531
Fax (408) 991-2265

Quality Semiconductor Inc.
851 Martin Ave.
Santa Clara, CA 95050
(408) 450-8061
Fax (408) 496-0591

Texas Instruments
8330 LBJ Freeway
M/S 8323
Dallas, TX 75265
(214) 997-5206
Fax (214) 997-5250

Toshiba America Electronic
Components Inc.
9775 Toledo Way
Irvine, CA 92718
(714) 455-2199
Fax (714) 859-3963

Manufacturers of Floppy Drives

Chinon America, Inc.
615 Hawaii Ave.
Torrance, CA 90503
(800) 441-0222
Fax (310) 533-1727

Epson America, Inc.
20770 Madrona Ave.
Torrance, CA 90509-2842
(800) 922-8911
Fax (310) 782-5220

Fujitsu Computer Products of America
2904 Orchard Pkwy.
San Jose, CA 95134
(800) 626-4686
Fax (408) 894-1709

IBM
Old Orchard Rd.
Armonk, NY 10504
(800) 426-2468

Mitsubishi Electronics America, Inc.
Information Systems Div.
5665 Plaza Dr.
Cypress, CA 90630
(800) 344-6352
Fax (714) 236-6171

Mitsumi Electronics Corp, Inc.
6210 N. Beltline Rd., Suite 170
Irving, TX 75063
(214) 550-7300
Fax (214) 550-7424

NEC Technologies, Inc.
1414 Massachusetts Ave.
Boxborough, MA 01719
(800) 632-4636
Fax (800) 366-0476

SONY Corporation of America
Computer Peripheral Products
655 River Oaks Pkwy.
San Jose, CA 95134
(800) 352-7669
Fax (408) 943-0740

TEAC America, Inc.
Data Storage Products Div.
7733 Telegraph Rd.
Montebello, CA 90640
(213) 726-0303
Fax (213) 727-7652

Toshiba America Information Systems, Inc.
Computer Systems Division
9740 Irvine Blvd.
Irvine, CA 92713-9724
(800) 334-3445
Fax (714) 587-6034

Manufacturers of DC-DC Converters

Abbott Electronics Inc.
2727 S. La Cienega Blvd.
Los Angeles, CA 90034
(213) 202-8820
Fax (213) 836-1027

Apex Microtechnology Corp.
5980 N. Shannon Rd.
Tucson, AZ 85741
(602) 690-8680
Fax (602) 888-3329

Astec America Inc.
401 Jones Rd.
Oceanside, CA 92054
(619) 757-1800
Fax (619) 439-4243

AT&T Microelectronics
555 Union Blvd.
Dept. 52AL040420
Allentown, PA 18103
(800) 372-2447
Fax (215) 778-4106

Burr-Brown Power
Convertibles
3450 S. Broadmont Dr., Suite 128
Tucson, AZ 85713
(602) 628-8292
Fax (602) 628-1602

Calex Mfg. Co. Inc.
2401 Stanwell Dr.
Concord, CA 94520
(510) 687-4411
Fax (510) 687-3333

Computer Products Inc.
7 Elkins St.
South Boston, MA 02127
(617) 268-1170
Fax (617) 268-0300

Conversion Devices Inc.
15 Jonathan Dr.
Brockton, MA 02401
(508) 559-0880
Fax (508) 559-9288

Datel Inc.
11 Cabot Blvd.
Mansfield, MA 02048
(508) 339-3000
Fax (508) 339-6356

Engineered Components Co.
Box 8121
San Luis Obispo, CA 93403
(805) 544-3800
Fax (805) 544-8091

International Power Sources Inc.
200 Butterfield Dr.
Ashland, MA 01721
(508) 881-7434
Fax (508) 879-8669

Interpoint Corp.
Box 97005
Redmond, WA 98073
(206) 882-3100
Fax (206) 882-1900

Linear Technology Corp.
1630 McCarthy Blvd.
Milpitas, CA 95035
(408) 432-1900
Fax (408) 434-0507

Newport Components Ltd.
Tanners Dr.
Blakelands North
Milton Keyes MK 14 5NA, UK
(0908) 615232
Fax (0908) 6175465

Powercube Corp.
8 Suburban Park Dr.
Billerica, MA 01821
(508) 667-9500
Fax (508) 667-6280

Power General
152 Will Dr.
Canton, MA 02021
(617) 828-6216
Fax (617) 828-3215

RO Associates Inc.
Box 61419
Sunnyvale, CA 94088
(408) 744-1450
Fax (408) 744-1521

Sierra West Power Systems
2615 Missouri Ave., Suite 5
Las Cruces, NM 88001
(505) 522-8828
Fax (505) 522-8828

Vicor Corp.
23 Frontage Rd.
Andover, MA 01810
(508) 470-2900
Fax (508) 475-6715

Wall Industries Inc.
5 Watson Brook Rd.
Exeter, NH 03833
(603) 778-2300
Fax (603) 778-9797

Manufacturers of Batteries

Chelsea/RS Electronics
34443 Schoolcraft
Livonia, MI 48150
(800) 366-7750

Duracell, Inc.
OEM Sales and Marketing Div.
Berkshire Industrial Pk.
Bethel, CT 06801

Gates Energy Products
555 Pointe Drive
Building Three, Suite 307
Brea, California 92621
(714) 529-2117

Sanyo
12980 Saratoga Ave.
Saratoga, CA 95070

Varta Batteries, Inc.
300 Executive Blvd.
Elmsford, NY 10523
(800) 468-2782

BIOS Vendors

AMI
1346, Oakbrook Drive, Suite 120
Norcross, Georgia 30093
(404) 263-8181
Fax (404) 263-9381

Award Software Inc.
130 Knowles Drive
Los Gatos, CA 95030-1832
(408) 370-7979
Fax (408) 370-3399

Phoenix Technologies Ltd.
40 Airport Parkway
San Jose, CA 95110
(408) 452-6590
Fax (408) 452-1985

System Software
313 Speen St.
Natick, MA 01760
(508) 651-0088
Fax (508) 651-8188

Manufacturers of Test Adapters

Emulation Technology, Inc.
2344 Walsh Ave., Building F
Santa Clara, CA 95051
(408) 982-0664
Fax (408) 982-0660

Pomona Electronics
1500 E. Ninth St.
P.O. Box 2767
Pomona, CA 91769
(714) 469-2900
Fax (714) 629-3517

Appendix

B

Hardware Emulation Using SMI*

One of the biggest potentials of SMM is the emulation of hardware in software. Software emulation of hardware can maximize the utilization of the CPU, and reduce the cost of the system as well. An example is the emulation of VGA graphics in software when running VGA-compliant applications using non-VGA-compatible graphics hardware.

The SMM architecture can be used to emulate VGA graphics hardware in software by making it transparent to the VGA applications. This requires some hardware support, where the hardware traps and latches the address and data of both the memory and I/O cycles. The traps will generate an SMI to the CPU.

In fact, all the accesses to the VGA memory mapped I/O (VGA frame buffer) and the I/O registers would appear to finish successfully to the VGA applications. In its minimal form, the base VGA mode 11 with a single plane can be emulated with the help of 64-Kbyte on-board system memory (0A0000H-0AFFFFH). All the reads to the VGA memory would finish successfully to this memory space, which in a way emulates a FIFO. Once an access to the VGA space is trapped, the SMI handler will translate the VGA accesses to those of a non-VGA-compatible frame buffer hardware. Thus, in effect, no secondary VGA frame buffer is needed. In most cases, the on-board DRAM of the system inside the VGA address space is not rolled over to the high memory areas. This unused memory area (64 Kbytes) can be used, without additional cost or real estate of the VGA graphics frame buffer, when VGA functionality is needed.

This concept can be extended to emulate a full-blown VGA graphics system hardware functionality with additional (but minimal and less expensive hardware) resources.

---

* Contributed by Suresh Marisetty, System Architect for Intel Corporation.

Appendix

C

Intel386™ SL Microprocessor DRAM Configurations

Case	Bank 0	Bank 1	Bank 2	Bank 3	MCBS	MCBSEXT	Total	Interleaving
1	1 MB	1 MB			32H		2 MB	0 & 1 in lower MB
2	1 MB	1 MB	2 MB		9332H	02H	4 MB	0 & 1 in lower MB
3	1 MB	1 MB		2 MB	0A332H	0302H	4 MB	0 & 1 in lower MB
4	1 MB	1 MB	2 MB	2 MB	3332H		6 MB	0 & 1, 2 & 3
5	1 MB	1 MB	8 MB		9532H	02H	10 MB	0 & 1 in lower MB
6	1 MB	1 MB		8 MB	0A532H	0502H	10 MB	0 & 1 in lower MB
7	1 MB	1 MB	8 MB	2 MB	0B532H	0302H	12 MB	0 & 1 in lower MB
8	1 MB	1 MB	2 MB	8 MB	3332H	0502H	12 MB	0 & 1 in lower MB
9	1 MB	1 MB	8 MB	8 MB	3532H		18 MB	0 & 1, 2 & 3
10	2 MB				8013H		2 MB	
11	2 MB		2 MB		9313H		4 MB	0 & 2 in lower MB
12	2 MB			2 MB	0A313H	0300H	4 MB	0 & 3 in lower MB
13	2 MB		2 MB	2 MB	0B313H	0300H	6 MB	2 & 3 in lower MB
14	2 MB		8 MB		9513H		10 MB	
15	2 MB			8 MB	0A513H	0500H	10 MB	
16	2 MB		8 MB	2 MB	0B513H	0300H	12 MB	0 & 3 in lower MB
17	2 MB		2 MB	8 MB	0B313H	0500H	12 MB	0 & 2 in lower MB
18	2 MB		8 MB	8 MB	0B513H	0500H	18 MB	2 & 3 above 2 MB
19	2 MB	2 MB			33H		4 MB	0 & 1 in lower MB
20	2 MB	2 MB	2 MB		9333H	03H	6 MB	0 & 1 in lower MB
21	2 MB	2 MB		2 MB	0A333H	0303H	6 MB	0 & 1 in lower MB
22	2 MB	2 MB	2 MB	2 MB	3333H		8 MB	0 & 1, 2 & 3
23	2 MB	2 MB	8 MB		9533H	03H	12 MB	0 & 1 in lower MB
24	2 MB	2 MB		8 MB	0A533H	0503H	12 MB	0 & 1 in lower MB
25	2 MB	2 MB	8 MB	2 MB	0B533H	0303H	14 MB	0 & 1 in lower MB
26	2 MB	2 MB	2 MB	8 MB	0B333H	0503H	14 MB	0 & 1 in lower MB
27	2 MB	2 MB	8 MB	8 MB	3533H		20 MB	0 & 1, 2 & 3
28	2 MB	8 MB			8033H	05H	10 MB	
29	2 MB	8 MB	2 MB		9333H	05H	12 MB	0 & 2 in lower MB
30	2 MB	8 MB		2 MB	0A333H	0305H	12 MB	0 & 3 in lower MB
31	0.5 MB	0.5 MB			31H		1 MB	0 & 1 in lower MB
32	0.5 MB	0.5 MB	2 MB		9331H	01H	3 MB	0 & 1 in lower MB
33	0.5 MB	0.5 MB		2 MB	0A331H	0301H	3 MB	0 & 1 in lower MB
34	0.5 MB	0.5 MB	2 MB	2 MB	3133H		5 MB	0 & 1 in lower MB
35	0.5 MB	0.5 MB	8 MB		9531H	01H	9 MB	0 & 1 in lower MB
36	0.5 MB	0.5 MB		8 MB	0A531H	0501H	9 MB	0 & 1 in lower MB

NOTE: The MCBSEXT bit (bit 15) of the MCBS register (306H, OMCU) is a don't care bit for equal bank size.

Appendix

D

Schematics for a Complete Notebook Computer Design*

* Contributed by Mike Wagner, Intel Corporation.

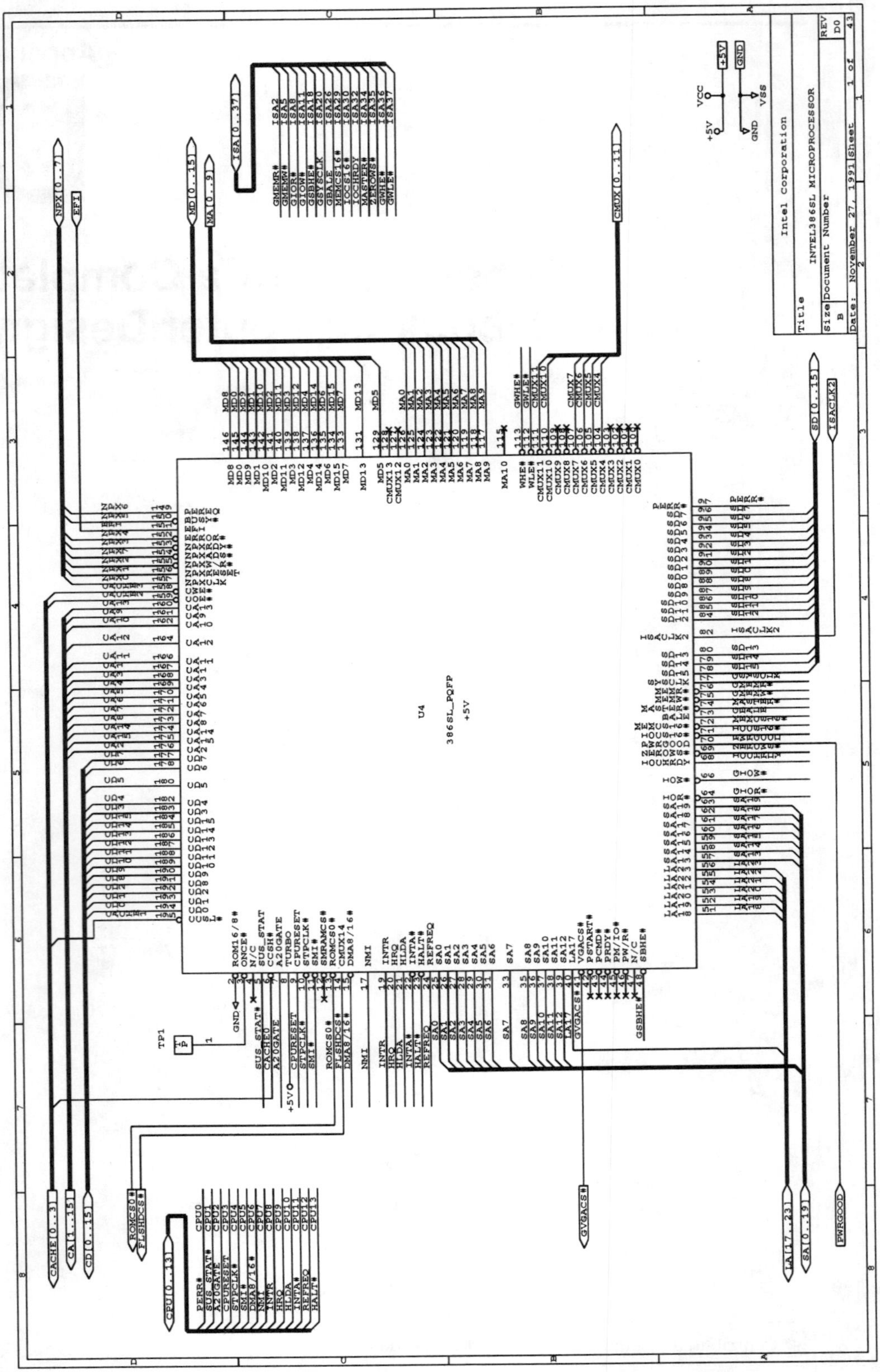
Intel Corporation
Title
INTEL386SL MICROPROCESSOR
Size
B
Document Number
REV
D0
Date: November 27, 1991
Sheet 1 of 43
U4
386SL_PQFP
+5V

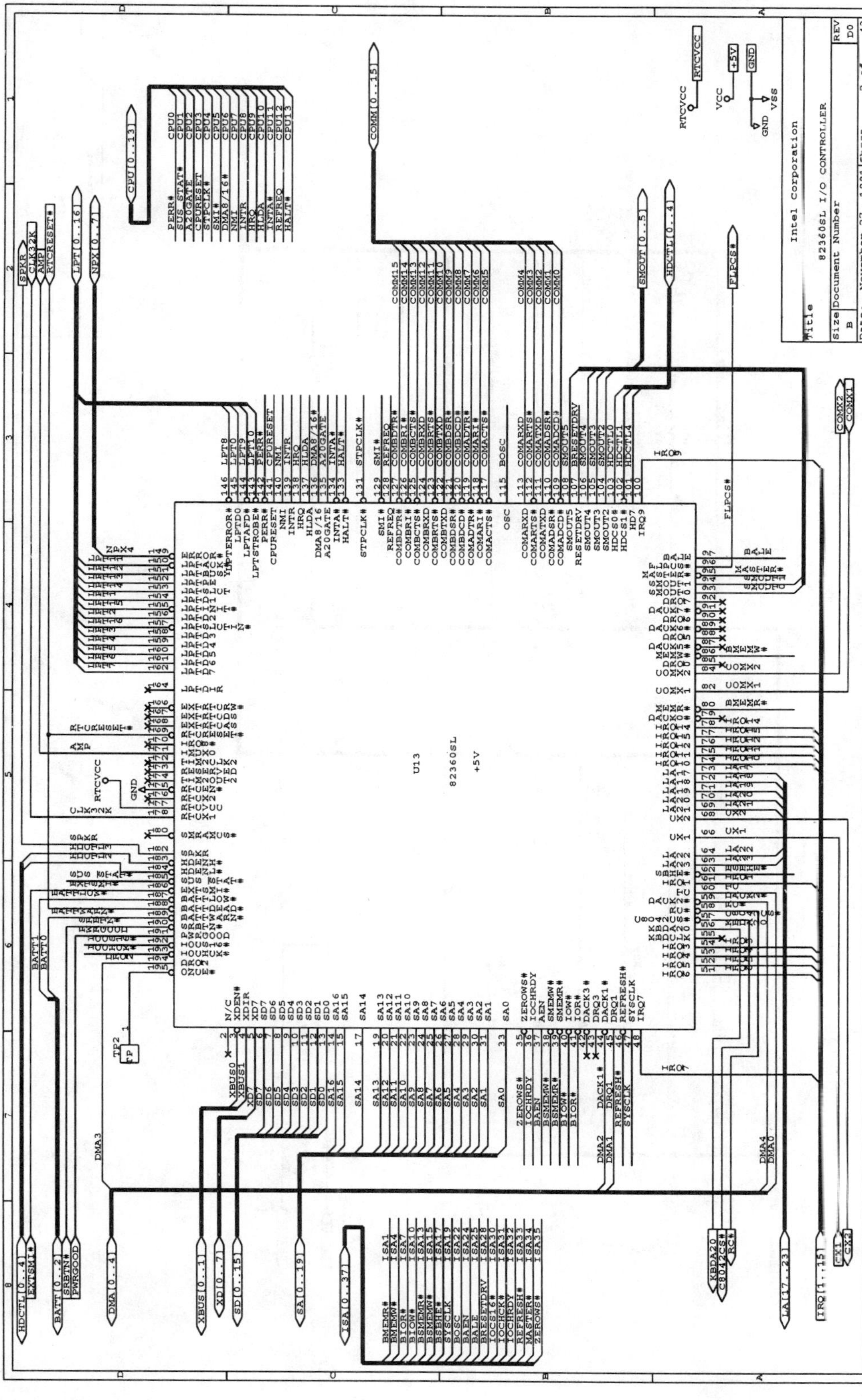
Intel Corporation
Title
82360SL I/O CONTROLLER
Size Document Number REV
B D0
Date: November 27, 1991 Sheet 2 of 43
U13
82360SL
+5V

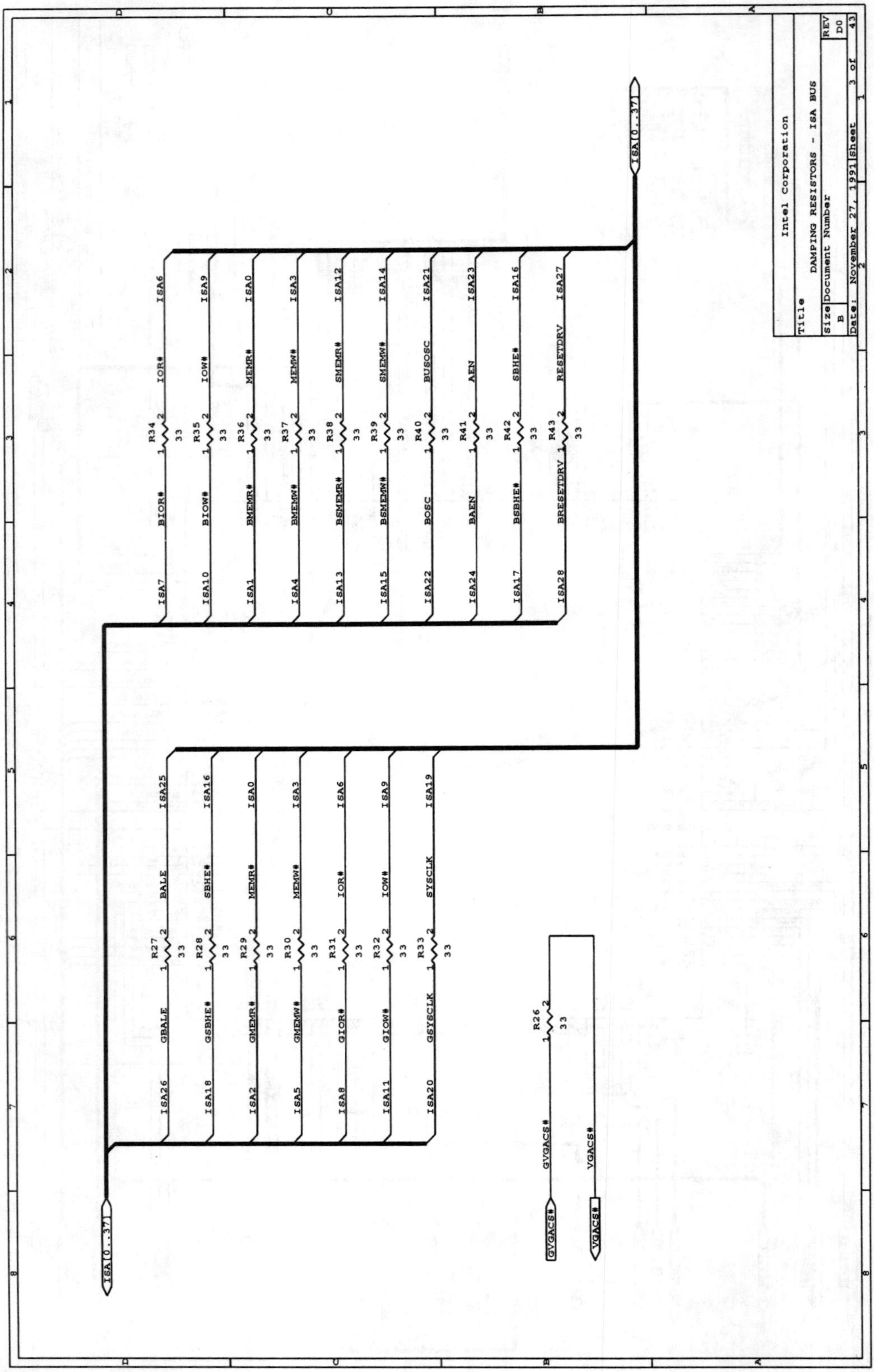
Intel Corporation
Title
DAMPING RESISTORS - ISA BUS
Size Document Number
B
REV
D0
Date: November 27, 1991 Sheet 3 of 43
ISA[0..37]
R34 BIOR# IOR# ISA7 ISA6 33
R35 BIOW# IOW# ISA10 ISA9 33
R36 BMEMR# MEMR# ISA1 ISA0 33
R37 BMEMW# MEMW# ISA4 ISA3 33
R38 BSMEMR# SMEMR# ISA13 ISA12 33
R39 BSMEMW# SMEMW# ISA15 ISA14 33
R40 BOSC BUSOSC ISA22 ISA21 33
R41 BAEN AEN ISA24 ISA23 33
R42 BSBHE# SBHE# ISA17 ISA16 33
R43 BRESETDRV RESETDRV ISA28 ISA27 33
R27 GBALE BALE ISA26 ISA25 33
R28 GSBHE# SBHE# ISA18 ISA16 33
R29 GMEMR# MEMR# ISA2 ISA0 33
R30 GMEMW# MEMW# ISA5 ISA3 33
R31 GIOR# IOR# ISA8 ISA6 33
R32 GIOW# IOW# ISA11 ISA9 33
R33 GSYSCLK SYSCLK ISA20 ISA19 33
R26 GVGACS# VGACS# 33
GVGACS#
VGACS#

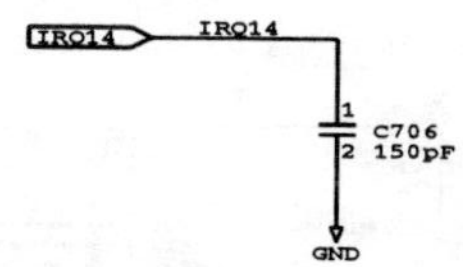

This is NOT a chip errata
but is needed to support some hard
drives because of noisy IRQ14 signals

Intel Corporation		
Title CPU/IO ERRATA		
Size B	Document Number	REV D0
Date: November 27, 1991	Sheet 4 of 43	

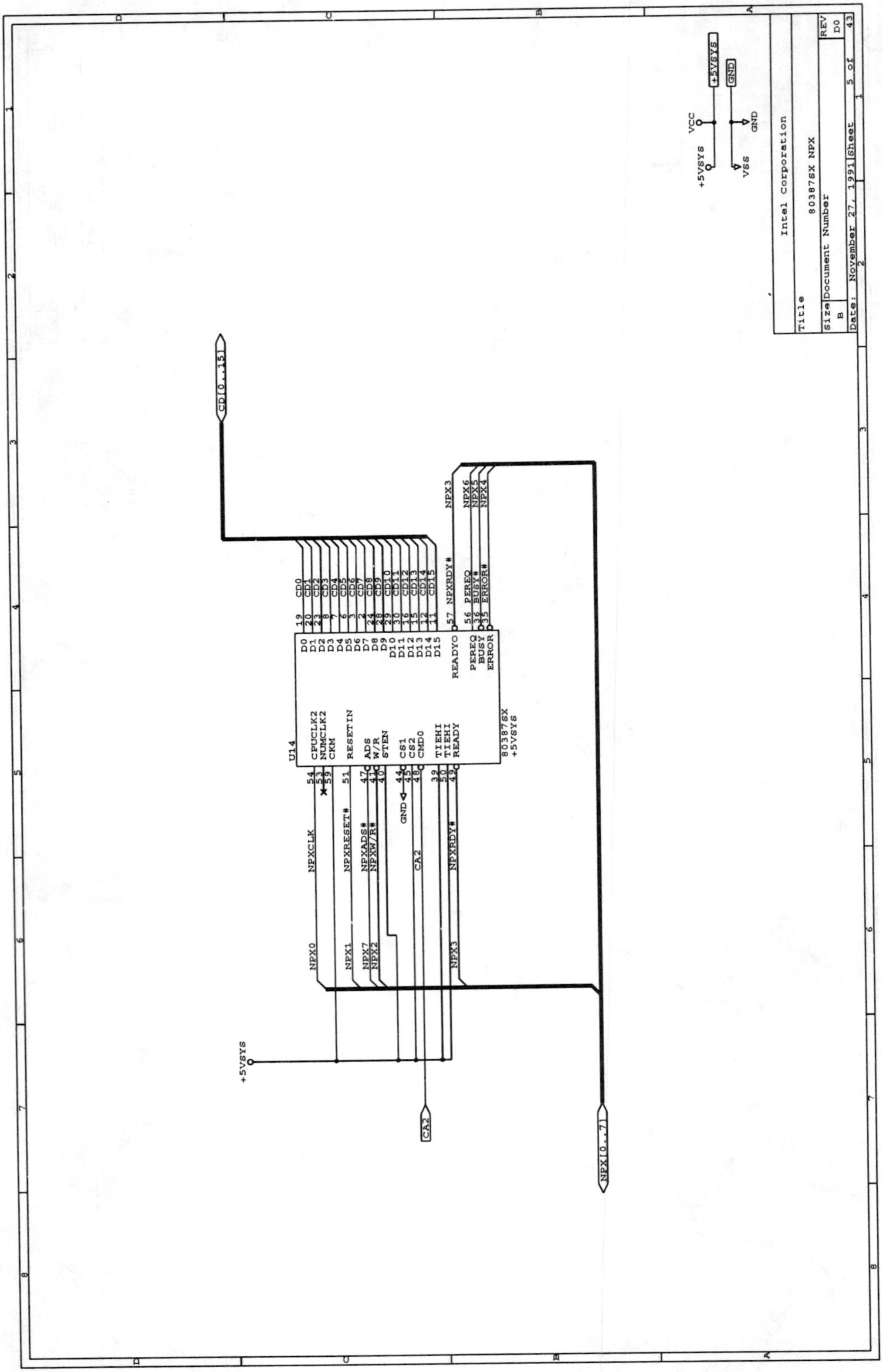

Intel Corporation
Title 80387SX NPX
Size B
Document Number
REV D0
Date: November 27, 1991
Sheet 5 of 43
+5VSYS
VCC
VSS
GND
U14
80387SX
+5VSYS
CPUCLK2
NUMCLK2
CKM
RESETIN
ADS
W/R
STEN
CS1
CS2
CMD0
TIEHI
TIEHI
READY
D0
D1
D2
D3
D4
D5
D6
D7
D8
D9
D10
D11
D12
D13
D14
D15
READYO
PEREQ
BUSY
ERROR
CD0
CD1
CD2
CD3
CD4
CD5
CD6
CD7
CD8
CD9
CD10
CD11
CD12
CD13
CD14
CD15
NPXRDY#
PEREQ
BUSY#
ERROR#
NPXCLK
NPXRESET#
NPXADS#
NPXW/R#
CA2
NPXRDY#
NPX0
NPX1
NPX7
NPX2
NPX3
NPX6
NPX5
NPX4
CD[0..15]
NPX[0..7]

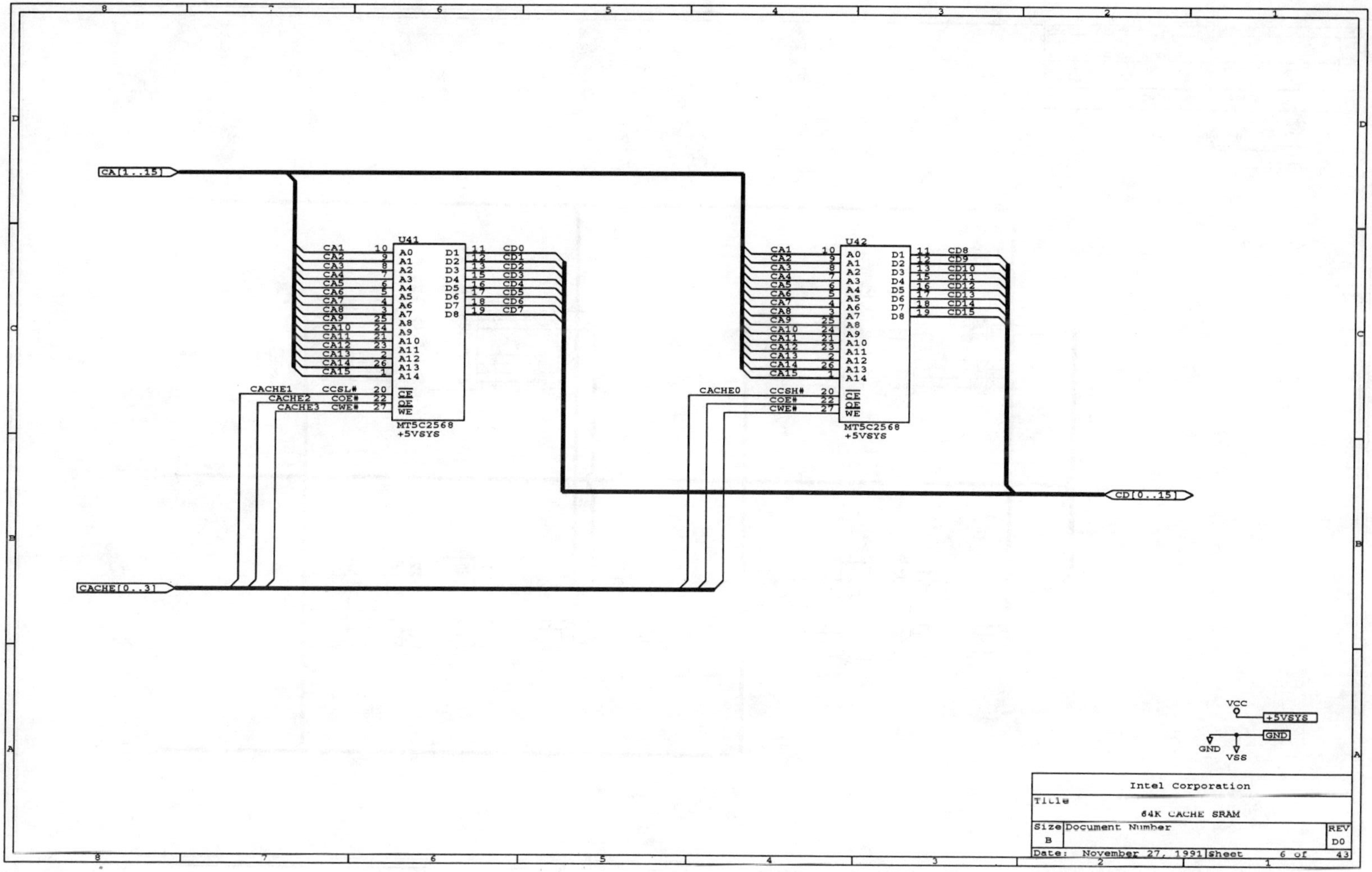
CA[1..15]
U41
CA1 CA2 CA3 CA4 CA5 CA6 CA7 CA8 CA9 CA10 CA11 CA12 CA13 CA14 CA15
10 9 8 7 6 5 4 3 25 24 21 23 2 26 1
A0 A1 A2 A3 A4 A5 A6 A7 A8 A9 A10 A11 A12 A13 A14
D1 D2 D3 D4 D5 D6 D7 D8
11 12 13 15 16 17 18 19
CD0 CD1 CD2 CD3 CD4 CD5 CD6 CD7
CACHE1 CCSL# 20 CE
CACHE2 COE# 22 OE
CACHE3 CWE# 27 WE
MT5C2568
+5VSYS
U42
CA1 CA2 CA3 CA4 CA5 CA6 CA7 CA8 CA9 CA10 CA11 CA12 CA13 CA14 CA15
10 9 8 7 6 5 4 3 25 24 21 23 2 26 1
A0 A1 A2 A3 A4 A5 A6 A7 A8 A9 A10 A11 A12 A13 A14
D1 D2 D3 D4 D5 D6 D7 D8
11 12 13 15 16 17 18 19
CD8 CD9 CD10 CD11 CD12 CD13 CD14 CD15
CACHE0 CCSH# 20 CE
COE# 22 OE
CWE# 27 WE
MT5C2568
+5VSYS
CD[0..15]
CACHE[0..3]
VCC
+5VSYS
GND
GND
VSS
Intel Corporation
Title
64K CACHE SRAM
Size B
Document Number
REV D0
Date: November 27, 1991
Sheet 6 of 43

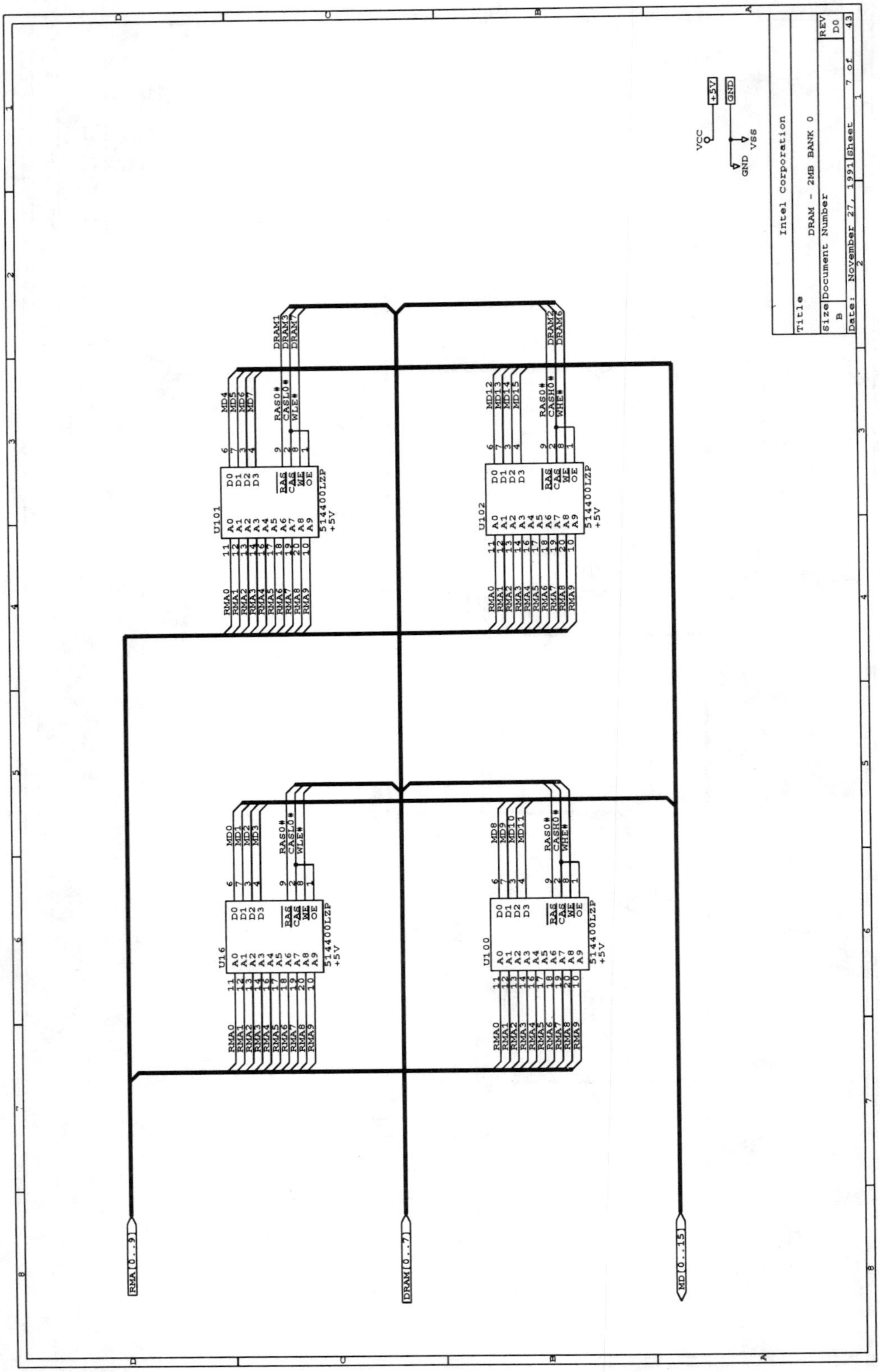
Intel Corporation
Title
DRAM - 2MB BANK 0
Size
B
Document Number
REV
D0
Date: November 27, 1991
Sheet 7 of 43
VCC
+5V
GND
VSS
U101
U102
U16
U100
514400LZP
+5V
RMA[0..9]
DRAM[0..7]
MD[0..15]

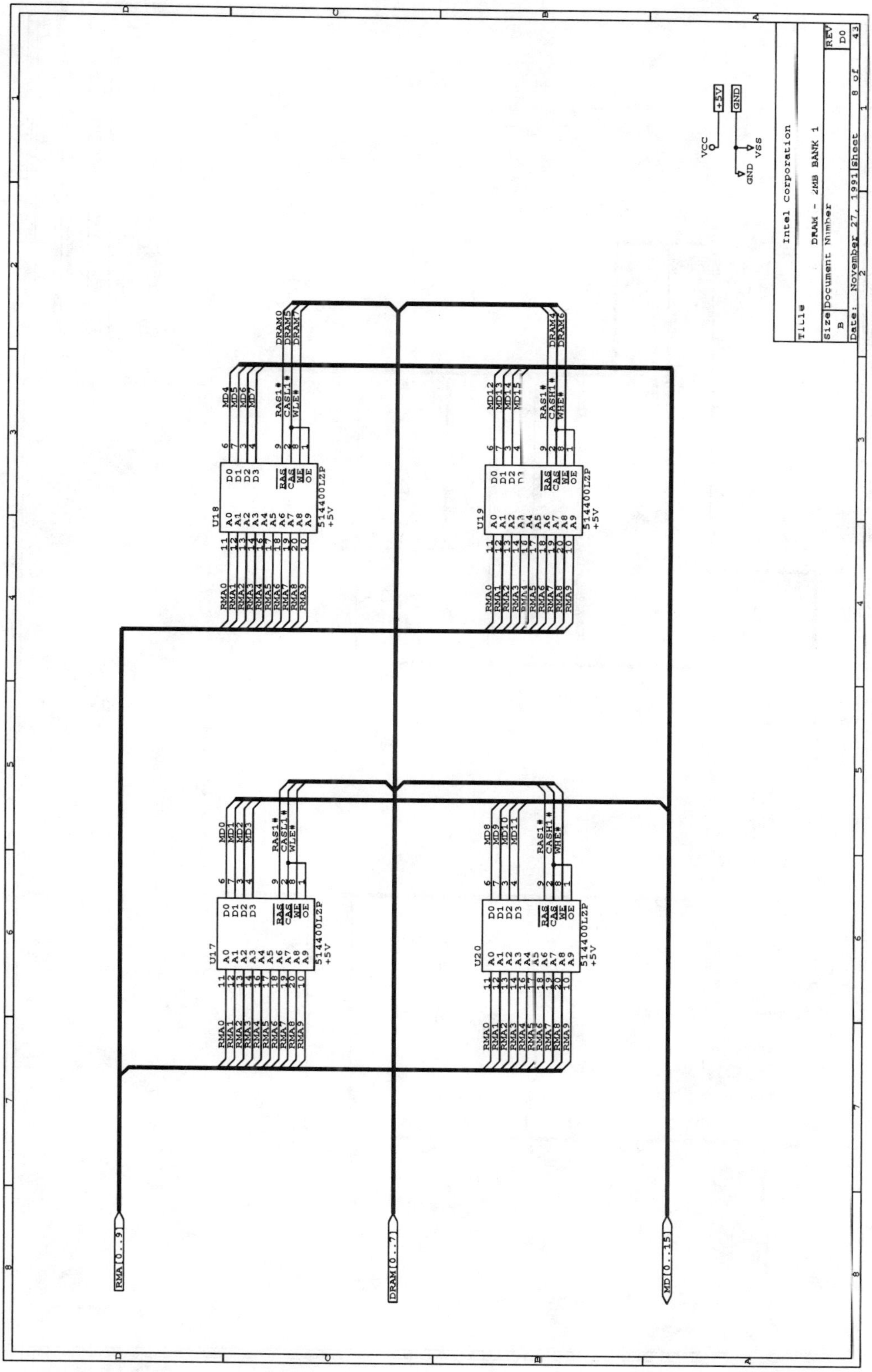
Intel Corporation
Title DRAM - 2MB BANK 1
Size B
Document Number
REV D0
Date: November 27, 1991
Sheet 8 of 43
VCC
+5V
GND
VSS
U17
U18
U19
U20
514400LZP
+5V
RMA0
RMA1
RMA2
RMA3
RMA4
RMA5
RMA6
RMA7
RMA8
RMA9
A0
A1
A2
A3
A4
A5
A6
A7
A8
A9
D0
D1
D2
D3
RAS
CAS
WE
OE
MD0
MD1
MD2
MD3
MD4
MD5
MD6
MD7
MD8
MD9
MD10
MD11
MD12
MD13
MD14
MD15
RAS1#
CASL1#
CASH1#
WLE#
WHE#
DRAM0
DRAM4
DRAM5
DRAM6
DRAM7
RMA[0..9]
DRAM[0..7]
MD[0..15]

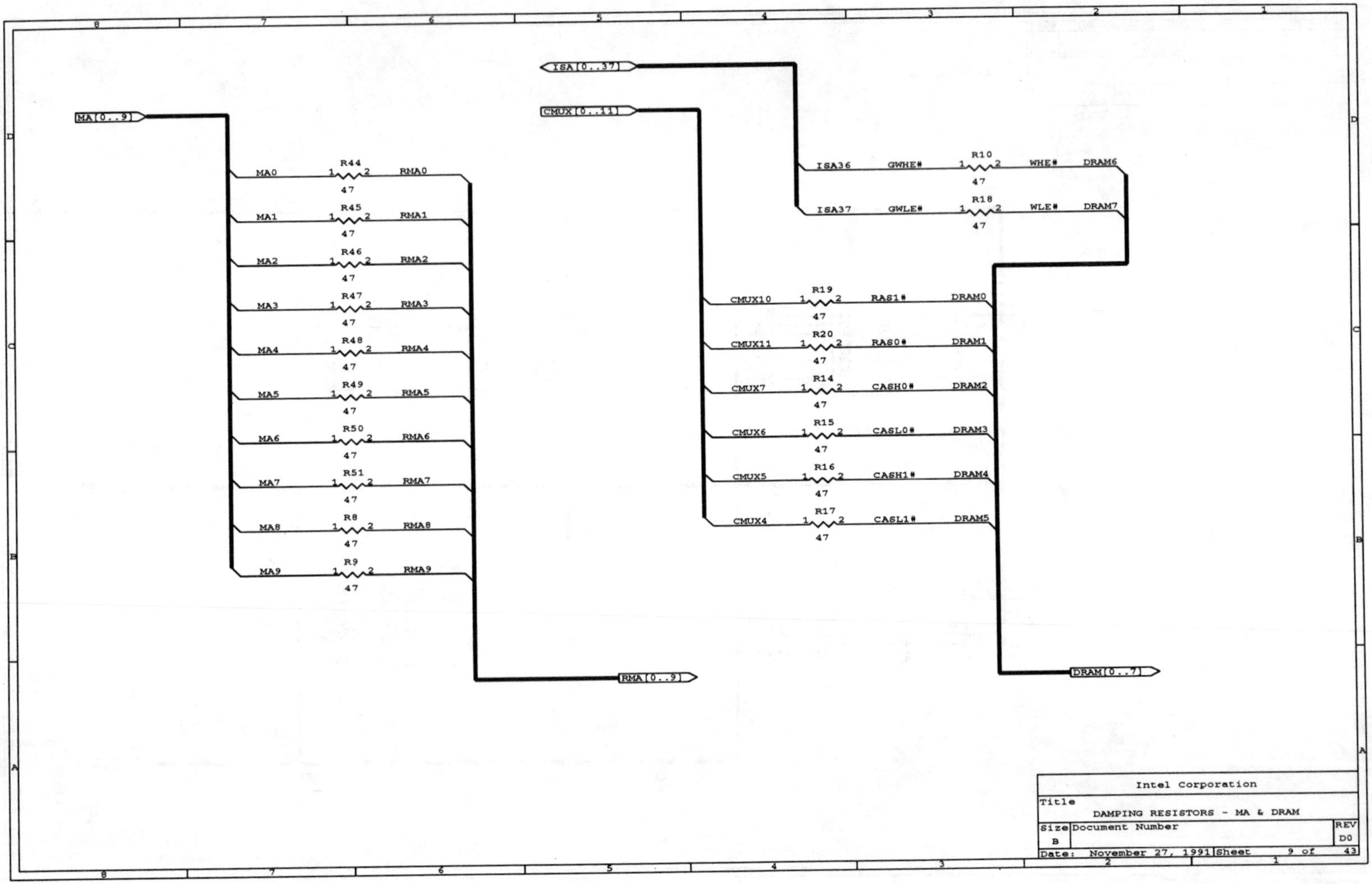
MA[0..9]
MA0 R44 47 RMA0
MA1 R45 47 RMA1
MA2 R46 47 RMA2
MA3 R47 47 RMA3
MA4 R48 47 RMA4
MA5 R49 47 RMA5
MA6 R50 47 RMA6
MA7 R51 47 RMA7
MA8 R8 47 RMA8
MA9 R9 47 RMA9
RMA[0..9]
ISA[0..37]
CMUX[0..11]
ISA36 GWHE# R10 47 WHE# DRAM6
ISA37 GWLE# R18 47 WLE# DRAM7
CMUX10 R19 47 RAS1# DRAM0
CMUX11 R20 47 RAS0# DRAM1
CMUX7 R14 47 CASH0# DRAM2
CMUX6 R15 47 CASL0# DRAM3
CMUX5 R16 47 CASH1# DRAM4
CMUX4 R17 47 CASL1# DRAM5
DRAM[0..7]
Intel Corporation
Title
DAMPING RESISTORS - MA & DRAM
Size B
Document Number
REV D0
Date: November 27, 1991
Sheet 9 of 43

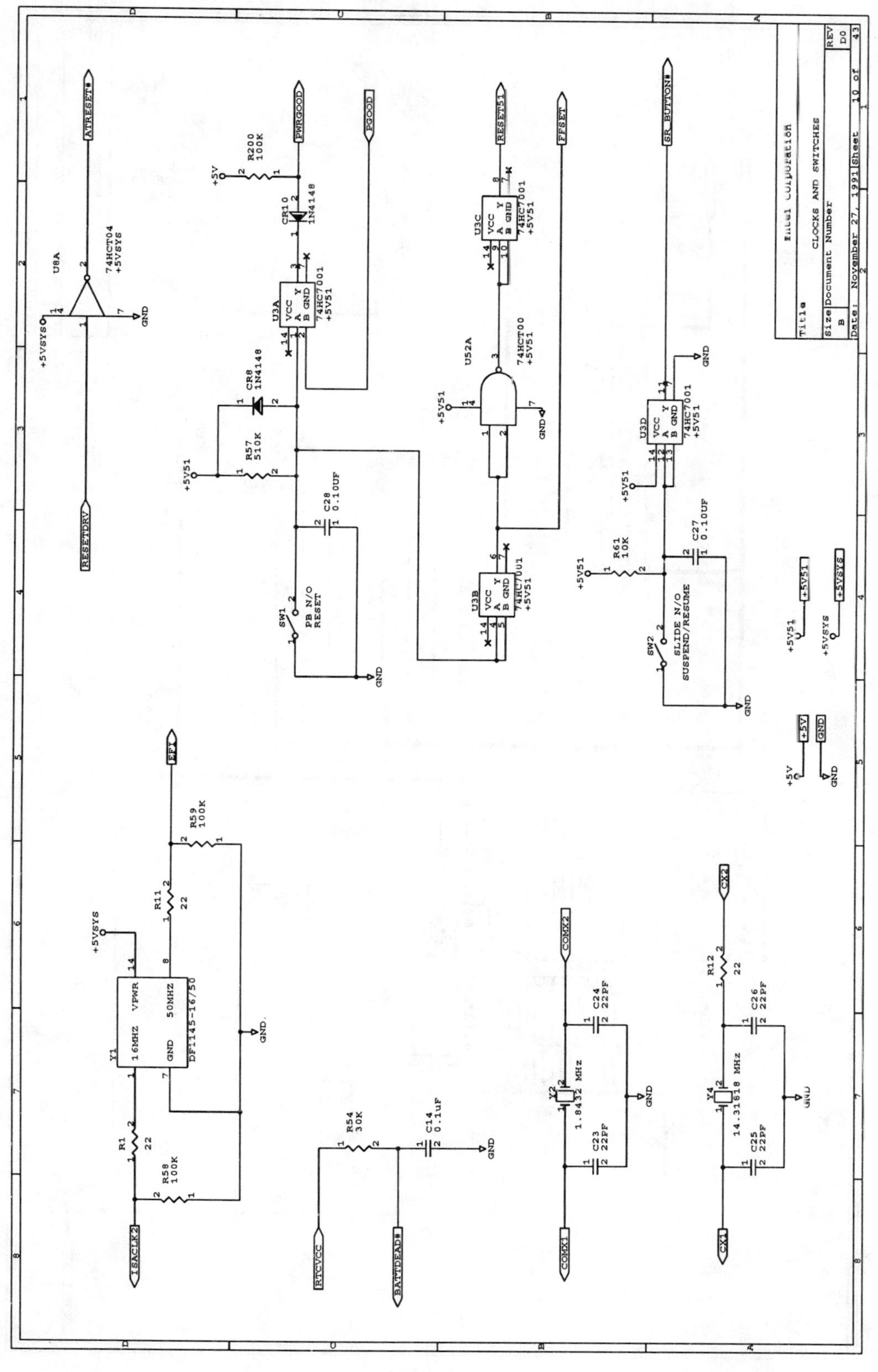

Intel Corporation
Title CLOCKS AND SWITCHES
Size B
Document Number
REV D0
Date: November 27, 1991
Sheet 10 of 43
U8A 74HCT04 +5VSYS
ATRESET#
RESETDRV
+5VSYS
GND
PWRGOOD
PGOOD
R200 100K
+5V
CR10 1N4148
U3A 74HC7001 +5V51
CR8 1N4148
R57 510K
+5V51
C28 0.10UF
SW1 PB N/O RESET
RESET51
FFSET
U3C 74HC7001 +5V51
U52A 74HCT00 +5V51
U3B 74HC7001 +5V51
SR_BUTTON#
U3D 74HC7001 +5V51
R61 10K
C27 0.10UF
SW2 SLIDE N/O SUSPEND/RESUME
+5V51
+5VSYS
+5V
EF1
R59 100K
R11 22
Y1 16MHZ VPWR 50MHZ GND DF1145-16/50
R1 22
R58 100K
ISACLK2
RTCVCC
BATTDEAD#
R54 30K
C14 0.1uF
COMX2
C24 22PF
Y2 1.8432 MHz
C23 22PF
COMX1
CX2
R12 22
C26 22PF
Y4 14.31818 MHz
C25 22PF
CX1

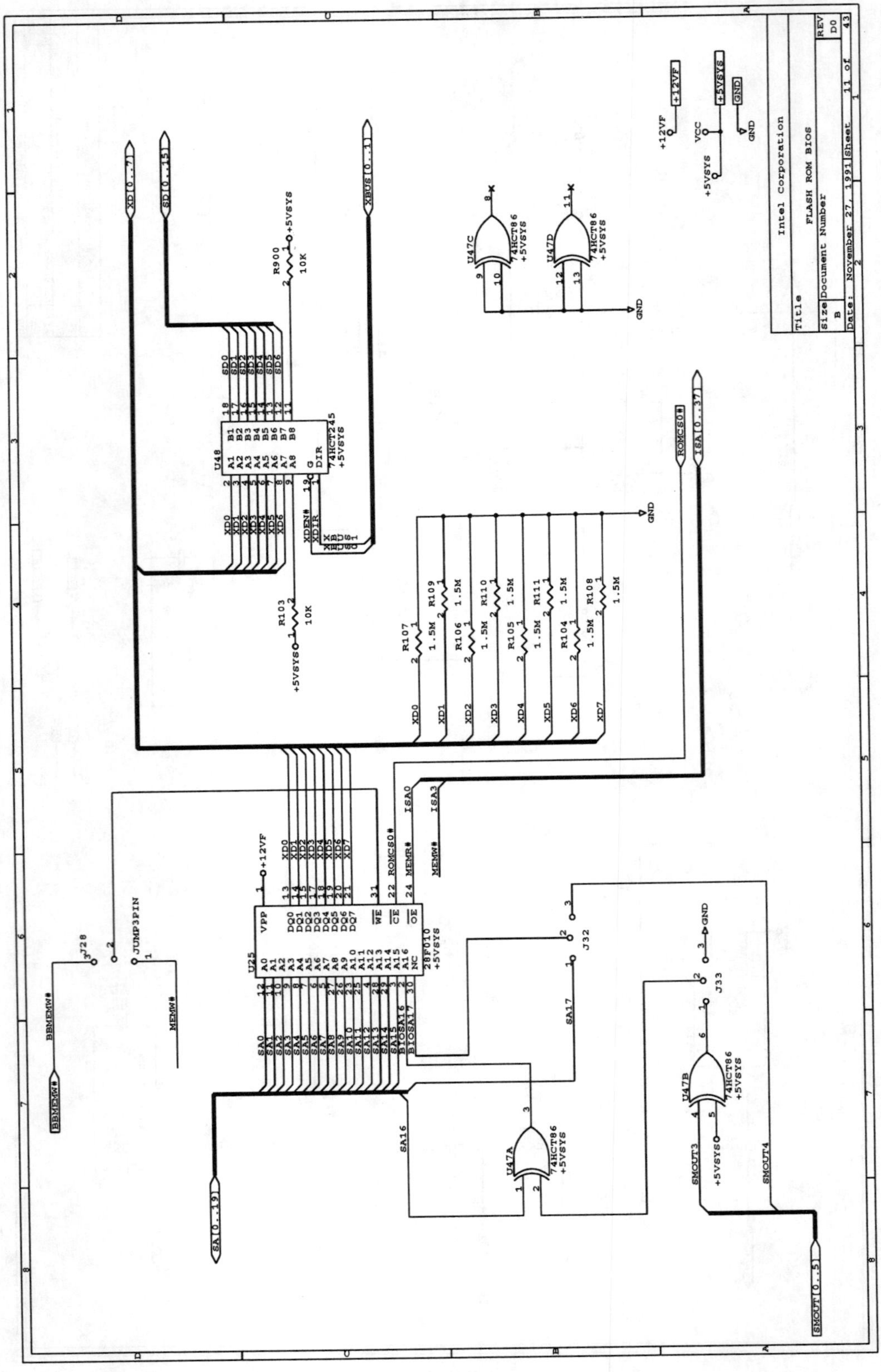
Intel Corporation
Title FLASH ROM BIOS
Size B
Document Number
REV D0
Date: November 27, 1991
Sheet 11 of 43
U25
28F010
+5VSYS
VPP
+12VF
U48
74HCT245
+5VSYS
U47A
U47B
U47C
U47D
74HCT86
R900
10K
R103
10K
R104
R105
R106
R107
R108
R109
R110
R111
1.5M
J28
JUMP3PIN
J32
J33
XD[0..7]
SD[0..15]
XBUS[0..1]
SA[0..19]
ISA[0..37]
ROMCS0#
SMOUT[0..5]
BBMEMW#
MEMW#
MEMR#
XDEN#
XDIR
SA16
SA17
BIOSA16
BIOSA17
ISA0
ISA3
SMOUT3
SMOUT4
GND
VCC
+12VF
+5VSYS

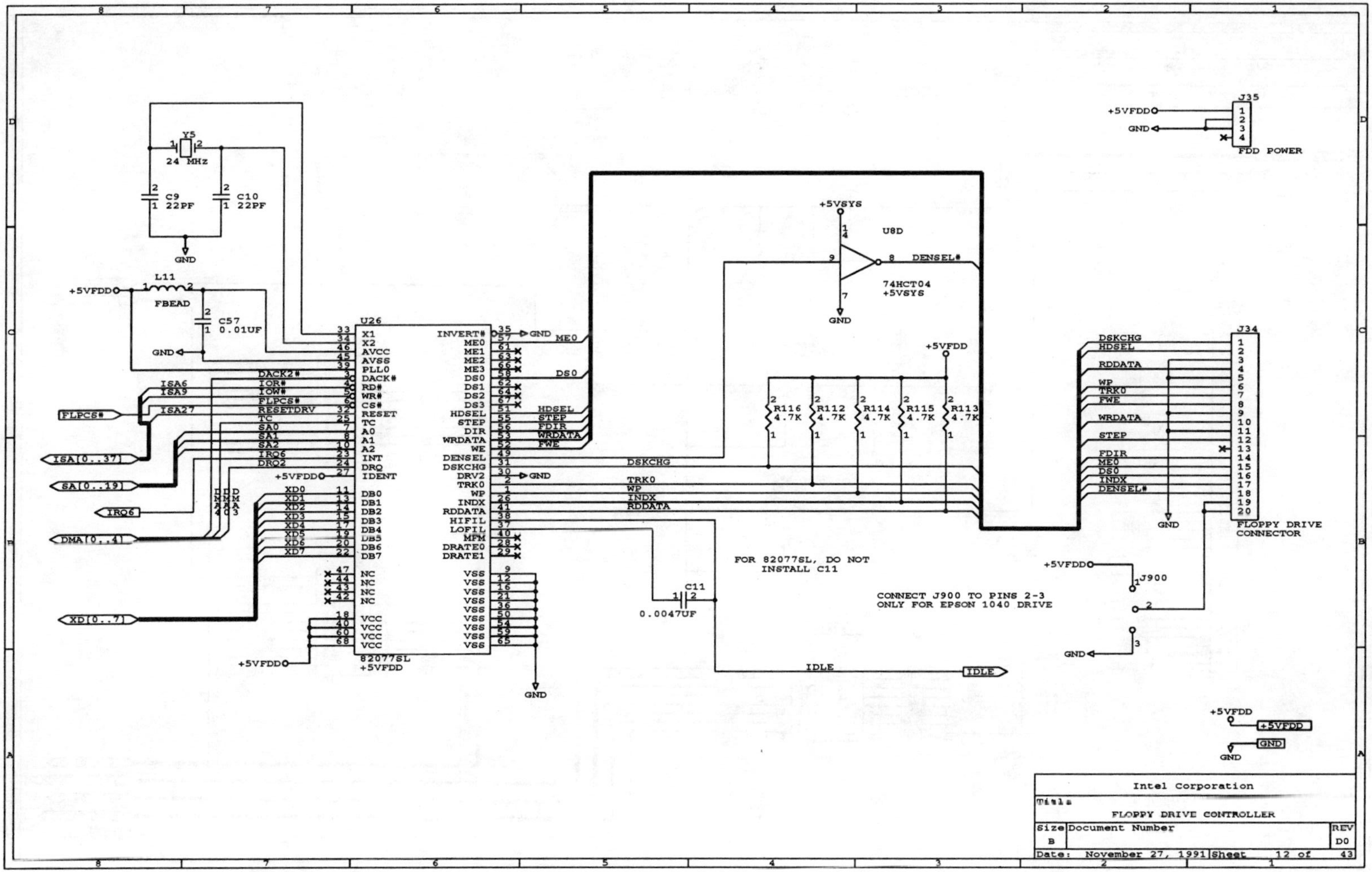
Intel Corporation
Title
FLOPPY DRIVE CONTROLLER
Size B
Document Number
REV D0
Date: November 27, 1991
Sheet 12 of 43
FOR 82077SL, DO NOT INSTALL C11
CONNECT J900 TO PINS 2-3 ONLY FOR EPSON 1040 DRIVE
J35
FDD POWER
J34
FLOPPY DRIVE CONNECTOR
U26
82077SL
+5VFDD
U8D
74HCT04
+5VSYS
DENSEL#
Y5
24 MHz
C9
22PF
C10
22PF
L11
FBEAD
C57
0.01UF
C11
0.0047UF
R116 4.7K
R112 4.7K
R114 4.7K
R115 4.7K
R113 4.7K
J900
IDLE
GND
+5VFDD
FLPCS#
ISA[0..37]
SA[0..19]
IRQ6
DMA[0..4]
XD[0..7]
X1
X2
AVCC
AVSS
PLL0
DACK#
RD#
WR#
CS#
RESET
TC
A0
A1
A2
INT
DRQ
IDENT
DB0
DB1
DB2
DB3
DB4
DB5
DB6
DB7
NC
VCC
INVERT#
ME0
ME1
ME2
ME3
DS0
DS1
DS2
DS3
HDSEL
STEP
DIR
WRDATA
WE
DENSEL
DSKCHG
DRV2
TRK0
WP
INDX
RDDATA
HIFIL
LOFIL
MFM
DRATE0
DRATE1
VSS
DACK2#
IOR#
IOW#
RESETDRV
ISA6
ISA9
ISA27
SA0
SA1
SA2
DRQ2
FDIR
FWE

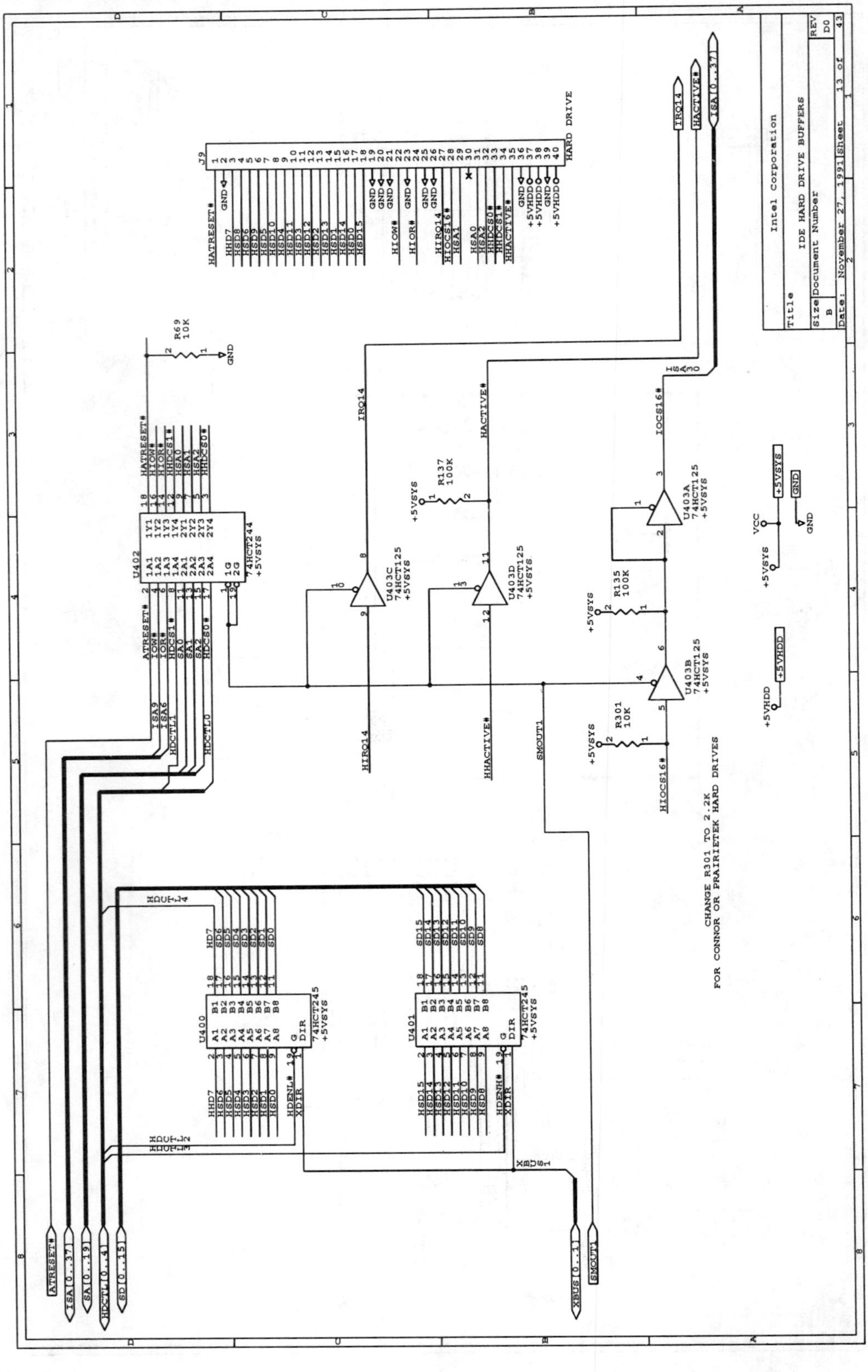
Intel Corporation
Title IDE HARD DRIVE BUFFERS
Size B
Document Number
REV D0
Date: November 27, 1991 Sheet 13 of 43
CHANGE R301 TO 2.2K
FOR CONNOR OR PRAIRIETEK HARD DRIVES
J9
HARD DRIVE
U400
U401
U402
74HCT245
74HCT244
U403A
U403B
U403C
U403D
74HCT125
+5VSYS
+5VHDD
R69 10K
R137 100K
R135 100K
R301 10K
VCC
GND
ATRESET#
ISA[0..37]
SA[0..19]
HDCTL[0..4]
SD[0..15]
XBUS[0..1]
SMOUT1
IRQ14
HACTIVE#

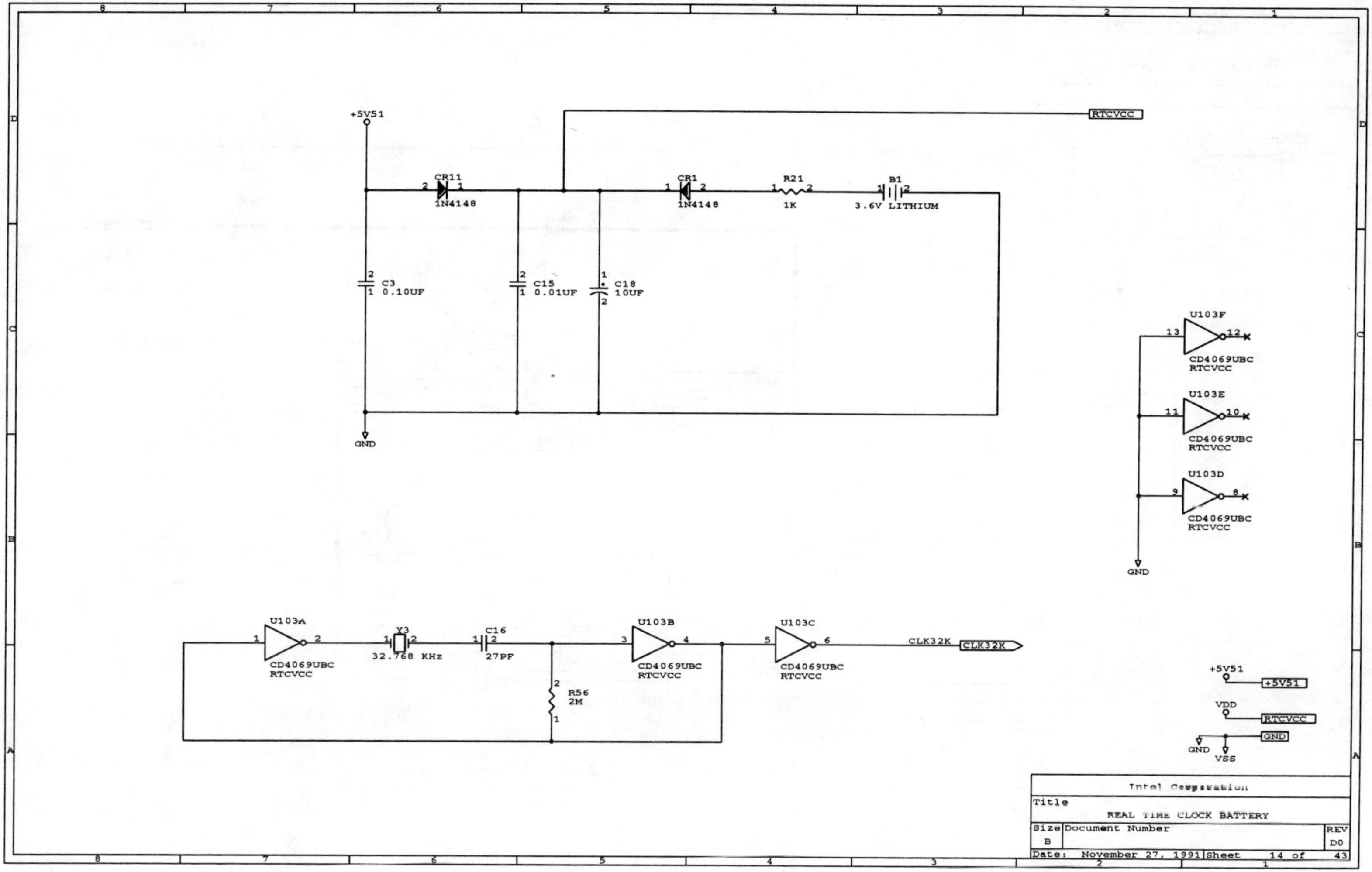
+5V51
RTCVCC
CR11
1N4148
CR1
1N4148
R21
1K
B1
3.6V LITHIUM
C3
0.10UF
C15
0.01UF
C18
10UF
GND
U103F
U103E
U103D
CD4069UBC
RTCVCC
U103A
U103B
U103C
Y3
32.768 KHz
C16
27PF
R56
2M
CLK32K
VDD
VSS
Title
REAL TIME CLOCK BATTERY
Size B
Document Number
REV D0
Date: November 27, 1991
Sheet 14 of 43

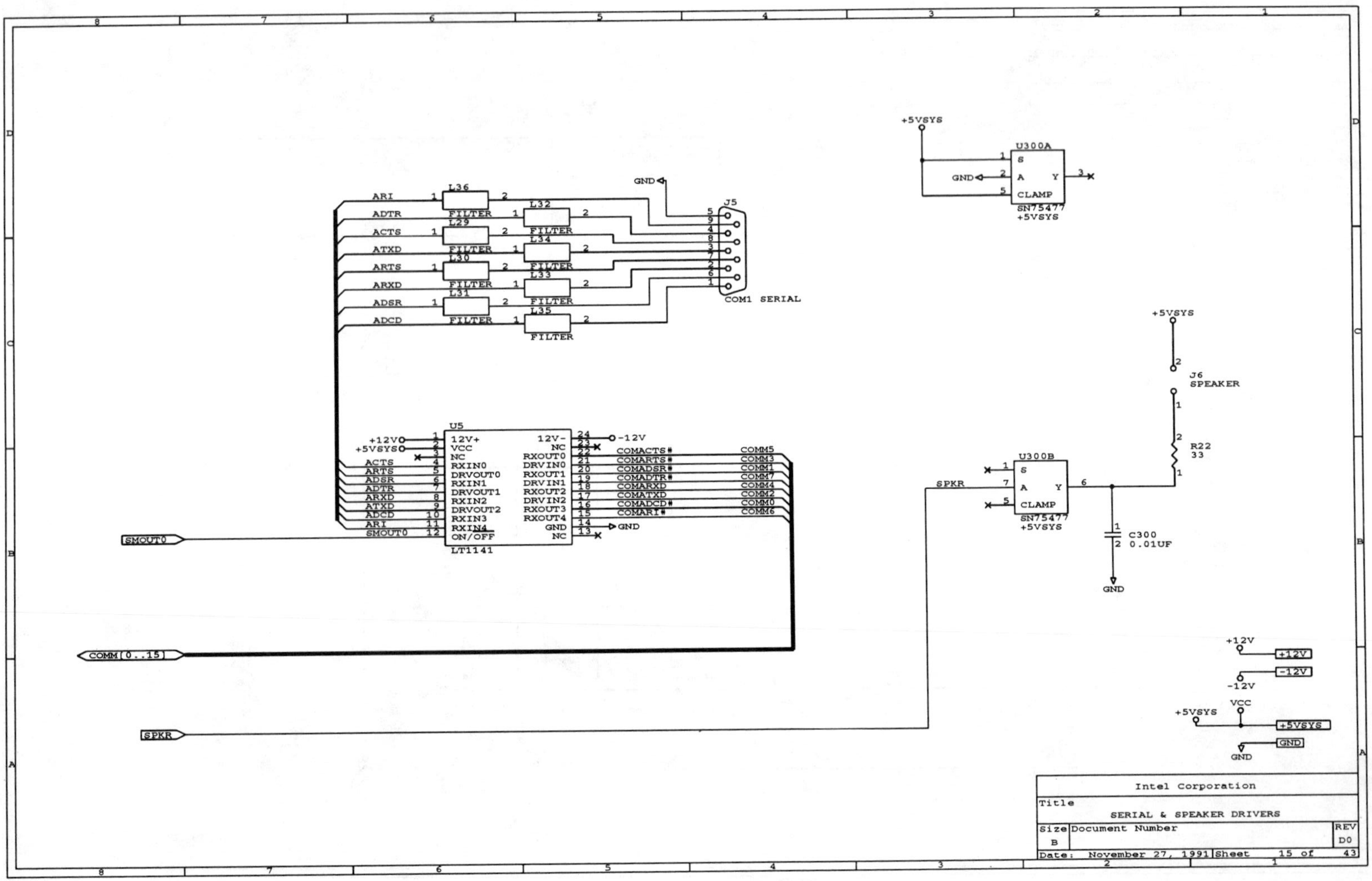
U300A
SN75477
+5VSYS
J5
COM1 SERIAL
L36
L29
L30
L31
L32
L34
L33
L35
FILTER
ARI
ADTR
ACTS
ATXD
ARTS
ARXD
ADSR
ADCD
U5
LT1141
12V+
VCC
NC
RXIN0
DRVOUT0
RXIN1
DRVOUT1
RXIN2
DRVOUT2
RXIN3
RXIN4
ON/OFF
12V-
RXOUT0
DRVIN0
RXOUT1
DRVIN1
RXOUT2
DRVIN2
RXOUT3
RXOUT4
GND
COMACTS#
COMARTS#
COMADSR#
COMADTR#
COMARXD
COMATXD
COMADCD#
COMARI#
COMM5
COMM3
COMM1
COMM7
COMM4
COMM2
COMM0
COMM6
SMOUT0
COMM[0..15]
SPKR
J6
SPEAKER
R22
33
U300B
C300
0.01UF
+5VSYS
+12V
-12V
VCC
GND
Intel Corporation
Title
SERIAL & SPEAKER DRIVERS
Size
B
Document Number
REV
D0
Date: November 27, 1991
Sheet 15 of 43

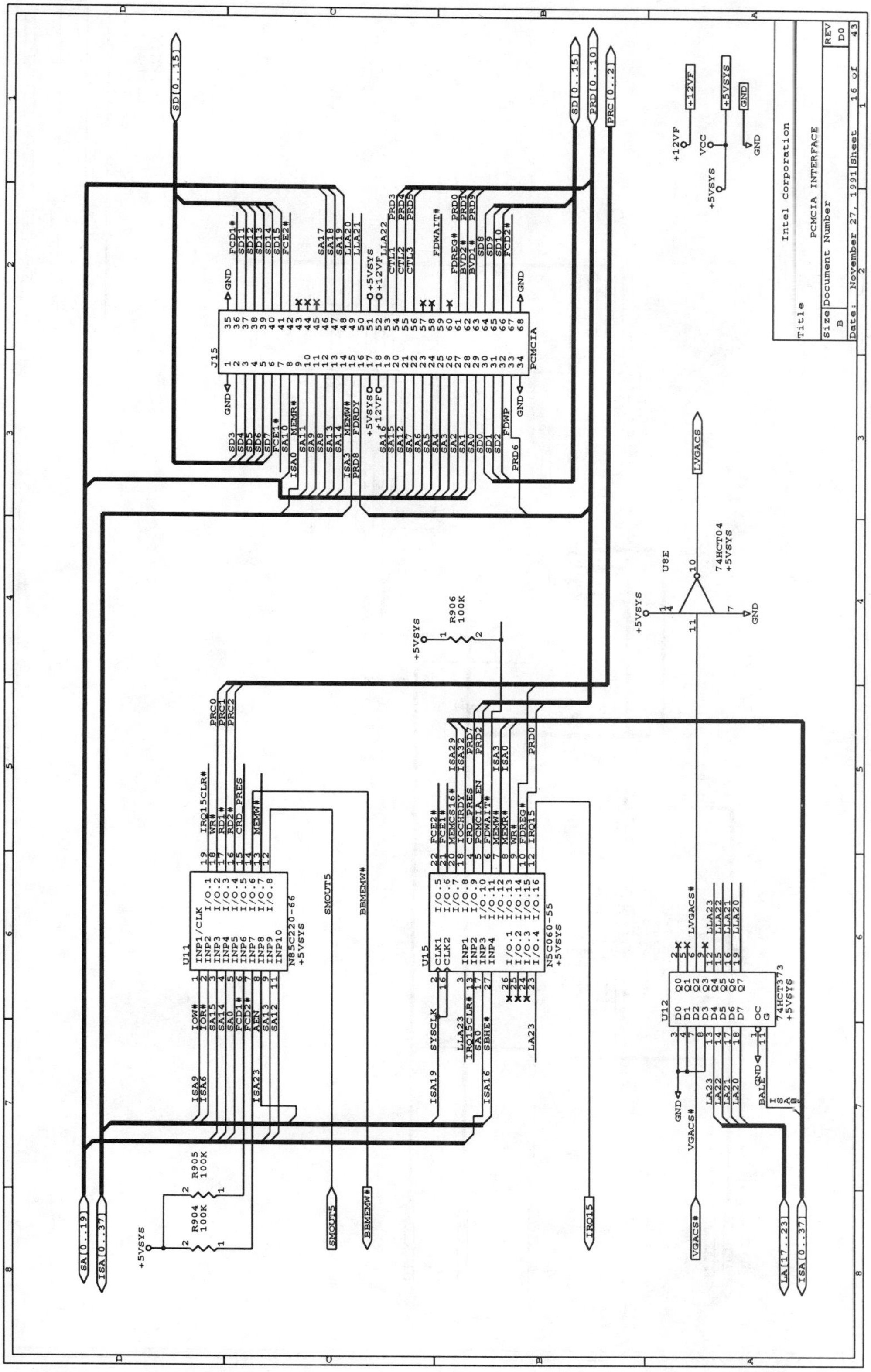
Intel Corporation
Title PCMCIA INTERFACE
Size Document Number REV
B D0
Date: November 27, 1991 Sheet 16 of 43
J15
PCMCIA
U11
N85C220-66
U15
N5C060-55
U12
74HCT373
U8E
74HCT04
R904 100K
R905 100K
R906 100K
SD[0..15]
PRD[0..10]
PRC[0..2]
SA[0..19]
ISA[0..37]
LA[17..23]
VGACS#
LVGACS
SMOUT5
BBMEMW#
IRQ15
+12VF
+5VSYS
GND

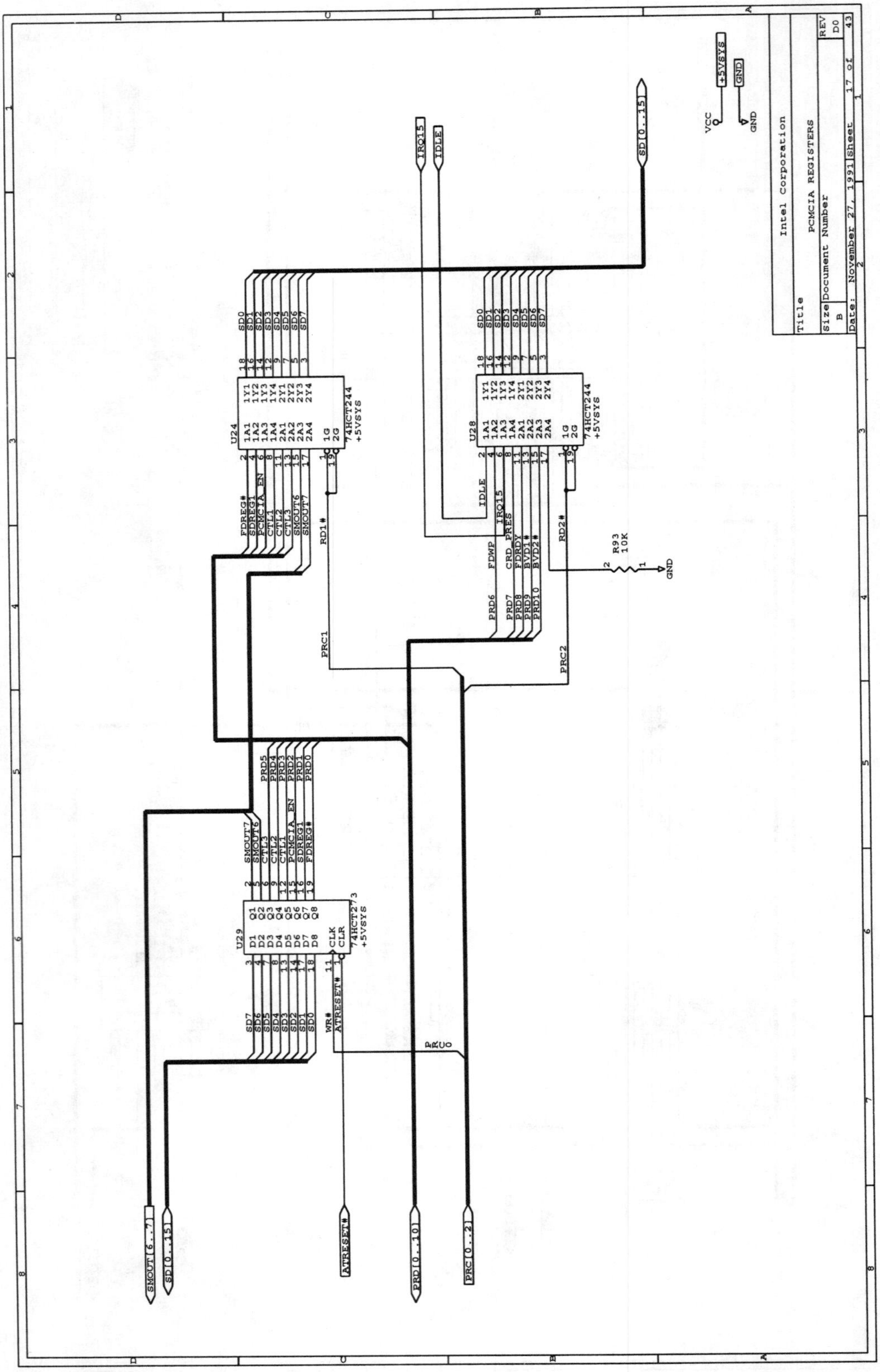

Intel Corporation
Title
PCMCIA REGISTERS
Size B
Document Number
REV D0
Date: November 27, 1991 Sheet 17 of 43
VCC
+5VSYS
GND
SD[0..15]
IRQ15
IDLE
U24
74HCT244
+5VSYS
U28
74HCT244
+5VSYS
U29
74HCT273
+5VSYS
R93
10K
FDREG#
SDREG1
PCMCIA_EN
CTL1
CTL2
CTL3
SMOUT6
SMOUT7
RD1#
RD2#
FDWP
CRD_PRES
FDRDY
BVD1#
BVD2#
PRC1
PRC2
WR#
ATRESET#
SMOUT[6..7]
ATRESET#
PRD[0..10]
PRC[0..2]

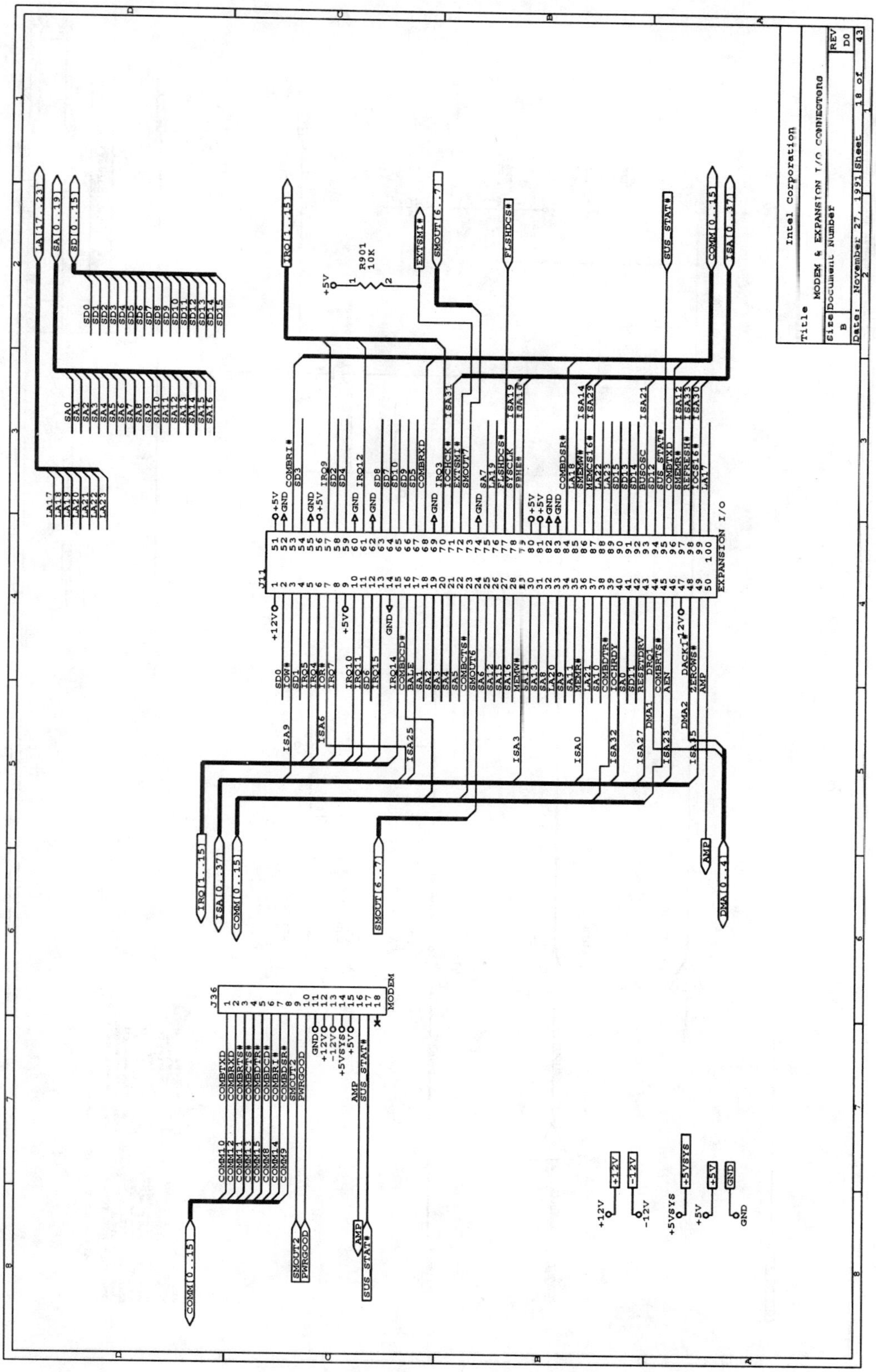
Intel Corporation
Title
MODEM & EXPANSION I/O CONNECTORS
Size
B
Document Number
REV
D0
Date: November 27, 1991
Sheet 18 of 43
J11
EXPANSION I/O
J36
MODEM
R901
10K

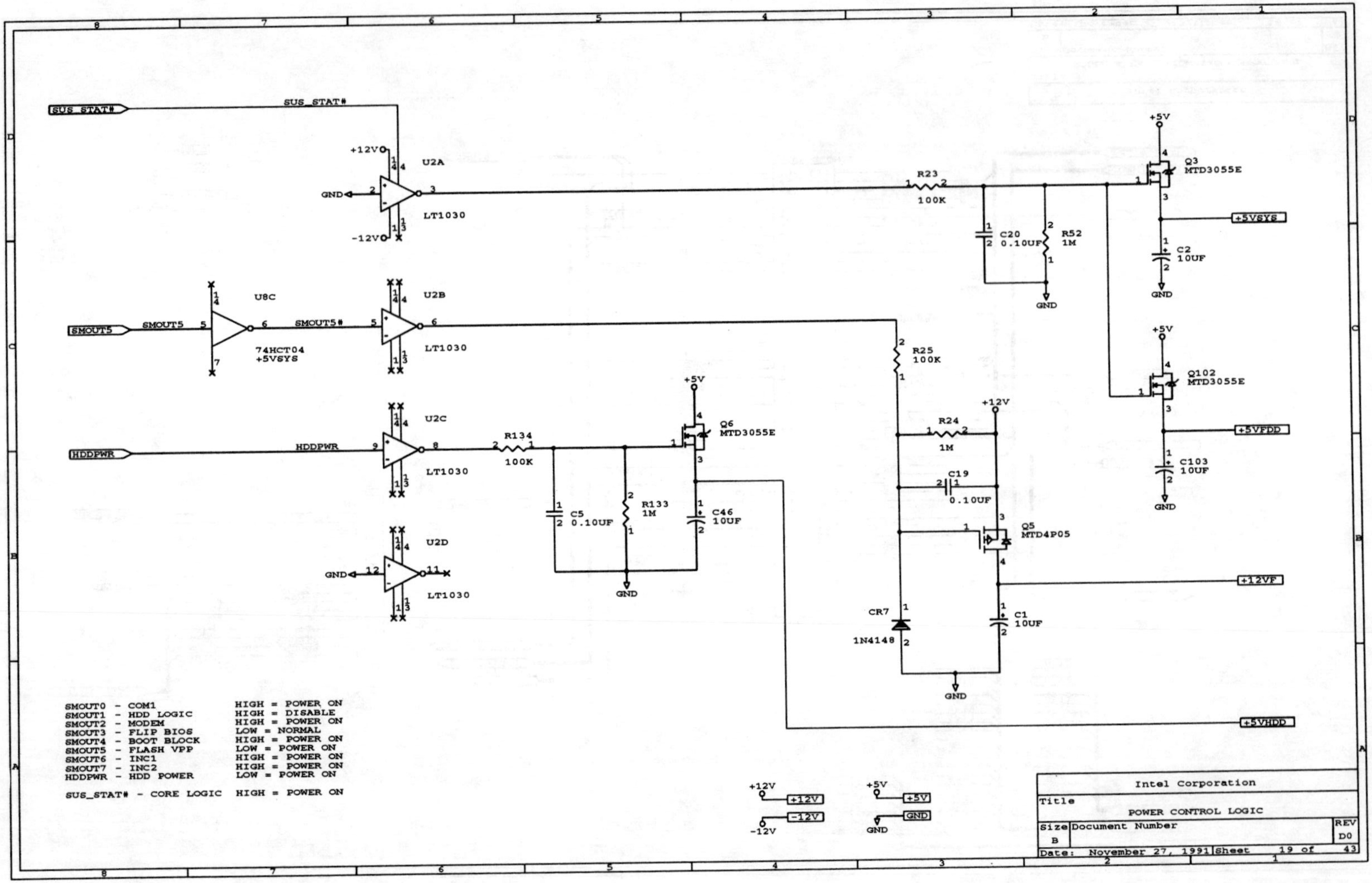
SUS_STAT#
SMOUT5
SMOUT5#
HDDPWR
U2A
U2B
U2C
U2D
U8C
LT1030
74HCT04
+5VSYS
R23 100K
R25 100K
R134 100K
R24 1M
R52 1M
R133 1M
C20 0.10UF
C19 0.10UF
C5 0.10UF
C2 10UF
C103 10UF
C46 10UF
C1 10UF
Q3 MTD3055E
Q102 MTD3055E
Q6 MTD3055E
Q5 MTD4P05
CR7 1N4148
+5VSYS
+5VFDD
+12VF
+5VHDD
+5V
+12V
-12V
GND
SMOUT0 - COM1 HIGH = POWER ON
SMOUT1 - HDD LOGIC HIGH = DISABLE
SMOUT2 - MODEM HIGH = POWER ON
SMOUT3 - FLIP BIOS LOW = NORMAL
SMOUT4 - BOOT BLOCK HIGH = POWER ON
SMOUT5 - FLASH VPP LOW = POWER ON
SMOUT6 - INC1 HIGH = POWER ON
SMOUT7 - INC2 HIGH = POWER ON
HDDPWR - HDD POWER LOW = POWER ON
SUS_STAT# - CORE LOGIC HIGH = POWER ON
Intel Corporation
Title POWER CONTROL LOGIC
Size B
Document Number
REV D0
Date: November 27, 1991
Sheet 19 of 43

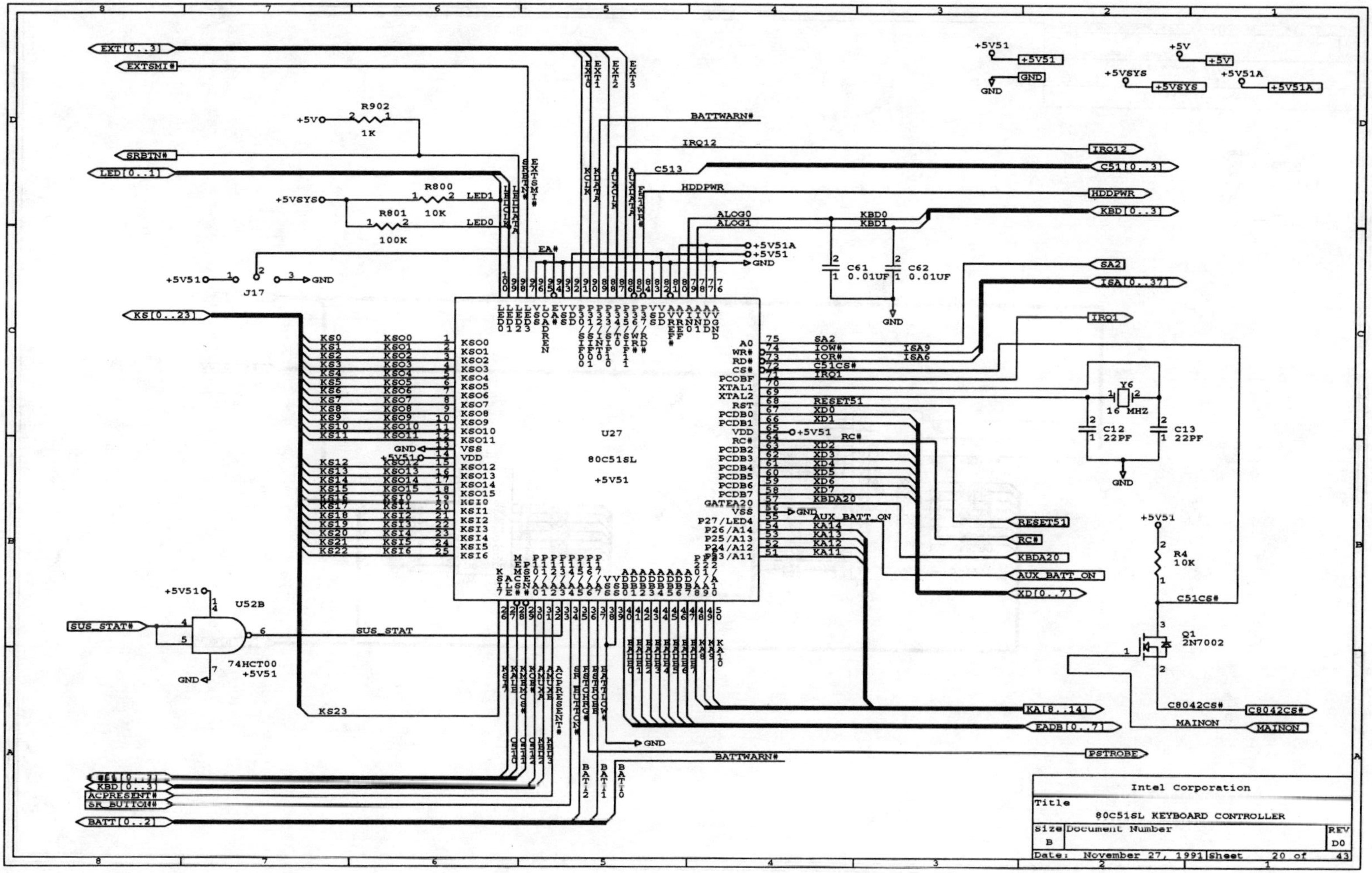
Intel Corporation
Title 80C51SL KEYBOARD CONTROLLER
Size B Document Number REV D0
Date: November 27, 1991 Sheet 20 of 43
U27
80C51SL
+5V51
U52B
74HCT00
Q1 2N7002
Y6 16 MHZ
R902 1K
R800 10K
R801 100K
R4 10K
C61 0.01UF
C62 0.01UF
C12 22PF
C13 22PF
J17

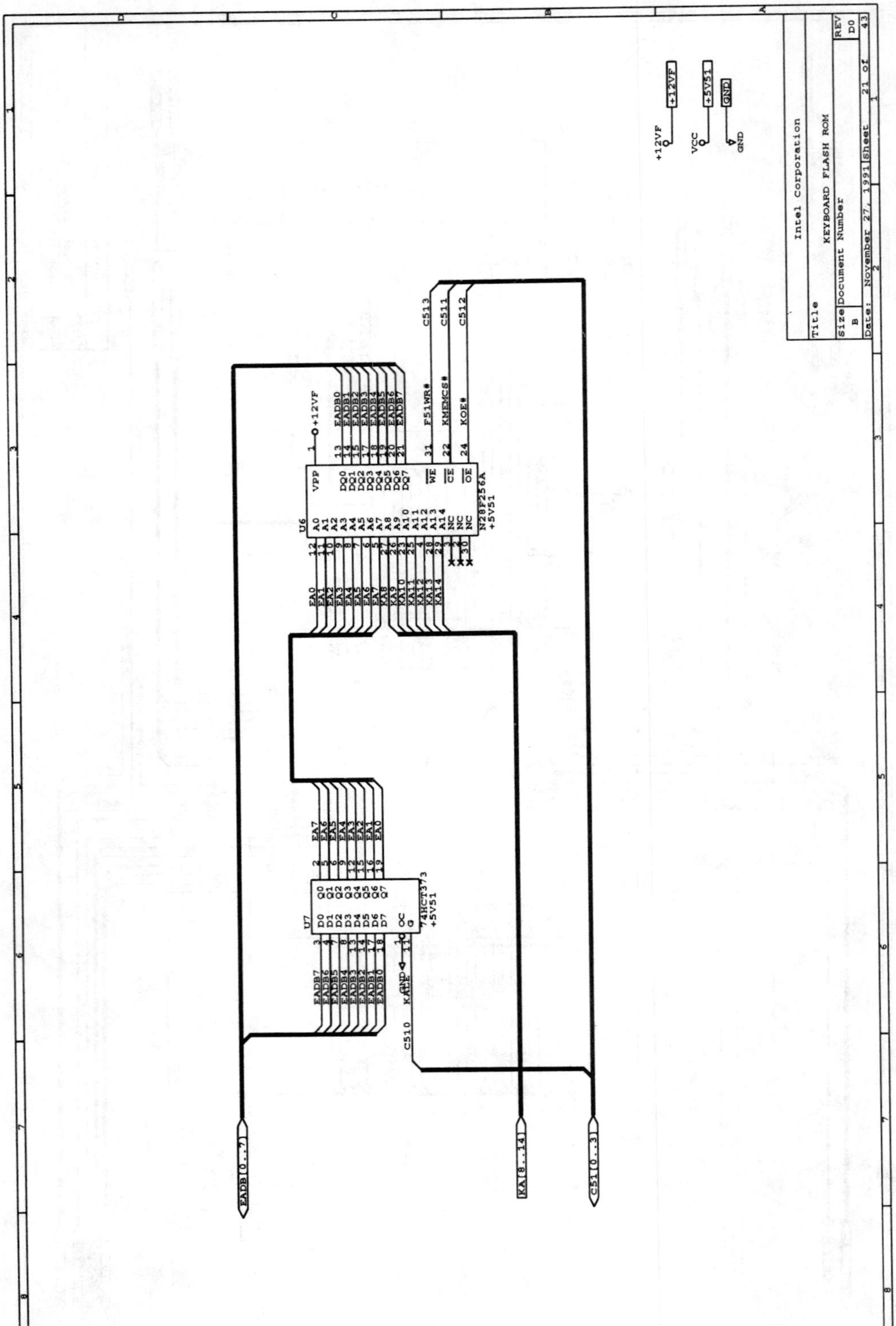
Intel Corporation
Title
KEYBOARD FLASH ROM
Size B
Document Number
REV D0
Date: November 27, 1991
Sheet 21 of 43
+12VF
VCC
GND
+5V51
U6
N28F256A
U7
74HCT373
EADB[0..7]
KA[8..14]
C51[0..3]
F51WR#
KMEMCS#
KOE#
C510
C511
C512
C513

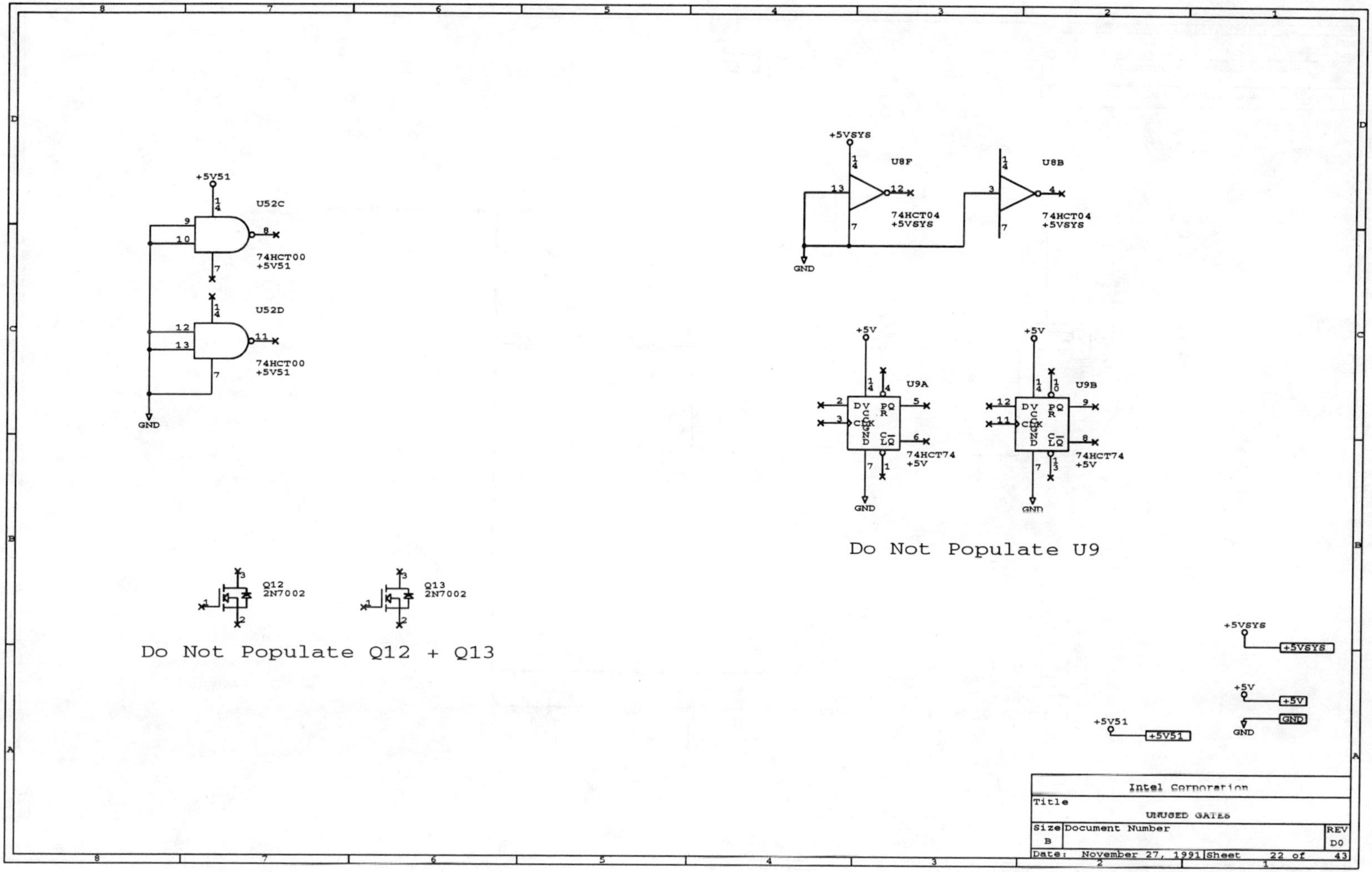
+5V51
U52C
74HCT00
+5V51
U52D
74HCT00
+5V51
GND
+5VSYS
U8F
74HCT04
+5VSYS
U8B
74HCT04
+5VSYS
GND
+5V
U9A
74HCT74
+5V
U9B
74HCT74
+5V
GND
Do Not Populate U9
Q12
2N7002
Q13
2N7002
Do Not Populate Q12 + Q13
+5VSYS
+5V
GND
+5V51
Intel Corporation
Title
UNUSED GATES
Size Document Number
B
REV
D0
Date: November 27, 1991 Sheet 22 of 43

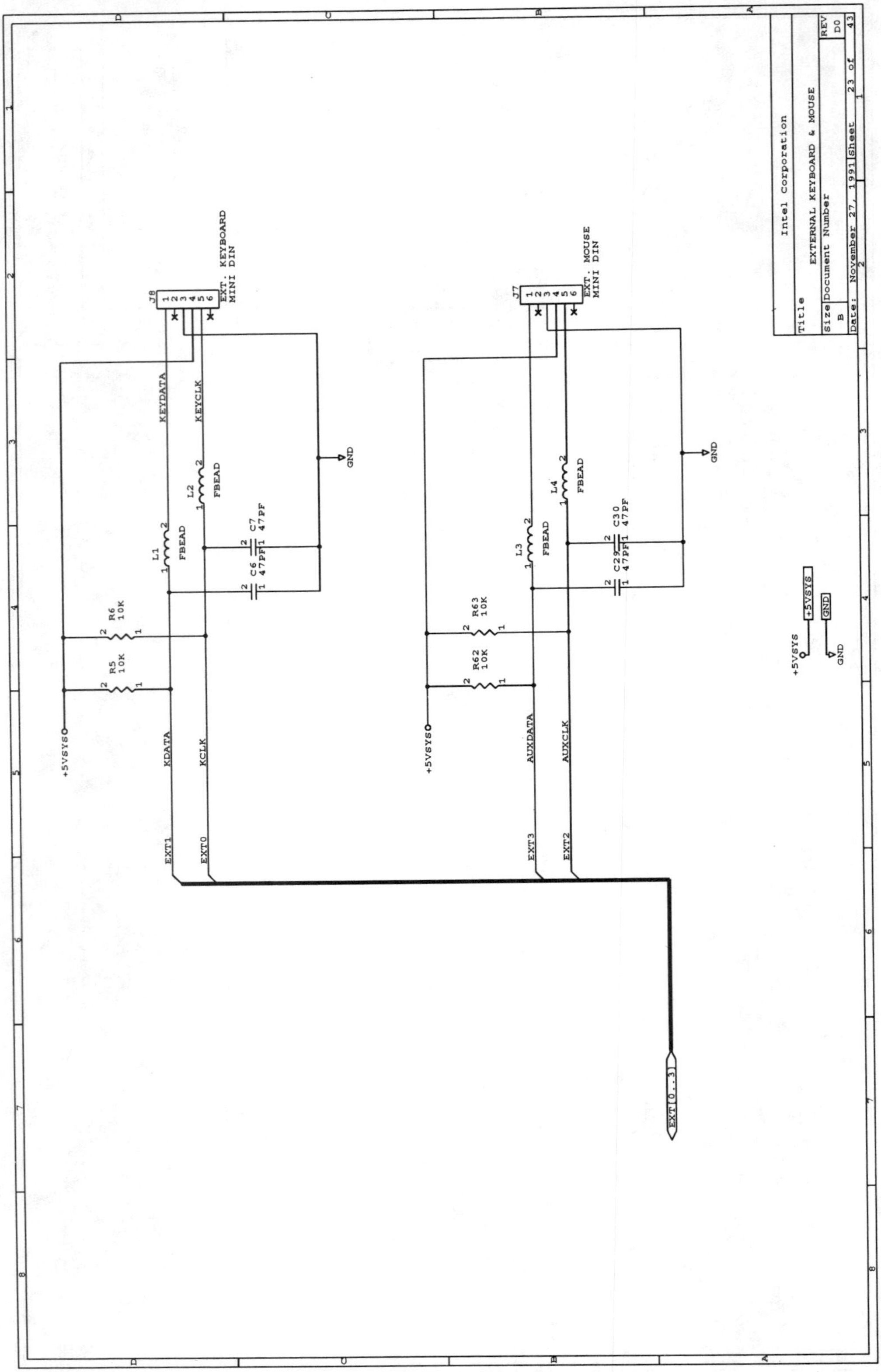
Intel Corporation
Title
EXTERNAL KEYBOARD & MOUSE
Size Document Number
B
REV
D0
Date: November 27, 1991 Sheet 23 of 43
J8
EXT. KEYBOARD
MINI DIN
J7
EXT. MOUSE
MINI DIN
KEYDATA
KEYCLK
L1
L2
L3
L4
FBEAD
C6
47PF
C7
47PF
C29
47PF
C30
47PF
R5
10K
R6
10K
R62
10K
R63
10K
GND
+5VSYS
KDATA
KCLK
AUXDATA
AUXCLK
EXT1
EXT0
EXT3
EXT2
EXT[0..3]

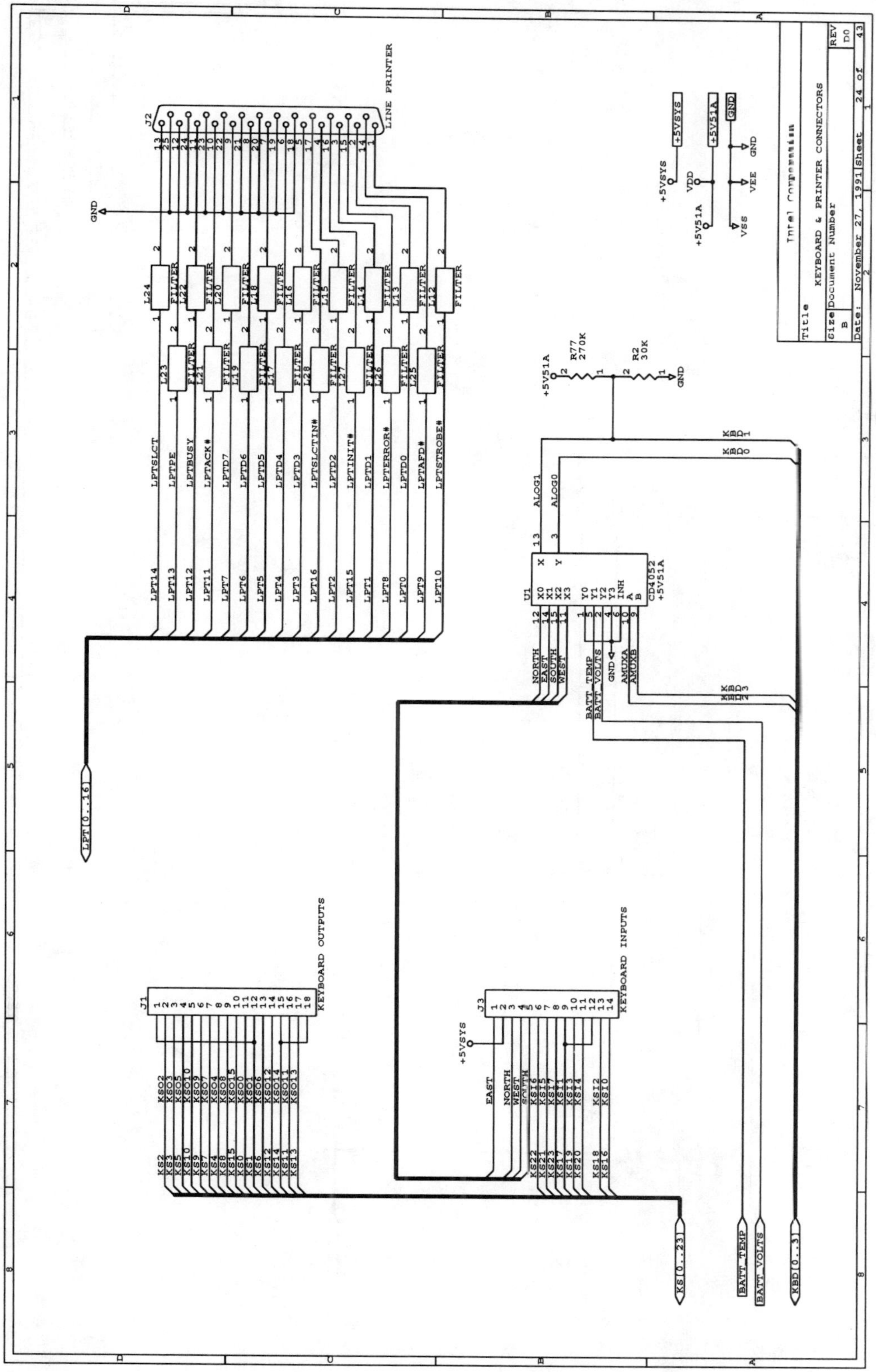
LINE PRINTER
J2
GND
LPT[0..16]
KEYBOARD OUTPUTS
J1
KEYBOARD INPUTS
J3
+5VSYS
U1
CD4052
+5V51A
R77
270K
R2
30K
ALOG1
ALOG0
KS[0..23]
BATT TEMP
BATT VOLTS
KBD[0..3]
Intel Corporation
Title
KEYBOARD & PRINTER CONNECTORS
Size
B
Document Number
REV
D0
Date: November 27, 1991
Sheet 24 of 43

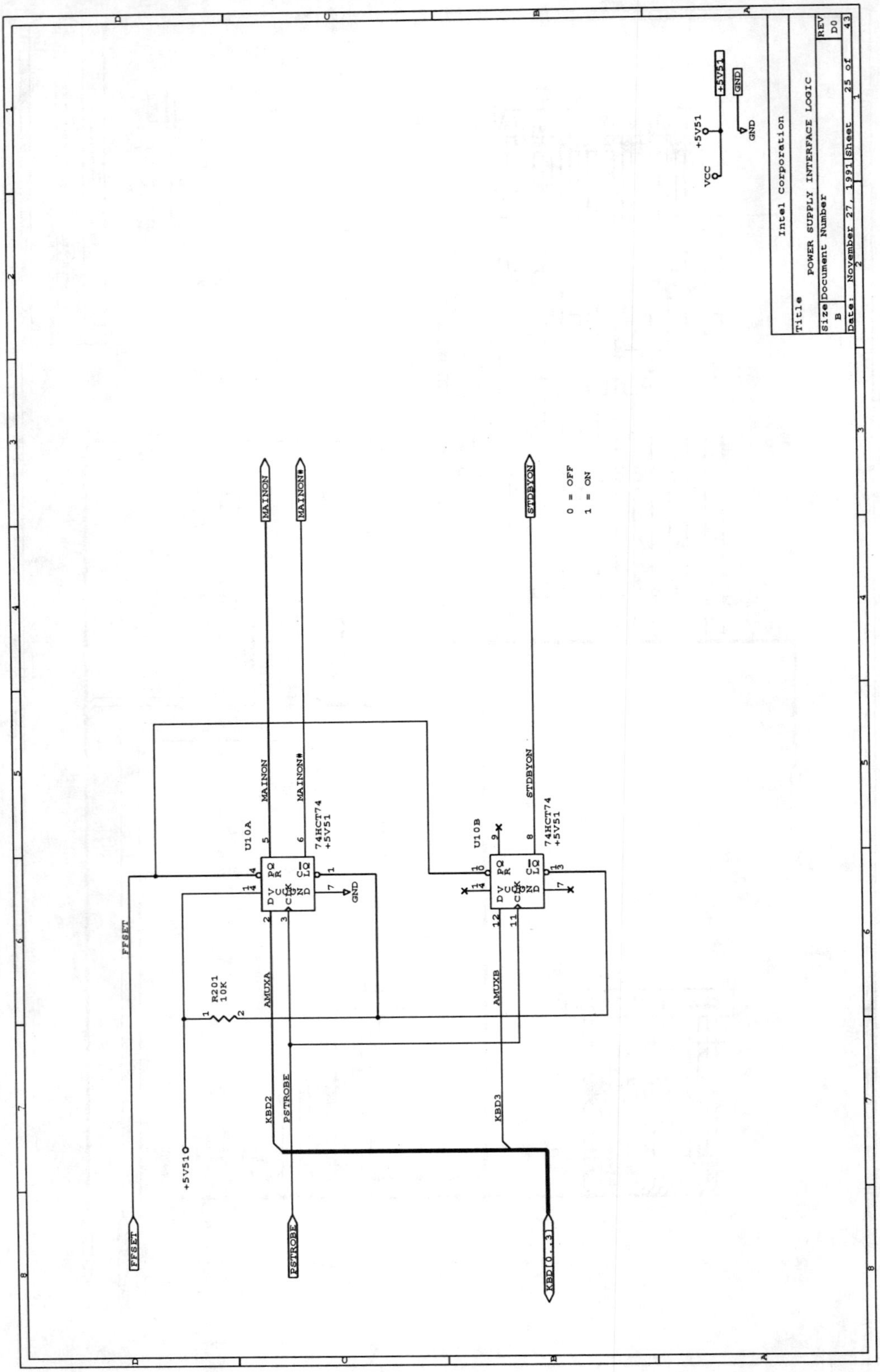
Intel Corporation
Title
POWER SUPPLY INTERFACE LOGIC
Size
B
Document Number
REV
D0
Date: November 27, 1991
Sheet 25 of 43
VCC
+5V51
GND
MAINON
MAINON#
STDBYON
0 = OFF
1 = ON
U10A
U10B
74HCT74
R201
10K
FFSET
PSTROBE
KBD[0..3]
KBD2
KBD3
AMUXA
AMUXB

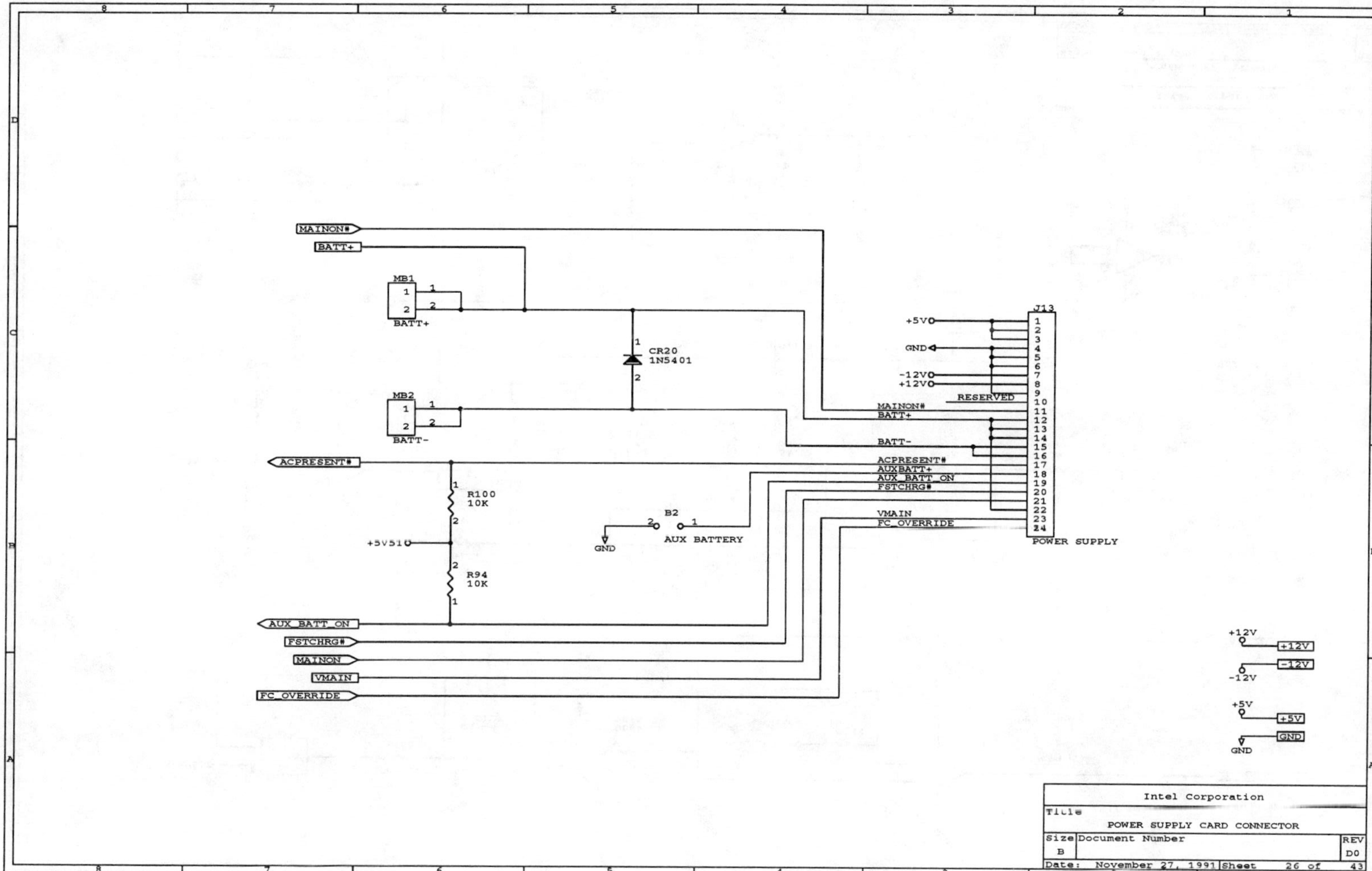
MAINON#
BATT+
MB1
BATT+
MB2
BATT-
CR20
1N5401
ACPRESENT#
R100
10K
+5V51
R94
10K
B2
AUX BATTERY
GND
AUX_BATT_ON
FSTCHRG#
MAINON
VMAIN
FC_OVERRIDE
J13
POWER SUPPLY
+5V
GND
-12V
+12V
RESERVED
MAINON#
BATT+
BATT-
ACPRESENT#
AUXBATT+
AUX_BATT_ON
FSTCHRG#
VMAIN
FC_OVERRIDE
+12V
-12V
+5V
GND
Intel Corporation
Title
POWER SUPPLY CARD CONNECTOR
Size B
Document Number
REV D0
Date: November 27, 1991
Sheet 26 of 43

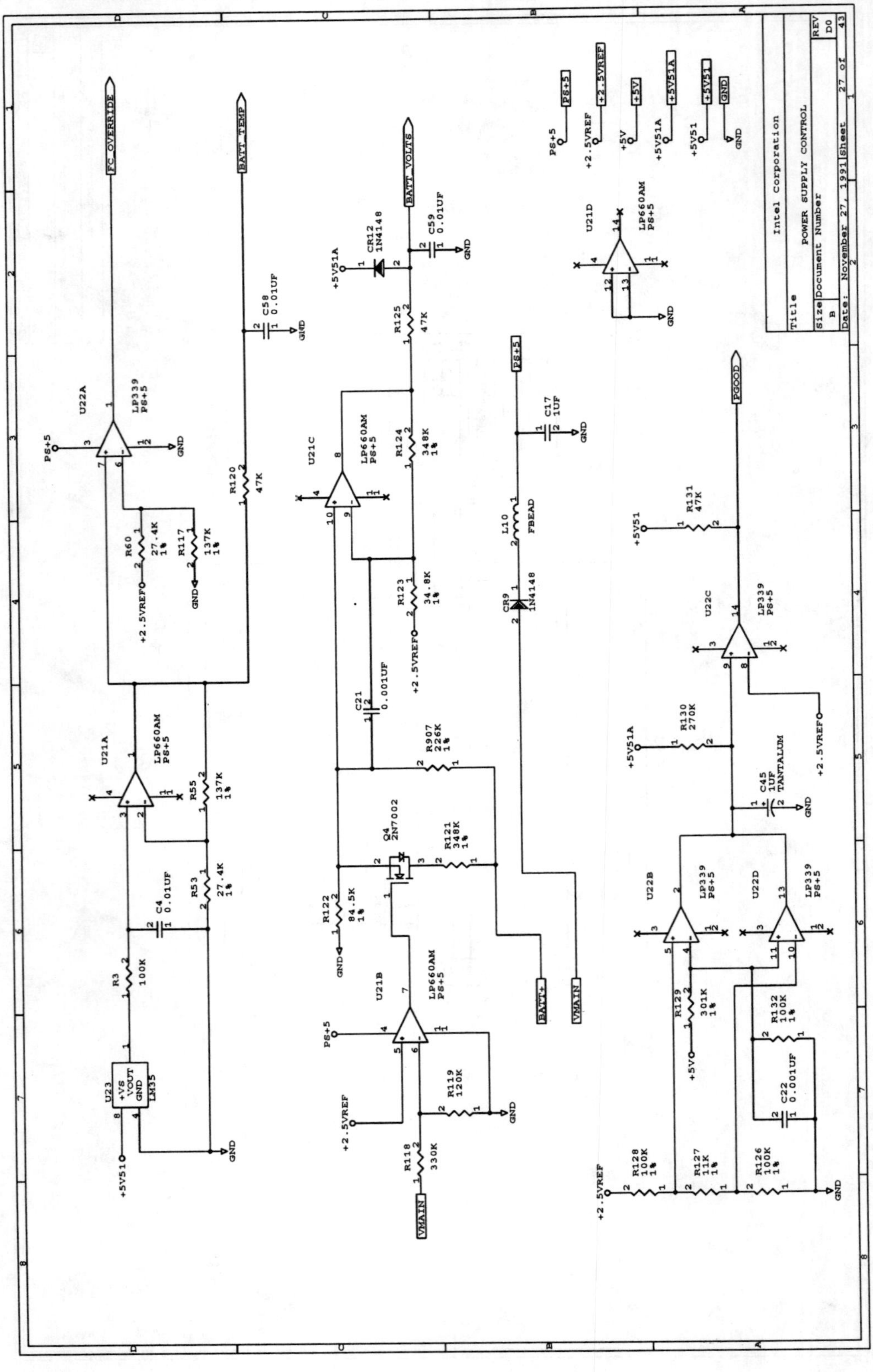
Intel Corporation
Title
POWER SUPPLY CONTROL
Size
B
Document Number
REV
D0
Date: November 27, 1991
Sheet 27 of 43
FC_OVERRIDE
BATT_TEMP
BATT_VOLTS
PGOOD
BATT+
VMAIN
PS+5
+2.5VREF
+5V
+5V51A
+5V51
GND
U22A LP339 PS+5
U21A LP660AM PS+5
U21B LP660AM PS+5
U21C LP660AM PS+5
U21D LP660AM PS+5
U22B LP339 PS+5
U22C LP339 PS+5
U22D LP339 PS+5
U23 +VS VOUT GND LM35
Q4 2N7002
CR12 1N4148
CR9 1N4148
L10 FBEAD
C58 0.01UF
C59 0.01UF
C17 1UF
C4 0.01UF
C21 0.001UF
C22 0.001UF
C45 1UF TANTALUM
R3 100K
R53 27.4K 1%
R55 137K 1%
R60 27.4K 1%
R117 137K 1%
R120 47K
R125 47K
R124 348K 1%
R123 34.8K 1%
R907 226K 1%
R121 348K 1%
R122 84.5K 1%
R119 120K
R118 330K
R131 47K
R130 270K
R129 301K 1%
R132 100K 1%
R128 100K 1%
R127 11K 1%
R126 100K 1%

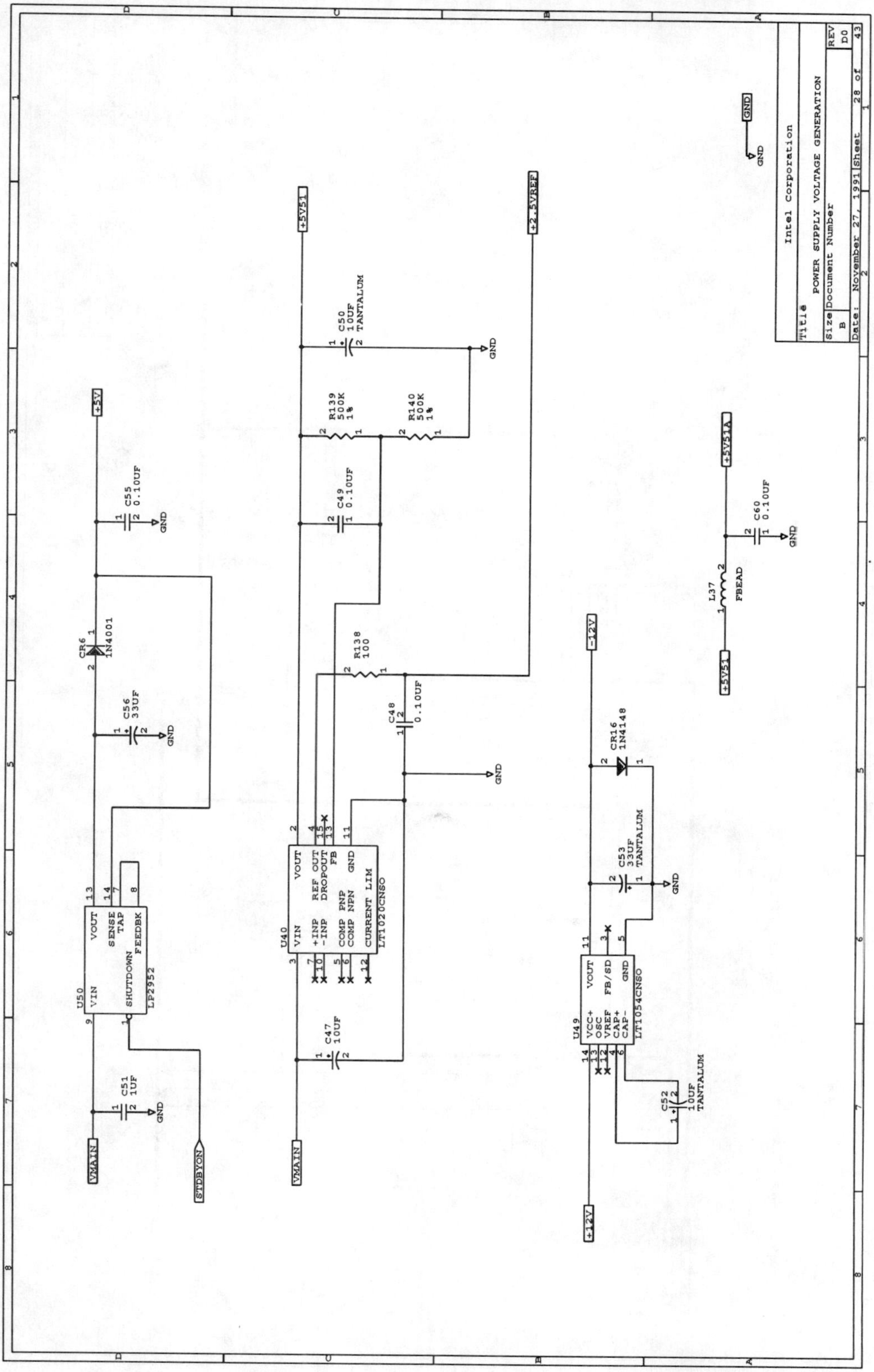

Intel Corporation
Title
POWER SUPPLY VOLTAGE GENERATION
Size B
Document Number
REV D0
Date: November 27, 1991
Sheet 28 of 43
U50
LP2952
VIN
VOUT
SENSE
TAP
SHUTDOWN
FEEDBK
VMAIN
STDBYON
+5V
C51 1UF
C55 0.10UF
C56 33UF
CR6 1N4001
U40
LT1020CNSO
VIN
VOUT
+INP
-INP
COMP PNP
COMP NPN
CURRENT LIM
REF OUT
DROPOUT
FB
GND
+5V51
+2.5VREF
C47 10UF
C48 0.10UF
C49 0.10UF
C50 10UF TANTALUM
R138 100
R139 500K 1%
R140 500K 1%
U49
LT1054CNSO
VCC+
OSC
VREF
CAP+
CAP-
VOUT
FB/SD
GND
+12V
-12V
C52 10UF TANTALUM
C53 33UF TANTALUM
CR16 1N4148
L37 FBEAD
C60 0.10UF
+5V51A
GND

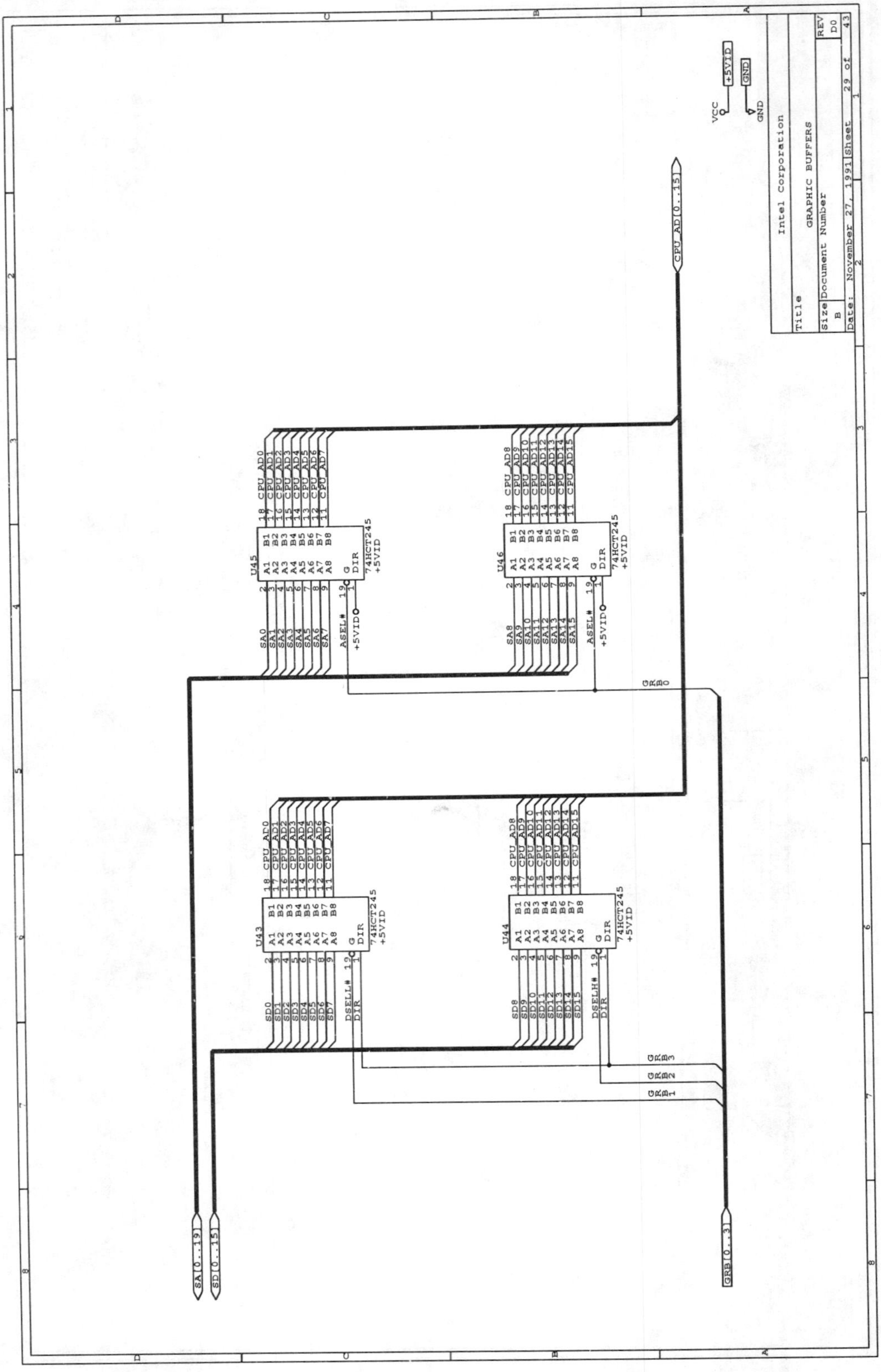
Intel Corporation
Title GRAPHIC BUFFERS
Size B
Document Number
REV D0
Date: November 27, 1991
Sheet 29 of 43
VCC
+5VID
GND
CPU_AD[0..15]
SA[0..19]
SD[0..15]
GRB[0..3]
U45
U46
U43
U44
74HCT245
ASEL#
DSELL#
DSELH#
DIR

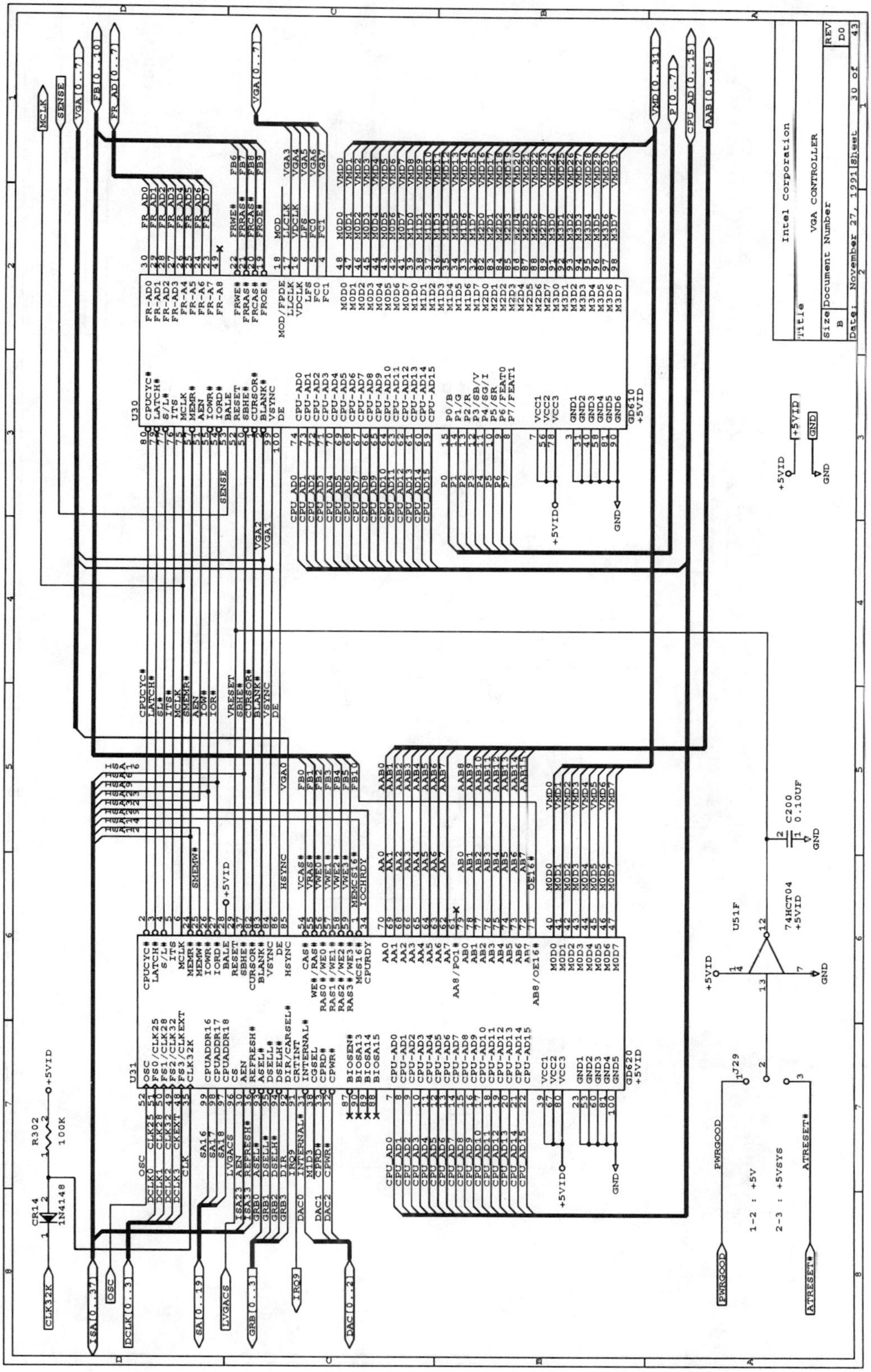
Intel Corporation
Title VGA CONTROLLER
Size B
Document Number
REV D0
Date: November 27, 1991 Sheet 30 of 43

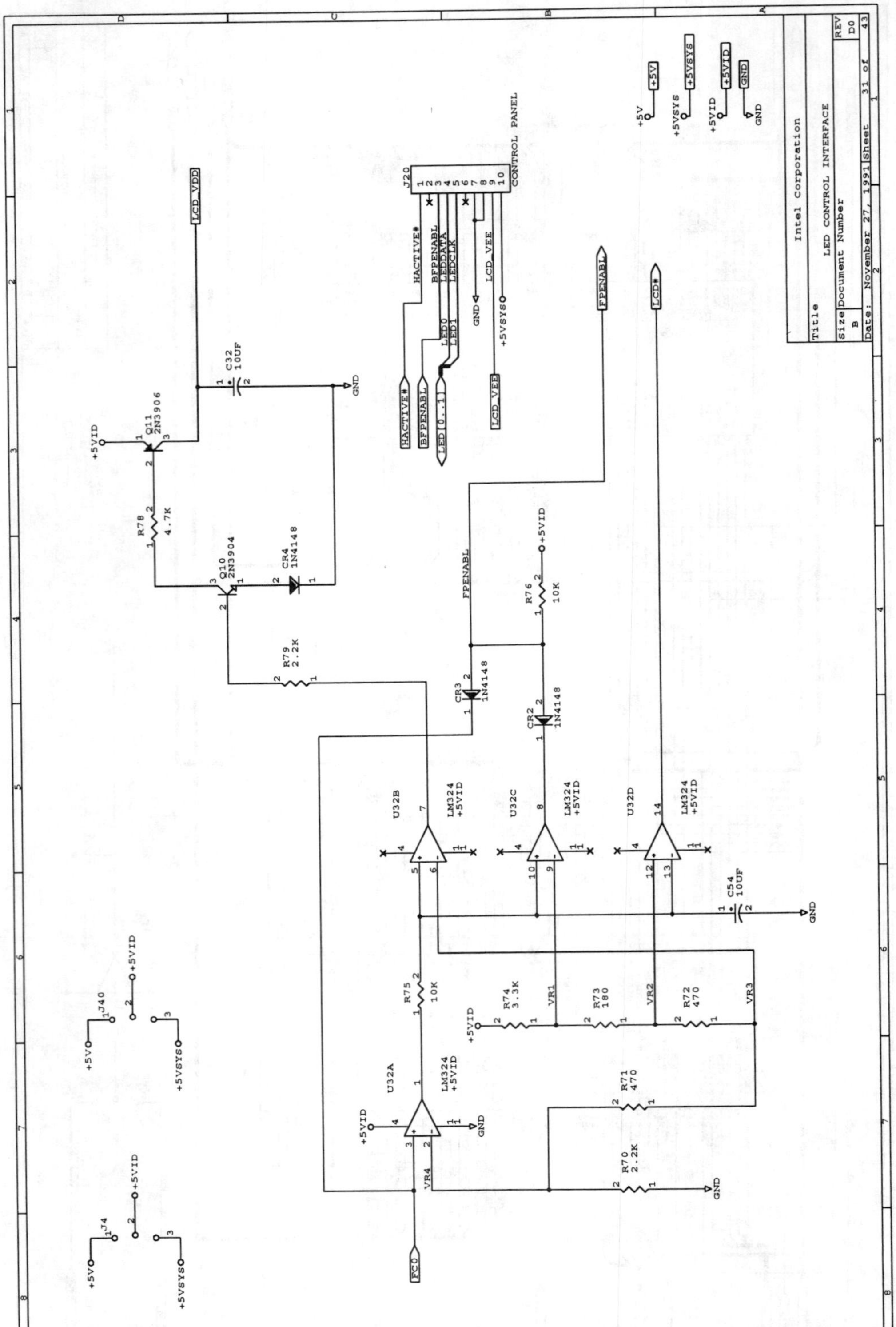
Intel Corporation
Title
LED CONTROL INTERFACE
Size Document Number
B
REV
D0
Date: November 27, 1991 Sheet 31 of 43
CONTROL PANEL
J20
HACTIVE#
BFPENABL
LEDDATA
LEDCLK
LCD VEE
LCD VDD
FPENABL
LCD#
FC0
U32A
U32B
U32C
U32D
LM324
Q11
2N3906
Q10
2N3904
CR4
CR3
CR2
1N4148
R78
4.7K
R79
2.2K
R76
10K
R75
10K
R74
3.3K
R73
180
R72
470
R71
470
R70
2.2K
C32
10UF
C54
10UF
J40
J4
+5V
+5VSYS
+5VID
GND

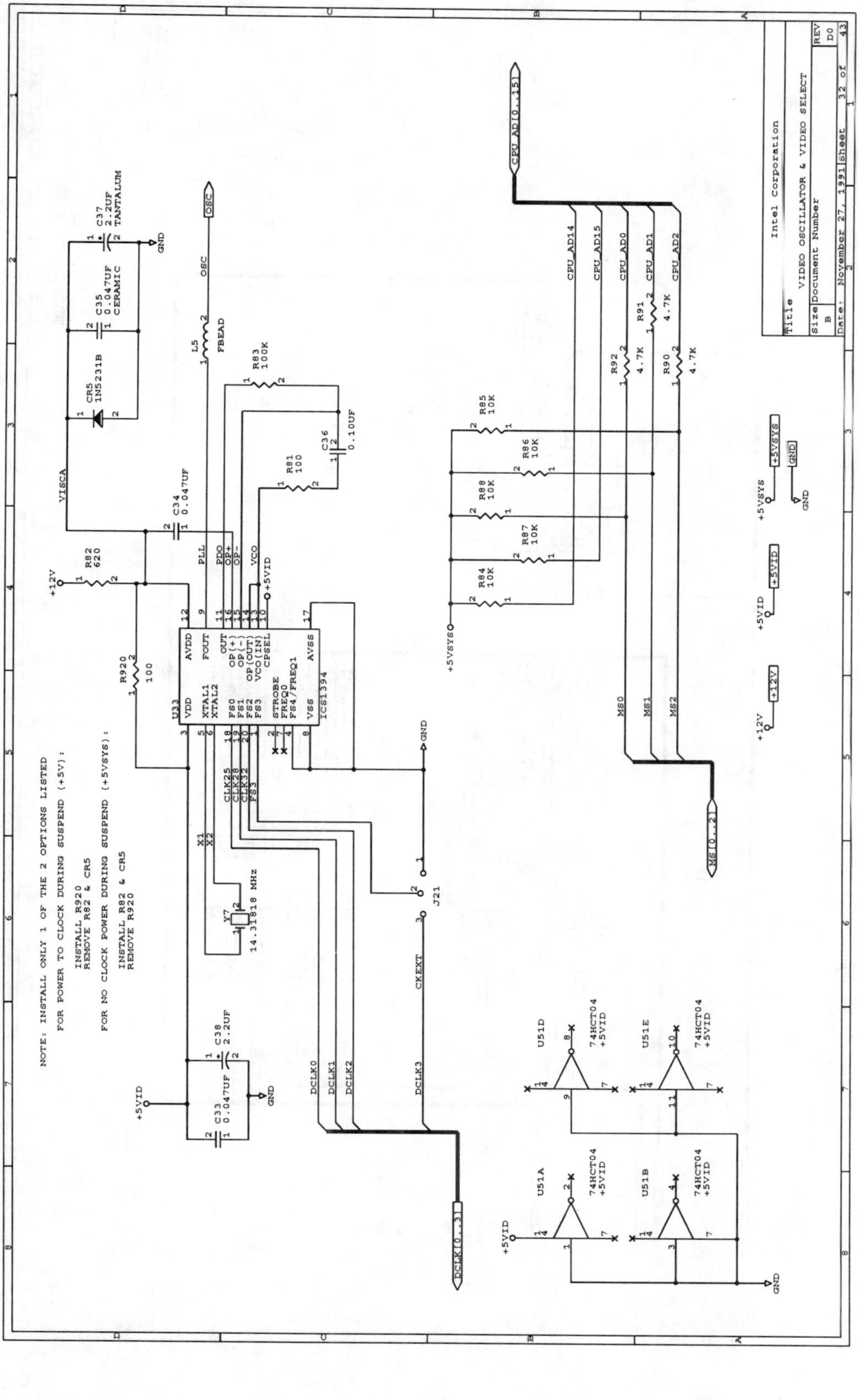
Intel Corporation
Title
VIDEO OSCILLATOR & VIDEO SELECT
Size Document Number
B
REV
D0
Date: November 27, 1991 Sheet 32 of 43
NOTE: INSTALL ONLY 1 OF THE 2 OPTIONS LISTED
FOR POWER TO CLOCK DURING SUSPEND (+5V):
INSTALL R920
REMOVE R82 & CR5
FOR NO CLOCK POWER DURING SUSPEND (+5VSYS):
INSTALL R82 & CR5
REMOVE R920
U33
ICS1394
VDD
XTAL1
XTAL2
FS0
FS1
FS2
FS3
STROBE
FREQ0
FS4/FREQ1
VSS
AVDD
FOUT
OUT
OP(+)
OP(-)
OP(OUT)
VCO(IN)
CPSEL
AVSS
C37
2.2UF
TANTALUM
C35
0.047UF
CERAMIC
CR5
1N5231B
L5
FBEAD
OSC
R83
100K
C36
0.10UF
R81
100
C34
0.047UF
VISCA
R82
620
R920
100
+12V
+5VID
+5VSYS
GND
PLL
PDO
OP+
OP-
VCO
Y7
14.31818 MHz
X1
X2
CLK25
CLK28
CLK32
FS3
J21
CKEXT
C38
2.2UF
C33
0.047UF
DCLK0
DCLK1
DCLK2
DCLK3
DCLK[0..3]
U51A
U51B
U51D
U51E
74HCT04
R84
R85
R86
R87
R88
10K
R90
R91
R92
4.7K
CPU_AD[0..15]
CPU_AD14
CPU_AD15
CPU_AD0
CPU_AD1
CPU_AD2
MS0
MS1
MS2
MS[0..2]

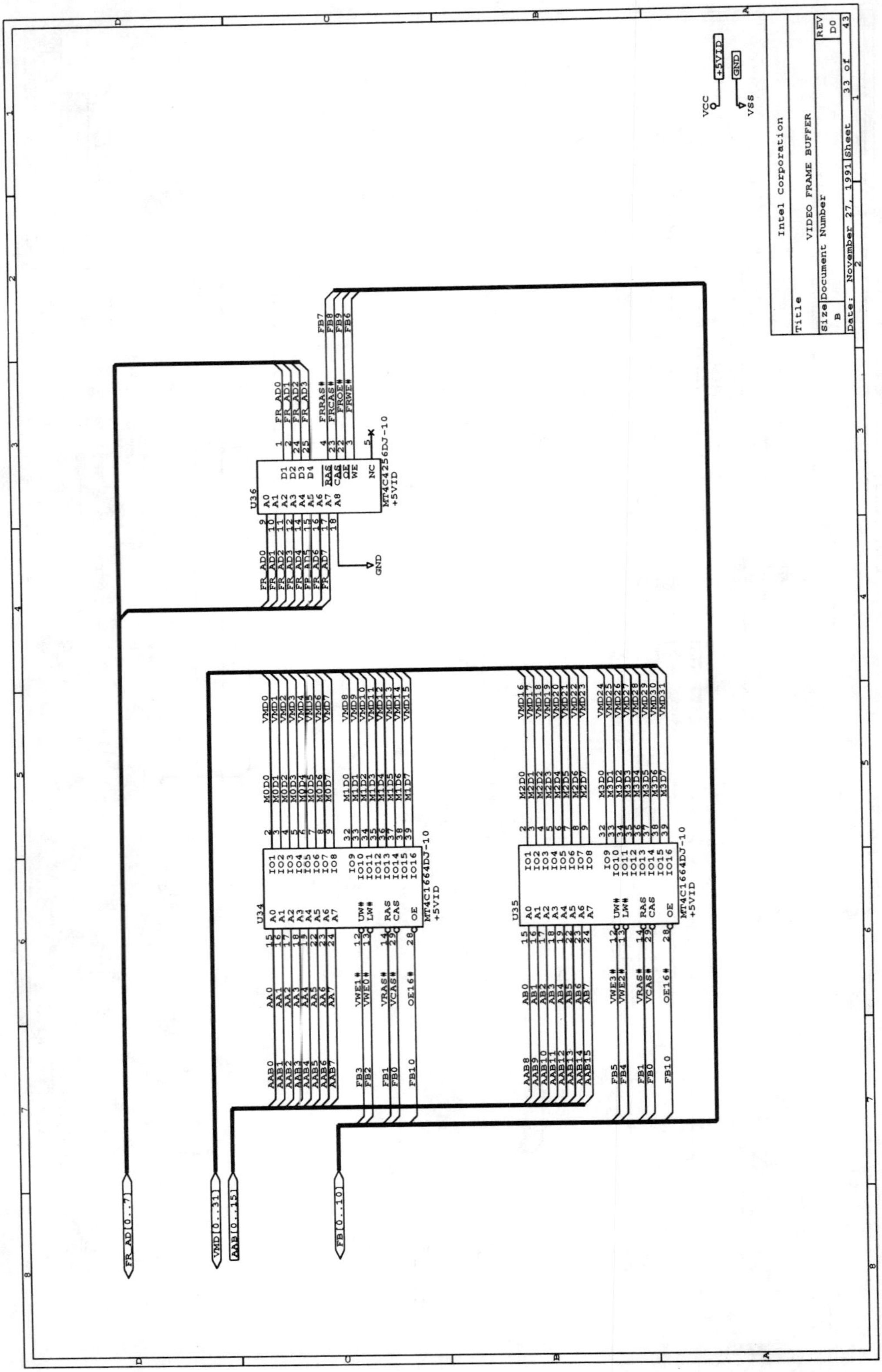
Intel Corporation
Title VIDEO FRAME BUFFER
Size B
Document Number
REV D0
Date: November 27, 1991
Sheet 33 of 43
VCC
+5VID
GND
VSS
U36
MT4C4256DJ-10
U34
MT4C1664DJ-10
U35
MT4C1664DJ-10
FR_AD[0..7]
VMD[0..31]
AAB[0..15]
FB[0..10]

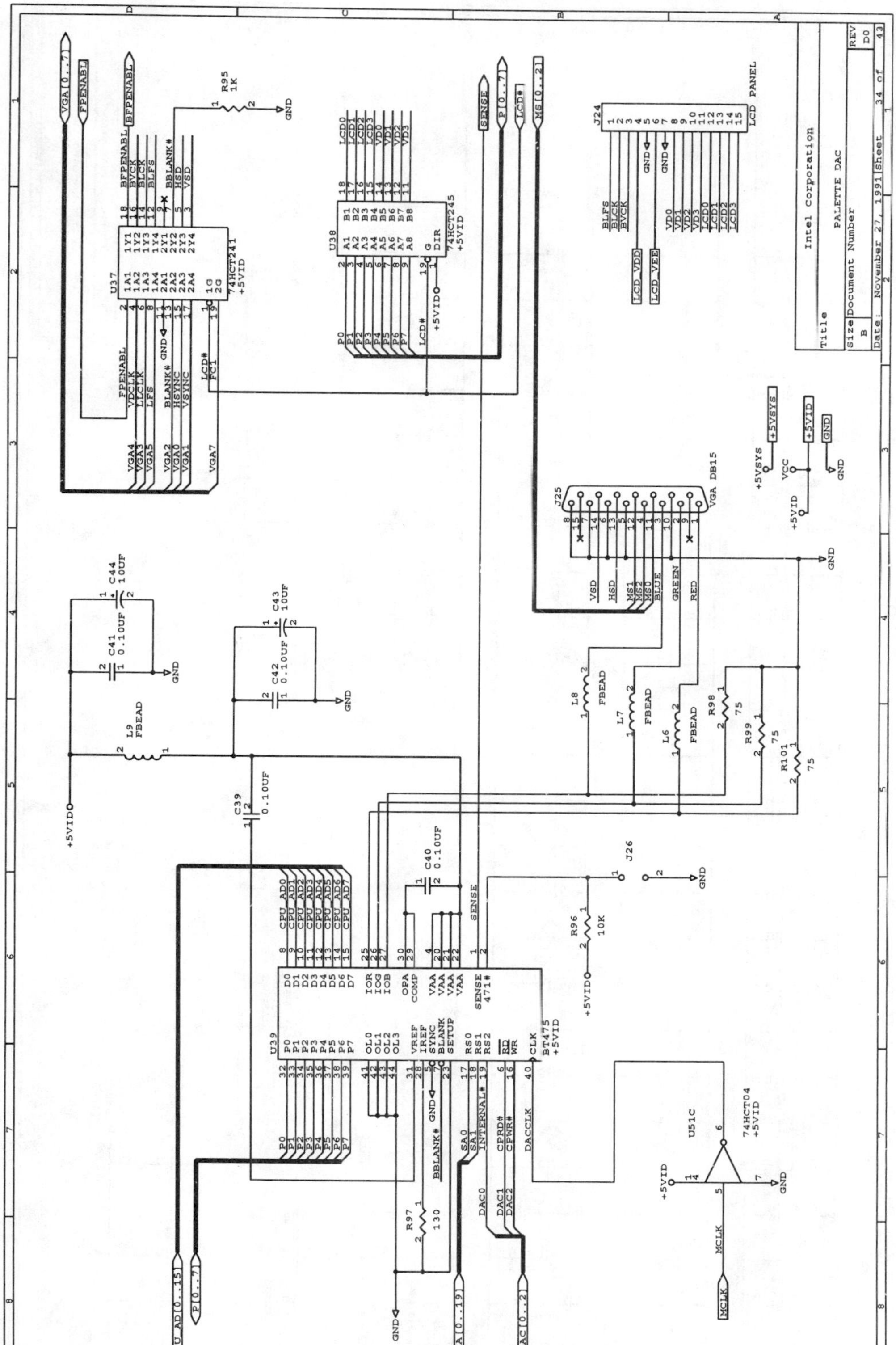
Intel Corporation
Title
PALETTE DAC
Size Document Number
B
REV
D0
Date: November 27, 1991 Sheet 34 of 43

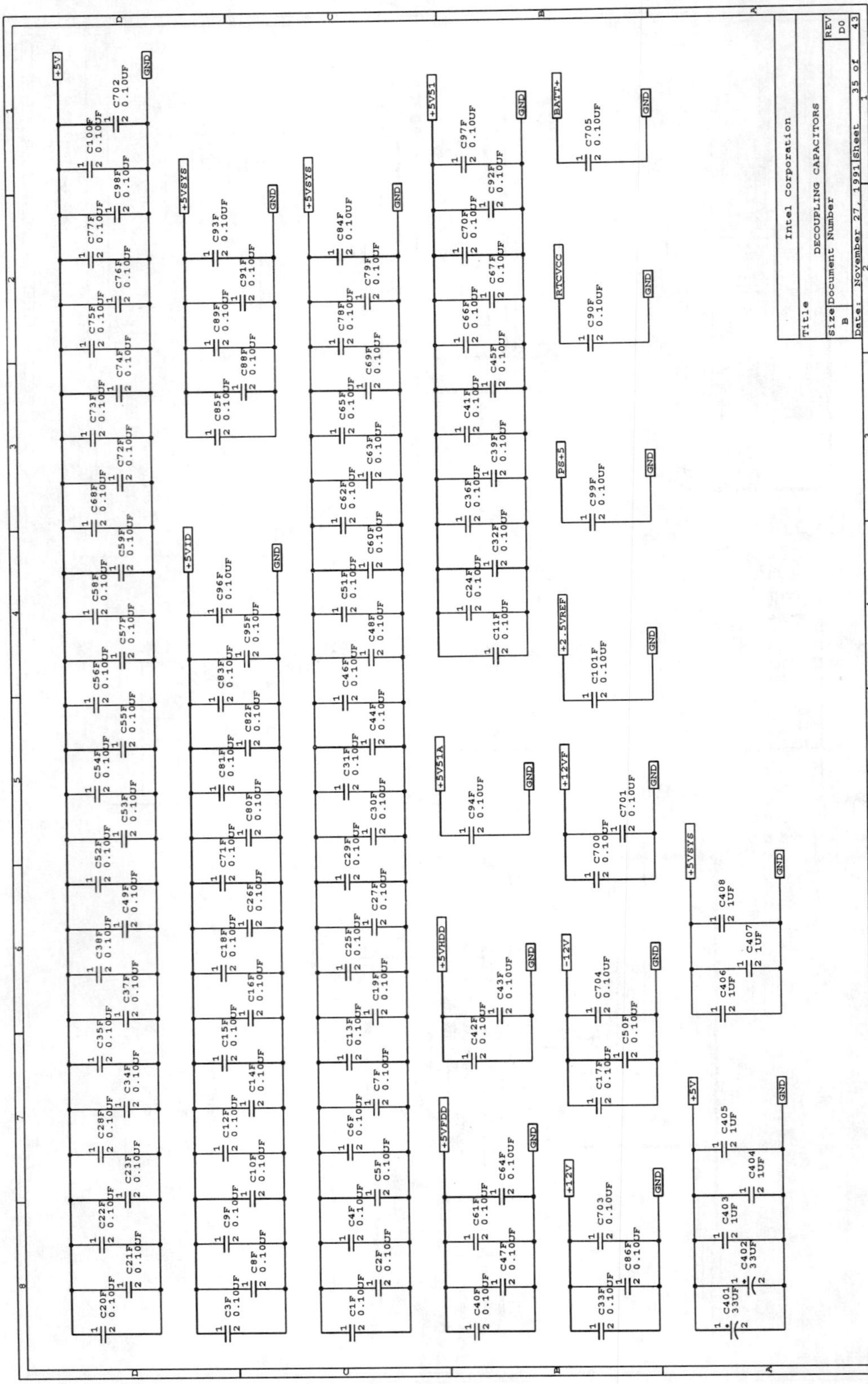
Intel Corporation
Title
DECOUPLING CAPACITORS
Size Document Number
B
REV
D0
Date: November 27, 1991 Sheet 35 of 43
+5V
GND
+5VSYS
+5VID
+5V51
BATT+
RTCVCC
PS+5
+2.5VREF
+5V51A
+12VF
+5VHDD
-12V
+5VFDD
+12V

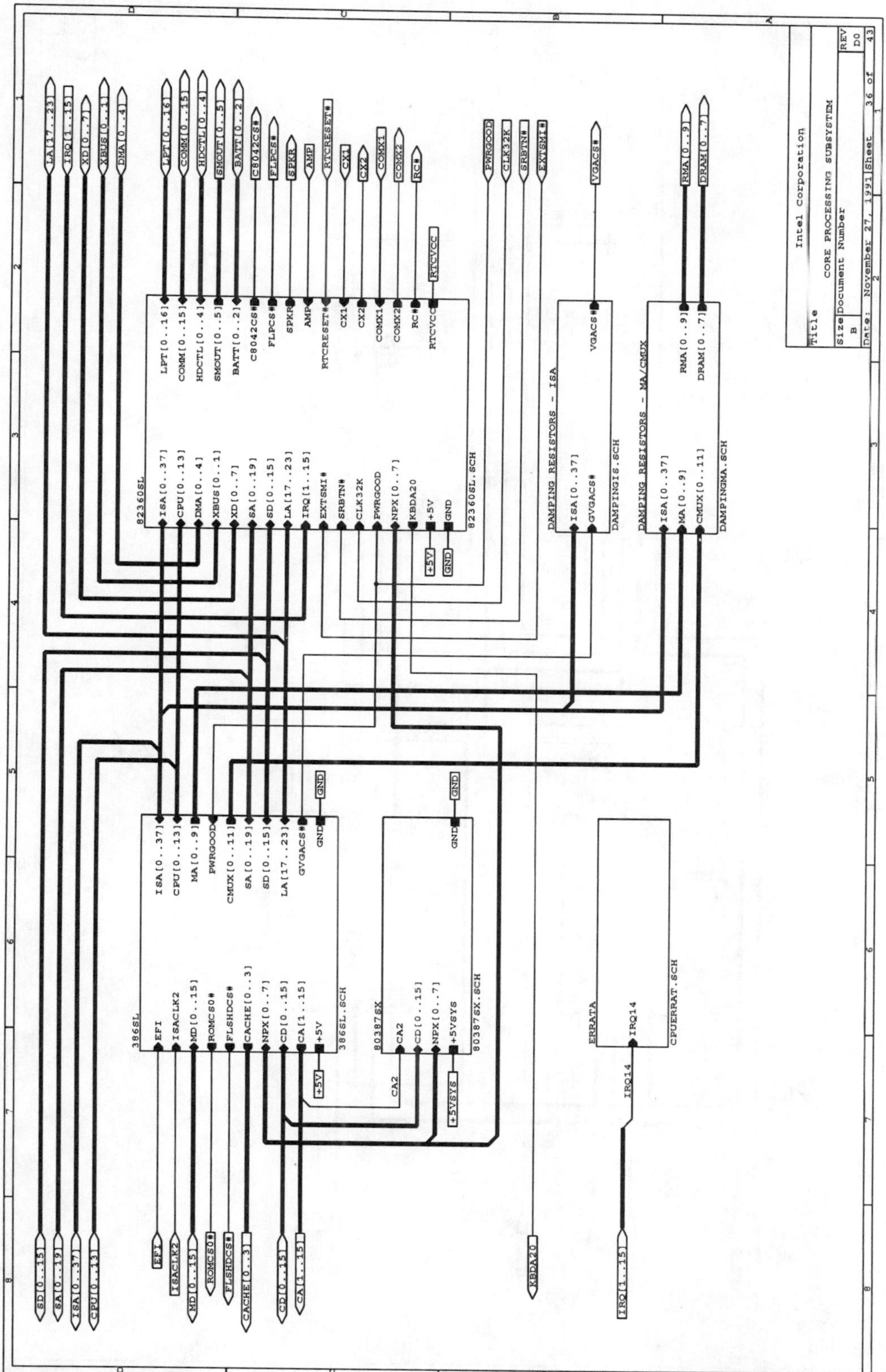
Intel Corporation
Title CORE PROCESSING SUBSYSTEM
Size B
Document Number
REV D0
Date: November 27, 1991
Sheet 36 of 43
82360SL
82360SL.SCH
386SL
386SL.SCH
80387SX
80387SX.SCH
DAMPING RESISTORS - ISA
DAMPINGIS.SCH
DAMPING RESISTORS - MA/CMUX
DAMPINGMA.SCH
ERRATA
CPUERRAT.SCH
LA[17..23]
IRQ[1..15]
XD[0..7]
XBUS[0..1]
DMA[0..4]
LPT[0..16]
COMM[0..15]
HDCTL[0..4]
SMOUT[0..5]
BATT[0..2]
C8042CS#
FLPCS#
SPKR
AMP
RTCRESET#
CX1
CX2
COMX1
COMX2
RC#
RTCVCC
PWRGOOD
CLK32K
SRBTN#
EXTSMI#
VGACS#
RMA[0..9]
DRAM[0..7]
ISA[0..37]
CPU[0..13]
SA[0..19]
SD[0..15]
NPX[0..7]
KBDA20
+5V
GND
GVGACS#
MA[0..9]
CMUX[0..11]
EFI
ISACLK2
MD[0..15]
ROMCS0#
FLSHDCS#
CACHE[0..3]
CD[0..15]
CA[1..15]
CA2
+5VSYS
IRQ14

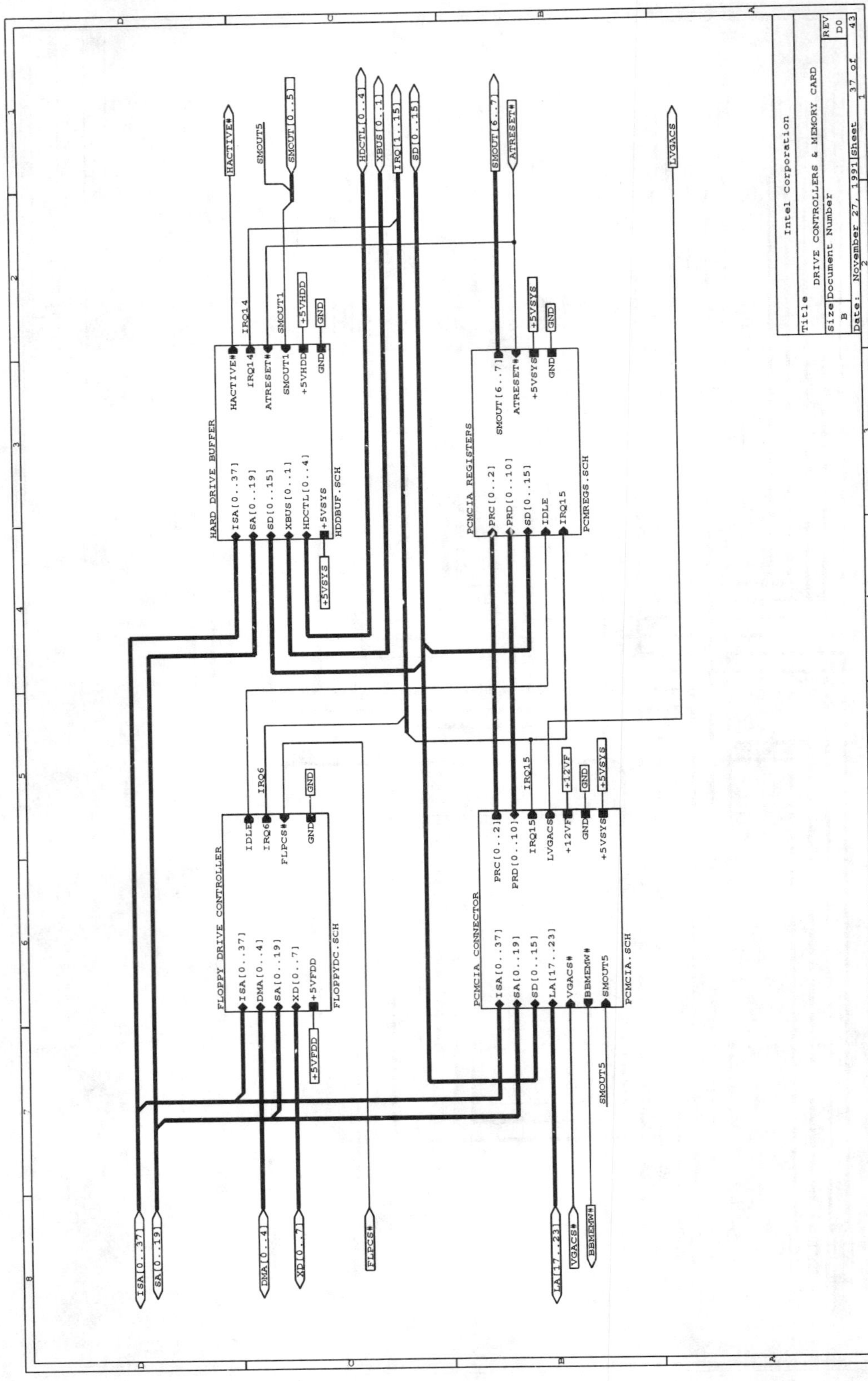
Intel Corporation
Title
DRIVE CONTROLLERS & MEMORY CARD
Size B
Document Number
REV D0
Date: November 27, 1991
Sheet 37 of 43
HARD DRIVE BUFFER
ISA[0..37]
SA[0..19]
SD[0..15]
XBUS[0..1]
HDCTL[0..4]
+5VSYS
HDDBUF.SCH
HACTIVE#
IRQ14
ATRESET#
SMOUT1
+5VHDD
GND
PCMCIA REGISTERS
PRC[0..2]
PRD[0..10]
SD[0..15]
IDLE
IRQ15
PCMREGS.SCH
SMOUT[6..7]
ATRESET#
+5VSYS
GND
FLOPPY DRIVE CONTROLLER
ISA[0..37]
DMA[0..4]
SA[0..19]
XD[0..7]
+5VFDD
FLOPPYDC.SCH
IDLE
IRQ6
FLPCS#
GND
PCMCIA CONNECTOR
ISA[0..37]
SA[0..19]
SD[0..15]
LA[17..23]
VGACS#
BBMEMW#
SMOUT5
PCMCIA.SCH
PRC[0..2]
PRD[0..10]
IRQ15
LVGACS
+12VF
GND
+5VSYS
HACTIVE#
SMOUT5
SMOUT[0..5]
HDCTL[0..4]
XBUS[0..1]
IRQ[1..15]
SD[0..15]
SMOUT[6..7]
ATRESET#
LVGACS
ISA[0..37]
SA[0..19]
DMA[0..4]
XD[0..7]
FLPCS#
LA[17..23]
VGACS#
BBMEMW#

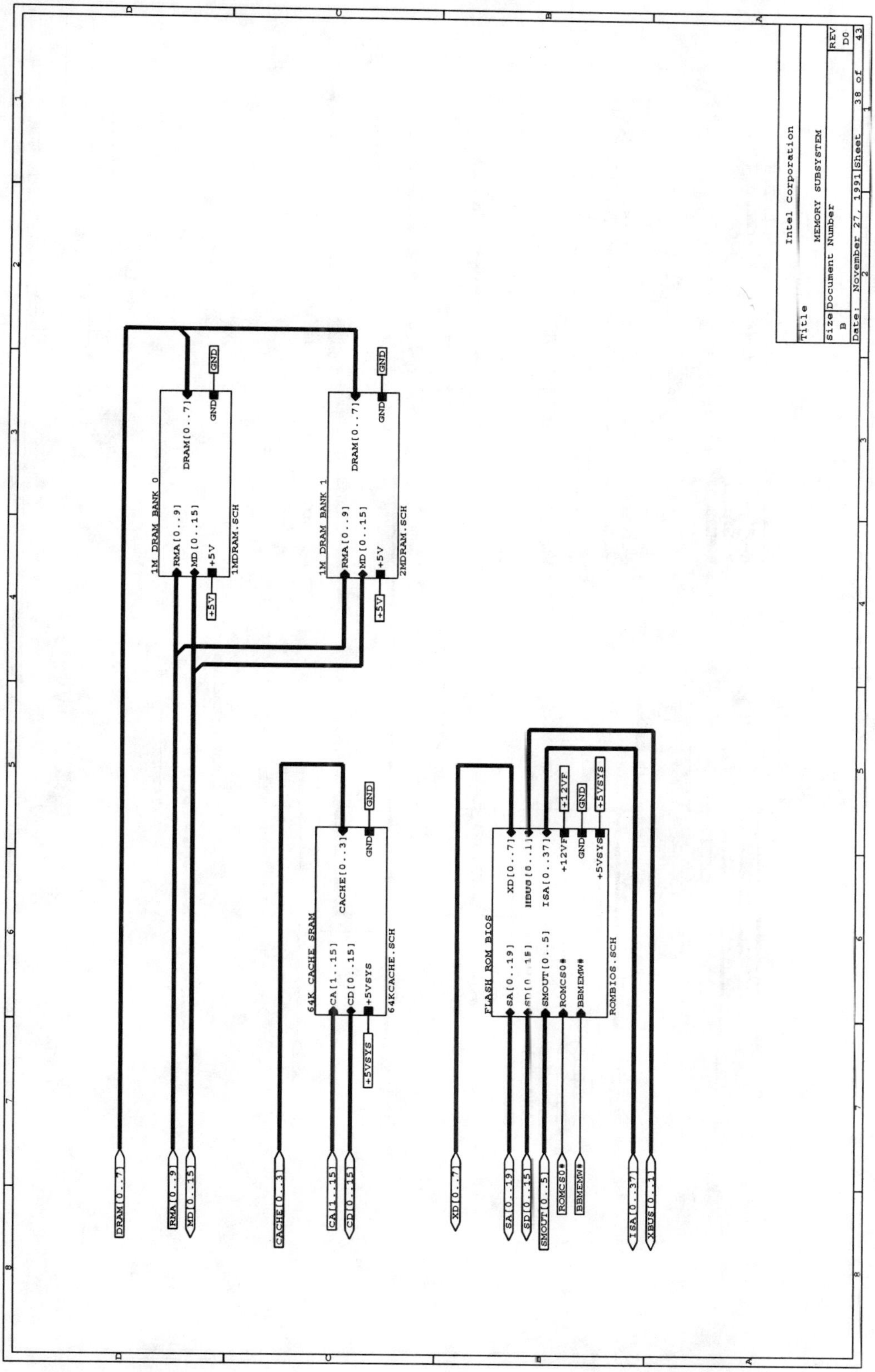
Intel Corporation
Title MEMORY SUBSYSTEM
Size B
Document Number
REV D0
Date: November 27, 1991
Sheet 38 of 43
1M DRAM BANK 0
RMA[0..9]
MD[0..15]
+5V
DRAM[0..7]
GND
1MDRAM.SCH
1M DRAM BANK 1
RMA[0..9]
MD[0..15]
+5V
DRAM[0..7]
GND
2MDRAM.SCH
64K CACHE SRAM
CA[1..15]
CD[0..15]
+5VSYS
CACHE[0..3]
GND
64KCACHE.SCH
FLASH ROM BIOS
SA[0..19]
SD[0..15]
SMOUT[0..5]
ROMCS0#
BBMEMW#
XD[0..7]
XBUS[0..1]
ISA[0..37]
+12VF
GND
+5VSYS
ROMBIOS.SCH
DRAM[0..7]
RMA[0..9]
MD[0..15]
CACHE[0..3]
CA[1..15]
CD[0..15]
XD[0..7]
SA[0..19]
SD[0..15]
SMOUT[0..5]
ROMCS0#
BBMEMW#
ISA[0..37]
XBUS[0..1]

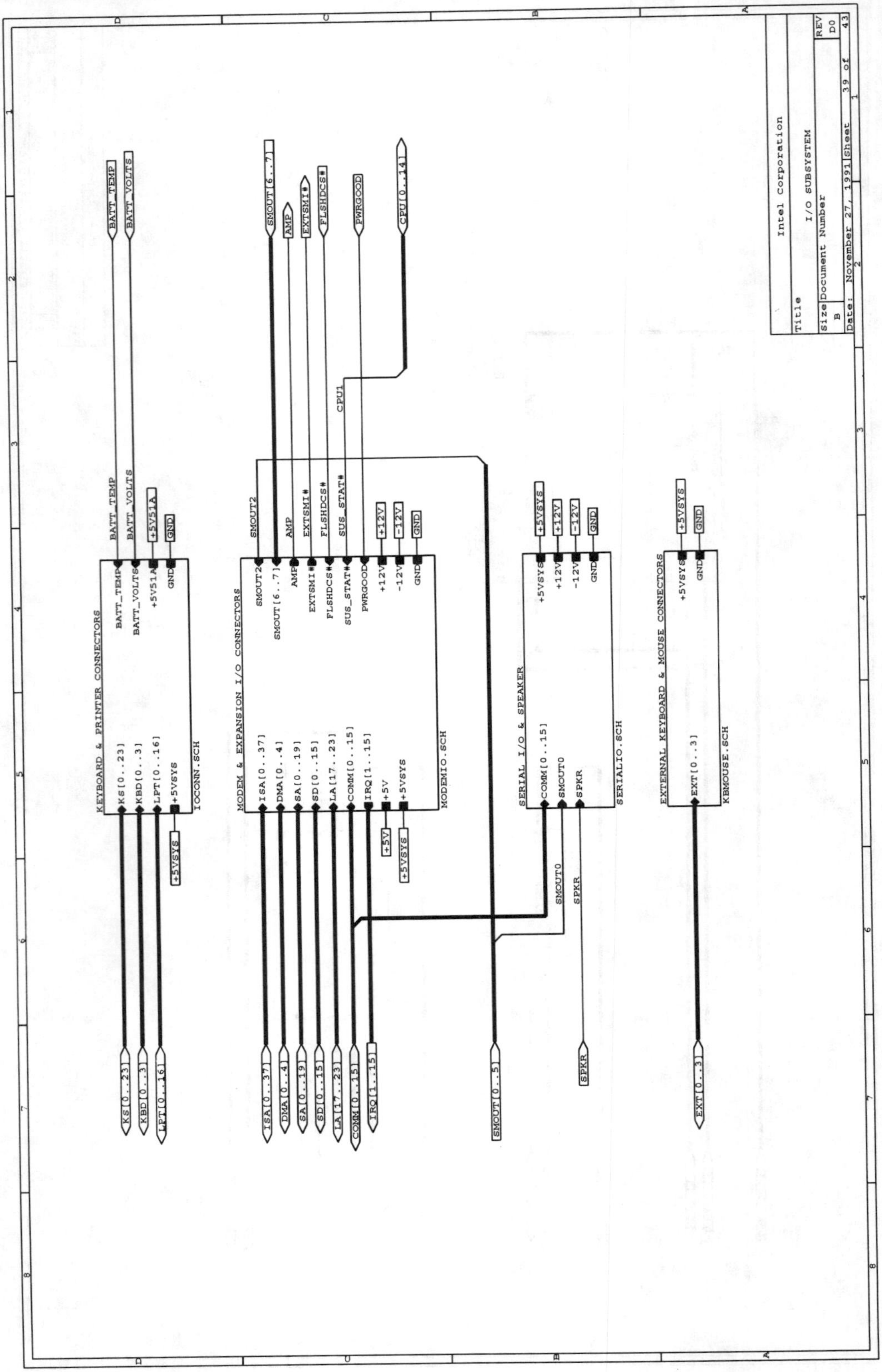

Intel Corporation
Title
I/O SUBSYSTEM
Size
B
Document Number
REV
D0
Date: November 27, 1991
Sheet 39 of 43
KEYBOARD & PRINTER CONNECTORS
IOCONN.SCH
BATT_TEMP
BATT_VOLTS
+5V51A
GND
KS[0..23]
KBD[0..3]
LPT[0..16]
+5VSYS
MODEM & EXPANSION I/O CONNECTORS
MODEMIO.SCH
SMOUT2
SMOUT[6..7]
AMP
EXTSMI#
FLSHDCS#
SUS_STAT#
PWRGOOD
CPU1
CPU[0..14]
+12V
-12V
ISA[0..37]
DMA[0..4]
SA[0..19]
SD[0..15]
LA[17..23]
COMM[0..15]
IRQ[1..15]
+5V
SERIAL I/O & SPEAKER
SERIALIO.SCH
SMOUT0
SPKR
SMOUT[0..5]
EXTERNAL KEYBOARD & MOUSE CONNECTORS
KBMOUSE.SCH
EXT[0..3]

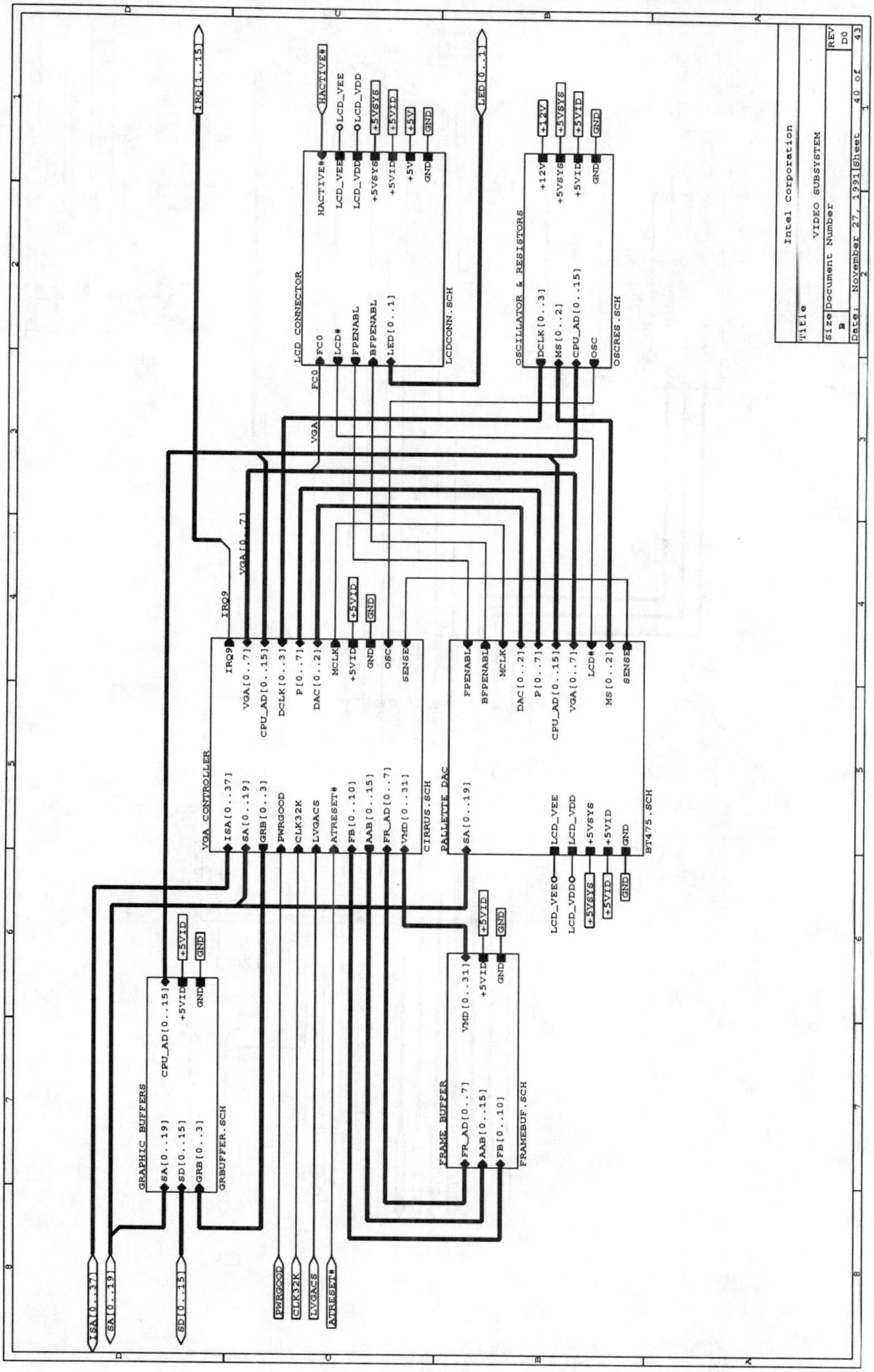

Intel Corporation
Title VIDEO SUBSYSTEM
Size B
Document Number
REV D0
Date: November 27, 1991
Sheet 40 of 43
VGA CONTROLLER
CIRRUS.SCH
ISA[0..37]
SA[0..19]
GRB[0..3]
PWRGOOD
CLK32K
LVGACS
ATRESET#
FB[0..10]
AAB[0..15]
FR_AD[0..7]
VMD[0..31]
IRQ9
VGA[0..7]
CPU_AD[0..15]
DCLK[0..3]
P[0..7]
DAC[0..2]
MCLK
+5VID
GND
OSC
SENSE
PALLETTE DAC
BT475.SCH
FPENABL
BFPENABL
LCD_VEE
LCD_VDD
+5VSYS
LCD#
MS[0..2]
LCD CONNECTOR
LCDCONN.SCH
FC0
LED[0..1]
HACTIVE#
+5V
OSCILLATOR & RESISTORS
OSCRES.SCH
+12V
GRAPHIC BUFFERS
GRBUFFER.SCH
SD[0..15]
FRAME BUFFER
FRAMEBUF.SCH
IRQ[1..15]

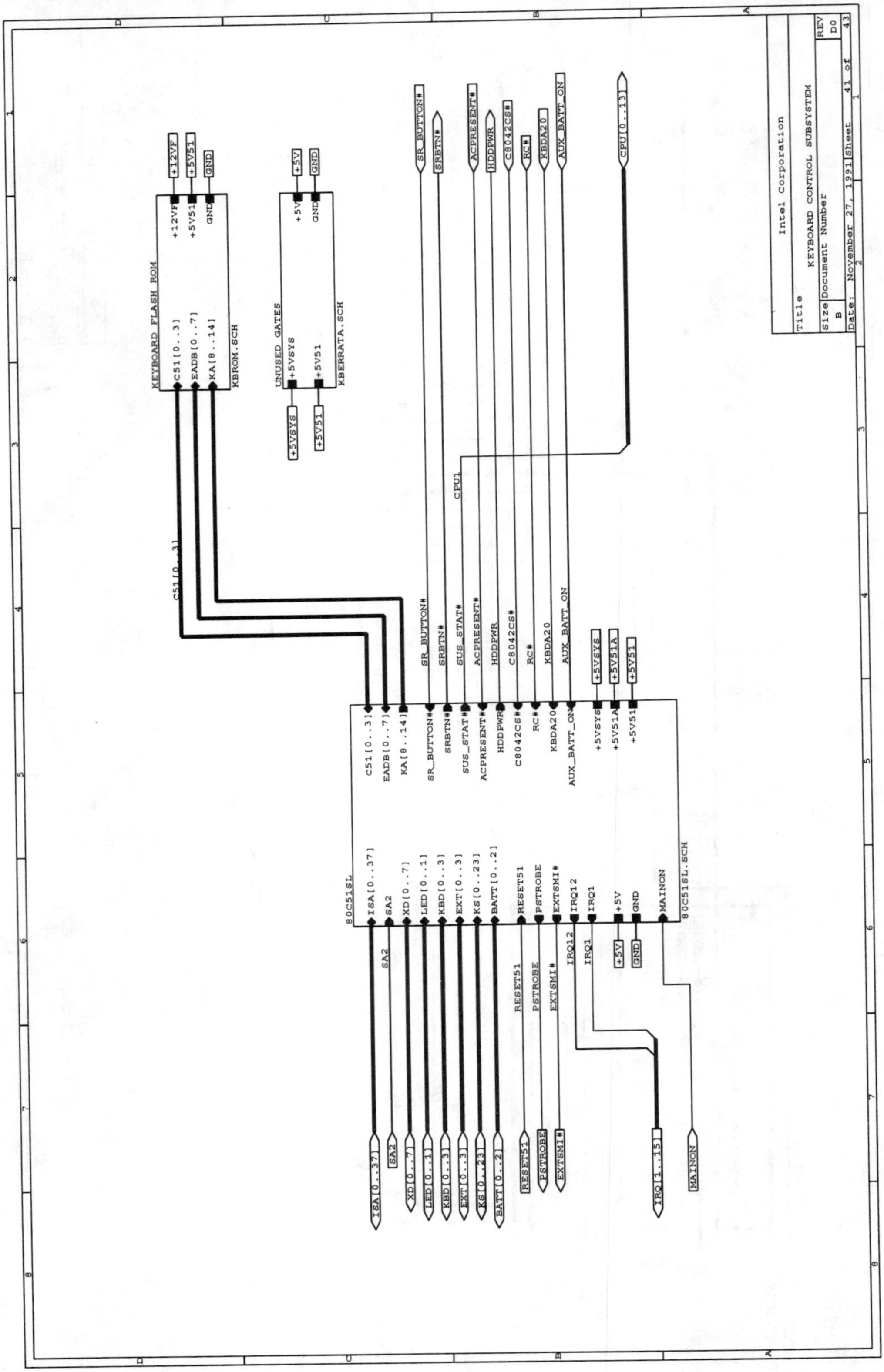
Intel Corporation
Title KEYBOARD CONTROL SUBSYSTEM
Size B
Document Number
REV D0
Date: November 27, 1991
Sheet 41 of 43
KEYBOARD FLASH ROM
KBROM.SCH
C51[0..3]
EADB[0..7]
KA[8..14]
+12VF
+5V51
GND
UNUSED GATES
KBERRATA.SCH
+5VSYS
+5V51
+5V
GND
80C51SL
80C51SL.SCH
ISA[0..37]
SA2
XD[0..7]
LED[0..1]
KBD[0..3]
EXT[0..3]
KS[0..23]
BATT[0..2]
RESET51
PSTROBE
EXTSMI#
IRQ12
IRQ1
IRQ[1..15]
MAINON
SR_BUTTON#
SRBTN#
SUS_STAT#
ACPRESENT#
HDDPWR
C8042CS#
RC#
KBDA20
AUX_BATT_ON
+5VSYS
+5V51A
+5V51
CPU1
CPU[0..13]

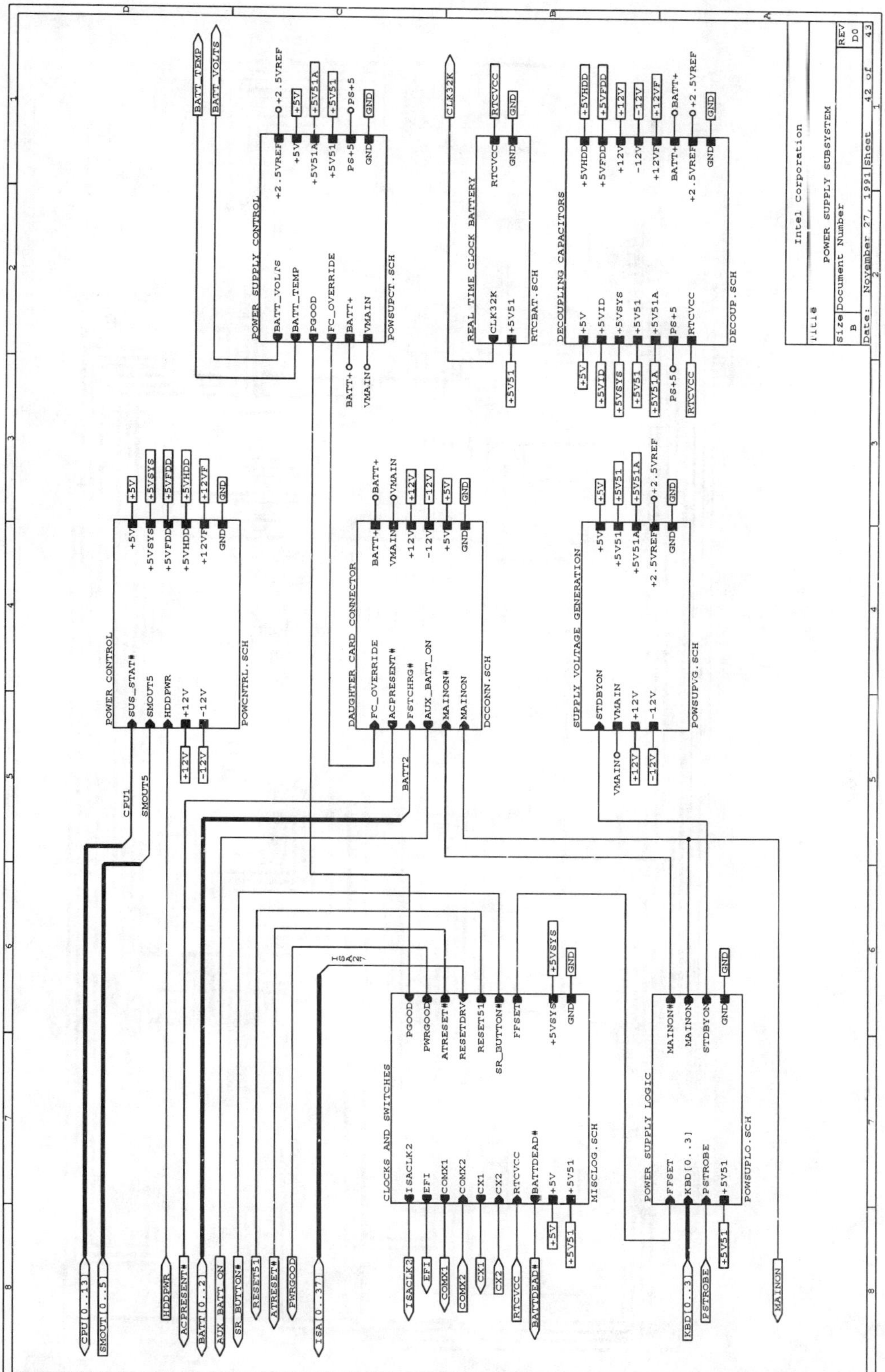
Intel Corporation
Title POWER SUPPLY SUBSYSTEM
Size B
Document Number
REV D0
Date: November 27, 1991 Sheet 42 of 43
POWER SUPPLY CONTROL
POWSUPCT.SCH
BATT_VOLTS
BATT_TEMP
PGOOD
FC_OVERRIDE
BATT+
VMAIN
+2.5VREF
+5V
+5V51A
+5V51
PS+5
GND
REAL TIME CLOCK BATTERY
RTCBAT.SCH
CLK32K
RTCVCC
DECOUPLING CAPACITORS
DECOUP.SCH
+5VHDD
+5VFDD
+12V
-12V
+12VF
+5VID
+5VSYS
POWER CONTROL
POWCNTRL.SCH
SUS_STAT#
SMOUT5
HDDPWR
CPU1
DAUGHTER CARD CONNECTOR
DCCONN.SCH
ACPRESENT#
FSTCHRG#
AUX_BATT_ON
MAINON#
MAINON
BATT2
SUPPLY VOLTAGE GENERATION
POWSUPVG.SCH
STDBYON
CLOCKS AND SWITCHES
MISCLOG.SCH
ISACLK2
EFI
COMX1
COMX2
CX1
CX2
BATTDEAD#
PWRGOOD
ATRESET#
RESETDRV
RESET51
SR_BUTTON#
FFSET
POWER SUPPLY LOGIC
POWSUPLO.SCH
KBD[0..3]
PSTROBE
ISA27
CPU[0..13]
SMOUT[0..5]
BATT[0..2]
AUX BATT ON
ISA[0..37]

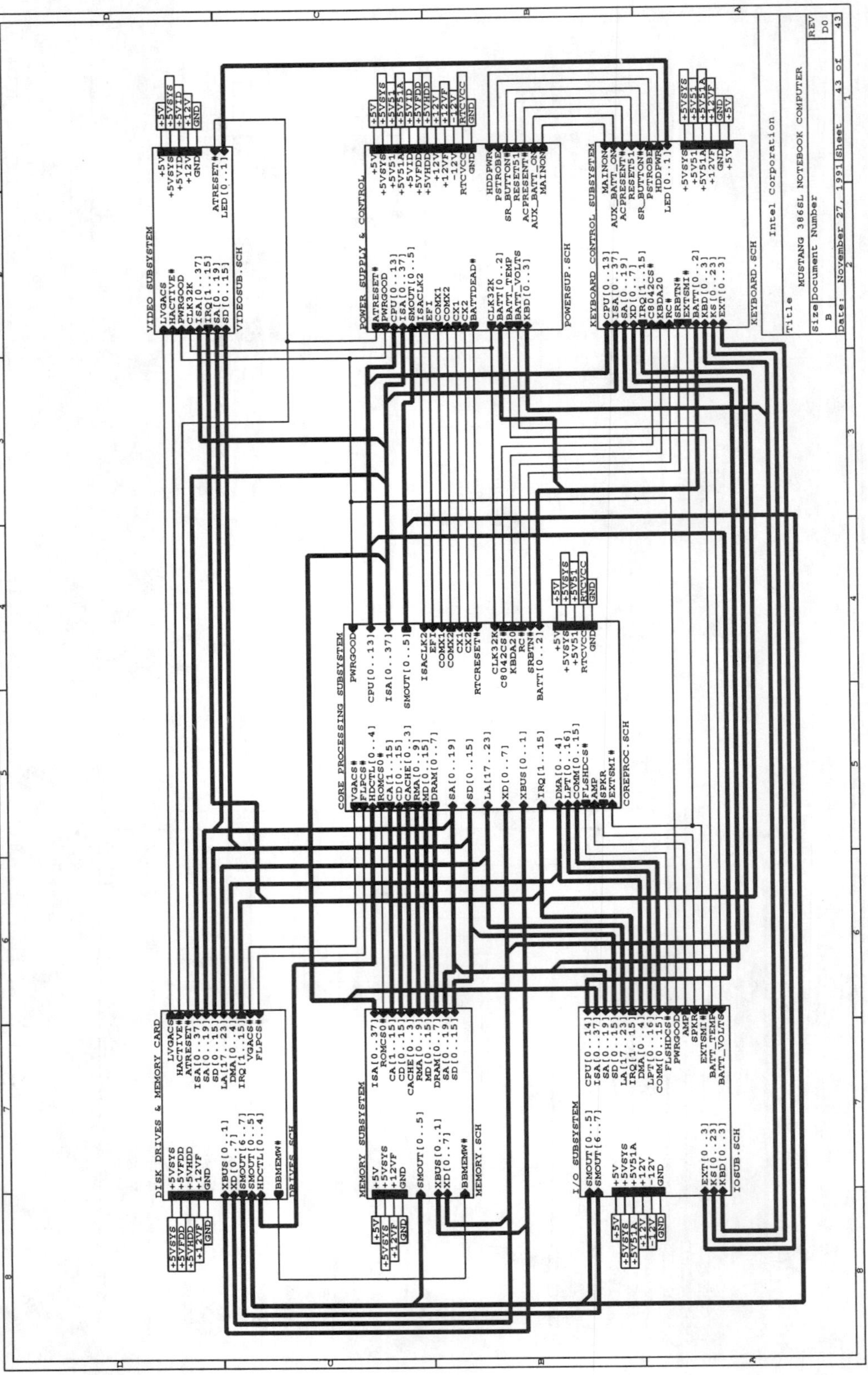

VIDEO SUBSYSTEM
VIDEOSUB.SCH
POWER SUPPLY & CONTROL
POWERSUP.SCH
KEYBOARD CONTROL SUBSYSTEM
KEYBOARD.SCH
CORE PROCESSING SUBSYSTEM
COREPROC.SCH
DISK DRIVES & MEMORY CARD
DRIVES.SCH
MEMORY SUBSYSTEM
MEMORY.SCH
I/O SUBSYSTEM
IOSUB.SCH
Intel Corporation
Title MUSTANG 386SL NOTEBOOK COMPUTER
Size Document Number REV
B D0
Date: November 27, 1991 Sheet 43 of 43

Glossary

auto power off A feature to turn power off automatically when the system is inactive for a long period of time.

BIOS Basic Input and Output System. System initialization software embedded inside nonvolatile memory device such as flash memory.

bus A group of communication lines for transferring data between the processor and the peripherals.

cache flush An operation which invalidates all cache lines.

de-turbo mode A mode where the CPU executes at a slower speed. De-turbo mode in the SL architecture can be controlled by either hardware or software.

DMA Direct Memory Access. Data stored in memory is accessed without going through the CPU.

BIOS shadowing A mechanism that copies information from flash memory to the RAM for faster code execution speed.

expanded memory Memory in the CPU memory address space that is accessed through a 64-Kbyte memory address window.

flash memory Nonvolatile memory which augments EPROM functionality with in-circuit electrical erasure and reprogramming.

flash BIOS Flash memory used for storing BIOS software to allow easy upgrade.

global standby A mode where the system removes power to selected power-hungry devices and stops the CPU clock to the CPU core inside the SL architecture CPU.

I/O cycle recovery time Delay time inserted after the trailing edge of any I/O command and before the next consecutive I/O command.

I/O trap A mechanism to detect access to an I/O port.

internal bus unit An SL architecture CPU control unit which directs bus cycles between the CPU core, the external bus unit, the cache unit, and the on-board memory control unit.

ISA-sliding window A mechanism that allows access to the entire 16-Mbyte of system address space on the ISA bus or PI bus in real mode.

ISA bus An industry standard bus interface for PC system based on IBM PC AT's 8-MHz expansion bus.

LIM EMS Lotus/Intel/Microsoft Expanded Memory Manager Specification. This specification was developed to provide more memory for applications software running in real mode.

local standby A mode in which an idle device controlled by the SL CPU is optionally powered down.

lower memory Memory located below the 1-Mbyte system address space limit.

MCP Intel387SL math coprocessor.

on-board memory Memory controlled by the memory controller inside the SL CPU which is not the same as ISA-bus memory.

ONCE A special mode for the SL CPU which is activated by asserting the ONCE# signal. When asserted, it causes all the outputs on the SL CPU to float.

parity checking A method of verifying the accuracy of data by adding a binary digit to a group of binary digits that indicates parity.

PI bus Peripheral Interface bus. A high speed bus which shares the same address and data bus with the ISA-bus interface.

power-on password A PS/2-compatible security option to prevent illegal access to system.

register shadowing A process in which the contents of write-only registers are saved to read-only registers so that the write-only registers can be restored to their previous states after they are reset.

resume A process of restoring the system to its previous state prior to suspend.

RSM A new microprocessor instruction to restore the CPU to its previous state prior to entering system management mode. The opcode for this instruction is 0FAAH.

SIGNATURE register A 16-bit register which provides revision number, family code, and family member code of the SL CPU.

SMRAM Memory used for storing system management code.

special feature set A set of functions for controlling CPU reset, A20 GATE, CPU speed, and shadowing.

SRAM Static Random Access Memory.

stop break event An event that can cause a stopped CPU clock to restart.

suspend The lowest power state of the SL architecture required to maintain the state of the system. There are three kinds of suspends and they are characterized by the state of the Vcc to the SL CPU and 82360SL during suspend. In a 5-volt suspend, the Vcc to the SL CPU and 82360SL remains at 5 volts during suspend. With 3-volt suspend, the Vcc to the SL CPU and 82360SL is running at 3 volts during suspend. When both the SL CPU and the 82360SL are powered down, the system is in a 0-volt suspend. Typically, the state of the system is saved to a nonvolatile memory device.

suspend refresh A special type of slow DRAM refresh to retain data in DRAM during suspend.

system event An event that indicates the system is not idle and keeps the system from going into global standby mode.

suspend/resume button An input pin to the 82360SL which can be used as a button to put the system in suspend state or resume from a suspend state.

tag The part of a cache line which holds the address information used to determine if a memory operation is a hit or miss on that cache line.

turbo mode A mode in which CPU is running at full speed.

wait state The number of additional clock cycles in addition to the minimum number of clock cycles to complete a read or write access.

write through A form of caching in which memory writes load both the cache memory and main memory.

Index

ABOUT THE AUTHOR

Desmond Yuen is a Senior Applications Engineer at Intel Corporation. A member of the IEEE, he chaired the IEEE P1284 Enhanced Parallel Port subcommittee in 1992. Intel has filed three patent applications related to System Management Mode based on Mr. Yuen's work. In addition, he has written several Intel manuals, including the *Intel386 SL Microprocessor Programmer's Reference Manual* and the *Intel486 SL Microprocessor Programmer's Reference Manual.* The author has been directly involved with the SL architecture and its advanced power management features since June 1989, and he has worked extensively with OEM manufacturers and software vendors to develop SL architecture–based portable computer systems.

DISK WARRANTY

This software is protected by both United States copyright law and international copyright treaty provision. You must treat this software just like a book, except that you may copy it into a computer to be used and you may make archival copies of the software for the sole purpose of backing up our software and protecting your investment from loss.

By saying, "just like a book," McGraw-Hill means, for example, that this software may be used by any number of people and may be freely moved from one computer location to another, so long as there is no possibility of its being used at one location or on one computer while it is being used at another. Just as a book cannot be read by two different people in two different places at the same time, neither can the software be used by two different people in two different places at the same time (unless, of course, McGraw-Hill's copyright is being violated).

LIMITED WARRANTY

McGraw-Hill warrants the physical diskette(s) enclosed herein to be free of defects in materials and workmanship for a period of sixty days from the purchase date. If McGraw-Hill receives written notification within the warranty period of defects in materials or workmanship, and such notification is determined by McGraw-Hill to be correct, McGraw-Hill will replace the defective diskette(s). Send request to:

Customer Service
TAB/McGraw-Hill
13311 Monterey Avenue
Blue Ridge Summit, PA 17294-0850

The entire and exclusive liability and remedy for breach of this Limited Warranty shall be limited to replacement of defective diskette(s) and shall not include or extend to any claim for or right to cover any other damages, including but not limited to, loss of profit, data, or use of the software, or special, incidental, or consequential damages or other similar claims, even if McGraw-Hill has been specifically advised to the possibility of such damages. In no event will McGraw-Hill's liability for any damages to you or any other person ever exceed the lower of suggested list price or actual price paid for the license to use the software, regardless of any form of the claim.

McGRAW-HILL, INC. SPECIFICALLY DISCLAIMS ALL OTHER WARRANTY, EXPRESS OR IMPLIED, INCLUDING BUT NOT LIMITED TO, ANY IMPLIED WARRANTY OF MERCHANTABILITY OR FITNESS FOR A PARTICULAR PURPOSE. Specifically, McGraw-Hill makes no representation or warranty that the software is fit for any particular purpose and any implied warranty of merchantability is limited to the sixty-day duration of the Limited Warranty covering the physical diskette(s) only (and not the software) and is otherwise expressly and specifically disclaimed.

This Limited Warranty gives you specific legal rights; you may have others which may vary from state to state. Some states do not allow the exclusion of incidental or consequential damages, or the limitation on how long an implied warranty lasts, so some of the above may not apply to you.